The Economics of Essential Medicines

The Royal Institute of International Affairs is an independent body which promotes the rigorous study of international questions and does not express opinions of its own. The opinions expressed in this publication are the responsibility of the authors.

The Economics of Essential Medicines

Edited by
BRIGITTE GRANVILLE

**THE ROYAL INSTITUTE OF
INTERNATIONAL AFFAIRS**
International Economics Programme

© Royal Institute of International Affairs, 2002

First published in Great Britain in 2002 by
Royal Institute of International Affairs, 10 St James's Square, London SW1Y 4LE
(Charity Registration No. 208 223)

Distributed worldwide by
The Brookings Institution, 1775 Massachusetts Avenue NW,
Washington, DC 20036-2188, USA

All rights reserved. No part of this publication may be reproduced or transmitted in any form or by any means, electronic or mechanical including photocopying, recording or any information storage or retrieval system, without prior permission in writing from the publishers.

British Library Cataloguing in Publication Data
A CIP catalogue record for this book is available from the British Library.

ISBN 1 86203 143 6 hardback
ISBN 1 86203 138 X paperback

Typeset in Garamond by Koinonia
Printed and bound in Great Britain by the Chameleon Press Limited
Cover design by Matthew Link

CONTENTS

Preface xiii
Contributors xv
Glossary, acronyms and abbreviations xvii

PART I: TRIPS AND ESSENTIAL MEDICINES

1 A Market Perspective on Recent Developments in the TRIPS and Essential Medicines Debate 3
   Owen Lippert
   Introduction 3
   Background 4
   Economic analysis of patents and 'market failure' 6
      Accusation of market failure 6
      Definition of market failure and welfare loss 7
      Not market failure but an affordability problem 8
   WHO and Africa Group proposals 9
      The WHO proposals 9
      Potential market interventions in the WHO proposals 11
      Market concerns with the WHO proposals 12
      The Africa Group proposal 13
   From Geneva to Doha 17
      Doha 17
   Impact of Doha Declaration on TRIPS and public health 18
   Looking towards 2005 19
      Reassessing the potential welfare of higher levels of patent protection 19
   Assessing the long-term dynamic gains 23
      Investment 24
      Indigenous innovation 24

	Enhanced institutional performance	25
	India is already seeing the industrial benefit in pursuing original research over compulsory licensed exports	26
	Adding up the costs and benefits	28
	Conclusion	28

2 The Economics of TRIPS Options for Access to Medicines 32
F. M. Scherer and Jayashree Watal

	Introduction	32
	Implications of TRIPS-compatible policy options for developing countries with access to patented medicines	33
	Compulsory licensing and government use	34
	Parallel trade	38
	Price controls	49
	Conclusion	53
	References	55

3 Parallel Trade in Pharmaceutical Products: Implications for Procuring Medicines for Poor Countries 57
Keith E. Maskus and Mattias Ganslandt

	Introduction	57
	Empirical evidence on differential prices	60
	International price differentials	60
	Why might prices be higher in poor countries?	68
	Evidence from the EU on the extent and effects of PT	69
	Evidence on PI and R&D performance	76
	Conclusions and policy recommendations	77
	References	79

4 Fatal Side Effects: Medicine Patents Under the Microscope 81
Oxfam

	Introduction	81
	The health crisis	83
	How much will the new patent rules increase prices?	85
	Is TRIPS 'flexible' enough, and are the public health safeguards adequate?	88
	'TRIPS plus'	90
	Will patenting in developing countries stimulate research into the diseases of poverty?	92
	Is TRIPS good for development and poverty reduction?	95
	The IP that TRIPS does not protect	96
	Corporate social responsibility	97
	Oxfam's principal recommendations	99

5	Patents, Patients and Developing Countries: Access, Innovation and the Political Dimensions of Trade Policy	100
	Harvey E. Bale Jr	
	Introduction	100
	The role of industry and of intellectual property rights	102
	Developing countries and TRIPS – the role of patents	104
	Weakening patent rules versus access partnerships	106
	Should increased R&D into AIDs and other infectious diseases be encouraged?	108
	A brief comment on the Doha WTO ministerial meeting	112

PART II: STATE RESPONSES

6	Developing States' Responses to the Pharmaceutical Imperatives of the TRIPS Agreement	115
	Jillian Clare Cohen	
	Introduction	115
	Costs and benefits of intellectual property protection	118
	The WTO	122
	To accept or to shirk? The costs and benefits of TRIPS	124
	The optimal policy choice	127
	Country comparisons: the spectrum of commitment	128
	Romania	130
	Brazil	131
	India	133
	Conclusions	135

7	The Pharmaceutical Sector: The Generics Development Trajectory	137
	Brigitte Granville and Carol Leonard	
	Introduction	137
	Pharmaceutical development across regions	138
	Pharmaceutical production and IP protection	145
	India	147
	Brazil	147
	China	148
	The learning and feedback mechanisms in pharmaceutical production and trade	149
	Conclusion	155
	References	158

8 The Development Trilemma and the South African Response   161
W. Duncan Reekie

    The development trilemma: patents, price discrimination and   161
        parallel imports
        Patents   161
        Price discrimination   163
        Preventing parallel imports   166
    AIDS in South Africa   169
    The trilemma in South Africa   172
    Promoting access for the developing world   174
    Conclusions   176
    References   177

9 Expanding Access to Essential Medicines in Brazil: Recent   178
Economic Regulation, Policy-Making and Lessons Learnt
Jorge Bermudez

    Introduction   178
    Brazil: a profile   180
    Access to medicines: the essential background   183
    Recent regulation related to access to medicines   184
    Strengthening regulatory capacity and generic drugs policy   187
    Health issues involving intellectual property and trade   189
    Main highlights of the HIV–AIDS control programme   191
    Lessons learnt and the way forward   194
    References   196

10 Challenges in Widening Access to HIV–AIDS-Related Drugs   198
and Care in Uganda
Dorothy Ochola

    Introduction   198
    Health status   198
        HIV–AIDS situation   199
    Health care delivery   200
        The minimum health care package   200
    Essential medicines   201
        The UNAIDS–Ministry of Health HIV–AIDS Drug Access   202
           Initiative
    Challenges and lessons learnt   203
        Competeing demands for health care   204
    Conclusion   205

PART III: DELIVERING EFFECTIVE HEALTH

11 **Differential Pricing and the Financing of Essential Drugs** 209
WHO–WTO
    Introduction 209
        Access to essential drugs 209
        Financing health care and essential drugs 210
        Differential pricing is necessary and feasible 210
        The role of intellectual property rights 213
        Differential pricing and greater international funding 213
    Access to essential drugs in developing countries 214
    The role of financing in ensuring access to essential drugs 217
    Differential pricing 218
        The economic feasibility of differential pricing 219
        Giving effect to differential pricing 222
        Maintaining separate markets and preventing diversion 226
        Political feasibility 228
        Middle-income countries and well-to-do populations in poor countries 230
    The role of intellectual property rights 230
    Conclusion 231

12 **The International Effort for Anti-Retrovirals: Politics or Public Health?** 232
Louisiana Lush
    Introduction 232
    Access to ARVs: international political developments 234
    Neglect of practicalities at the national level 236
    From political posturing to practical steps: an agenda for action and research 238
    References 240

13 **Providing Health Care to HIV Patients in Southern Africa** 242
Markus Haacker
    Introduction 242
    The health sector in Southern Africa 243
    The impact of HIV–AIDS on the health sector 246
        The impact on existing health facilities 246
        The costs of prevention of opportunistic diseases and basic treatment 248
        The scope for improving access to anti-retroviral therapies 251
    Summary and conclusions 253
    References 254

14 Successful public–private partnerships in global health: lessons from the MECTIZAN Donation Program — 255
Jeffrey L. Sturchio and Brenda D. Colatrella

- A devastating disease — 256
- The discovery and development of MECTIZAN — 257
- Collaboration with the World Health Organization — 259
- The decision to donate MECTIZAN — 260
- Challenges and obstacles — 262
- Creation of the Merck MECTIZAN Donation Program — 262
- The evolution of a unique public–private partnership — 265
- The impact of the partnership — 266
- Lessons learnt — 266
  - *Partnerships* — 267
  - *Infrastructure* — 268
  - *Sustainability* — 268
  - *Capacity-building* — 269
  - *Implications for future access programmes* — 271
- Conclusions — 272
- References — 273

15 Street Price: A Global Approach to Drug Pricing for Developing Countries — 275
Anna Thomas

- Introduction — 275
- The context: high prices — 276
  - *Why is price important?* — 276
  - *The special nature of drugs* — 277
  - *New drugs, higher prices* — 277
  - *Why are prices high?* — 278
  - *Looking for a different approach* — 279
- Essential criteria for equity-pricing — 280
  - *The 10 criteria* — 281
  - *Additional issues* — 283
- Existing methods of acquiring lower-price drugs for developing countries — 284
  - *Situational factors* — 284
  - *Intentional initiatives* — 285
  - *'Price offers' by companies* — 288
  - *Donations* — 289
  - *Negotiation and purchase by international organizations* — 290
  - *Generic competition* — 290

A framework for global pricing that fits the criteria	291
The equity-pricing framework	292
Which drugs, countries and purchasers would be eligible for equity prices?	296
Recommendations	296
Conclusion and summary	298
References	300

PREFACE

This collection of articles results from a conference at Chatham House on 10 July 2001 organized by the International Economics Programme of the Royal Institute of International Affairs in cooperation with the London School of Hygiene and Tropical Medicine. The idea for this conference emerged from an initial consideration of issues related to the impact of trade-related aspects of intellectual property rights (TRIPS) on essential medicines and to concerns for what could be done to make essential medicines more accessible to the poor. This book does not aim to answer all questions, but it does intend to show the complexity of the debate from a variety of viewpoints – those of academics, policy-makers in wealthy and poor states, international and non-governmental organizations such as Oxfam and VSO, and the pharmaceutical industry.

I warmly thank our sponsors, without whom this conference and this publication would not have been possible: Merck, the Ashden Trust, the World Bank and the International Policy Network. I would especially like to thank the speakers, most of whom covered their own costs, in view of the difficulties of obtaining funding for this conference. The Royal Institute of International Affairs is an independent body that promotes the rigorous study of international questions but does not express opinions of its own. It is a charity and therefore relies on external funding for all its activities. This conference was in the spirit of Chatham House, free of partisan lines, and I hope that this volume fully reflects that spirit.

I would also like to thank Joann Fong, Zhen Kun Wang and Louisiana Lush for helping me to organize the conference, and Dr Kim Mitchell for his meticulous work on the text. The publication of this volume has been made possible by the work of Margaret May, head of the publications department, and Matthew Link, who designed the cover.

May 2002   B.G.

CONTRIBUTORS

Michael Bailey, Policy Department, Oxfam

Dr Harvey Bale, Director-General, International Federation of Pharmaceutical Manufacturers Association

Professor Jorge A.Z. Bermudez, Director of the National School of Public Health, Oswaldo Cruz Foundation, Brazilian Ministry of Health

Dr Jillian Clare Cohen, World Bank Pharmaceutical Policy, Consultant

Brenda D. Colatrella, Director, Worldwide Product Donation Policy & Programs

Andrew Creese, Senior Health Economist, Policy, Access and Rational Use, Essential Drugs and Medicines Department, World Health Organization

Dr Mattias Ganslandt, Research Fellow, The Research Institute of Industrial Economics, IUI, Stockholm

Dr Brigitte Granville, Head of the International Economics Programme, The Royal Institute of International Affairs

Markus Haacker, Economist in the World Economic Studies Division, Research Department, International Monetary Fund

Dr Carol Leonard, Fellow, St Antony's College, Oxford University; Associate Fellow, International Economics Programme, The Royal Institute of International Affairs

Dr Owen Lippert, Senior Fellow in Law and Markets, The Fraser Institute, Canada

Dr Louisiana Lush, Lecturer in Health and Population Policy, Health Policy Unit, Department of Public Health and Policy, London School of Hygiene and Tropical Medicine

Professor Keith Maskus, Professor of Economics, University of Colorado

Dr Dorothy Ochola, National Coordinator of the UNAIDS/Ministry of Health HIV/AIDS Drug Access Initiative, Uganda

Professor Duncan W. Reekie, E.P. Bradlow Professor of Industrial Economics at the University of the Witwatersrand, South Africa

Professor F. M. Scherer, Aetna Professor of Public Policy Emeritus, Harvard University and Visiting Professor at Princeton University

Dr Jeffrey L. Sturchio, Executive Director, Public Affairs Europe, Middle East and Africa, Merck & Company

Anna Thomas, Senior Advocacy Officer, Global Education and Advocacy Department, VSO

Jayashree Watal, Counsellor, Intellectual Property Division, WTO

GLOSSARY, ACRONYMS AND ABBREVIATIONS

ACAME	African Association of Central Medical Stores
AIDS	Acquired immunodeficiency syndrome
ANDA	Abbreviated new drug application
APOC	African Programme for Onchocerciasis Control
ARV	Anti-retroviral
ASEAN	Association of Southeast Asian Nations
BERD	Business expenditures on research and development
CAGR	Compound annual growth rate
CC	Conversion cost: labour, energy, R&D etc.
CDTI	Community-directed treatment with ivermectin
DPCO	Drug price control order
DSB	Dispute Settlement Board (WTO)
ED	Excise duty
EDLU	Essential Drugs List of Uganda
EU	European Union
FSTI	Fond de Solidarité Thérapeutique Internationale
GATT	General Agreement on Tariffs and Trade
GAVI	Global Alliance for Vaccines and Immunization
GDP	Gross domestic product
GFFATM	Global Fund to Fight AIDS, Tuberculosis and Malaria
GNP	Gross national product
GSK	GlaxoSmithKline, the world's second-largest pharmaceutical company
HAARTs	Highly active anti-retroviral therapies
HIV	Human immunodeficiency virus
IAVI	International AIDS Vaccine Initiative
ICH	International Conference on Harmonization
IFPMA	International Federation of Pharmaceutical Manufacturers Association

IP	Intellectual property. The concept includes patents, copyright, trade marks and geographical denominations.
IPRs	Intellectual property rights
ISIC	International Standard Industrial Classification
LDCs	Least developed countries. This UN classification is based on income, health and education standards, and economic vulnerability. There are currently 49 LDCs.
MAPE	Maximum allowable post-manufacturing expenses, including distribution and retail margins
MC	Material cost, including bulk pharmaceuticals used and allowance for wastage
MDP	MECTIZAN Donation Program
MDR	Multi-drug-resistant
MEC	MECTIZAN Expert Committee
MMV	Medicines for Malaria Venture
MOH	Ministry of Health
MRA	Mutual Recognition Agreement
MSF	Médecins Sans Frontières
MTCT	Mother-to-child transmission
NAFTA	North American Free Trade Agreement
NCE	New chemical entity
NGDO	Non-governmental development organization
NGO	Non-governmental organization
NMEs	New molecular entities
NOTF	National Onchocerciasis Task Force
OCP	Onchocerciasis Control Programme
OECD	Organization for Economic Cooperation and Development
OEPA	Onchocerciasis Elimination Programme of the Americas
OTC	Over-the-counter
PhRMA	Pharmaceutical Research and Manufacturers of America
PI	Parallel imports
PMPRB	Patented Medicine Prices Review Board
PPP	Purchasing power parity
PT	Parallel trade
R&D	Research and development
STD	Sexually transmitted diseases
TB	Tuberculosis
TNCs	Transnational corporations
TRIPS	WTO Agreement on Trade-Related Aspects of Intellectual Property Rights, agreed at the end of the Uruguay Round of trade talks in 1994

UNAIDS	Joint United Nations Programme on HIV–AIDS
UNDP	United Nations Development Programme
UNFPA	United Nations Fund for Population Activities
UNGASS	UN General Assembly Special Session on HIV/AIDS
UNICEF	United Nations Children's Fund
UNIDO	United Nations Industrial Development Organization
USTR	United States Trade Representative. The Office of the USTR deals with trade policy and represents the United States at the WTO.
VCT	Voluntary counselling and testing
WHO	World Health Organization
WTO	World Trade Organization

PART I
TRIPS AND ESSENTIAL MEDICINES

1 A MARKET PERSPECTIVE ON RECENT DEVELOPMENTS IN THE TRIPS AND ESSENTIAL MEDICINES DEBATE

Owen Lippert

INTRODUCTION

The Royal Institute of International Affairs' in-depth conference in July 2001 highlighted the varied perspectives on the debate over access to essential medicines, specifically HIV–AIDS drugs in developing countries and in particular sub-Saharan Africa. This contribution seeks to provide a market perspective on the issue, a standard welfare economic analysis.

A need to re-state the standard welfare analysis is evident from the uncritical assumption made by several individuals and organizations that drug access in sub-Saharan Africa represents a 'market failure.' The contention made is that TRIPS (Trade-Related Aspects of Intellectual Property Rights) has globalized the patent monopoly position of international pharmaceutical companies, thus leading to a market abuse in the pricing of drugs.

Two sets of proposals emerged during 2001 to counter this alleged 'market failure'.

- The World Health Organization (WHO) 'proposed' an expanded international regulatory framework for drugs that would lower prices in developing countries through differential pricing.
- Several African countries with strong support from India and Brazil brought to the TRIPS Council the proposal to expand the latitude in TRIPS for the compulsory licensing of drugs and the export of copied on-patent drugs (through parallel importation) to sub-Saharan Africa and other countries. Various non-governmental organizations (NGOs) have long advocated this approach. These proposals framed the discussion of the Declaration on TRIPS made at the World Trade Organization (WTO) meeting held in November in Doha, Qatar.

Not far from the surface of the above debate is the question of what will happen in 2005 when developing countries, primarily India, are scheduled to implement TRIPS. What will be the welfare impact of higher patent protection standards?

This chapter will discuss the questions:

- Do higher standards of patent protection lead to 'market failure' in terms of access to drugs in developing countries?
- From a market perspective, how effective are the Africa Group and the WHO proposals?
- What might be the welfare impact of higher patent protection standards in India?

Overall, this chapter will argue that the debate over patent protection and drug access has led to the false choice between upholding TRIPS or denying drugs to HIV–AIDS sufferers. Such a choice overlooks the obvious point that science funded through the lawful exercise of patent rights has made progress towards both a vaccine and greater access.

A debate over access to HIV–AIDS drugs exists only because the drugs were discovered in the first place. Patents provided the incentive to discover and develop better AIDS drugs. Profits funded the research that found a pharmaceutical response when many scientists believed it was not possible to do so.

Affordability remains a problem, but it is misguided compassion to undermine the legal system that made it a question in the first place. Hot-housing production of first-generation drugs through state-created generic companies can only provide a short-term gain with possibly serious long-term effects.

To address immediate needs, Amir Attaran and Lee Gillespie-White have proposed a dramatic increase in donor aid to Africa to supply essential medicines. Certainly, more donor money would help. Their proposal, nonetheless, deliberately sidesteps the serious public policy choice that must be made. How should developing countries participate fully in the global knowledge economy with all its benefits and costs?

BACKGROUND

The question of access to essential medicines and the role of TRIPS arises because of the disparity in treatment of diseases between the developed and the developing world. Few people in North America, Western Europe, Japan or Singapore die, for instance, from malaria or tuberculosis.

According to the World Health Organization (WHO) there are 300 to 500 million clinical cases of malaria each year, resulting in 1.5 to 2.7 million deaths.[1] About 40 per cent of the world's population – some two billion people – are at risk in about 90 countries and territories. Between 80 and 90 per cent of malaria deaths occur in sub-Saharan Africa, where 90 per cent of the infected people

---

[1] The Malaria Control Programme, World Health Organization at *http://www.idrc.ca/books/reports/1996/01-07e.html.*

live. The disease kills at least one million people there each year. According to some estimates, 275 million of 530 million people have malaria parasites in their blood, although they may not develop symptoms. Malaria is responsible for as many as half the deaths of African children under the age of five. In regions of intense transmission, 40 per cent of toddlers may die of acute malaria.

About one-third of the world's population is infected by M. tuberculosis.[2] Worldwide in 1995 there were about nine million new cases of the disease, with three million deaths. M. Tuberculosis kills more people than any other single infectious agent. Deaths from tuberculosis comprise 25 per cent of all avoidable deaths in developing countries. Ninety-five per cent of tuberculosis cases and 98 per cent of tuberculosis deaths are in developing countries.

Even though far more people in the developing world die of tuberculosis and malaria, it is AIDS that has focused attention on the disparity between the developed world and the developing world in terms of access to drugs. As of the end of 2000, an estimated 36.1 million people worldwide – 34.7 million adults and 1.4 million children younger than 15 years – were living with HIV–AIDS.[3] More than 70 per cent of these people (25.3 million) live in sub-Saharan Africa; another 16 per cent (5.8 million) live in South and Southeast Asia. Worldwide, approximately one in every 100 adults aged 15 to 49 is HIV-infected. In sub-Saharan Africa, about 8.8 per cent of all adults in this age group are HIV-infected. In 16 African countries, the prevalence of HIV infection among adults aged 15 to 49 exceeds 10 per cent. An estimated 5.3 million new HIV infections occurred worldwide in 2000, about 15,000 infections each day. More than 95 per cent of these new infections occurred in developing countries.

In all of North America and Western Europe, it is estimated that there are 1.5 million children and adults infected with HIV–AIDS and that they are living longer since the introduction of anti-retroviral therapies.[4] In the United States, mortality from HIV infection, which dropped more than 70 per cent in 1996–98, continued this trend in 1999 by decreasing by nearly 4 per cent.[5] HIV–AIDS is no longer ranked among the leading causes of death there: HIV–AIDS mortality declined by 26 per cent in 1996, by 48 per cent in 1997 and by 21 per cent in 1998. Death rates across Europe among patients infected with HIV-1 have been falling since September 1995, and at the beginning of 1998 they were less than one-fifth of their previous level. New treatments or combinations of treatments can explain much of the reduction in mortality.[6] The

[2] WHO at *http://www.who.int/gtb/publications/gmdrt/foreword.html*.
[3] National Institutes of Health at *http://www.niaid.nih.gov/factsheets/aidsstat.htm*.
[4] See the Avert Organization at *http://www.avert.org/worldstats.htm*.
[5] US Department of Health and Human Services at *http://www.cdc.gov/nchs/releases/01news/declindea.htm*.
[6] A. Morcroft et al., 'Changing Patterns of Mortality across Europe in Patients Infected with HIV-1', *Lancet*, Vol. 352, No. 9142 (November 1998), pp. 1725–30.

WHO estimates that although the number of people with access to essential drugs has doubled in the past 20 years, one-third of the world's population does not have access, with this figure rising to over 50 per cent in Asia and Africa.[7]

ECONOMIC ANALYSIS OF PATENTS AND 'MARKET FAILURE'

Accusation of market failure

Dr James Orbinski, President of the International Council of Médecins Sans Frontières (MSF), states that 'The market has failed … In fact, the pharmaceutical record is the clearest evidence of any form of market failure.'[8] Dr Gro Harlem Brundtland, Director General of the World Health Organization, adds: 'Let us be frank about it: essential and life-saving drugs exist while millions and millions of people cannot afford them. This amounts to a moral problem, a political problem and a problem of credibility for the global market system.'[9]

The alleged failure of the market in the developing world has two parts. First, the international pharmaceutical companies are accused of abusing their market power conferred by patent rights to overcharge for HIV–AIDS drugs. Second, these companies have failed to produce pharmaceuticals for tuberculosis and malaria and other tropical diseases because the sufferers are poor and therefore an unprofitable market.

The discussion of TRIPS, patented pharmaceuticals and the developing countries goes back to the Uruguay Round negotiations in the late 1980s. The final text was agreed upon, if not ratified, in 1991. However, not until the agreement was signed did complaints arise within the broader arena of public policy. After the implementation of TRIPS, the case made against the agreement was that it imposed both short-term and long-term losses on developing countries. Consumers in developing countries would face higher prices and thus a welfare loss.[10] Producers would lose industrial benefits by being denied the 'imitation' phase of economic development.

---

[7] World Health Organization, 'The Impact of Essential Drugs', found at *http://www.who.int/medicines/strategy/whozip16e/ch04.htm*.

[8] Closing comments, conference on 'Access to Essential Medicines in a Global Economy', 24–25 November 1999, at *http://www.haiweb.org/campaign/novseminar/orbinski.html*.

[9] Statement by the Director General to the Executive Board at its 105th session, found at *http://www.who.int/director-general/speeches/2000/20000124_eb.html*.

[10] See generally Carlos A. Primo Braga, 'The Developing Country Case For and Against Intellectual Property Protection', in Wolfgang Siebeck (ed.), *Strengthening Protection of Intellectual Property in Developing Countries: A Survey of the Literature* (Washington, DC: The World Bank, 1990), pp. 69–87. See also the interesting discussion by Arvind Subramanian, 'TRIPs and the Paradigm of the GATT: A Tropical, Temperate View', *World Economy*, No. 13 (1990), pp. 509–21.

The response, as to how TRIPS has contributed to market success in the developing world, has taken some time to be properly presented. In its absence, the public policy debate over TRIPS has been one-sided. The latest accusation is that TRIPS has contributed to a 'market failure' in the access of developing countries to essential medicines.

Definition of market failure and welfare loss

In approaching the question of whether or not a 'market failure' exists, it is important to draw the distinction between 'market failure' and 'welfare loss.' A 'market failure' always involves a 'welfare loss', but a 'welfare loss' does not always imply a 'market failure'.

To define 'market failure', one must first define market success. The standard definition of market success is that all gains from trade have been exhausted. Individuals have bought and sold a product to the point at which the marginal cost of production is equal to the marginal benefit of consumption. Any further production and consumption would not make the consumer better off without making the producer worse off. This allocation of resources is said to be 'Pareto efficient'. The efficiency of a market defines whether it has succeeded or failed.

A market failure can occur under two conditions. First, a deficiency in the market structure systematically prevents a market from moving towards Pareto efficiency. The classic example is the presence of either a producer or a consumer monopoly. A monopoly, by stifling competition, prevents the efficient convergence of the marginal cost of production with the marginal benefit of consumption. A second source of market failure lies in external costs or benefits not being properly included in the price, thus leading to a misallocation of resources.

The important point is that unmet demand does not, in itself, constitute a market failure. A market may still be efficient even if the cost of a product is unaffordable to many.

A welfare loss, which can apply to either a producer or a consumer, does not necessarily reflect on the efficiency of a market. Welfare losses result from a market intervention that shifts the point at which price meets supply (where marginal cost of production equals marginal benefit of consumption) from the point at which they would intersect under competitive conditions. A welfare loss can result from either a price intervention or a supply intervention. The most common source of welfare losses is taxes that add a wedge to either the cost of making a product or of consuming it, or both. Taxes do not necessarily prevent producers and consumers from arriving efficiently at a mutual price point. Taxes do, however, redistribute income, which at some point have an impact on the efficiency of a market.

The central question is whether a patent represents a monopoly, and therefore potentially a source of market failure, or whether a patent, by virtue of the exchange of disclosure for exclusivity, represents an acceptable trade-off of short-term welfare loss for long-term dynamic gain. The key to this question is how you define a monopoly. Is it just the concentration of market power or is it a condition of the market's structure preventing the free entry of new competitors? The standard neo-classical answer is that a monopoly can only occur when there is an artificial barrier to market entry. As patents do not prevent new inventions from coming into the market to provide the same functional product use, they are generally not considered monopolies.

All that said, a patent could provide its holder with the opportunity – but only the opportunity – for charging a price above the marginal cost of production because of the right to control the supply of the product.

The important point is that while a patent may incur a static welfare loss as a result of exclusivity, that loss may be offset in two ways. The product itself may provide overall benefits that would not have been possible before. Also dynamic market gains from the increased incentive to innovate and to invest may in the long term exceed the limited term loss. Indeed, the market failure most associated with intellectual property goods is that of underproduction owing to an inability of producers to achieve economic returns.[11]

In short, patents do not present a market failure. They may present an ambiguous welfare loss in isolation if the overall intellectual property system systematically fails to stimulate innovation and investment.

As Professor Keith Maskus has written: 'The main goal of an intellectual property system should be to create economic incentives that maximize the discounted present value of the difference between the social benefits and the social costs of information creation, including the cost of administering the system.'[12]

Not market failure but an affordability problem

Even if patents do not create a market failure in access to essential drugs in developing countries, the affordability of those drugs certainly remains a serious problem. The question of affordability involves many actors, not just the producers of drugs. Government policies have a major impact on affordability. Jayashree Watal, a consultant to the WTO, points to several government-induced price interventions:

---

[11] See Wendy J. Gordon, 'Asymmetric Market Failure and Prisoner's Dilemma in Intellectual Property', *University of Dayton Law Review*, Vol. 17 (1992), pp. 853–4.
[12] Keith E. Maskus, *Intellectual Property Rights in the Global Economy* (Washington, DC: Institute for International Economics, 2000), p. 31.

- Distribution margins and taxes can contribute up to 80 per cent of the consumer price in developing countries – twice the level of developed countries.
- Tariffs on pharmaceuticals and active ingredients add to the consumer price.
- Poor spending controls in some African countries have led to only 12 per cent of expenditure achieving effective results.[13]

If affordability is the problem, it should be addressed. The point, as will be shown next, is that the proposed solution by the Africa Group and the WHO deals less with fundamental issues of affordability and more with the structure of the pharmaceutical market by authorizing generic market entrants at the expense of the basic patent system. Some NGOs have gone as far as arguing for this state intervention in pharmaceutical markets independently of any advances in affordability. Jean-Marie Kindermans of MSF said in a recent interview: 'The logic of the pharmaceutical industry is not the logic of social action' and 'The solution for AIDS is not to have five big donors reducing their prices – we need pressure for a political agreement, not a charitable one.'[14] Charity is a market-based solution to the affordability problem in that it is a voluntary act.

WHO AND AFRICA GROUP PROPOSALS

Taken as a whole, the WHO and Africa Group proposals centre on three actions:

- Increased use of compulsory licences in developing countries. Domestic generic manufacturers producing a patented drug would pay the original patent-holder only a small royalty fee.
- The export and import of compulsorily licensed generic copies of patented drugs between developing countries.
- Some combination of carrots and sticks to multinational companies to price their products radically differently between developed and developing markets.

The WHO proposals

The various proposals of the WHO arise from a background of institutional scepticism as to the merits of TRIPS. The WHO has long complained that countries did not consult with them and other international organizations during the negotiation of TRIPS.[15] The WHO now seeks recognition of a role

---

[13] Jayashree Watal, Background Note prepared for WHO–WTO workshop on Differential Pricing and Financing of Essential Drugs, held in Høsbjør, Norway on 8–11 April 2001, available on WTO website.

[14] http://www.unesco.org/courier/2001_02/uk/droits.htm.

[15] Carlos Correa, 'Health and Intellectual Property Rights', *Bulletin of the World Health Organization*, Vol. 79, No. 5 (2001) at http://www.who.int/bulletin/pdf/2001/issue5/editorial.pdf.

in which it monitors the health impact of the TRIPS Agreement. This has led to a conflict with the United States. The US views, for instance, the WHO's efforts to create an international database of pharmaceutical prices as a move towards global drug price regulation.

At the outset, one should concede that the WHO proposals constitute less of a coherent plan and more of a toolbox of potential regulatory interventions. They may be found in the background paper 'More Equitable Pricing for Essential Drugs: What Do We Mean and What are the Issues?' prepared for the WHO–WTO secretariat workshop on differential pricing and the financing of essential drugs held in Høsbjør, Norway from 8 to 11 April 2001, and reproduced in this volume (Chapter 11).

The particular style of the WHO proposals reflects the institutional nature of the organization itself. Given the WHO's collective management and funding, the organization cannot take firm policy stands, though it may muse about them. The background paper uses the format of asking questions and answering them in orderly but opaque language while denying that there is any objective other than to stimulate discussion. Many of the WHO proposals deal with bureaucratic issues that do not apply directly to the structure of pharmaceutical markets. The full scope of the WHO's proposals deserves careful attention. The passage in question, from the second half of the paper, is entitled 'Framework for dialogue: questions, principles and options'. It addresses the following 10 questions, with draft principles and options as a framework for dialogue:

Priorities – *Which health problems and products should be priorities for differential pricing?* The burden of disease and comparative safety and efficacy of alternative treatments – standard criteria for selecting essential drugs for national lists – are primary considerations. Cost-effectiveness analysis may contribute to decision-making. Diagnostics for common health problems should also be considered.

Target countries – *Which countries should benefit?* If national income criteria are used, then the choice of countries could range from the 33 countries (654 million people) in the 'low' category of the Human Development Index to the 78 countries (2,326 million people), which are IDA-eligible (GNP less than $885).

Mechanisms – *How can differential pricing be achieved in the context of international agreements?* Differential pricing can be achieved through normal market mechanisms, negotiated price discounts, or licensed competitive production. Each of these options can be pursued within international agreements, national law and available safeguards.

Price reduction – *What else will contribute to lower prices?* Adequate and sustainable domestic and international financing, therapeutic competition, concentration of demand through pooled procurement arrangements, improved distribution efficiency, elimination of tariffs and taxes, better governance and other factors can each contribute to achieving the best possible prices.

Target price – *Should a 'target price' be set for individual products?* Setting a target price, though technically difficult and perhaps undesirable to some stakeholders, can be invaluable in negotiation, in other price reduction strategies, and in monitoring progress. Possible benchmarks include marginal cost of production, existing therapeutic alternatives, a specified level of developed-country prices (e.g. under 5%), or a ratio of annual treatment cost to per capita GNP.

Financing – *How could differentially priced drugs be financed?* Increased domestic public financing, expanded social health insurance, greater employer health spending, use of debt relief resources, and substantial increases in international donor funding for the poorest countries could each contribute.

Purchasing and distribution – *Who should purchase and distribute differentially priced drugs?* Potential purchasers include public-sector national health services, non-governmental organizations, private health services and private pharmaceutical supply channels. International purchasing funds can play an important role in achieving better prices and attracting donor funding.

Preventing diversion – *How can diversion away from intended countries and populations be prevented?* Preventing diversion to unintended markets, especially back-flow to high-income countries, will be critical to the long-term viability of differential pricing schemes. Manufacturers' market segmentation technology, purchaser undertakings, and regulation all have roles.

Ensuring political support – *How can developed countries be persuaded not to demand the same low prices?* Adding a high-volume, low-margin market in developing countries would not be expected to raise prices in developed countries. Advocacy and public awareness are needed.

Sustainability and dependability – *What mechanisms are needed to ensure sustained and dependable differential pricing?* Existing discretionary decisions by individual companies could be supported by tax or other financial incentives, international agreements on differential pricing for low-income countries, monitoring and publication of companies' performance on differential pricing.[16]

Potential market interventions in the WHO proposals

As the WHO proposals present a range of options, a range of consequences becomes possible. The result is that it is difficult to critique them without falling vulnerable to the accusation of exaggeration.

The key WHO proposal is for developing countries to claim 'public health' exemptions (allowed by TRIPS under specific conditions) for a list of essential medicines, on- and off-patent. Countries would then grant compulsory licences

---

[16] WHO, 'More Equitable Drug Pricing', p. 17, found at *http://www.who.int/medicines/library/edm_general/who-wto-hosbjor/equitable_pricing.doc*.

for these pharmaceuticals to at least five generic or international companies for manufacture. (The WHO claims to have discovered the 'rule-of-fives' whereby prices tend to be lowest when five or more companies compete. This may be true, but jigging the structure of an industry, although long a favourite of industrial planners, rarely works in practice. A more likely outcome is either a single state company or, as in Canada, a less than fully competitive duopoly.)

The WHO proposes setting a target price for a drug, then working backwards through the production chain to reduce costs to meet that pre-specified price level. The only concession to the original rights-holders is that they would be paid small royalties.

An international agency, presumably the WHO itself, funded by increased aid donations, would then buy these drugs. As part of its pressure on the price level, the agency would force deep discounts through bulk purchases.

The agency would set retail prices through one or more complicated formulas. The range includes a cost-plus calculation, a target of five per cent of the price in developed countries or a comparison with therapeutic equivalents.

Essentially the plan would establish indirectly drug price controls for developing-nation markets. This would create differential or tiered pricing of pharmaceuticals between developed and developing countries.

The drugs would be distributed in developing countries through a network of NGOs and local health organizations instead of normal commercial channels of distribution.

To prevent the compulsorily licensed drugs from being parallel-imported back to the developing world, the developed countries themselves would have to strengthen their import controls. Moreover, the generic manufacturers could receive funding not to export production.

Market concerns with the WHO proposals

The WHO proposals, if implemented, would fall foul of their own complexity, increase corruption and distort global markets. They would risk undermining the research effort for truly effective vaccines and cures. For all that, they would have only a marginal impact on access to essential medicines in the developing world. The WHO has failed to consider that greater market freedom and stronger intellectual property rights could lead to more differential pricing, not less.

The WHO scheme would also create multiple opportunities for corruption. The critical points for the exercise of corruption are the decision to subject a patented pharmaceutical to compulsory licensing, the awarding of licences to manufacturers, the setting of the purchase price, the distribution of the drugs and, last but not least, the ability to overcharge the ultimate user. The expectation that local generic manufacturers could be persuaded not to export their products through tax and financial inducements is naïve at best and cynical at worst.

This scheme is ultimately unworkable, however well intentioned. The WHO lacks the institutional capacity to carry out the global regulation of the pharmaceutical market. As Adetokunbo Lucas writes in the *Lancet*,

> WHO's performance has been closely scrutinized in recent years. Although some of this scrutiny has been related to the increasing concern about the efficiency of the United Nations (UN) system as a whole, specific criticisms have been levelled at the quality of WHO's leadership and the effectiveness of its programmes. There is also concern that WHO's strength lies mainly in supporting traditional programmes for disease control, and that the organization is not equipped to respond to the current needs of the more advanced developing countries.[17]

Although the WHO proposals surely mean well, they reflect an abstract and bureaucratic understanding of how markets work. Real markets are rarely as tidy and predictable. As the more advanced developing countries adopt health care systems with more sophisticated private-sector delivery, the WHO's proposals for 'command and control' drug markets appear contradictory.

The Africa Group proposal

The most significant development in the debate over access to medicines and TRIPS arose at the meeting of the TRIPS Council in Geneva on 18–22 June 2001. At that meeting, the document 'TRIPS and Public Health' was submitted by the Africa Group and Barbados, Bolivia, Brazil, Dominican Republic, Ecuador, Honduras, India, Indonesia, Jamaica, Pakistan, Paraguay, Philippines, Peru, Sri Lanka, Thailand and Venezuela.[18] This document – the joint submission by a substantial portion of the developing world, many states of which are still in the throes of conforming to the TRIPS agreement – deserves careful consideration.

The basic purpose of the Africa Group proposal is to restrict developed countries from taking trade actions against developing countries should they engage in compulsory licensing and parallel importation. Various rationales are offered. A new complaint is that TRIPS inhibits developing countries from responding to health crises by way of the compulsory licensing of essential medicines. Countries fear using the legitimate exclusions for public health contained in TRIPS. They worry about developed countries launching trade dispute actions. Potential trade retaliation has created the international equivalent of 'litigation chill'.

[17] Adetokunbo Lucas, 'World Health: WHO at the Country Level', *Lancet*, Vol. 351, Issue 9104 (1998), pp. 743–7.
[18] Statement by Africa Group et al., WTO document IP/C/W/296 available at *www.wto.org*.

Compulsory licensing[19]

TRIPS itself does allow for compulsory licensing under certain narrow conditions. Just what latitude the agreement provides has been a source of great controversy. The best guide probably remains what the WTO itself states are the limits:[20]

> The agreement allows compulsory licensing as part of the agreement's overall attempt to strike a balance between promoting access to existing drugs and promoting research and development into new drugs. But the term 'compulsory licensing' does not appear in the TRIPS Agreement. Instead, the phrase 'other use without authorization of the right holder' appears in the title of *Article 31*. Compulsory licensing is only part of this since 'other use' includes use by governments for their own purposes.
>
> Compulsory licensing and government use of a patent without the authorization of its owner can only be done under a number of conditions aimed at protecting the legitimate interests of the patent holder. For example: Normally, the person or company applying for a licence must have first attempted, unsuccessfully, to obtain a voluntary licence from the right holder on reasonable commercial terms – *Article 31b*. If a compulsory licence is issued, adequate remuneration must still be paid to the patent holder – *Article 31h*.
>
> However, for 'national emergencies', 'other circumstances of extreme urgency' or 'public non-commercial use' (or 'government use') or anti-competitive practices, there is no need to try for a voluntary licence – *Article 31b*.
>
> Compulsory licensing must meet certain additional requirements. In particular, it cannot be given exclusively to a single licensee, and usually it must be granted mainly to supply the domestic market. Compulsory licensing cannot be arbitrary.

The TRIPS Agreement does not list the reasons that might be used to justify compulsory licensing. In Article 31, it does mention national emergencies, other circumstances of extreme urgency and anti-competitive practices – but only as grounds when some of the normal requirements for compulsory licensing do not apply, such as the need to try for a voluntary licence first.

In order to get around the strictures of Article 31 the Africa Group proposes that it 'be read in light of the objectives and principles set forth in Articles 7 and 8'.

---

[19] See also Chapter 2 by Scherer and Watal in this volume.
[20] Found under 'Information about TRIPS' at *www.wto.org*.

Article 7
Objectives
The protection and enforcement of intellectual property rights should contribute to the promotion of technological innovation and to the transfer and dissemination of technology, to the mutual advantage of producers and users of technological knowledge and *in a manner conducive to social and economic welfare, and to a balance of rights and obligations.* [Italics added]

Article 8
Principles
Members may, in formulating or amending their laws and regulations, adopt measures necessary to protect health and nutrition, and to promote the public interest in sectors of vital importance to their socio-economic and technological development, provided that such measures are consistent with the provisions of this Agreement.[21]

This interpretation is possible, the Africa Group claims, because of the 1969 Vienna Convention on the Law of Treaties, which states that a 'treaty shall be interpreted in good faith in accordance with the ordinary meaning to be given to the terms of the treaty in their context and in light of its object and purpose'.

The Africa Group brief pursues the 'reading in' argument further in its interpretation of Article 31 with reference to compulsory licensing. It argues that 'Where confronted with specific situations where the patent rights over medicines are not exercised in a way that meets the objectives of Article 7, Members may take measures to ensure that they will be achieved – such as the granting of compulsory licenses.'

Very important to the Africa Group is the objective of technology transfer, which it views as 'the development of domestic production of pharmaceutical products'. Taken at face value, this means that if a pharmaceutical company does not start local production of a drug, 'Members may take measures to ensure transfer and dissemination of technology to provide better access to pharmaceuticals'.

Article 8 of the Africa Group brief proceeds in the same fashion: 'Nothing in the TRIPS Agreement will prevent Members from adopting measures to protect public health, as well as from pursuing the overarching policies defined in

---

[21] The WTO website says of Article 7 that it 'recognizes that the protection of intellectual property should contribute to the promotion of technological innovation and to the transfer and dissemination of technology, to the mutual advantage of users and producers of technological knowledge and in a manner conducive to social and economic welfare and to a balance of rights and obligations'. Similarly, it says of Article 8, dealing with public health, that it 'makes it clear that WTO Members may, in formulating or amending their rules and regulations, adopt measures necessary to protect public health and nutrition, provided that such measures are consistent with the provisions of the Agreement'.

Article 8.' It appears as if the brief is reading the objectives of Article 8 to override its important qualification 'provided that such measures are consistent with the provisions of this Agreement'.

Parallel importing[22]

The TRIPS Agreement simply says that none of its provisions, except those dealing with non-discrimination ('national treatment' and 'most-favoured-nation treatment'), can be used to address the issue of exhaustion of intellectual property rights in a WTO dispute. In other words, even if a country allows parallel imports in a way that might violate the TRIPS Agreement, this cannot be raised as an issue of dispute in the WTO unless fundamental principles of non-discrimination are involved. As the relevant article in TRIPS (Article 6) says little about parallel trade, the Africa Group brief simply states that 'Members should therefore confirm their right of applying regimes of exhaustion of rights in their jurisdiction'.

What is novel in the Africa Group submission is the explicit connection between compulsory licensing and parallel trade. In short, it calls for the explicit repudiation of Article 31(f), which reads 'any such use shall be authorized predominantly for the supply of the domestic market of the Member authorizing such use'. The brief states that 'the reading of Article 31(f) should confirm that nothing in the TRIPS Agreement will prevent Members to grant compulsory licenses to supply foreign markets'. This position clearly is to the benefit of the larger signatories such as India and Indonesia. They would require the latitude to issue a compulsory licence on a drug and then to export it to other developing countries with impunity.

One should also note that 'foreign markets' *would potentially include developed as well as developing markets.*

Differential pricing

One surprise in the Africa Group brief was the dismissal of differential pricing. The brief suggested that differential pricing was not an issue to discuss in the context of TRIPS. It suggested other forums such as the WHO as more appropriate. The one concern in the brief about differential pricing was that a potential agreement might blunt the effort to redefine TRIPS itself. The relevant passage reads: 'In no way should discussions on differential pricing be prejudicial to the right of Members to make use of the provisions of the TRIPS Agreement, such as parallel imports and compulsory licenses.'

Such a remark reinforces the concern that the focus is more on restructuring pharmaceutical markets than on the question of affordability.

[22] See Chapter 3 by Maskus and Ganslandt in this volume for more details on parallel imports.

FROM GENEVA TO DOHA

Throughout the summer of 2001, the Africa Group countries as well as India and Brazil pushed hard for the then upcoming WTO ministerial summit in Doha to address the issues raised in the submission. At a two-day meeting of the TRIPS Council, in Geneva on 28 and 29 September, delegates discussed a potential declaration concerning TRIPS and public health. It was decided to make a declaration at Doha separate from, but together with, the main ministerial declaration.

By this time, the division between countries was clearly apparent. India, Brazil and many African countries proposed a draft declaration based on the Africa Group submission. The United States and Switzerland proposed a far more limited agenda for discussion. For instance, they were reluctant to see discussed revisions to the interpretation of what is contained in TRIPS in regard to compulsory licences. They were supported by Canada, Australia and New Zealand.

The European Union attempted to straddle the divide and act as a broker. Germany and the United Kingdom had reason to worry that the EU's stance might compromise their own pharmaceutical industries. The division continued until the meeting of the TRIPS Council in Doha.

Doha

If you had polled the delegates to the WTO meeting in Doha as they arrived, many would have said that they expected the discussion of TRIPS to pose a 'deal breaker'. In my conversations with delegates, there was great concern over whether sufficient momentum existed for launching a new round such that a compromise could be reached in the scheduled Declaration on TRIPS.

On 10 November at Doha, the Council of the Whole (COW) heard the initial presentations. As predicted, deadlock seized the proceedings. The Chair then designated a committee to find compromise language between the two competing options. Its composition caused some controversy. Of the original nine members, including India, Brazil and Zimbabwe, seven were pushing for Option 1.

Option 1 proposed no threshold in terms of public health criteria to justify a state invoking its right under TRIPS to issue a compulsory licence. In the same vein, it proposed no restriction on a country achieving the same result by importing patented drugs copied in countries in which patents were not held as valid. India pushed this point, as it hoped to export copied drugs to Africa at least until 2005, when it too should, according to its TRIPS obligations, stop copying newly patented drugs.

The United States and New Zealand were the only two committee members proposing Option 2. This proposed thresholds for the issuance of compulsory licences. Although it did not go into great detail, it suggested the use of words such as 'health care crisis' and 'pandemic'. Consistent with this position, Option 2 proposed that parallel importation of copied patented drugs should occur only as a last alternative in the event of a crisis.

The Chair, after protests from Canada and Switzerland, agreed to add the EU and Japan to the 'compromise' committee. On the night of 11 November, the committee heard and rejected various proposals. Though no agreement appeared in sight, the situation remained fluid.

The critical moment came when the US negotiators held a bilateral meeting with the Brazilian negotiators. Brazil had sent a very large and politically important delegation including the minister of health, Jaime Serra. Out of the meeting came an agreement by the US to seek a compromise declaration based on Option 1, with the exception of the parallel importation provisions.

The US decision did not resolve all the issues, however. Negotiations continued over the language of the ministerial declaration, in particular the sentence 'We agree that the TRIPS Agreement does not and should not prevent Members from taking measures to protect public health.'[23] India and Brazil had pushed for the imperative phrase 'does not and shall not', which has a stronger legal meaning in international treaties. They had also wanted the above clause to read that TRIPS should 'ensure' rather than 'promote' access to medicines. They did not succeed.

On parallel importation, no agreement could be found. It was decided to refer the issue of countries with insufficient or no pharmaceutical manufacturing capacity to the TRIPS Council. It is to report back to the General WTO Council before the end of 2002.

Another notable part of the declaration was that the least developed countries in Africa could push their accession to TRIPS back to 2015.

IMPACT OF DOHA DECLARATION ON TRIPS AND PUBLIC HEALTH

For all the discussion that went into the Declaration on TRIPS, it is not clear what may happen as a result of it. The declaration is a political statement, not a renegotiation of TRIPS. In that sense it merely restates for clarification what was already in TRIPS. The declaration did not alter TRIPS, nor did it add new issues to the TRIPS framework, although there had been some NGO pressure to exempt life forms and genetic codes from TRIPS disciplines.

The declaration will have a direct impact only if a complaint involving a developing country's issuance of a compulsory licence reaches a WTO dispute resolution panel. In that case, the panel would refer to the declaration in coming to a decision. The panel would probably follow the Declaration's broader understanding of an acceptable compulsory licence.

[23] See Doha Ministerial Declaration at *www.wto.org*.

In a broad sense, Doha put TRIPS to the test of political opposition, and TRIPS survived. Even the critics of TRIPS, India and Brazil, did not suggest that they would remove their signatures from the agreement. Still, the declaration does raise the possibility that India and Brazil may seek to issue compulsory licences and to use domestic production as a source for export sales to developing countries without a manufacturing capacity. The key country to watch is India, given its well-developed domestic pharmaceutical industry.

LOOKING TOWARDS 2005

The Doha Declaration on TRIPS will certainly not be the last word on the relationship between TRIPS and access to essential medicines, nor on the structure of the international pharmaceutical market. The next date of significance is 1 January 2005 when the middle tier of developing countries is scheduled to have passed TRIPS implementation legislation. India is the largest and most important country in this group.

As Keith Maskus laid out in an earlier quotation, the key question for India and other developing countries is whether the static welfare losses of higher new drug prices can be matched and exceeded by dynamic welfare gains in investment, technology and institutional improvements.

The literature into this question has reached massive proportions. Claims and counter-claims fly back and forth. Even ardent proponents of robust intellectual property right protections must admit the definitive empirical proof of long-term net welfare gain deriving from higher standards of enforcement remains incomplete. Space and time do not allow here for a full review of the literature. What can be done is to point to a few suggestive studies and trends. From these emerge a strong basis for hope that India and other developing countries will benefit by adopting TRIPS-level intellectual property right protections.

Reassessing the potential welfare of higher levels of patent protection

First it is important to point out that when a country accedes to TRIPS, the protections only extend to drugs in which the patent is still in force and to future drugs. Drugs that are off-patent will not be affected. For example, the WHO's Model List of Essential Drugs lists some 300 drugs. Jayashree Watal estimates that less than five per cent, or fewer than 20 drugs, are under patent protection anywhere in the world.[24] Professor Heinz Redwood has calculated that at the time of its implementation, TRIPS would have covered (according to value of sales) only 10.4 per cent of the drugs sold in India and 13 to 15 per cent

---

[24] See Jayashree Watal, 'Background Note', found at *http://www.who.int/medicines/library/edm_general/who-wto-hosbjor/wto_background_e.doc.*

of those sold in Brazil.[25] This is not too surprising. In developed countries patented pharmaceuticals account for under 25 per cent of the total market for prescription drugs. For instance, of the 200 top-selling prescription drugs in the United States in 1994, 95 per cent were off-patent.[26]

Still, one would expect that pharmaceutical patent-holders would seek patent protection in developing countries for drugs still under patent and for new drugs. The impact of TRIPS protection on the price of those patented drugs depends on three factors:

1. Market structure before and after the newer IPR come into force. This includes elements such as the number of firms (domestic and foreign) competing with rights-holders, the type of competition, the ease of market entry and exit, quality differentiation among products, openness to trade and wholesale and retail distribution mechanisms.
2. Demand elasticity or 'what the market will bear', a key variable determining market power, may vary markedly across countries and over time.
3. The presence of substitute off-patent therapeutic treatments.

Keith Maskus, among others, has cited the structure of market competition before the introduction of new IPR as the single most critical factor in the potential impact on drug prices.[27]

Demand elasticity depends largely on a country's income. Typically, the wealthier a country is, the higher is the price. Lower drug prices are related with lower national incomes. This is a result of price discrimination by pharmaceutical manufacturers. The United Kingdom's Office of Fair Trading describes this process as follows:

> There are many areas of business where [price discrimination] is a usual and legitimate commercial practice. For example ... in industries where there are large fixed costs and low marginal costs (the cost of supplying each additional unit of output is very small compared to the initial investment to set up the business). In most markets undertakings are normally expected to set prices equal to their marginal cost but in industries with high fixed costs an undertaking which did so might never be able to recover its fixed costs. It may therefore be more efficient to set higher prices to customers with a higher willingness to pay.

---

[25] Cited in J. Watal and Heinz Redwood, *New Horizons in India: The Consequences of Pharmaceutical Patent Protection* (Felixstowe, Suffolk: Oldswicks Press, 1994) and *Brazil – The Future Impact of Pharmaceutical Patents* (Felixstowe, Suffolk: Oldswicks Press, 1995).
[26] Cited in J. Watal and Graham Dukes, 'Change and growth in Generic Markets in Developed and Developing Countries', in Félix Lobo and Germán Velásquez (eds), *Medicines and the New Economic Environment* (Madrid: World Health Organization and University Carlos III, 1998).
[27] Maskus, *Intellectual Property Rights in the Global Economy*, pp. 160–1.

In general price discrimination will not be an abuse in such industries if it leads to higher levels of output than an undertaking could achieve by charging every customer the same price.[28]

Price discrimination is a benefit to developing countries less able or unable to pay the normal, uniform profit-maximizing price. They gain access to products otherwise unavailable. New medicines, for example, can be made available at a lower cost in developing countries if companies are able to discriminate in setting prices across countries.

The ability to practise price discrimination depends, of course, on the ability to preserve market segments as distinct markets. This requires, in innovative markets, the presence of a degree of exclusivity – in the form either of patents or of other types of intellectual property (IP). By extension, the ability to practise discriminatory pricing also depends on lack of arbitrage (leakage between segments). The firm can charge different prices in the segments only if it is not possible for a third party to come along and buy at one price in a market and sell the product at another price in another market.

As to the third factor, the presence of substitute off-patent therapeutic treatments, very few drugs do not have some substitute therapeutic treatment.

The combination of these factors may lead to very limited price impacts on on-patent drugs currently in the market. A case in point is the experience of Canada.[29] In preparation for the signing of the North American Free Trade Agreement (NAFTA), in 1993 Canada upgraded its intellectual property laws. Specifically, the new law, known popularly as Bill C-91, ended the practice of compulsory licensing of patented pharmaceutical drugs developed by foreign drug companies.[30] The fear at the time was that these companies would exploit their 'monopoly' position and force up the price of patented drugs.[31] But ever since 1993, the average price of patented drugs has increased below the rate of inflation.

For the past two years, prices have dropped by an average annual rate of two per cent.[32] In Canada, the difference between the prices of patented and generic

---

[28] Office of Fair Trading, Chapter 11, 402 (March 1999), cited in Julian Morris, Rosalind Mowatt and W. Duncan Reekie, *Ideal Matter: Globalisation and the Intellectual Property Debate* (New Delhi: Liberty Institute, 2001), pp. 51–4. The discussion here of price discrimination draws from this recent work.

[29] See Owen Lippert, Bill McArthur and Cynthia Ramsay, 'A Submission Prepared by the Fraser Institute for the House of Commons Industry Committee Concerning Bill C-91 (A Bill to Amend the Patent Act)', at *http://www.fraserinstitute.ca.*

[30] See Patent Act Amendment Act of 1992, S.C., ch. 2, §3 (1993) (Can.).

[31] See Greg Ip, 'State Intervention, Canadian-Style: There's a Right Way and Wrong Way to Guide Markets', *The Financial Post*, 31 December 1994, p. 39 (discussing positive effects of patent, including Canadian pharmaceutical companies' increase in research and development of new products and emphasis on export).

[32] Patented drug prices decreased by approximately 2 per cent in 1995. Barrie McKenna, 'Ottawa seeks Prescription for Drug Patent Battle', *Globe and Mail*, 17 February 1997, p. B4.

drugs is now about 20 per cent.[33] Although the claim is made that the Patented Medicine Prices Review Board (PMPRB), set up by Bill C-91 to monitor drug prices and, if necessary, to roll them back, has contributed to price restraint, the actual number and scope of PMPRB interventions have been modest. Of more importance, one could claim, has been the consistently competitive nature of the pharmaceutical drug market in Canada, which the PMPRB has no mandate to regulate. In 1993, there were 45 drug companies in Canada providing therapeutic-class drugs. The largest held an eight per cent market share.[34] The same is true today.

Canada's experience of relatively benign effects on the prices of pharmaceutical drugs from increased patent production is not unique, at least according to a major new study of nine post-IPR reform countries in the developing world conducted by Richard P. Rozek and Ruth Berkowitz.[35] They found no evidence of unusual price increases for existing on-patent pharmaceutical products in, for example, South Korea, Mexico, Taiwan and Hungary. They cited, but did not analyse, factors such as competition within therapeutic classes, price regulation, government bulk purchasing and state competition policies.

Economists have attempted to simulate the likely price effects of the introduction of product patents for the patentable segment of the pharmaceutical market in Argentina and India. The results of these studies are highly sensitive to the methodologies used and the assumptions made. Watal calculated the potential price effects of introducing patents in India under the high-cost assumption that the domestic market for patented drugs would revert completely to multinational companies.[36] She estimated that the weighted-average price increase for patented drugs could be as low as 26 per cent, although she stresses that other assumptions could lead to other results. One should add, however, that in the case of new breakthrough drugs, if it were not for the fact of the patent incentive in the first place, they might never have come to market.

World Bank economist Carsten Fink, building on Watal's work, developed a partial equilibrium model to simulate the effects of introducing patent protection for pharmaceutical products in India. His work examined how stronger patent rights might affect prices, static consumer welfare and the profits of

---

[33] Owen Lippert, 'Submission to Patented Medicine Prices Review Board', 1999, available at www.pmprb.gc.ca.

[34] See 'IMS Canada Reports New Treatments Push Canadian Pharmaceutical Sales Up 10% Over 1997', *Canada Newswire*, 17 March 1998, available in *Westlaw*, 17 March 1998 and *Canwire*, 20 October 2000.

[35] See Richard P. Rozek and Ruth Berkowitz, 'The Effects of Patent Protection on the Prices of Pharmaceutical Products: Is Intellectual Property Protection Raising the Drug Bill in Developing Countries?', *Journal of World Intellectual Property*, Vol. 1, No. 2, 1998, pp. 179–243.

[36] Jayashree Watal, 'Introducing Product Patents in the Indian Pharmaceutical Sector: Implications for Prices and Welfare', *World Competition*, 20 (1999), pp. 5–21.

multinational enterprises.³⁷ He found that 'if future drug discoveries are mainly new varieties of already existing therapeutic treatments, the impact is likely to be small. If newly discovered drugs are medical breakthroughs, however, prices may be significantly above competitive levels and static welfare losses relatively large.'³⁸ Thus, the ability of firms to raise prices may be restrained by the availability of 'close, off-patent therapeutic substitutes'. His research suggested that the availability of therapeutic substitutes could contain these price increases to as low as 12 per cent. The price change for individual drugs, of course, could vary.

Earlier studies, using less detailed data, arrived at higher price increase estimates. As Maskus himself admits, the more recent studies estimating a lower range of price increases reflect greater attention to the existing market structure.³⁹ An important feature of drug markets, it must be recognized, is that they are not monopoly markets, as there are few regulatory barriers to entry.

ASSESSING THE LONG-TERM DYNAMIC GAINS

Improved intellectual property protection should bring dynamic economic gains in at least three areas:

- Increased investment, licensing and technology transfer,
- Indigenous innovation, and
- Enhanced institutional performance.

Robert E. Evenson and Carlos A. Primo Braga ably reviewed the literature on this subject to 1990 in a World Bank study.⁴⁰ It is fair to say that the findings up to then were tentative. Newer studies, however, have begun to demonstrate a consistently positive correlation between more robust intellectual property protections and desirable economic benefits.⁴¹

---

³⁷ Carsten Fink, *How Stronger Patent Protection in India Might Affect the Behaviour of Transnational Pharmaceutical Industries*, World Bank Working Paper No. 2352 (2000).
³⁸ Ibid., p. 29.
³⁹ Maskus, *Intellectual Property Rights in the Global Economy*, p. 164.
⁴⁰ See Carlos A. Primo Braga, 'Guidance from Economic Theory', and Robert E. Evenson, 'Survey of Empirical Studies', in World Bank Discussion Papers (1990).
⁴¹ See Richard T. Rapp et al., 'Benefits and Costs of Intellectual Property Protection in Developing Countries,' *Journal of World Trade*, Vol. 24, No. 75 (1990), pp. 77–90 (discussing costs and benefits of intellectual property protection in developing countries); see also Robert M. Sherwood, *Intellectual Property and Economic Development* (Boulder, CO: Westview Press, 1990) pp. 190–99 (examining the relationship between economic development and intellectual property). For correlations between intellectual property rights and economic growth, see Johan Torstensson, 'Property Rights and Economic Growth: An Empirical Study', *Kyklos*, Vol. 47, No. 2 (1994), pp. 231–47.

Investment

Special mention must go to the pioneering work of Edwin E. Mansfield of the University of Pennsylvania. In 1994 Mansfield published an empirical study of the impact of intellectual property rights protection on foreign direct investment and licensing.[42] He examined 100 major US firms operating in six different industries. He found a correlation, if not perhaps a direct causal link, between the intellectual property protection of a country and the extent and variety of foreign direct investment and technology licensing. In short, the higher a country's level of intellectual property protection, the more likely companies were to invest in higher stages of production and transfer more technology.

Since Mansfield's initial work, there have been a large number of finer-grained studies seeking to explore the relationship between the intellectual property rights protection of developing countries and the specific types of investment or licensing undertaken by foreign corporations. Keith Maskus, Carlos A. Primo Braga and Carsten Fink have done a lot of work in this area. A recent publication provides a good overview of their research.[43] The topic possesses many intricacies and unanswered questions. Still the basic insight of Mansfield has not been challenged. Companies invest in and transfer technology more readily to countries with higher levels of intellectual property protection.

Indigenous innovation

A peculiar circular logic appears embedded in the discussion of technological innovation in developing countries. On the one hand, developing countries have stated support and interest in local inventions. On the other, they have been reluctant to establish the kind of intellectual property regime to uphold local innovation, preferring instead access to foreign innovation through unrestricted imitation. The missing point is that protection of local innovation requires at the same time protection of foreign innovation.

Granted, many countries have not had the experience of strong intellectual property rights protection and may not fully understand its positive effects on indigenous technology.[44] Still, there is no reason to assume that these countries

---

[42] Edwin Mansfield, *Intellectual Property Protection, Foreign Direct Investment, and Technology Transfer*, International Finance Corporation, Discussion Paper 19, Washington, DC, 1994; and *Intellectual Property Protection, Direct Investment, and Technology Transfer: Germany, Japan and the United States*, International Finance Corporation, Discussion Paper 27, Washington, DC, 1995.

[43] Carlos A. Primo Braga and Carsten Fink, 'The Relationship between Intellectual Property Rights and Foreign Direct Investment', *Duke Journal of Comparative and International Law*, Vol. 9, Issue 1, Fall 1998, pp. 163–88; and, in ibid., Keith Maskus, 'The Role of Intellectual Property Rights in Encouraging Foreign Direct Investment and Technology Transfer', pp. 109–61.

[44] Robert Sherwood, 'Intellectual Property in South America: How Soon Will it Work?', *NAFTA: Law and Business Review of the Americas*, Vol. 4, No. 2 (Spring 1998), pp. 77–90.

could not generate as many advances in knowledge on a per capita basis as any other country. The problem lies not in the intelligence and creativity of their citizenry but in the institutional protection afforded the fruits of their labour.

There are a significant number of influential patented innovations coming from the developing world. The problem is that they are being patented in the US. Margalit Edelman, in her survey of inventors in developing countries, found that inventors throughout the developing world incur the cost of a US patent only because they do not believe their own country provides adequate protection.[45] Having made the effort to secure a US patent, the tendency is, therefore, to seek to develop the product in the US. This was the case recently with two Indian scientists who received a US patent for an analgesic compound.[46]

At the conference, Dr. R.A. Mashelkar, Director General of India's Council of Scientific and Industrial Research, lamented that only $US 3 billion is spent on research in India. Though many reasons may explain that low figure, certainly the lack of patent protection has to be one of them. India's patent office estimates that approximately $US 2 billion worth of discoveries are registered abroad by resident and non-resident Indians.[47] The United Nations Development Programme estimates that India loses $2 billion in resources owing to its 'brain drain' to the United States.[48] India has the resources but not the patent protection infrastructure to create a strong enough incentive for its most talented researchers to patent in their own country.

Enhanced institutional performance

Intellectual property rights are part of a legal and institutional framework that, by lowering transaction costs, can create the conditions necessary for technological development. If strong protections can be created and held in place, contractual efficiency should ensure that new local technology will be discovered and, more importantly, that domestic and international technology can be fully exploited.

Maskus, for example, comments: 'IPRs (Intellectual Property Rights) are an important component of the general regulatory system, including taxes, investment regulations, production incentives, trade policies and competition rules. As such, it is joint implementation of a pro-competitive business environment that matters overall for FDI.'[49]

---

[45] Margalit Edelman, 'Why Foreign Inventors Want to Patent in the US', *Fraser Forum*, February 2001.
[46] 'US Patent Granted', found at *http://www.pharmabiz.com/archives/July2001/pat290.asp*.
[47] V.K. Shashikumar, 'Registered Overseas', *The Week*, 4 April 1999 at *http://www.theweek.com/99apr04/biz2.htm*.
[48] UNDP, *Human Development Report 2001*, found at *http://www.undp.org/hdr2001/pr5.pdf*.
[49] Keith Maskus, 'The Role of Intellectual Property Rights in Encouraging Foreign Direct Investment and Technology Transfer', Paper for the Conference 'Public–Private Initiative After TRIPS: Designing a Global Agenda' (1997), p. 13.

Contractual efficiency should also lower the costs and improve the results of local industries receiving, adapting and utilizing foreign technology. A society's overall contractual efficiency, however that may be measured, may prove critical in its ability both to adapt and to invent new technology. Walter Park and Carlos Ginarte have found a strong correlation between a country's ability to define and to enforce intellectual property rules and economic growth. They posit that the fundamental growth mechanism is the ability to absorb and generate new technology.[50]

In sum, intellectual property rights are just one, perhaps small, part of the complete package of individual rights upon which economic opportunity and development ultimately depend. Adopting stronger intellectual property rights protection contributes overall to a country's institutional capacity to define, monitor and enforce all property rights. The public costs include the upgrading of judicial, legal and administrative systems, the training of the legal community and the bolstering of private managerial competence to contract and license technology. These are comparatively small costs in dollar terms, but much larger ones in the sense that they depend on the political courage to convey a vision of why and how short-term welfare losses will lead to long-term dynamic economic gains.

India is already seeing the industrial benefit in pursuing original research over compulsory licensed exports

As a document, TRIPS has been in existence since 1991. For a decade, the rules in TRIPS on compulsory licensing and parallel importing have been known to developing countries. What is different from 1991 is that there is now a generic pharmaceutical industry in the developing world, specifically India, that has yet to grapple with the implementation of TRIPS.

One can understand the dilemma of the Indian pharmaceutical industry. The industry confronts a domestic market that works and intellectual property laws that do not. Domestic competition is fierce. India has over 200 national drug companies and as many as 20,000 regional ones.'[51] As no patent law functionally exists, new generic companies pop up rapidly to challenge the existing generic companies such as Dr Reddy's Cipla. Existing companies need to export in order to survive, as export profit margins are higher than for domestic sales.[52]

[50] Walter G. Park and Carlos Ginarte, 'Intellectual Property Rights and Economic Growth', *Contemporary Economic Policy*, No. 15 (1997), pp. 51–61.
[51] See Noel J. de Souza, 'Overview of the Indian Pharmaceutical Industry', *Pharmaceutical News*, Vol. 5, No. 6, 1998 available at *www.gbhap.com/magazines/pharmanews/selections.htm*.
[52] See Atul Rastogi, 'Dr. Reddy's 20-F Insight', at *http://www.indiainfoline.com/phar/feat/drre.html*.

Yet the wholesale expansion of compulsory licensing and parallel importing would provide only a short-term gain for generic drug companies in developing countries. The competition they face at home would be just as strong as from abroad. Already, disputes have arisen among developing countries about trade access for generic drugs. Argentina, a significant generic producer, did not sign the Africa Group submission to the TRIPS Council. One speculates that this had something to do with India's complaint before the WTO that Argentina is blocking the sale there of copied Indian drugs.

Undermining TRIPS will ultimately not help India's drug companies. Companies can enter the market with relative ease. As generic drugs do not lend themselves to product differentiation, competition drives the price of drugs down to the marginal cost of production. Indian companies face the same problem as other producers of bulk commodities – declining prices and thin profits.

Even if the TRIPS Council concludes in favour of the parallel importation of copied under-patent drugs, Indian companies may still not see profit relief. Instead of domestic competition, they will face international competition from Brazil, Argentina and, on the horizon, China. Just as in India, drug prices in developing countries will move towards the marginal price of production. Furthermore, an aggressive stance on compulsory licensing will not help Indian companies to secure legitimate access to US and EU markets. Lawful sales of generic drugs to the United States and the European Union offer Indian companies an opportunity for above-average returns. They have a comparative advantage in low labour and production costs. EU regulators and US will look dimly on Indian requests if the same companies copy and sell patented drugs in developing markets.

India's best pharmaceutical companies have figured this out. K. Balaji writes: 'companies like Ranbaxy, Cipla, Cadila and Wockhardt have shifted their R&D focus from process research to discovering new molecules ... Drug discovery costs in India are low ... This represents a huge competitive strength waiting to be encashed.'[53]

TRIPS offers India the opportunity to employ its most important comparative advantage, a skilled, educated people. India has the capacity to earn above-marginal-cost revenues on new products. Why then compete against China and Brazil simply on the basis of low wage rates?

---

[53] K. Balaji, 'Post Patent Expiry Era: An Indian Pharmaceutical Industry Perspective,' May 2001, at *www1.frost.news*.

ADDING UP THE COSTS AND BENEFITS

Clearly, the transition towards more robust intellectual property protection does not come without a cost. There may be a static loss owing to potentially higher drug costs. It is important, however, to keep in mind the following considerations:

- Potential price increases affect only patented drugs.
- The patented drugs affected are generally new introductions to the market, as market structure, demand elasticity and substitutes contain increases.
- The prices of new drugs, although they may be higher than for copied drugs, are still conditioned by market factors.
- Differential pricing and large-scale purchasing may moderate entry prices.

The welfare cost of limited increases in drug prices should be offset by the dynamic gains, including increased foreign direct investment, increased technology transfer and greater domestic innovation because of increased incentives. The key consideration is to view intellectual property rights as part of the institutional infrastructure of a country.

CONCLUSION

Finally one has to return to the hard case that has led to the questioning of TRIPS as an impediment to access to essential medicines, the HIV–AIDS drug situation in sub-Saharan Africa. For a start, one must recognize that the crisis in southern Africa is unprecedented in modern public health. The uniqueness of the situation has led to awkward responses from both government and industry.

Two points stand out and are discussed elsewhere in this volume. Pharmaceutical companies have responded, perhaps not as quickly as they might have, with substantial resources.[54] The SmithGlaxoKline, Pfizer and Merck corporations, as well as the Bill and Melinda Gates Foundation, are providing genuine assistance. Their combined contributions rival the current pledges to the UN AIDS Fund.

Amir Attaran and Lee Gillespie-White make a strong case that patent protection is not the most significant issue in the sub-Saharan HIV–AIDS crisis.[55] They point instead to a lack of donor financing of treatment programmes.

---

[54] See Chapter 5 by Harvey Bale in this volume.
[55] Amir Attaran and Lee Gillespie-White, 'Do Patents for Antiretroviral Drugs Constrain Access to AIDS Treatment in Africa?', Special Communication, *Journal of the American Medical Association*, Vol. 286, No. 15, pp. 1886–92, 17 October 2001. See also Amir Attaran and Jeffrey Sachs, 'Defining and Refining International Donor Support for Combating the AIDS Pandemic', *The Lancet*, vol. 357, Issue 9249, 6 January 2001, p. 57.

Is it just money that stands between the current HIV–AIDS crisis in southern Africa and an effective response? Certainly, the money pledged by governments of developed countries seems small in comparison with their other priorities. The developed countries pay out each day $US 700 million in farm subsidies. The European Union, in particular, spends billions of dollars every year on export subsidies for food that contribute to a shattering of domestic African agricultural capacity. If the EU redirected those subsidies to African health care, the effect would be doubly efficacious. African farmers could achieve sustainable incomes and Africans as a whole would have a stronger health care infrastructure.

Yet dollars and donations often do not achieve the desired result either in Africa or in any other country. Of the entire range of means to improve life, two stand out as the most effective in the long term – science and markets. As the WHO itself has documented,

> Today, through a combination of public and private health systems, nearly two-thirds of the world's people are estimated to have access to full and effective treatment with the medicines they need. In absolute terms, the number of people with access to essential drugs grew from roughly 2.1 billion in 1977 to 3.8 billion in 1997.[56]

Part of responsibility for solving the HIV–AIDS crisis in southern Africa must be borne by the research-based pharmaceutical industry. Working together with public researchers, the industry has an obligation to find a vaccine or, if that is not possible, a simpler, less expensive drug maintenance regime. It is a legitimate argument that undermining global patent law in order to hothouse the production of first-generation drugs undermines the incentive for the research-based industry to commit its resources and expertise to AIDS research. Companies, even big ones, ultimately are responsible to their shareholders. It is difficult to justify billions of dollars to research when a risk exists that the final result will be immediately expropriated.

James Love of CPTECH suggests that governments could direct much of the research and development of HIV–AIDS drugs. He correctly points out that already governments fund much of the basic research. The corollary to that observation is that reducing drug prices through compulsory licensing and price controls would thus have little impact on innovation.[57] MSF in its recent statement to the WHO Executive Board makes this suggestion about drugs for

---

[56] World Health Organization, *Revised Drug Strategy. WHO's Work in Pharmaceuticals and Essential Drugs*. Geneva, World Health Organization, 1998 (document reference EB/RDS/RC/1).
[57] See presentation by James Love at *http://www.cptech.org/ip/health/rnd/carrotsnsticks.html*, and also by Ralph Nader at *http://www.cptech.org/ip/health/econ/govrnd.html*.

other diseases: 'Not-for-profit drug development initiatives should be explored to take drug R&D for neglected diseases out of the marketplace altogether.'[58]

Two responses can be made to this suggestion. First, the research phase of discovering a new medicine accounts for only about 36 per cent of the total costs of research and development.[59] The other 63 per cent are largely regulatory costs, including government-mandated testing and extensive and detailed market entry regulations. As well as the regulatory costs, there is the risk that governments will not act decisively to prevent unauthorized copying. Ultimately, prices reflect the high-cost and high-risk environment.

Secondly and more importantly, the modern history of medicine is characterized not just by scientific advances but also by the translation of knowledge into improved health care through the dynamic of a market economy in physician care, medical technology and pharmaceutical drugs. The efficiency of the health delivery system is as important to health outcomes as is the state of medical knowledge. Like them or not, private markets have historically proved to be more efficient than governments in the delivery of services. At the very least, one can argue that high levels of both private and public investment into pharmaceutical research will provide the quickest solutions to health care challenges.

To lower prices and spur further research, more legitimate competition within the pharmaceutical industry itself is needed. Achieving this requires less government micro-management of pharmaceutical markets and stronger intellectual property rights. The irony is that government market interventions and tenuous intellectual property rights have led to the consolidation of research-based pharmaceutical companies into large entities. Big government has created big 'Pharma'.

If the free market view prevailed, the large companies of today would face much stiffer competition from new-entry entrepreneurial companies. Also, it would probably create a shareholder demand to split up the big companies. The theory goes as follows. Large companies tend to have disproportionately large transaction costs. The efficiencies of scale are overwhelmed by the inefficiencies of managing a large organization whose internal operations are separate from market price signals. In a market-place with less risk of government intervention and the appropriation of intellectual property, shareholders may correctly surmise that greater value lies in having separate companies with more efficient and focused management.

---

[58] 14 January 2002 found at *http://www.accessmed-msf.org/prod/publications.asp?scntid =1412021123512&contenttype=PARA&*.
[59] The allocation of research and development spending is found at *http://www.phrma.org/ publications/publications/profile01/chapter2.phtml#allocation*.

A freer, more secure international pharmaceutical market would, moreover, address many of the pricing concerns now raised in discussions about access to essential drugs. Upholding the integrity of TRIPS is vital to securing real and sustainable improvements in the health of millions of people.

The Doha Declaration on TRIPS should be considered the final word on the issue. The TRIPS Council should not endorse parallel importation except in the case of a genuine crisis. The generic drug industries in India and Brazil should explore ways to compete not only in the legitimate generic market but also in the market for patented pharmaceuticals. All companies should focus on a vaccine. Developed countries should pledge more in donations. Developing countries should support, not hinder, the effective working of the market in health care. International agencies such as the WHO should help them gain the knowledge to make their health care markets work. The WHO should not saddle the developing world with the dysfunctional legacy of state 'command and control' health care. To be sure, there is a role for the public sector – as a source of funds to address affordability, not as arbiter of market structure and outcomes.

2 THE ECONOMICS OF TRIPS OPTIONS FOR ACCESS TO MEDICINES

F. M. Scherer and Jayashree Watal

INTRODUCTION

The agreement on Trade-Related Aspects of Intellectual Property Rights (TRIPS) entered into force with the formation of the World Trade Organization (WTO) in January 1995.[1] TRIPS lays down the minimum obligatory standards for the protection of intellectual property rights (IPRs), including the patenting of pharmaceutical processes and products. Some fear that TRIPS could lead to higher prices for patented medicines in poor countries. Others argue that TRIPS contains sufficient flexibility to safeguard the public health needs of those countries. The WTO, at its fourth Ministerial Meeting in Doha, Qatar in November 2001 agreed to a Declaration on the TRIPS Agreement and Public Health which clarified the flexibility contained in this Agreement, and is currently undertaking work on some remaining aspects.[2]

This chapter explores the economic implications and limitations of policy instruments permitted under TRIPS, specifically compulsory licences (and their use by government), parallel imports and price controls. It does not deal with the legal interpretations of these provisions nor with other TRIPS provisions relevant to pricing in the pharmaceuticals sector such as trademark protection for brand names, copyright protection for labels or the protection of test data and trade secrets.

This contribution is excerpted from an earlier paper (Scherer and Watal (2001)) written for Working Group 4 of the Commission for Macroeconomics and Health of the World Health Organization. The views expressed herein are those of the authors and not attributable to any organization or institution with which they are or were associated. In particular, these views should not be attributed to the WTO or the WTO Secretariat.

[1] The text of TRIPS is available at *www.wto.org*.
[2] See *www.wto.org* for a text of the declaration and for the latest developments in the work undertaken in the WTO on TRIPS and access to medicines.

IMPLICATIONS OF TRIPS-COMPATIBLE POLICY OPTIONS FOR DEVELOPING COUNTRIES WITH ACCESS TO PATENTED MEDICINES

How the introduction of product patents will change developing countries' access to low-price medicines will vary with their pre-TRIPS patent regimes and drug procurement strategies. In the pre-TRIPS period, products still protected by patents in the most industrialized countries were available in lower-cost generic versions from at least some countries that had a vibrant domestic industry producing generic drugs,[3] called below the supplier countries, e.g. Italy in the 1960s and 1970s and Brazil, China, India, Korea and Israel more recently. These sources could dry up for patented pharmaceutical inventions that fall into the TRIPS net, i.e. those that meet the criteria of patentability in the supplier countries that did not protect pharmaceutical product patents as of January 1995.[4] The countries most significantly affected by the new TRIPS environment will be not only these supplier countries but also those that, lacking domestic production, actively encouraged the importation and use of generic substitutes from countries with export-oriented generic suppliers. Countries that relied mainly on research-oriented multinational pharmaceuticals enterprises for their drug supplies, either through production by local subsidiaries or importation, tended to pay relatively high (and often unnecessarily high) prices for state-of-the-art medicines before TRIPS was negotiated, and, in the absence of policy changes, they will continue to do so in the new environment.

The key question is what measures less developed countries[5] might adopt in the new TRIPS environment to enhance low-cost access to the newest drugs while either retaining benefits they enjoyed pre-TRIPS if they had pursued aggressive generic substitution policies or capturing some of those benefits if they have belatedly recognized the advantages of pro-substitution policies. Several policy options, notably compulsory licensing, utilizing parallel trade and enforcing price controls, might be adopted without running afoul of the obligations imposed by TRIPS. We analyse those options here.

---

[3] In this context a generic drug is a copy of the original patented drug (i.e. the drug manufactured by or with the consent of the patent-owner). Such drugs may have their own brand names and are sometimes called 'branded generics'.

[4] One provision of TRIPS allows developing countries time up to January 2005 to introduce product-patent protection (and up to 2006 for least developed countries to enact this and all other provisions of TRIPS). But another requires the acceptance of product-patent applications for pharmaceuticals and agricultural chemicals by January 1995 and the grant of five-year exclusive marketing rights until the patent is granted or rejected, whichever is sooner, upon the fulfilment of certain conditions.

[5] This term is used throughout the chapter to include both developing and least developed countries.

Compulsory licensing and government use

For developing countries to achieve economical access to patented drugs once TRIPS has been fully implemented, one option is the issuance of compulsory licences, which are authorizations permitting a third party to make, use or sell a patented invention without the patent-owner's consent. Another, related policy instrument is the use of patents by the government or persons authorized by it for public non-commercial use. Although no examples are given, public non-commercial use might occur when national health authorities distribute drugs at no price or at cost through public health care networks.

TRIPS does not define or limit the circumstances under which patented inventions can be subjected to compulsory licensing or use by government. An important condition listed under Article 31 of TRIPS is that a prospective licensee should have been unsuccessful within a reasonable time in negotiating to obtain authorization from the patent-holder to use the patented invention 'on reasonable commercial terms and conditions'. The failed negotiations clause can be waived in the case of national emergency or extreme urgency or for non-commercial public use. Further, any use of compulsory licences must be 'predominantly for the supply of the domestic market' (Article 31 (f)) of the authorizing country, and the user must pay the patent-holder 'adequate remuneration', taking into account 'the economic value of the authorization'. TRIPS also states that in cases where compulsory licences are granted to correct anti-competitive practices, the need to do so may be taken into account in determining the amount of remuneration to be paid to the patent-holder. Thus, payments might be less than in other compulsory licensing cases. Also, such compulsory licences could, unlike others, be granted predominantly or even solely for export.

The extent to which price-reducing competition can arise through compulsory licensing depends critically upon the criteria imposed to determine the magnitude of the compensation paid. What guidance can economists give on the amount of remuneration to be paid?

Determining licence compensation rates

The US Patent Code, 35 US Code 284, provides that in cases of patent infringement, the damages awarded shall be '... *adequate to compensate* for the infringement but in no event less than a *reasonable royalty* for the use made of the invention by the infringer, together with interest and costs' [emphasis added].

One implication, confirmed by court decisions in the United States, is that there are two potentially different standards, with the 'reasonable royalty' standard tending to be less generous and/or second-best.

Figure 2.1 shows how the US Appellate Court for the Federal Circuit has interpreted the 'adequate to compensate' provisions of US statutory law. Suppose the

Figure 2.1: Royalty determination under profits lost standard

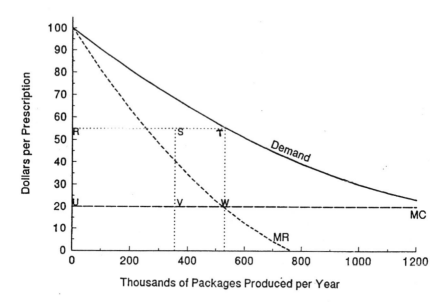

Source: Author.

demand curve for a drug product is as marked in Figure 2.1[6] and marginal production costs are $20 per standard prescription package. Without competition, the patent-holder is in effect a monopolist in the sale of its product.[7] It derives its marginal revenue function (dashed line marked MR), equates marginal revenue with marginal cost and sets a price of $55 per package, producing 530,000 packages to satisfy demand. Its contribution to profits and the repayment of research and development costs is 530,000 x (55 − 20) = $18.55 million per year. If another firm enters and supplies VW packages (= 175,000), inducing the patent-holder to reduce its output to 355,000 packages, the infringer deprives the patent-holder of profits measured by the area rectangle STWV, or 175,000 x (55 − 20) = $6.125 million per year. Under the 'adequate to compensate' law as interpreted, that is the initial measure on the basis of which damages are computed. If assessed on an *ad valorem* basis, the royalty would approximate 64 per cent of the infringer's sales.

[6] It has the equation $P = 100 - 0.1 Q + .00003 Q2$, where P is price and Q is the quantity sold (in thousands of packages).
[7] This does not mean that there are no other chemically different products with similar therapeutic effects; it means only that the products are sufficiently differentiated that the drug's patent-holder faces a downward-sloping demand curve that takes into account the availability of imperfect substitutes.

Suppose, however, that because it lacks a well-known brand name or other first-mover advantages, the infringer can obtain only a price of $40 per package for its version of the drug. Then the highest royalty it could agree to in arm's-length negotiations would be $20 per package. If the courts accepted those facts as a basis for awarding royalty, the royalty rate would be reduced to 50 per cent *ad valorem* on the infringer's lower-priced sales (which is 36 per cent relative to the patent-holder's price). If the infringer's lower price forced the patent-holder to reduce its price (which is unlikely, given evidence that branded-drug sellers tend not to reduce their prices in the face of generic competition), under a 'profits lost' standard the court would count as additional damages to be paid by the infringer the profit loss per package still sold by the patent-holder as a result of price suppression times the number of packages sold by the patent-holder. Given a downward-sloping demand curve, however, the lower price will lead to higher unit sales by the patent-holder, complicating the damages assessment problem in ways beyond the value of further exploration here.[8]

Two things are evident from this elementary exposition. First, if 'adequate remuneration' were to be construed under the simplest of the 'profits lost' tests analysed here, compulsory licensing would impose such high royalty payments on the licensed producer that there could be no price reduction and hence no expansion of drug availability at all. If the purpose of compulsory licensing schemes is to increase competitive supply and reduce prices, the 'profits lost' test cannot logically be the standard to be met in determining compensation for compulsory licensing. Second, it is evident from a large number of cases that the royalties awarded in actual compulsory licensing cases have been much lower than the 50 to 64 per cent *ad valorem* rates derived in our simple 'profits lost' example.

The United Kingdom and Canada provide the leading examples of compulsory licensing of drug patents without a finding that the anti-monopoly laws have been violated. Low royalty rates, as in the Canadian experience – typically four per cent of the licensee's sales – could provide the basis, assuming that other conditions are satisfied, for competitive drug supplies while compensating patent-holders at least to some extent for their research and development (R&D) contributions. The choices made in industrialized countries provide ample precedent for royalty-setting on the modest side of the range of possibilities.

---

[8] For an analysis showing that price suppression and loss of output by a dominant patent-holder tend not to coincide, see the declaration of F. M. Scherer submitted in the matter of Mahurkar Double Lumen Hemodialysis Catheter Patent Litigation, MDL-853, US Federal District Court for the Northern District of Illinois, September 1992.

Other obstacles

The longer the issuance of compulsory licences is delayed after patented drugs enter the market-place, the less time licensees have to recover their start-up costs and the more difficult it is to achieve effective competition among multiple generic-substitute suppliers. Thus, if compulsory licensing is to be successful, expeditious licensing procedures are a necessity. TRIPS Article 31 requires judicial or other independent review of the decisions taken by the licensing authority. Here the experience of Canada is relevant. The licensing authority there was required to reach its decisions within 18 months of a licence application. In fact, the median time to decision was 10 months for applications filed between 1969 and 1977.[9] It will also be essential for the designated authorities to establish clear and transparent precedents in early cases, as was done in Canada, so that they can perform subsequent reviews efficiently. In developing countries where the courts are overburdened with cases of all kinds and the time taken for disposal is very long, it may be advisable to designate independent administrative authorities to hear appeals on compulsory licensing cases.

The requirement under TRIPS that any compulsory drug-patent licence be authorized predominantly for the supply of the domestic market is most likely to pose serious problems to less developed countries that lack the infrastructure and technical capabilities to build a domestic industry able to supply modern pharmaceutical products reliably. Even Canada, with a high per capita income, excellent universities and a population in the 1970s of roughly 22 million, found it necessary to import most of the bulk pharmaceuticals ultimately supplied under compulsory licences. Thus, smaller less developed countries will have to issue their compulsory licences mainly for importation rather than for domestic production. This in turn requires that competitive supply sources exist in the world market. The term 'predominantly' in Article 31(f) above clearly implies that some exportation under compulsory licence in the exporting country will be allowed. Some developing-country WTO members are seeking to clarify this provision of the TRIPS Agreement, and the subject is currently under discussion in the WTO TRIPS Council following the Doha Declaration on the TRIPS Agreement and Public Health.

Compulsory licences should not, however, be seen as a magic wand for obtaining affordable access to patented medicines in developing countries, as there are three basic limitations. First, compulsory licensees must have the capability to 'reverse-engineer' or import the product without the cooperation of the patent-owner.[10] Increasingly, larger domestic companies in developing

---

[9] Gorecki (1981), p. 41.
[10] Transfer of technology, often recommended as a solution, requires the active cooperation of the patent-owner or, in the context of South–South cooperation, of its competitors.

countries are raising their R&D investments and are collaborating with multinational companies in order to achieve advanced capabilities and reach more markets. This cooperation may be accompanied by tacit agreement to restrict competition in some markets. Second, exports of compulsorily licensed products from large markets to small least developed countries can work only where the disease patterns are common to both markets. Third, compulsory licensees will be attracted only to large and profitable drug markets. Thus essential medicines with small potential volumes or mostly poor patients will not attract many applicants, however important it is from the perspective of public health. Manufacture in government-owned facilities may be a solution in these cases, although an element of public subsidy may be necessary.

Parallel trade

Parallel trade occurs when a product covered by intellectual property rights sold by or with the rights-holder's consent in state A is resold in state B without the rights-holder's authorization.[11] The incentive for this is a difference in price between the price paid by the first purchaser and the price charged in state B sufficient to cover shipping and other transaction costs and still offer gains to both the shipper and the state B buyer. It is therefore a form of arbitrage, tending to reduce differences in prices across diverse markets. For the incentive to engage in parallel trade to exist, there must be underlying market imperfections, e.g. ones stemming from monopoly power attributable to unique product patents, strong brand image differentiation or lack of price transparency, which are exploited by the original seller through a strategy of price discrimination.

Patents on drug products offering unique therapeutic features often give the drug's seller sufficient pricing discretion to engage in the cross-state price discrimination that creates incentives for parallel trade. So also may trademarks signalling the reputation a well-known multinational drugs-producer enjoys *vis-à-vis* legitimate generic imitators. However, even when parallel importation is permitted under relevant laws, it may be thwarted by differences in product approval and labelling standards enforced by national regulatory authorities, by differences in physical product characteristics such as pill shape or colour or by trademark names in diverse markets.

Because price discrimination is widely practised by multinational pharmaceuticals firms and because the costs of shipping drugs from one country to another are modest in relation to product prices, incentives for parallel trade emerge. For reasons that will become clear, parallel trade reduces the profitability of original-

---

[11] There are some who believe that this covers any product sold legitimately in country A, i.e. even when the product is sold under a compulsory licence or when intellectual property rights do not exist in that country.

drugs manufacturers and thus has been vigorously opposed by them. The conflict of interest between drug sellers and ultimate buyers has led to considerable controversy over national and international policies governing parallel trade.

National and international policies

Parallel trade in patented articles is legally permissible under what is called the exhaustion of rights doctrine. This doctrine states that once the producer of a patented product or its agent has sold its product in good faith to an independent party, the patent-holder's right to determine the conditions under which the product is resold is exhausted. If there are price differences among customers of the original manufacturer, any customer can engage in arbitrage transactions that exploit those differences.

Where controversy emerges is over the rights of a patent-holder to limit parallel trade in its products across national borders. Jurisdictions that allow only national exhaustion as distinguished from international exhaustion maintain that although the first sale in a market exhausts rights within that market, the rights-holder can still exclude unauthorized transactions from another national market to the one allowing only national exhaustion. Neither the Paris Convention on industrial property nor the TRIPS Agreement established rules determining when cross-border parallel trade could occur or be restrained. As a result, widely varying national policies exist among countries and between different intellectual property regimes within countries. For instance, the provisions on exhaustion differ *inter alia* for goods protected by trademarks (with parallel imports allowed by most countries) as compared to patents (with parallel imports discouraged by most developed states and now by many developing countries).

The underlying theory

To understand why parallel trade is such an important and controversial issue, one must know why prices are set at widely varying levels in different national markets and what the consequences of this price discrimination are. Figures 2.2(a) and 2.2(b) tell the basic theoretical story.

They assume two countries, A and B, with roughly equal numbers of cases in which the use of a particular drug product might be indicated. Thus at a zero price, equal quantities of the drug – one million prescriptions (Rx) per month – would be demanded. However, A is assumed to have a high average per capita income and B to have a low average per capita income. This 'income effect' leads to different demand curves, assumed for illustrative purposes to be straight lines, for the two countries, with the demand curve for A being higher and (at any given positive price) less price-elastic than the demand curve

Figure 2.2: Price discrimination between markets of differing weath

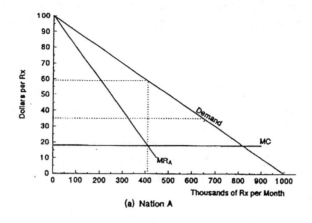

(a) Nation A

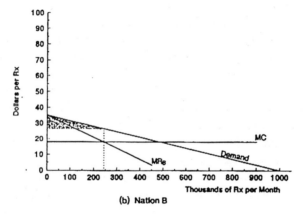

(b) Nation B

Source: Author.

for B.[12] We assume also that the drug can be produced and distributed at a constant marginal cost of $18 per Rx, shown by the horizontal lines marked *MC*.[13] Patent protection permits the drug's producer to maximize its profits, given demand and cost, in each market separately or in both markets together. In wealthy country A, the firm will derive its marginal revenue curve MR_A, equate marginal cost with marginal revenue at an output of 410(000) Rx and set

[12] Where Q is quantity consumed per month and P is the price, the inverse demand curve for country A is assumed to be $P_A = 100 - 0.1\ Q_A$ and the curve for country B is $P_B = 35 - 0.035\ Q_B$.
[13] Economies of scale or cost savings through learning by doing might invalidate this assumption, strengthening incentives for parallel trade and in some cases leading to price reductions in the countries paying high prices. For vaccine production, there is evidence of substantial cost savings with high-volume production. See case study 14-98-1450.1, 'Vaccines for the Developing World: The Challenge to Justify Tiered Pricing (Sequel)', John F. Kennedy School of Government, Harvard University (1998).

the corresponding price at $59 per Rx, earning a contribution to the repayment of its research and development outlays and to its profits measured by the rectangular area (59 − 18) × (410,000) = $16.8 million per month.

If it must charge a uniform price in every national market, the drug's producer recognizes that at the price-maximizing profits in A, it can sell nothing in low-income B, as the $59 price is higher than the maximum $35 price any consumer in B is able and willing to pay. To sell anything at all in B under a uniform price policy, the firm must reduce its price in A to less than $35, entailing a profit and R&D cost recovery sacrifice in A of at least (59 − 35) × (410,000) less (35 − 18) × (240,000) (i.e. the surplus of a $35 price less the marginal cost on additional sales of 240,000 Rx) = $5.76 million. This sacrifice is larger than the zero profit the firm could make at a $35 price in B. For prices lower than $35, it can be shown, the sacrifice in A also exceeds the gain in B, given the assumed demand functions.[14] Thus, if forced to charge a uniform price, the firm will not sell in B.

If, however, the firm can engage in price discrimination, selling in both markets will be profitable. It will derive its marginal revenue curve MR_B in national market B, equate marginal cost with marginal revenue at an output of approximately 243,000 Rx and set a much lower, $26.50, price, which maximizes profits in B. Relative to selling only in country A, this is clearly profitable for the drug's producer. It contributes incrementally to the firm's profits and R&D cost recoupment by (26.50 − 18) × (243,000) = $2.07 million. Relative to the no-sales-in-B case, it is also beneficial to the citizens of B, adding consumers' surplus measured by the dot-shaded triangular area, or approximately $1.04 million per month. Ignoring any fixed costs that might be incurred in setting up a sales outlet in country B, the drug's producer will find it worthwhile to sell at a relatively low price in B as long as at least part of B's demand curve lies above the marginal cost line − a condition, to be sure, that may not be satisfied in the very poorest countries.

Thus, under the plausible conditions assumed here, both less developed country consumers and the drugs-producer are better off with price discrimination than under uniform pricing. Although not valid under all plausible conditions, this case is typical of a broad range of economic situations conducive to what is called Ramsey–Baumol–Bradford pricing or, more simply, Ramsey pricing.[15]

---

[14] If demand for the drug at relatively low prices in country B were many times higher than demand at the same prices in country A, an exception to this uniform price case could arise, and profits would be maximized by selling in both markets at a price much lower than the price that maximizes profits in country A.

[15] The relevant theory, attributable to Frank P. Ramsey (1903–30), was after long neglect brought back to the forefront of interest by Baumol and Bradford (1970), pp. 265–83. The simpler version analysed here was actually proposed in 1839 by a railway engineer, Charles Ellet Jr, in *An Essay on the Laws of Trade* (New York: Kelley reprint, 1966). In transportation circles it has been called 'value of service' pricing. Its application to the parallel trade aspects of drug pricing has been proposed *inter alia* by Yarrow in Towse (ed.) (1995), pp. 1–11, and Danzon (1997), Chapter 7.

In the classic formulation, it is necessary to recover a substantial block of fixed costs (e.g. for research and development) by setting prices in diverse markets with differing demand elasticities. It can be shown that the most efficient solution is the one in which the more prices are elevated above the marginal costs of production, the less elastic demand is in any given market. 'Most efficient' in this sense means that the fixed costs are recovered and that the sum of the producer's surplus (e.g. contributions to fixed costs and profits) plus the consumers' surplus (i.e. the amount consumers are able and willing to pay less what they actually pay) is maximized.[16] Discriminatory pricing along Ramsey lines approaches an ideal price-setting method in an intrinsically imperfect world as closely as one can reasonably hope.

Parallel trade is relevant to this analysis because it takes advantage of the fact that prices are set lower in some markets than in others, reallocating output from the low-price markets to the higher-price markets. Its consequences are analysed in Figure 2.3, which reproduces Figure 2.2(a) with additional assumptions. It is assumed that 15,000 units of output (Rx) are diverted monthly from low-price country B to high-price country A. This shifts the demand curve remaining to be satisfied locally in A to the left by 15,000 units, yielding the new, more elastic demand curve D*. The drug's producer, confronted with this change in demand conditions, will reconsider its pricing decision, deriving marginal revenue MR* and maximizing profits by equating revised marginal revenue with marginal cost at an output of 335,000 Rx; this leads to the reduced price of $51.50, which is still high enough to attract parallel imports from B. The producer's contribution to profits and R&D cost reimbursement in national market A is reduced by the dot-shaded L-shaped area in Figure 2.3, whose magnitude is $(59 - 51.50) \times (410,000) + (51.50 - 18) \times (75,000) = \$5.59$ million. Recognizing that parallel exports from market B are significantly eroding its surplus in market A, a rational drugs-producer will reduce the quantity it offers for sale in B. This will lead to some combination of decreased supply to and reduced parallel exports from B, the first effect implying (if there is no ceiling price regulation) a price increase in B. Consumers in B are made worse off by this reaction, at least by the reduction in quantities available domestically and also (if there are no price controls) by an increase in domestic prices. If the drugs-producer recognizes that it cannot control the quantities obtained by B's parallel exporters and that the parallel export process will progress to such an

---

[16] Under the form of Ramsey pricing proposed for regulated utility price-setting by Baumol and Bradford (1970), the regulator can squeeze the producer's profits down to the point at which only normal returns on investment are realized. When profits are subjected to such a squeeze, the so-called Ramsey number has a value of less than unity. When firms are allowed to engage in price discrimination of the type illustrated here with no profit constraint, the Ramsey number has a value of unity, in which case it conforms to the model originally proposed by Ellet in 1839.

Figure 2.3: How parallel imports affect prices in market A

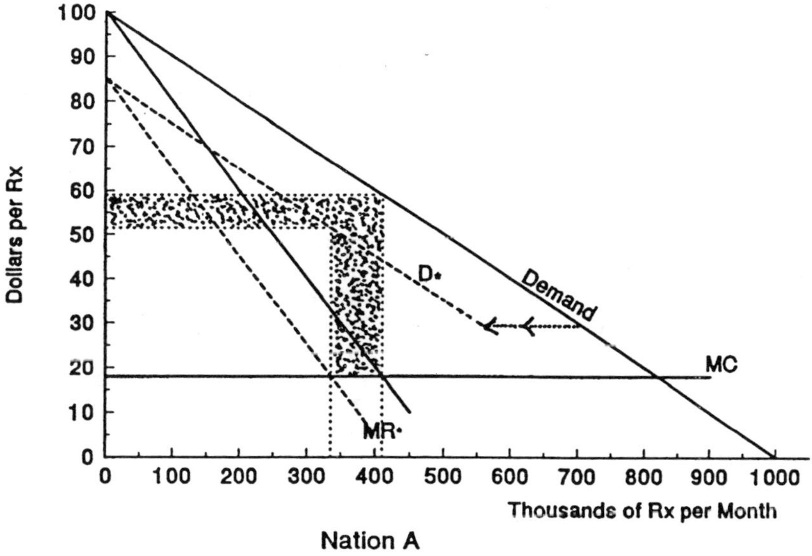

Nation A

Source: Author.

extent that perfect arbitrage occurs, the situation reverts to the uniform price case discussed above. Under the demand conditions postulated, the drugs-producer, forced to accept a uniform price, will maximize its profits by ceasing to supply low-income B altogether.

It follows that in the absence of the complications ignored thus far, low-income countries are more likely to receive patented pharmaceuticals at lower prices when drug-producers engage in cross-national price discrimination than when parallel trade narrows price differences and forces prices towards uniformity. For those who are concerned, as we are, about achieving the largest feasible supply of life-saving, debility-reducing drugs to less developed countries, parallel trade can plausibly be seen as doing more harm than good.

Complications

One complication in the analysis so far is suggested by a possible mismatch between the theory and some salient facts. If systematic price discrimination works to the benefit of lower-income countries but generates incentives for the products sold at low prices in those countries to be re-exported to high-income, high-price countries, why does a relatively poor country such as South Africa adopt policies *encouraging* parallel imports? An answer could be that for some drugs, the multinational drugs companies do not set their wholesale prices on

Figure 2.4: Market segmentation within a national market

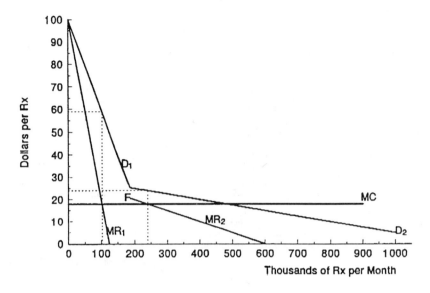

Source: Author.

the unambiguous assumption that South Africa is a low-income state. Income in South Africa is unequally distributed, unusually so: a small minority enjoys industrialized-country income levels while most of the population is poor. The affluent minority tends also to have comprehensive health insurance that covers *inter alia* prescription-drug purchases. Under these circumstances, demand conditions in South Africa are best portrayed (in Figure 2.4) by the kinked demand curve D_1D_2, the upper segment representing the demands of well-off citizens and the lower segment those of the poorer majority. The corresponding marginal revenue function begins as MR_1 and then jumps at point F to MR_2. There is a uniform-price, local profit-maximizing equilibrium that entails selling to both consumer groups at a price of $24 per Rx, at which price 240,000 Rx are filled monthly. However, the drugs-supplier finds it more profitable to sell only to the more affluent minority.[17] Thus a price of $59 is set, leading to the sale (only in market 1) of 102,500 Rx per month.[18] Profits under

---

[17] The situation here is quite similar to what happens after patents expire in a wealthy nation, such as the United States, and the original drugs-producer, with a brand image that commands sales from loyal and risk-averse prescribing physicians, finds the market for its chemical entity bifurcating into low- and high-elasticity segments. See Scherer (1996), p. 377.

[18] The price here is identical to that charged for country A in Figure 2.1 because the demand function is linear and pivoted inward from a vertical intercept value of 100. With constant marginal costs, such demand curve shifts yield unchanged prices.

Figure 2.5: Price discrimination under Cobb-Douglas demand functions

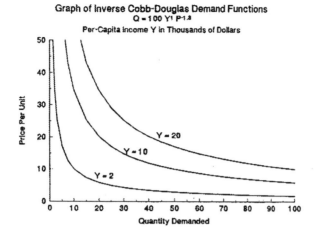

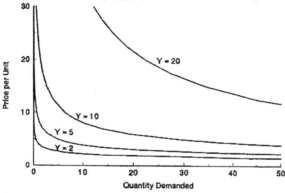

Source: Author.

this high-price strategy are (59 − 18) x (102,500) = $4.2 million per month, compared to (24 − 18) x (240,000) = $1.44 million per month under the low-price strategy. Market segmentation of this sort has apparently engendered incentives for parallel imports of some drugs by South Africa from middle-income countries such as Spain and Portugal.[19] In such cases, parallel trade confers upon low-income countries benefits in the form of reduced prices to affluent consumers and perhaps, but with less certainty, the possibility that some less affluent citizens will be able to afford the drug.

---

[19] See 'South Africa's Bitter Pill for World's Drug Makers', *New York Times*, 29 March 1998, sec. 3, p. 1. We have also benefited from conversations with a South African government official.

A second complication is that the demand functions confronting pharmaceutical manufacturers may not be linear, as assumed thus far. Economic theory textbooks often assume for reasons of mathematical tractability that demand functions are of a curvilinear form known as Cobb–Douglas. Figure 2.5(a) shows the demand relationships that would exist with the simplest Cobb–Douglas demand curves, assuming a consistent income elasticity of unity (i.e. a 100 per cent increase in per capita income leads to a 100 per cent increase in consumption, all else being equal) and constant price elasticities of −1.3. In such cases, as the demand curves have the same price elasticity at all relevant points, the same profit-maximizing price prevails regardless of the assumed income elasticity; e.g., with marginal costs of $10 per unit, the same $43.15 price will be set in every market. In this special case, no price discrimination will be observed. It is not necessary, however, to have invariant price elasticities with demand curves of the general shape shown. Figure 2.5(b) illustrates an alternative case, in which the price elasticity (the exponent of the P variable, in parentheses) becomes lower in absolute value with higher per capita income. In this case, profits will be maximized by setting lower prices in the markets with lower incomes. Real-world demand curves probably have shapes somewhere between the extremes of Figures 2.2 and 2.5. The demand curves in Figures 2.5 (a) and (b) are unrealistic in implying that prices can be raised to nearly infinite levels without choking off all demand and in assuming a huge expansion of quantity demanded as prices are reduced within the lowest range of possible values.

There is a third complication: parallel trade may occur not because prices are kept low to satisfy demand in low-income, high-elasticity countries but because some countries, however affluent they may be, impose more stringent government controls on prices than do others. The possibilities here are quite complex, but Figures 2.6(a) and 2.6(b) capture their core tendencies. We assume two countries, A and B, of equal size and with equal per capita incomes and the same straight-line free-market demand curves as those assumed for country A in Figure 2.2. If there are no price controls and parallel imports from less affluent countries, a rational firm enjoying patent protection in both countries on some more or less unique drug would set prices at the identical $59 level in the two markets. Now suppose the government of A sets a $40 ceiling price in its home market. Readers with only a faint exposure to economic theory may be surprised to learn that, because the price ceiling nullifies a monopolist's ability to benefit by restricting output, the drug's producer has an incentive to expand its supply in the price-controlled market so that the full demand of 600,000 Rx per month at the $40 price is satisfied.[20] The immediate consequence of this price control is a reduction in market A's contribution to the

---

[20] An early proof of this proposition is found in Robinson (1934), Chapter 13.

Figure 2.6: Parallel trade under price controls

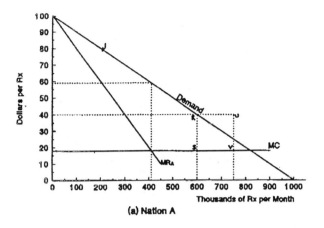

(a) Nation A

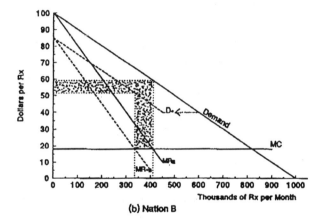

(b) Nation B

Source: Author.

producer's fixed R&D costs and profits by the amount of the rectangle (59 – 40) x (410,000) less the (necessarily smaller) rectangle (40 –18) x (190,000), or by a total of $3.61 million. Thus, consumers in the price-controlled market pay less than their Ramsey-efficient contribution to the coverage of R&D costs.[21] If such controls are expected to be applied to future (i.e. new) products, R&D investments are likely to be cut back.[22] If, on the other hand, the controls are believed

---

[21] The negative contribution impact might be reduced if, under the Dorfman–Steiner theorem, lower profit margins lead to lower expenditures on advertising and other forms of product promotion such as direct company-to-physician 'detailing'.
[22] For the analytic apparatus needed to demonstrate this point, see Scherer (1996), pp. 364–6.

to be 'one-off' and not to be imposed on future products, the reduction in profits represents pure expropriation with few direct R&D investment implications.

The difference in prices between national markets may lead to parallel exports from country A to country B. If (paralleling the analysis of Figure 2.3) 15,000 units are transferred to B, the demand curve in it (Figure 2.6(b)) will be shifted to the left and, after new marginal revenue calculations are completed, the price in B will be reduced from $59 to $51. Consumers in B benefit, but there is a further reduction (dot-shaded area) in the contribution to the producing firm's profits and R&D reimbursement. From our analysis of Figure 2.3, we know that this reduction amounts to $5.59 million per month. What happens then in country A depends upon how the producer reacts to the product diversions of its middlemen. If it increases output by 15,000 units monthly to keep A's market fully satisfied, there are no further ramifications, although the additional profit contribution RUVS in A ((40 − 18) x (15,000) = $330,000) partly, but less than fully, compensates for the loss of profits (dot-shaded area) from the impact of parallel imports on prices and quantities in B. If, more plausibly, the producer restricts its supply to less than 600,000 Rx (needed to satisfy demand in A) plus 15,000 and if 15,000 units continue to be diverted to the higher-price market B, there will be 'shortages' in A: supply in A will be less than the 600,000 units demanded. The welfare consequences of those shortages depend upon the mechanism used to ration scarce drug supplies among consumers willing and able to purchase them. It is not implausible that some consumers to whom the drug has very high value, e.g. consumers located at point J on country A's demand curve, will be deprived.[23] If so, substantial losses of consumers' surplus in the price-controlling country can occur.[24]

The correlation of prices with per capita income may also deteriorate when countries use a method of price control known as external reference pricing – that is, setting local price ceilings on the basis of prices observed in other (notably, low-price) countries. In this case, drug-producers rationally fear that charging lower prices in low-income countries could rebound and hurt them by influencing prices in more affluent countries imposing this price control. This could happen even if the external reference pricing is not linked to a formal price control system, e.g. when drugs procurement officers or politicians in the high-price country insist: 'You're setting much lower prices in low-income countries; you should do the same for us or we will make your life unpleasant here.' In either situation, willingness to offer lower prices in less affluent countries will be curbed.

---

[23] This applies unless black markets materialize, in which case matters become even more complex.
[24] This inference depends upon the assumption that ability and willingness to pay measure the social value of a drug's provision – a debatable proposition. However, without a rationing system that reliably allocates scarce supplies to those most 'in need', it remains true that appreciable welfare losses ensue.

Implications

To sum up, there is much to be said for price discrimination in multinational drugs markets. By setting prices lower in low-income countries than in high-income, low-price-elasticity markets achieve two desirable ends: they helps low-income countries' consumers to obtain vital drug supplies and they enhance drug-producers' net revenues, which, if accurately foreseen, stimulate investment in the research and development of new drugs. To the extent that parallel trade interferes with the attainment of these results, there is reason to discourage it. We make the following nuanced policy recommendations, which make the best of an inherently imperfect situation:

- To encourage the low-price provision of drugs to low-income nations, low-income countries should be allowed to bar parallel exports of drugs received at preferential prices. Pharmaceutical manufacturers should be given the legal means to discourage parallel importation into high-income markets of the patented drugs they have sold at lower prices in countries identified as less developed under United Nations criteria.
- To reduce the adverse consequences from multinational drug-providers' niche-pricing strategies, parallel imports into low-income states should be allowed.
- To reduce the product misallocations and impairment of research and development capacity caused by price controls in affluent countries, parallel exports should not be permitted from price-controlled jurisdictions. High-income states should also agree not to base the prices they allow under their price control regimes on the prices observed in low-income nations, i.e. to limit the geographic scope of any controls based on external reference prices. As forgoing external reference pricing may not be in the interest of high-income countries, an international covenant may be required to achieve this desirable result.

Price controls

Many countries, developed and developing alike, regulate the prices of pharmaceutical products. The primary objectives of price control programmes are to make drugs affordable to the local population and to control public expenditure on drugs. However, some countries also use price control programmes to achieve secondary industrial policy objectives such as encouraging local investment, employment or R&D within their jurisdictions.[25] Controls on producer prices of pharmaceuticals have been conveniently classified into three categories:

Cost-plus pricing: prices are fixed product by product on the basis of the costs of production and distribution, with 'reasonable' profit margins added;

---

[25] Danzon (1997), Chapter 3.

Reference pricing: product-by-product maximum price reimbursements or price ceilings are based on prices of comparable products either in other, similarly placed countries (external reference pricing) or in the same therapeutic class within the national market (internal reference pricing); and

Profit-based price controls: ceilings are placed on profits or returns on capital invested for each pharmaceutical company, taking account of the company's R&D expenditure.[26]

In most developed countries, with the notable exception of the United States, pharmaceutical expenditures are covered extensively by public health insurance. Even in the United States, out-of-pocket expenses fell from 54 per cent of total national out-patient drug expenditure in 1987 to 29 per cent in 1997.[27] In the OECD countries as a group, almost 75 per cent of pharmaceutical expenditures are reimbursed in some way.[28] With the power to include or exclude new drugs in formularies for authorized or reimbursed drugs, national authorities can negotiate lower initial prices or extract assurances that prices will not be raised above the introductory levels. Some, such as the United Kingdom, also impose profit controls. Canada has a Patented Medicines Price Review Board that closely monitors the prices of patented medicines through external reference pricing and takes steps to check 'excessive' pricing. Australia, New Zealand and, since 1989, Germany have set reference prices for reimbursement of the cost of medicines, using the prices of similar medicines within the therapeutic group to do so. Maximum reimbursement limits are set, and if a choice is made for a higher-priced drug, the difference has to be borne by the patient.[29]

In contrast, few developing countries have universal public health insurance schemes or public drug reimbursement systems. Government hospitals and dispensaries are chronically underfinanced and suffer from drugs shortages. Private health insurance, where available, benefits only a small proportion of the population. In addition, governments have weak infrastructure for monitoring the costs of production or prices. Despite these problems, some developing-country governments have attempted to regulate prices, typically using cost-plus methods. We draw from the experiences of Colombia and India.

Colombia attempted comprehensive control of drugs prices beginning in 1968. After many changes, it focused in 1992 on 'critical drugs', defined as those with fewer than five suppliers. These comprised about 20 per cent of the total pharmaceuticals supply. The manufacturers of these drugs had to inform

[26] WHO (1997), pp. 53–6.
[27] US General Accounting Office (1999).
[28] OECD (2000), p. 4.
[29] A study of the change in Germany from a flat fee per prescription to this reference pricing system has shown that producers reacted by lowering prices by 10 to 30 per cent. See Pavcnik (2000).

the government in advance of price changes. Government price monitors could require cost data and impose the price they deemed to be appropriate. However, because it lacked the ability to follow price changes, Colombia returned in 1994 to cost-plus pricing, setting a ceiling price of 3.4 times the production cost.[30] It is not clear whether this generous limit of 240 per cent over production cost would have reduced prices from profit-maximizing prices set by producers.

India has one of the most extensive pharmaceutical price control regimes among developing countries. Until changes were implemented in 1995, over 70 per cent of the total pharmaceutical market was under price control.[31] Even after the new Drugs Prices Control Order (DPCO) of 1995, 50 per cent of the market remained under price control.[32] Prices are fixed for each dosage form and pack size for the bulk drugs selected for price control by the government.[33] Under Section 7 of DPCO, the maximum retail price calculation for a pharmaceutical formulation under the cost-plus method is as follows:

Retail price = (MC + CC + PM + PC) x (1+ MAPE/100) + ED, where
MC = material cost, including bulk pharmaceuticals used and allowance for wastage
CC = conversion cost: labour, energy, R&D etc.
PM and PC = packing materials and packing charges
MAPE = maximum allowable post-manufacturing expenses, including distribution and retail margins (100 per cent at present[34])
ED = excise duty

Under India's new drugs policy announced at the end of 1994, a drug is subject to price control if its annual turnover in the audited retail market is more than Rs 40 million (approximately $900,000 at the current exchange rate). Drugs with turnover above this minimum revenue level may be exempted if there are at least five bulk producers and at least 10 formulators, none with more than 40 per cent of the audited retail market. Any bulk drug with a turnover above Rs 10 million ($200,000) and with one formulator supplying 90 per cent or more of the market is also subject to price control. Given this last criterion,

---

[30] WHO (1997), p. 58.
[31] Redwood (1994), p. 4.
[32] Lanjouw (1998), p. 52.
[33] In addition to price ceilings, maximum returns are fixed at 18 per cent on net worth (defined as paid-up share capital plus free reserves or readily deployable surpluses) or 26 per cent on capital employed, where production is from the basic bulk drugs manufacturing stage. This part of DPCO has not come into operation, as no firm's profitability comes close to these limits. See Lanjouw (1998), p. 53.
[34] The previous drugs policy, of 1986, allowed only 75 per cent margins for essential drugs required under national health programmes.

all patented pharmaceuticals would be subject to price control unless they were widely licensed, which is unlikely.[35]

Lanjouw surveys the disputes in India between government and industry over DPCO criteria, data provision, definition of wastage etc. and identifies a general lack of cooperation by industry in the price control exercises.[36] Under these circumstances, further reduction of the profit margins under MAPE is not a realistic option. In addition, a maximum MAPE of only 50 per cent of the landed cost (c.i.f. price plus customs duty and clearing charges) is allowed in the case of an imported formulation.[37] This, however, is probably not an effective way to counter the manipulation of sale prices between the parent multinational company and its local subsidiary, as the landed transfer price can usually be raised to offset price regulators' actions.

Developing countries must strike a fine balance between lower prices and the availability of patented medicines. A strictly enforced price control regime may scare away potential production of patented pharmaceuticals within the country, or even lead to a decision not to supply the market through imports. On the other hand, if price controls are typically lax, the administrative costs of establishing and maintaining an effective price control regime over *all* patented pharmaceuticals may outweigh the benefits. Even if, for the sake of assumption, costs can be ascertained correctly and prices fixed on a cost-plus basis, the experience of monitoring costs and enforcing prices has been poor, as India's and Colombia's attempts to regulate drugs prices show. The alternative external or internal reference pricing method may be ineffective for a developing country that does not have extensive public health insurance coverage or substantial public expenditure on drugs. However, simulating price controls by applying the Indian formula to 1994 price data shows that such controls, where effective, do leave consumers better off while leaving patent-owners only negligibly worse off. Price decreases for widely used patented pharmaceuticals that have few substitutes increase consumers' surplus significantly.[38] Thus, selective cost-plus price controls on a few patented medicines in developing countries, with relatively strict limits on distribution and profit mark-ups (i.e. with Indian, not Colombian, mark-ups), may work towards maintaining a satisfactory balance between benefits and costs. In addition, as seen in the previous section, parallel imports from price-controlled countries in the developed world may allow countries to benefit from whatever monopsony (or exclusive buying) power they might

---

[35] There is a possibility that patent-owners may defeat the purpose of DPCO by licensing several small formulating units and selling the bulk drug to them, thus effectively controlling the final sale price.
[36] Lanjouw (1998), p. 13 and pp. 52–3.
[37] This is a more likely scenario, as TRIPS now obliges non-discrimination on patent rights between imported and locally produced products.
[38] Watal (2000), pp. 740–2.

possess. The threat of compulsory licensing can also enhance states' bargaining power. With the spreading introduction of private and public health insurance schemes in the developing world, some countries may be able to use reference-pricing systems.

CONCLUSION

The TRIPS Agreement is important. How it is interpreted and implemented may have life or death consequences for some citizens in less developed countries. Some countries – especially those that in the past have actively encouraged generic substitution for drugs protected elsewhere by patents – will experience a larger economic shock, compensated to some unknown degree by an increase in pharmaceuticals innovation, than countries that have not pursued active generic substitution policies. But the consequences of this shock may well resound throughout the world health system. The intent of this chapter has been to explore policies consistent with the TRIPS Agreement that minimize the adverse consequences for the world's least affluent inhabitants.

Generic drugs must play a crucial role in any set of future policies. Thousands of effective medicines are available without the protection of recently or long-expired patents. A vigorously competitive supply of these drugs can do much to extend the benefits of modern pharmaceutical technology to a wider range of consumers. This is not merely an admonition, in the spirit of Marie Antoinette, to 'Let them take generics.' Even in the United States, whose consumers' ability to pay is great and whose respect for intellectual property is exceeded by few other countries, generics fill nearly half of all prescriptions. Many less developed countries have hurt themselves by not taking full advantage of the opportunities for encouraging generic substitution. Some labour at a disadvantage in this respect because their markets are too small and their technological resources too limited to support broad-based indigenous suppliers of generic drugs. For them, a vigorous international trade in generic drugs must provide a solution – inhibited, to be sure, by limited purchasing power and binding foreign exchange constraints. Policy-makers responsible for setting the rules governing international trade should make every effort to ensure that the trade in generic drugs is not restricted and that vigorously competitive world markets emerge.

The TRIPS Agreement affects the evolution of generic drugs supplies by delaying the opportunities for producing generic versions of the newest, most technologically advanced drugs until patents have expired. This is a real constraint, but it is not absolute. TRIPS allows compulsory licensing of drugs (and other) patents under specified conditions. In order to make life-saving new drugs available at affordable prices and to strengthen the development of internationally competitive generic drugs industries, the compulsory licensing opportunities opened up by TRIPS should be seized selectively and imaginatively. This will require *inter alia* the creation of national regulatory and judicial institutions that ensure expeditiously that the TRIPS rules are respected.

Two issues are likely to be particularly important in determining the scope and effectiveness of compulsory licensing programmes. First, WTO member countries cannot simply draw without expense on the research and development efforts of multinational pharmaceutical enterprises; they must pay appropriate compensation for the patents subjected to licensing. The question is, how much compensation is appropriate? It seems clear from precedents established in industrialized countries that a 'reasonable' royalty is one that is higher than zero but much less than the royalty that would compensate a patent-holder fully for the loss of whatever monopoly position it might enjoy by virtue of the patent. Within that range, considerable discretion exists for national decision-makers to do what is right.

Second, as we have argued above, vigorous international trade that respects the principles of comparative advantage is essential if the smallest, least affluent countries are to be supplied with generic drugs, *inter alia*, under compulsory licences. This necessity may conflict with the TRIPS requirement that compulsory licences be issued 'predominantly for the supply of the domestic market' of the authorizing country. This problem can be resolved only in the WTO in future dispute settlements or negotiations.

Parallel trade and patent rights intersect in important ways. In an ideal world, pharmaceutical manufacturers would engage in Ramsey–Baumol–Bradford discrimination, setting relatively high prices for their patented products in order to recover drug discovery and development investments in the most affluent countries and to sell drugs at only a modest mark-up above marginal production and distribution cost in countries with the least ability to pay. For a variety of reasons, the world is much less than ideal. Parallel exportation of drugs sold at low prices in less developed countries could undermine the willingness of pharmaceutical manufacturers to sell at those low prices or even to supply low-income markets at all. To avoid these ill effects, there should be an international agreement or understanding to bar parallel imports to high-income states from low-income or price-controlled states while allowing parallel exports to low-income countries, including exports from price-controlled countries. This agreement would allow low-income countries to permit parallel imports and prohibit parallel exports whenever it is in their interest to do so.

The logic of parallel trade also conflicts with the propensity of countries, both rich and poor, to solve domestic health budget problems by imposing price controls on drug products. If the controls were coordinated to ensure that the most affluent countries pay the highest mark-ups of wholesale prices over costs, severe inequities could be avoided. But coordination is politically infeasible.

Thus, some of the world's most affluent countries impose stringent controls and attempt to take advantage of the contributions of others, rich and poor. In an imperfect world, each country is likely to advance its own narrow interests and impose controls (unless much emphasis is placed on avoiding the other market-distorting tendencies of controls). For less developed countries, this means that price controls can be an additional instrument for moderating health care costs, assuming that the controls are not implemented so clumsily that they drive supplies of critical drugs from the local market altogether. Feasible improvements of the status quo might be achieved through multilateral accords that (1) allow low-income countries to import price-controlled medicines from higher-income countries and that (2) bar national price control systems in high-income countries from using the uncontrolled prices set by multinational drugs-producers in low-income countries as external reference prices.

Ultimately, it must be recognized that the poorer citizens of the world's least affluent countries cannot pay even the marginal cost of drugs that might save their lives or permit them to become productive workers. Here, the only alternative to death or debility is charity. Charity, like high-technology drugs, is often in short supply. It could be facilitated if corporate income tax laws, at least in the leading countries investing in pharmaceuticals R&D, are interpreted so that outright donations of essential drugs confer tax advantages sufficiently large as to impose no net cost on the donor, with the burden falling upon the tax collector. Charity through non-transparent tax expenditures is often more feasible politically than outright governmental gifts and grants. It should be exploited aggressively as a means of increasing the supply of life-saving drugs to the world's poor.

REFERENCES

Baumol, William J. and David Bradford (1970), 'Optimal Departures from Marginal Cost Pricing', *American Economic Review*, 60 (June), pp. 265–83.

Danzon, Patricia (1997), *Pharmaceutical Price Regulation: National Policies versus Global Interests*. Washington, DC: AEI Press.

Gorecki, Paul K. (1981), *Regulating the Price of Prescription Drugs in Canada: Compulsory Licensing, Product Selection, and Government Reimbursement Programs*, Technical Report No. 8. Ottawa: Economic Council of Canada.

Lanjouw, Jean. O. (1998), 'The Introduction of Pharmaceutical Product Patents in India: "Heartless Exploitation of the Poor and Suffering"?', National Bureau of Economic Research, Working Paper Series, no. 6366, 1–53.

OECD (2000), 'Pharmaceutical Policies in OECD Countries: Reconciling Social and Industrial Goals', DEELSA/ELSA/WD(2000)1.

Pavcnik, Nina (2000): 'Do Pharmaceutical Prices Respond to Insurance?', National Bureau of Economic Research, Working Paper Series, no. W7865, August, available at http://papers.nber.org/papers/W7865.

Redwood, Heinz (1994), *New Horizons in India: The Consequences of Pharmaceutical Patent Protection*. Felixstowe, England: Oldswicks Press.

Robinson, Joan (1934), *The Economics of Imperfect Competition*. London: Macmillan.
Scherer, F. M. (1996), *Industry Structure, Strategy, and Public Policy*. New York: HarperCollins.
Scherer, F. M. and Jayashree Watal (2001), 'Post-TRIPS Options for Access to Patented Medicines in Developing Countries', prepared for Working Group 4, Commission for Macroeconomics and Health, available at *http://www.cmhealth.org/docs/wg4_paper1.pdf.*
Towse, Adrian (ed.) (1995), *Industrial Policy and the Pharmaceutical Industry*. London: Office of Health Economics.
Watal, Jayashree (2000), 'Pharmaceutical Patents, Prices and Welfare Losses: A Simulation Study of Policy Options for India under the WTO TRIPS Agreement', *The World Economy*, 23 (5), pp. 733–52.
World Health Organization (1997), 'Public-Private Roles in the Pharmaceutical Sector: Implications for Equitable Access and Rational Drug Use', available at *www.who.org*.
US General Accounting Office (1999), *Medicare: Beneficiaries Prescription Drug Coverage*, Testimony Before the Subcommittee on Health and Environment, Committee on Commerce, House of Representatives, GAO/T-HEHS-99-198, 28 September.
Yarrow, George (1995), 'CEC and EC Member State Industrial Policy and the Pharmaceutical Industry', in Towse (ed.) (1995), pp. 1–11.

3 PARALLEL TRADE IN PHARMACEUTICAL PRODUCTS: IMPLICATIONS FOR PROCURING MEDICINES FOR POOR COUNTRIES

Keith E. Maskus and Mattias Ganslandt

INTRODUCTION

Parallel trade (PT), also called grey-market trade, is the act of taking goods placed into circulation in one market, where they are protected by a trademark, patent or copyright, and shipping them to a second market without the authorization of the local owner of the intellectual property right. For example, it is permissible for a trading firm to purchase quantities of prescription drugs in Spain and import them into Sweden or Germany without the approval of the local distributor owning licensed patent rights. Note that these goods are authorized for original sale; they are not counterfeited or pirated merchandise. Thus, parallel imports (PI) are identical to legitimate products except that they may be packaged differently and may not carry the original manufacturer's warranty.

Parallel trade is profitable to the extent that the difference between the cost of acquiring medicines in one market and the price at which they can be sold in another market is large enough to cover the costs of achieving regulatory approval and transporting and marketing the drugs. This is most likely to be the case when one country, such as Italy, has rigorous price controls in place at the wholesale level, permitting parallel traders to procure drugs at the regulated price, while another country, such as Sweden or the United Kingdom, permits higher prices or does not control prices at all. It also arises when prices differ because original manufacturers choose to market a drug in different countries under different terms. One might expect prices for drugs treating hypertension, for example, to be lower in Spain than in Germany to the extent that Spanish consumers have a lower per capita income and more elastic demand. Firms try to sustain this price differentiation through establishing different brand names and packaging for identical products in various countries. Recognizing this, however, a parallel trading firm could purchase the drugs in the lower-price nation and repackage them for the higher-price nation (or, more likely, develop its own brand name there).

This paper draws on Maskus (2001).

The ability of a right-holder to exclude PT legally from a particular market depends on the importing country's treatment of exhaustion of intellectual property rights (IPR). A regime of national exhaustion awards the right to prevent parallel imports; one of international exhaustion makes such imports legal. To illustrate, national exhaustion is given effect by the 'first-sale doctrine', under which the sale of a good to a domestic agent ends the right of the manufacturing firm to control its subsequent disposition. Put most simply, once a product has been bought, its purchaser owns it and can resell it within a country without restraint. However, rights to control international trade in the good are not exhausted, and imports or exports are illegal. For patented goods, the United States pursues national exhaustion. International exhaustion extends this doctrine to first sale anywhere, including foreign markets. Thus, for example, if a drug is sold under patent or trademark to a parallel trading firm in Spain, it could be resold in the United Kingdom without restraint as long as it is profitable to do so. The European Union (EU) follows a policy of 'regional exhaustion', under which parallel trade within it is permitted; parallel imports from outside the EU are not permitted.

Regulation of PT in the pharmaceuticals area has become a critical issue in the global trading system. Advocates of strong international patent rights for new medicines support a global policy of banning PT, arguing that if this trade were widely allowed it would reduce profits in the research-intensive pharmaceutical sector and ultimately slow down innovation of new drugs. Moreover, PT could make it difficult for health authorities in different countries to sustain differential price controls and regulatory regimes. However, public health authorities in many countries argue that it is important to be able to purchase drugs from the cheapest sources possible, which requires an open regime of parallel imports. Whether or not such imports actually occur, the threat that they might come in could force distributors to charge lower prices. It is evident that policy-makers, in most developing countries especially, would place a greater weight on affordability of medicines than on promoting research and development (R&D) abroad. The reason is that, with few exceptions, developing countries do not have research-intensive pharmaceutical firms that would benefit from strong intellectual property protection. In such an environment, providing market power to international pharmaceutical firms through restraints on PI could raise prices of medicines without generating much domestic R&D. It is conceivable that precluding PI would make international pharmaceutical firms more willing to supply poor countries, but available evidence does not provide much support for this view.[1]

---

[1] See Maskus (2001).

This controversy was illustrated by the lawsuit filed in 1998 (but suspended in 2001) by 39 South African licensed pharmaceutical distributors to overturn South Africa's 1997 Medicines Law. This legislation would permit South Africa's health minister to resort to parallel imports in cases where a drug protected by a patent is priced at excessive levels in South Africa. Further, pharmaceutical firms in industrialized countries that recently agreed to provide many of their HIV–AIDS drugs at low cost in sub-Saharan African countries remain concerned that these drugs might come into higher-priced markets through parallel exports. For example, Merck and Co. recently announced it would cut the prices of two AIDS-controlling drugs in Africa by 40 to 55 per cent, adding to sharp price cuts announced a year earlier. Abbott Laboratories offered to sell its two AIDS drugs Norvir and Kaletra at a price that would earn the company no profit. Many other firms, including Bristol-Myers Squibb Co. and GlaxoSmithKline PLC, have announced similar price cuts or even donations. However, at the centre of all these offers have been requests that the recipient countries take steps to ensure that these drugs, which would sell in Africa for a small fraction of their prices in the United States and the European Union, would not be re-exported. In another example, in 2000 the Clinton administration decided not to implement a new law that would have permitted PI of medicines from approved locations in Canada and other developed states.

For present purposes, the primary issue is the role of restraints on PT in supporting a regime of internationally differentiated prices. Economic theory claims that if firms were permitted to segment national markets, they would engage in price discrimination whereby the price charged would be inversely proportional to the elasticity of demand.[2] Put more simply, prices would be lowest in countries where demand is most sensitive to price. Thus, developing countries, with low purchasing power and limited insurance markets, would be expected to pay lower prices. Differential pricing is at the core of proposals to improve the access of poor countries to drugs at modest prices.

This chapter discusses these issues as they affect medicines. In the next section, we analyse available empirical evidence of trademarked medicines in countries at varying levels of economic development. Then we discuss recent work on the impacts of PT in medicines within the EU, which has an open internal regime. Lastly, we put forward conclusions about the benefits and costs of PT in developing countries and make a series of policy recommendations. The basic conclusion is that there is an important rationale for restricting parallel exports of medicines from low-income countries to high-income countries, although the former group could remain open to parallel imports. This idea

[2] Malueg and Schwartz (1994, 169–70); Scherer and Watal (2001, 34–37); Ganslandt and Maskus (2001, 4–45). The notion that prices would fall as demand becomes more elastic is also called 'Ramsey pricing'.

could be supplemented by regimes of regional exhaustion among poor countries in order to increase market size within which prices are integrated.

EMPIRICAL EVIDENCE ON DIFFERENTIAL PRICES

Parallel imports are rarely recorded separately in official trade statistics. The Swedish health authorities compile information on such imports of drugs, but they are an exception. It is thus exceedingly difficult to analyse their impacts on prices and competition in any general sense, although we present below some evidence from the Swedish data. Instead, investigators tend to take indirect approaches, looking at international differences in drugs prices in order to make tentative inferences about whether prices fit standard models of price discrimination and about what the potential for PT might be. Here we review that evidence and also put forward some econometric evidence on price impacts.

International price differentials

For reasons set out in Danzon and Kim,[3] it is difficult to compare pharmaceutical prices among countries. First, a clear difficulty arises if the researcher attempts to develop a comparable price index for patients in different countries. These indexes should include prices of generic substitutes and local 'me-too' drugs, the existence of which could affect the relative consumption of different drugs. Thus, the selection of appropriate weights to include in cross-country indexes is important. Second, the same range and quality of drugs may not be available to consumers in all countries, because of differences in preferences, information asymmetries and regulatory differences. Third, significant differences among countries in brand name, product forms, concentrations and pack sizes make it difficult to find precise drug products that exist in multiple jurisdictions. Indeed, this differentiation is one method by which pharmaceutical firms attempt to segment markets. Fourth, to the extent that regulations, taxes and mandated discounts extend to ex-manufacturers' prices, these differences can cloud cross-country comparisons. Finally, because original prices are quoted in local currencies, the choice of exchange rates at which to convert these prices into a common unit (usually US dollars) could have a significant impact on price comparisons among countries (although not among medicines within each country).

These problems are least significant for a researcher considering PT. In particular, they may be effectively mitigated if the researcher focuses solely on well-defined products, which we define here as a drug sold in identical concentrations,

[3] Danzon and Kim (1998, 117–19).

forms and pack sizes and marketed by the original manufacturer (or its licensees). The advantage of this narrow definition is that it avoids weighting problems among dosages, and the advantage of focusing only on drugs sold by the original manufacturer is that it avoids weighting problems associated with generics. In any case, the proper focus of a study of PT is international differences in ex-manufacturer's prices. Moreover, although variations in market exchange rates clearly affect prices, such exchange rate effects are an important reason why PT exists. Accordingly, narrow comparisons of prices converted at market exchange rates are appropriate for investigating the potential scope for PT.

In order to investigate how significantly prices differ across countries and whether they vary inversely with income levels, we analyse data on ex-manufacturer's prices and sales for major molecules in 14 countries in 1998. Table 3.1 presents information on per dosage prices in US dollars for 20 brand-name drugs for which prices in several countries could be identified. These are the prices charged by the manufacturing firm (or its direct licensees) that owns the brand name listed at the top of each column. They are the most direct measures available of international price variability in identical products, which may be the subject of PT.

For example, Norvasc cost $0.97 per 5-mg tablet in the United States in 1998, while other prices ranged from $0.09 in India to $0.83 in Brazil. Despite the potential for PT, there was considerable price variability within the EU, with the British price of $0.61 being 45 per cent higher than the price in Spain. In this simple context, it seems that the prospect of PT did not cause those prices to converge at the factory gate within the EU. Note further that Italy and Spain were in the European Monetary System in 1998 but that their mutually fixed exchange rates did not induce enough arbitrage to result in identical dollar prices, with the Italian price remaining 38 per cent above the Spanish price. Among the developing countries, prices in Mexico and Brazil were markedly higher than were those in Korea, Thailand, India and South Africa. Note that the South African price was 3.7 times higher than the Indian price.

These observations are largely consistent for most of the 20 drugs. However, some important differences exist. First, prices in many drugs are lower in a number of developed countries, especially Canada, Italy and Spain, than in Mexico, Brazil and South Africa. This fact reflects the existence of significant price controls in these developed countries.[4] Indeed, in 10 of the 18 cases for which prices existed in Italy and/or Spain, on the one hand, and in South Africa, on the other hand, the price was higher in South Africa. Note also that prices in developing countries sometimes exceed those in the United States, which

---

[4] Canada may have especially low recorded prices because of deterioration in the value of the Canadian dollar.

typically has the highest prices of any country. Thus, Sandimmun 100-mg capsules were 17 per cent more expensive in dollar terms in Mexico than they were in the United States. This difference also existed in Mexico and Brazil for Neoral; in Brazil for Cipro, Diflucan and Cozaar; and in Mexico, Brazil, the Czech Republic and Korea for Effexor. Taking the simple average of prices in the next to last column, it seems that Brazil and Mexico had the second-highest and third-highest average prices in the sample, markedly higher than Canada, Italy, Spain and Japan.[5] Noting that such averages may be biased by the different numbers of products available per country, in the final column we report for each country the average of prices relative to US prices, where a product exists in both places. Again, Brazil and Mexico are the highest-priced countries behind the United States, although by this measure their prices are barely above those in Sweden and Japan.

A central question in thinking about PI is whether multinational pharmaceutical firms do indeed set prices according to per capita income differences. The standard theory of price discrimination suggests, as noted earlier, that when markets are segmented, prices will be lower in those countries with lower and more elastic demand curves, which would ordinarily be associated with poor countries. If per capita income were a perfect index of demand elasticity, there should be a correlation of plus unity in comparing prices among countries with differences in per capita GNP.

The final cell in each column presents calculations for each drug and for average prices. The first entry in the cell is the correlation between dollar price and per capita GNP measured at market exchange rates, and the second entry is the correlation between dollar price and per capita GNP measured at purchasing power parity (PPP) exchange rates. The latter comparison is more appropriate for the present purpose (comparing price behaviour at different levels of demand), although both present similar results.

It will be seen from the computations that 17 of the 20 individual-drug correlations are significantly positive, ranging from 0.18 (Cozaar) to 0.90 (Imitrex). Two of the PPP correlations approach unity (Pulmicort and Imitrex), suggesting for those drugs that the brand-owner practises something like Ramsey pricing. Six more have correlations of at least 0.5, which might be considered to support the underlying pricing model. However, nine drugs have correlation coefficients that range between 0 and 0.5, and three are negative. Neoral and Imovane both display significantly negative correlations between income levels and prices. As noted in the penultimate column, the correlation between average prices and per capita GNP is clearly positive but well below unity.

---

[5] Caution should be exercised in comparing averages because these figures are not weighted by local consumption patterns.

Table 3.1: International comparison of per-dosage ex-manufacturer's prices ($), 1998

Country	Norvasc 5-mg tabs	Lipitor 10-mg tabs	Pulmicort 200mcg press aerosol	Sandimmun 100-mg caps	Neoral 100-mg caps	Cipro 500-mg tabs	Plendil 5-mg tabs	Imovane 7.5-mg tabs
United States	0.97	1.46	0.43	5.03	4.47	2.94	0.72	n.a.
Canada	0.79	1.04	0.19	n.a.	3.50	1.16	0.42	0.40
Mexico	0.71	1.17	n.a.	5.90	7.32	1.70	0.64	0.28
Brazil	0.83	0.89	n.a.	4.57	4.47	3.76	0.65	0.38
United Kingdom	0.61	0.98	0.27	3.69	3.69	2.06	0.43	0.23
Sweden	0.57	0.94	0.34	n.a.	n.a.	3.28	0.53	0.22
Italy	0.58	0.89	0.17	3.04	3.12	1.82	0.3	0.26
Spain	0.42	0.83	0.14	n.a.	2.61	1.79	0.33	0.13
Czech Republic	0.42	0.98	0.16	n.a.	2.98	1.70	0.28	0.13
Japan	0.65	n.a.	n.a.	n.a.	n.a.	n.a.	0.31	n.a.
Korea	0.40	n.a.	0.13	3	4.28	1.46	0.63	0.18
Thailand	0.43	n.a.	0.10	1.10	3.14	1.27	0.27	n.a.
India	0.09	n.a.	n.a.	n.a.	n.a.	0.14	0.07	n.a.
South Africa	0.34	n.a.	0.08	4.19	4.45	1.35	0.53	0.35
Correlations	0.56, 0.63	0.33, 0.45	0.88, 0.82	0.16, 0.18	-0.24, -0.29	0.47, 0.36	0.16, 0.22	-0.08, -0.19

Table 3.1: International comparison of per-dosage ex-manufacturer's prices ($), 1998, continued

Country	Diflucan 50-mg tabs	Lasix 40-mg tabs	Claritin 10-mg tabs	Cozaar 50-mg tabs	Zyprexa 10-mg tabs	Losec 20-mg C. or T.	Zantac 150-mg tabs	Risperdal 2-mg tabs
United States	3.47	0.20	1.70	0.92	6.48	2.99	1.38	2.94
Canada	3.07	0.07	0.54	0.70	4.40	1.39	0.69	1.26
Mexico	3.20	0.09	n.a.	0.84	4.39	1.64	0.26	0.98
Brazil	4.66	0.13	0.59	1.07	5.73	2.41	0.52	1.61
United Kingdom	3.44	0.12	0.38	0.89	5.47	1.59	0.68	1.93
Sweden	4.27	n.a.	0.35	0.77	5.26	1.74	n.a.	1.58
Italy	2.21	0.08	0.32	0.69	4.03	1.43	0.54	1.10
Spain	2.48	n.a.	0.23	0.69	4.08	1.42	0.43	n.a.
Czech Republic	2.77	n.a.	0.29	0.93	4.25	1.21	0.28	1.12
Japan	5.41	0.12	n.a.	1.45	n.a.	1.75	0.47	0.46
Korea	2.69	0.06	n.a.	0.65	2.38	1.22	0.41	1.06
Thailand	1.62	0.06	0.24	0.78	2.88	1.13	0.47	0.94
India	n.a.	0.01	0.21	n.a.	n.a.	n.a.	0.02	0.46
South Africa	2.75	0.21	0.65	0.75	1.79	1.19	0.54	0.96
Correlations	0.51, 0.28	0.33, 0.35	0.47, 0.52	0.36, 0.18	0.36, 0.57	0.45, 0.40	0.65, 0.75	0.43, 0.55

Table 3.1: International comparison of per-dosage ex-manufacturer's prices ($), 1998, continued

Country	Zoloft 50-mg tabs	Zocor 10-mg tabs	Imitrex 50-mg tabs	Effexor 75-mg tabs	Number of drugs	Common drugs Avg. price	Avg. price rel. to US
United States	1.70	1.52	11.36	0.92	19	2.72	1.00
Canada	1.01	1.13	8.17	1.00	19	1.63	0.63
Mexico	1.13	1.25	3.71	1.12	18	2.02	0.76
Brazil	1.29	0.97	3.02	1.08	19	2.03	0.81
UK	1.37	0.95	7.13	1.04	20	1.85	0.70
Sweden	1.03	0.82	5.69	1.19	16	1.79	0.73
Italy	0.92	0.95	4.21	1.07	20	1.39	0.55
Spain	0.80	0.62	5.03	0.86	17	1.35	0.52
Czech Republic	0.71	0.84	n.a.	1.09	17	1.18	0.56
Japan	n.a.	n.a.	n.a.	n.a.	8	1.33	0.74
Korea	0.76	0.65	3.26	1.13	18	1.35	0.54
Thailand	0.83	0.89	2.85	n.a.	17	1.12	0.41
India	n.a	n.a.	n.a.	n.a.	7	0.14	0.08
South Africa	0.79	1.21	3.23	0.76	19	1.37	0.58
Correlations	0.56, 0.50	0.22, 0.27	0.84, 0.90	0.06, 0.00		0.47, 0.56	

Sources: Constructed by authors from data provided by IMS Health. Purchasing power parity-adjusted GNP figures were taken from World Bank, *World Development Report 2000* (New York: Oxford University Press).

Table 3.2: Pharmaceutical price comparisons and parallel imports, 1996: omeprazole (20-mg tablets)

Country	Patent expiry	No. of firms	Average price per pile ($)	Sales ($m)	No. of PI firms	Average price per pill	Sales ($m)
Germany	03/04/1999	2	1.93	55.5	5	1.84	5.4
United Kingdom	03/04/1999	1	1.73	279.6	1	1.76	2.4
Italy	03/04/1999	4	1.59	151.6	n.a.	n.a.	n.a.
Spain	18/01/1995	24	1.52	161.2	n.a.	n.a.	n.a.
United States	05/04/2001	1	2.91	1289.0	n.a.	n.a.	n.a.
Brazil	no patent	10	1.60	41.6	n.a.	n.a.	n.a.
India*	no patent	35	0.06	15.1	n.a.	n.a.	n.a.

*1997 data. Prices are ex-manufacturer charges to wholesalers.
Source: IMS Health.

These results provide some support for the idea that prices for identical brand-name drugs are inversely related to per capita income levels. However, there are numerous exceptions to this rule, and several correlation coefficients are well below unity. It seems that other factors go into national pricing decisions by the multinational pharmaceutical companies.

Before considering what those factors might be, let us consider additional evidence. An important factor in explaining price differences is the nature of competition in various markets, including the prospects for PT. In Table 3.2 we provide evidence on the competitive structure of markets for omeprazole (20-mg tablets) in seven countries. In the table we show 1996 average prices for this drug (original brand name Losec or Prilosec) for all competing firms in each country. Included also are information about patent expiration date, number of domestic firms and number of parallel-importing firms, where available.

It is evident from Table 3.2 that price variations between countries are considerable, setting up some potential for parallel trade. The average price per pill was highest in the United States, where the product was on patent, prices were not controlled by the government and PT was not allowed. The price was about one-third cheaper in Germany, where prices were also not controlled, but parallel imports (from elsewhere in the EU) came in at a lower price and accounted for about 10 per cent of the market. The United Kingdom also experienced parallel imports, which actually sold at a slightly higher price in 1996 than pills from the original manufacturer had first sold there. Italy and

Spain had markedly lower prices than Germany. Note the large number of producers in Spain, where the patent had expired. Spain is a common source of PT within the EU. Finally, Brazil and India did not provide patents for omeprazole. Both markets were highly competitive, and the Indian price was extremely low in relation to those in the other countries. Again, therefore, were PT to be generally allowed in patented drugs it is likely that considerable volumes of this trade would emerge.

Additional evidence comes from Scherer and Watal,[6] who present similar price data for a number of AIDS anti-retroviral drugs sold under brand names by multinational pharmaceutical companies in 18 low-income and middle-income countries over the period 1994–8. They also found that international price variations roughly approximated Ramsey pricing, although the correlation between relative prices and GNP per capita was lower, at 0.21, than most of those found here for other drugs. Of all country–drug pairs they found that the average price relative to the US price was only 0.85, suggesting that prices in developing countries averaged just 15 per cent below those in the United States. Indeed, in 98 cases the prices in developing countries were higher. They also found a number of large price relatives that suggested a degree of randomness (or perhaps measurement error) in the data.

Scherer and Watal performed basic regression analysis, confirming that average prices rise slightly with the level of per capita income. Over time, the average prices tend to fall in all countries. However, they discovered that by interacting their income variable with the year dummy variable, the strong income effect was attenuated as time went on. They interpreted this finding to mean that as products become more widely available, the ability of pharmaceutical firms to sustain Ramsey-like pricing tends to diminish and the positive relationship between per capita income and prices becomes less pronounced. The authors also found a significantly negative relationship between prices and a variable indicating whether a country provided pharmaceutical product patents in the years in question. Their interpretation was that the result is an anomaly that must be traced to poor measurement of the patent variable. This interpretation is questionable. It may be that the provision of patents is highly correlated with efficient distribution mechanisms that permit more competitive pricing. Under this interpretation, developing countries need to make their distribution systems more efficient and competitive as they introduce pharmaceutical product patents.

---

[6] Scherer and Watal (2001, 38–45).

Why might prices be higher in poor countries?

A central question raised by this analysis is why ex-manufacturers' prices for identical drugs may be higher in lower-income countries. If national pharmaceutical markets are largely segmented, as they seem to be outside the European Union, the finding that prices are high in countries such as South Africa, Mexico and Brazil relative to those in Canada, Spain and Italy seems anomalous. Three factors may explain this phenomenon.

Perhaps most significantly, the notion that markets are externally segmented but internally integrated may be misleading. In particular, domestic markets could be bifurcated between high-income consumers, with a low degree of price sensitivity and a high ability and willingness to pay for new drugs, and low-income consumers, who are more price-sensitive and less able to pay. In such cases, the market demand curve can be 'kinked' between a low-volume, inelastic segment and a high-volume, elastic segment.[7] Then it is possible that a pharmaceutical firm with market power would find it more profitable to supply the inelastic segment of the market at a high mark-up and avoid supplying the elastic segment altogether. Indeed, the firm would prefer not to sell to low-income consumers at a low price for fear that the drugs would be resold to higher-income consumers via 'internal parallel imports'. This is a classic case in which an inability to price-discriminate among consumers within a country discourages firms from selling to poorer consumers, with a lower net supply offered as a result.

Thus, it is possible that higher prices in developing countries for particular products reflect a decision to sell low volumes at high mark-ups. This situation is common in other areas of products protected by IPRs and brand names. For example, it has been observed that legitimate copies of Microsoft Office sell at considerably higher prices in Taiwan, Hong Kong and China than in the United States.[8] In the former countries software licensees are willing to provide legitimate copies only to such users as foreign enterprises and government offices, which are less likely to infringe the copyright. In contrast, in the United States users may be segmented by underlying demand elasticity. Thus, it is feasible to offer discounts to academic users and students on the expectation that they will not resell or copy their products. Such price discrimination characterizes the US pharmaceutical market as well.

A second, and related, reason why prices may be high in poor countries is that distribution systems may be concentrated or monopolistic. In countries where pharmaceutical products are largely imported, the imports may come into the market through a small number of domestic distributors. Single wholesalers

---

[7] Scherer and Watal (2001, 46) present a simple graphical analysis.
[8] See Maskus (2000, 166).

would maximize profits by limiting their supply and gaining a monopolistic mark-up over import costs. Indeed, many developing countries regulate distribution in such a way that only one domestic firm is permitted to serve as a licensee for particular foreign brands. This combination of monopolistic distribution structure and limited intra-brand competition is anti-competitive.

The third reason is simply that some affluent countries may have stringent price controls in place that limit manufacturers' prices to levels below those in poorer countries. These price controls may be based on cost mark-ups or on reference prices, in which regulators look to prices abroad to set allowable charges. When parallel imports originate in countries with strict price regulations, they have complex potential impacts on economic welfare in both origin and destination countries.[9]

EVIDENCE FROM THE EU ON THE EXTENT AND EFFECTS OF PT

Because parallel imports are rarely recorded, it is difficult to undertake any formal study of their effects. A few studies shed some light on the issues we have identified in this chapter. The earliest was by REMIT Consultants,[10] under contract to the European Commission. The authors surveyed participants in the pharmaceutical sector of several countries about their perceptions of PT. Participants included manufacturers, wholesalers, PT firms, hospitals, pharmacists and government officials. The basic goal was to identify significant impediments to PT within the European Community as of 1990. In order to determine the importance of PT, they interviewed market audit organizations and parallel-importing firms with direct knowledge of trade volumes and patterns. They found that, as of 1990, parallel imports amounted to perhaps two per cent of the prescription drugs market in the EC overall, with penetration rates for particular countries ranging from one per cent in Germany to five to ten per cent in the Netherlands and eight per cent in the United Kingdom. Those drugs with large markets experienced considerably higher import volumes, consistent with the view that PT firms concentrate on 'blockbuster' medicines. Parallel exports came primarily from Belgium, France, Italy, Greece and Spain, with the last two countries rapidly increasing their shares of the business.

Primary impediments to expanded PT came from four sources. First, some hospitals and pharmacists resented parallel imports, believing them to be entrepreneurial only and not to add any value or technology to the drugs market. Second, manufacturers engaged in considerable differentiation of products across countries through differences in packaging, labelling, information inserts

---

[9] Scherer and Watal (2001, 47–49).
[10] REMIT Consultants (1991).

and so on. These practices raised the cost of PT considerably and seemed to limit its growth. Third, in those countries with concentrated wholesale distribution systems, distributors often implicitly colluded in refusing to supply parallel traders. These two factors are of particular relevance for developing countries considering relaxing restraints on parallel imports. Fourth, government regulations were at times aimed at reducing parallel imports. These regulations included licensing and approval delays and price 'claw-backs' from pharmacists that discouraged the use of parallel imports. At the same time, some countries provided financial incentives to encourage substitution of parallel imports for purchases from original manufacturers.

Although there were no substantive data to support these claims, survey results pointed to the following difficulties with PT from the standpoint of economic welfare. First, PT firms perform no R&D and undertake little capital investment. They exploit original R&D without cost and without taking a long-term view of the future of the pharmaceutical sector. Second, to the extent that PT is undertaken, the activity incurs wasteful transportation costs and repackaging costs. Third, parallel imports reduce profit margins for original manufacturers, perhaps significantly in drugs with large markets. These reduced margins are transferred to PT firms, distributors, pharmacists and hospitals. The extent to which ultimate patients, insurance firms or public health services benefit from lower prices was unclear in their study, but they found little evidence of significant savings.

On the beneficial side, no evidence could be found that parallel imports caused patients to suffer from ingesting sub-standard or wrongly used medicines. Thus, the regulatory system for PT was safe. Also beneficial for consumers was the fact that the threat of sourcing parallel imports seemed to raise the bargaining power of public health services and insurance firms in negotiating price concessions from manufacturers. Indeed, this seemed to be an important source of profit transfers from manufacturers to purchasers. This observation is also significant for health authorities in developing countries.

The EU is the natural location in which to study the potential for PT in pharmaceuticals because of their essentially free movement, subject to any informal impediments and trade costs. Despite this free movement, there remains considerable variability in identical, branded-drug products across the European Union. In Table 3.3, we present calculations using data from the Swedish Medical Products Agency for a basket of 90 brand-name drugs in 1998. Average prices in Greece were 28 per cent below the EU-wide average, and in Germany they were 11 per cent above the mean. Switzerland's average prices were still higher. These price gaps are undoubtedly wider than the associated costs of transporting and repackaging on the part of parallel traders. Simple regression analysis confirmed that these price differences are statistically significant across countries.

Table 3.3: Average percentage deviation from European mean prices in pharmaceutical products, 1998

Country	All 90 products	Products in all 15 countries
Greece	−28	−16
Spain	−20	−12
Portugal	−13	−4
Italy	−13	−4
France	−0	−1
Finland	−2	−2
Austria	−2	+0
Norway	−1	−5
Sweden	−1	−1
Belgium	−1	+0
Netherlands	+2	+3
Denmark	+3	+3
Germany	+11	+8
United Kingdom	+19	+12
Switzerland	+25	+17

Source: Authors' calculations using data from the Swedish Medical Products Authority.

Considering only the set of products that were traded in all 15 countries (an indication that identical products are sold in all markets and may be sourced from anywhere), there is still significant price variation. Average prices ranged from 16 per cent below the mean in Greece to 17 per cent above the mean in Switzerland and 12 per cent above the mean in the United Kingdom. However, these price differences are smaller than those in the first column, suggesting that the universal availability of products induces less international variation in prices. It is conceivable that this smaller variation is a result of actual or threatened PT.

It seems also from these data that individual companies choose different pricing strategies for different EU members. In a sample of 25 pharmaceutical manufacturers, the standard deviation of their product prices ranged from 0.12 to 0.31. This considerable variation in prices by company (and thus by product portfolio) suggests that firms may have different methods for dealing with the potential for PT.

A formal analysis of PT within the European Union was provided by Ganslandt and Maskus.[11] They analysed data on price variations for branded drugs within the EU and on the extent of parallel imports. This task was made

[11] Ganslandt and Maskus (2001, 13–21).

possible by the Swedish government's provision of data on approvals and sales of parallel-importing firms. Valued at wholesale prices, sales of pharmaceuticals in Sweden came to Skr 16.6 million in 1998. These sales were concentrated in a number of patented molecules, with the 50 best-selling molecules accounting for 37 per cent of sales in 1998.

Sweden joined the EU in January 1995 and began taking applications for approvals and licences for parallel importers. The first approval did not occur until late 1996, but approvals mounted rapidly after that time. Thus, parallel imports have increased substantially since Sweden joined the EU, in terms of both sales and approvals. By 1998, parallel imports had grown to Skr 1.007 million, corresponding to 6 per cent of the overall pharmaceutical market, and there were 226 approvals to engage in this trade. Parallel imports were 16 per cent of sales in the 50 best-selling molecules. In fact, among those products for which parallel imports existed, the median share of those imports in sales was barely above zero. However, they accounted for 54 per cent of sales in those drugs for which parallel imports were greatest. Thus, parallel-importing firms focus on those drugs for which the largest markets exist.

In 1997–8 the number of parallel-importing firms rose from four to 10. However, the top four firms in 1998 accounted for 96 per cent of PI sales. Parallel imports from 13 countries had been approved by 1998, but the sources were heavily concentrated in low-price countries in southern Europe. Spain, Italy and Greece were the exporters in 63 per cent of all cases of approved PT.

With these data it is possible to consider some effects of parallel imports on the Swedish market. In Table 3.4, we present a comparison between products that were subject to parallel imports (that is, products for which at least one approval was issued) and products that were not. The calculations show average percentage price changes for products between either 1994 or 1997 and 1998. Computations are made both for samples including parallel imports, referred to as 'Mean incl. PI', and for manufacturing firms' prices. The first pair of columns presents simple averages of price changes and the second pair of columns presents average price changes in which each product is weighted by its Swedish sales share in 1998.

Consider the unweighted average price changes. In the period 1994–8, prices increased by 6.6 per cent for all products, while manufacturers' prices rose slightly more, at 7.3 per cent. Average prices for products in which PI took place rose by 2.9 per cent, while manufacturers' prices for those goods increased by 6.4 per cent, a significant difference. Note, finally, that manufacturers' prices for non-PI products rose by 7.6 per cent, which was higher than the 6.4 per cent increase of manufacturing prices for goods facing the threat of PI. An initial conclusion, then, is that parallel imports limit price increases relative to other goods. The weighted average price changes show similar results. Recall that PI

Table 3.4: Percentage change of pharmaceutical prices in Sweden, 1994–98

	Unweighted average		Weighted average	
	1994–8	1997–8	1994–8	1997–8
All products				
Mean including PI	6.6	0.25	0.8	−1.4
Manufacturers' price	7.3	0.73	2.8	−0.16
PI products				
Mean including PI	2.9	−3.1	−4.4	−3.8
Manufacturers' price	6.4	−0.3	0.3	−0.67
Non-PI products				
Mean	7.6	0.96	3.6	0.15
Number of observations	125	151	125	151

Source: Authors' calculations using data from the Swedish Medical Products Authority.

tends to target high-sales products, so we would expect to find larger price-moderating impacts in this group, as we do. Thus, those products in which PI occurred actually saw prices decline by 4.4 per cent over the period, while manufacturers were able to raise prices only by 0.3 per cent on a weighted basis. In contrast, non-PI goods saw a 3.6 per cent price increase.

These differences were more pronounced over the shorter period 1997–8. Average prices increased by 0.25 per cent. The mean prices set by the manufacturing firms declined by 0.3 per cent for products subject to PI competition but rose by 0.96 per cent for non-PI goods. Prices of parallel-imported products fell by 3.1 per cent. These relative price changes carried over qualitatively to the weighted-average calculations as well.

This basic evidence confirms that the prices of parallel-imported products, and products facing their competition, fell in the Swedish import market relative to the prices of goods not subject to PI. The main effect, approximately 75 per cent of the average price decrease, resulted from parallel trade, while the remaining effect was a result of changes in the manufacturing firms' prices.

It is possible to test statistically the role of PI in this price moderation. At the simplest level, we use t-tests to see whether differences between the changes in the manufacturing firms' prices for products subject to PI and in their prices for products not subject to PI are significant. The null hypothesis of no difference in these price changes was not rejected at the 10 per cent level for the period 1994–8. However, this hypothesis was rejected at the 5 per cent level for 1997–8, confirming that the manufacturers' prices increased significantly less for products subject to PI than for other products, with the effect concentrated at the end of the period. A further t-test shows that the average price change for PI products was significantly lower than the average price change for non-PI products in both 1994–8 and 1997–8.

The essential inference here is that the data support a price-moderating impact from PI. Over the short period 1997–8 the change in the manufacturers' prices was significantly lower for products facing PI competition than for other drugs. Thus, manufacturing firms seem to react to the volume of arbitrage through PI with a lagged price adjustment rather than with an attempt to deter PI before they enter the market.

A further perspective is available from a simple regression analysis (not shown) of these price changes. Two variables are included in the regression: PI SHARE, which is the share of parallel trade in total sales for specific products, and APPROVAL, which is a dummy variable equal to one when there is at least one approval in 1998 to parallel-import the good, and zero otherwise. The dependent variable, defined at the individual product level, is the relative price change of the manufacturing firms' price over the periods 1994–8 and 1997–8.

Our regressions find that the coefficients of PI SHARE and APPROVAL have the expected negative sign in every case. However, the coefficients are insignificant for the longer period 1994–8. For the shorter period 1997–8 the coefficient on PI SHARE is –0.039 and is significantly negative at the one per cent level. Thus, an increase of one per cent in the share of a drug's sales that came from PI tended to reduce the average price increase by 3.9 per cent. The coefficient on APPROVAL is –0.0125, and significant at the 5 per cent level.

A further issue is whether parallel trade has an effect on the price differentials between the export and the import markets. One would anticipate some price convergence between the two markets. To test this hypothesis we used bilateral price comparisons between the Swedish market and the two main export markets, Italy and Spain. The data are wholesale prices in US dollars in 1994 and 1998. These figures incorporated at least one pair of prices for 28 of the top 50 molecules in Sweden. Nine of these products were subject to parallel exports from Spain, Italy or both. Particular product varieties in Sweden that did not have comparable products in the export market were excluded from the sample.

Prices were defined as those in export markets relative to those in Sweden for 1994 and 1998. The price change of interest was then the relative price in 1998 minus the relative price in 1994, with price convergence occurring where the relative price change was positive (assuming, as was true in all cases, that the Spanish and Italian prices were below the Swedish prices in 1994). Regressing relative price changes on a dummy variable PI TRADE (taking on the value one if there was any parallel trade, and zero otherwise), we found that the estimated

Table 3.5: Prices of parallel imports and parallel importing firms' markups, 1998

	PI price relative to manufacturing firm's price in Sweden (ratio)					
	PI to Sweden from Italy			PI to Sweden from Spain		
	Mean (std. dev.)	Max. Min.	No. of observations	Mean (std. dev.)	Max. Min.	No. of observations
PI price in Sweden	0.89 (0.01)	0.92 0.85	28	0.89 (0.01)	0.92 0.85	28
PI price in exporter	0.68 (0.11)	0.83 0.51	7	0.68 (0.07)	0.79 0.59	8
PI markup	0.21 (0.11)	0.39 0.09	7	0.21 (0.07)	0.31 0.09	8

Source: Authors' calculations using data from the Swedish Medical Products Authority.

coefficient was 0.0180 for Italy, 0.0206 for Spain and 0.0176 for the pooled sample. These figures would indicate that PI was responsible for small tendencies for prices to converge: 1.8 per cent for Italy, 2.1 per cent for Spain and 1.8 per cent overall. However, these impacts are statistically insignificant and, in any case, are small relative to underlying price differentials. On average in 1998, the prices of these goods in Italy and Spain were 68 per cent of those in Sweden. In this sample, then, PI showed little ability to establish even a tendency towards price convergence.

Finally, it is possible to estimate the difference between the prices in the export markets and the prices set by PI firms in the Swedish market. Table 3.5 summarizes the PI firms' prices for products subject to this trade. The relative prices are defined as the PI prices divided by the prices charged by the manufacturing firms for identical products. Thus, the average price charged by PI firms in 1998 was 89 per cent of the manufacturers' prices in Sweden. The minimum relative price was 85 per cent and the maximum was 92 per cent.

With these figures on prices in the export markets and in Sweden, we compute the PI firms' margin to be approximately 21 per cent of the original manufacturers' prices in the importing country. The margins for PI from Italy ranged from 9 to 39 per cent and the margins for PI from Spain ranged from 9 to 31 per cent. Rents to the PI firms, or alternatively real resources used up in arbitrage through PI, were therefore considerable compared to the small price reductions in the Swedish market.

These margins and price impacts may be used to compute the impact of PI on consumer surplus and the rents that are shifted from manufacturers to trading firms. Recall that the effect of PI on the manufacturing firms' prices was to permit them to rise by 1.2 per cent less (unweighted) and by 3.3 per cent less (weighted) than non-PI prices. Assuming that drugs are normal goods, we obtain an upper limit for the positive effect on consumer surplus by employing the quantity consumed at the lower, PI-induced prices. The difference between (notional) expected expenditure at the lower price and actual expenditure is the change in consumer surplus. With this approach, the effect of PI on consumer benefits in Sweden in 1998 was approximately Skr 150 million with unweighted price changes and Skr 199 million with weighted price changes.

In comparison, the rents to PI firms, which include transport and packaging costs, could be calculated from the actual margin between these firms' prices in Sweden and wholesale prices in the export markets, multiplied by the quantity of parallel-imported drugs. Using these margins, we calculate the rents to PI firms to be approximately Skr 188 million in 1998. Interestingly, and significantly, these rents are of the same magnitude as the consumer surplus gains. Put differently, the gains to Swedish consumers are effectively offset by payments to PI firms. The greater the share of PI rents that are actually transport costs and the greater the share of rents that are garnered by foreign PI firms, the smaller is the net gain (and the larger the net loss) to Sweden. With our figures, it seems that the static welfare impacts in Sweden (including the profit reductions imposed on Swedish pharmaceutical firms) are negative, even without considering the dynamic impacts on R&D.

Evidence on PI and R&D performance

The findings just reviewed are fairly pessimistic about the static impacts of PT, at least within the European Union.[12] If PT were also shown empirically to reduce the level of R&D effort among original manufacturers that compete with it, there would be a further dynamic reason to question their value. For this purpose one would need to correlate carefully the lagged price impacts of parallel imports, product by product, with the R&D performance of pharmaceutical firms. One would also wish to take account of global sales and profits when correlating PT with research spending; it is possible, for example, that an American firm is most damaged by parallel imports into Germany or Sweden. Unfortunately, the available data do not make such an effort possible.

The best we can offer at present is to look at crude indicators of relative R&D performance in the 1990s, a time of growing PT in the European Union.

---

[12] See also Darba and Rovira (1998, 32–4).

For this purpose, we have computed growth in business enterprise R&D in both local currencies and in purchasing power parity-adjusted terms in the pharmaceutical sectors of 10 OECD countries.[13] These data relate to International Standard Industrial Classification (ISIC) category 3522, 'Drugs and Medicines', and therefore includes R&D into both new drugs and generics.

In Italy, which is a source of parallel exports, R&D performance languished in the 1990s, but Spain saw an increase of about 80 per cent in its R&D spending. In local currency terms, Sweden registered the highest relative increase in R&D performance, despite being the recipient of extensive parallel imports. Denmark was in a similar situation. Germany's performance was stagnant until late in the decade. Canada, which does not permit parallel imports, registered large increases in R&D, in part because of a commitment by foreign pharmaceutical firms to increase research activity in their Canadian branches.

Overall, there is no detectable relationship between R&D in the pharmaceutical sector and permission for or the extent of parallel imports. Again, a company-level analysis focusing on basic R&D would be more appropriate if the data were available. At this simple level, however, there seems to be little reason to argue empirically that parallel imports clearly reduce R&D expenditures in pharmaceuticals.

CONCLUSIONS AND POLICY RECOMMENDATIONS

Parallel imports of patented and brand-name drugs arise for a variety of factors associated with price differences among markets: price discrimination by manufacturers, vertical price-setting within distribution systems and differential systems of price control. As may be expected, PT has complex effects on markets. There are many reasons to believe that price discrimination in competitive markets can be beneficial overall, so a presumption in favour of restraining parallel trade could be supported. However, under some circumstances ensuring access to cheaper imports is warranted.

It is useful by way of summary to list here the potential benefits and costs of permitting PI. The benefits of parallel imports are as follows.

1. As PI enables pharmacists, hospitals and insurance services to procure drugs from cheaper international sources, prices of brand-name drugs are directly reduced. Presumably, this reduction is passed on to final consumers (patients) to some degree. This price-reducing impact may be of particular benefit in developing countries where firms sell small volumes at high prices.

---

[13] The source of these data is the OECD (2001) data set for business enterprise research and development (BERD), various tables.

2. The threat of procuring PI drugs may be sufficient to give health providers enough negotiating leverage with original manufacturers that they would charge lower prices. Thus, PI can be a complement to price control programmes.
3. Parallel imports may be a source of technology transfer in that they could make products available on markets where firms could reverse-engineer their composition.

The costs of parallel imports are as follows.

1. To the extent that original manufacturers set prices according to local demand elasticity and market size, integrating markets through PI could raise the prices in exporting countries by reducing available supply there. Under plausible circumstances, firms could refuse to supply small markets altogether.
2. Parallel trade uses resources in transport costs and repackaging. These costs may take up a significant portion of any potential price advantages.
3. PI firms engage in no R&D and undertake little in the way of marketing investments. Thus, they are permitted to exploit without cost the marketing expenses of original manufacturers and their licensees, which could reduce the willingness of these firms to supply certain markets and products.
4. To the extent that PI reduces profitability for original manufacturers and that their R&D programmes are sensitive to profit reductions, the activity can slow down global drugs development. Because PI firms focus on the most successful drugs *ex post*, the relative returns for developing breakthrough or 'blockbuster' drugs are reduced.
5. It is conceivable that if developing countries were to make comprehensive and widespread resort to PI in drugs of particular interest they could offset incentives for more R&D to emerge from the TRIPS Agreement.

In the light of this background, the empirical evidence supports the following conclusions. First, there are substantial price differences between countries in identical brand-name drugs. Second, these prices roughly follow Ramsey pricing, but there are many instances of prices that are higher in developing countries than in developed countries. This fact may be attributed to imperfectly competitive distribution systems and a decision by firms to sell small volumes at high mark-ups to price-insensitive consumers in poor countries. Third, PI in drugs within the EU, particularly in the more successful products, reached substantial proportions in the 1990s. Despite that, significant price differences remain between countries, and there is little evidence of price convergence caused by PI. In that context, the activities of PI firms seem to incur transport costs and earn rents while failing to provide much benefit to drug-consumers, at least in Sweden. Finally, there is no detectable relationship between parallel imports and R&D performance within OECD countries, but the data available to check for this relationship are crude.

In view of the theory and findings set out in this report, the policy recommendations below seem to be supportable and sensible. These recommendations are consistent with those in Scherer and Watal,[14] but also extend them.

1. In order to avoid price spillovers associated with price discrimination, high-income countries could be encouraged to prohibit parallel imports in pharmaceuticals. However, they could permit parallel exports from their markets to poor countries in essential drugs.
2. If a desirable regime of differential pricing is to be established, the richer countries cannot use prices in low-income jurisdictions as references for their own price controls. Thus, an agreement not to set reference pricing schemes on the basis of prices in low-income economies would be beneficial for maintaining the integrity of the system and for sustaining R&D incentives.
3. Parallel importation by low-income countries should be permitted if they wish it, in order to avoid problems with high prices charged in low-volume products. These countries should also be permitted to ban parallel exports to high-income economies, in order to keep supply available locally.
4. To the extent that high domestic prices in developing countries are caused by exclusive distributorship regulations, these requirements should be eliminated, in order to complement the effects of parallel imports.
5. The fact that parallel trade incurs transport costs implies that it should be limited to regional exhaustion regimes among poor countries. In such integrated markets (say in sub-Saharan Africa, Central America, the Andean countries and ASEAN) there would be free parallel trade among the members. The threat of PI within these regions would discipline country-specific monopoly pricing. However, these regional groupings would be expected to prevent parallel exports from their regions.

Having reviewed the evidence available on parallel trade in pharmaceutical products, we are persuaded that modified restraints on this trade would advance the global interest in increasing the availability of essential medicines at low prices in the least developed countries.

REFERENCES

Danzon, Patricia M. and Jeong Kim (1998), 'International Price Comparisons for Pharmaceuticals: Measurement and Policy Issues', *Pharmacoeconomics*, 14, 115–28.

Darba, Josep and Joan Rovira (1998), 'Parallel Imports of Pharmaceuticals in the European Union', *Pharmacoeconomics*, 14, Supplement: 129–36.

---

[14] Scherer and Watal (2001, 60–64). See also Chapter 2 in this volume.

Ganslandt, Mattias and Keith E. Maskus (2001), 'Parallel Imports of Pharmaceutical Products in the European Union', manuscript, University of Colorado.
Malueg, David A. and Marius Schwartz (1994), Parallel Imports, Demand Dispersion, and International Price Discrimination, *Journal of International Economics*, 37, 167–96.
Maskus, Keith E. (2000), *Intellectual Property Rights in the Global Economy* (Washington, DC: Institute for International Economics).
Maskus, Keith E. (2001), 'Parallel Imports in Pharmaceuticals: Implications for Competition and Prices in Developing Countries', Report to the World Intellectual Property Organization.
Organization for Economic Cooperation and Development (2001). *R&D Expenditures in Industry: 1987/1999*. (Paris: OECD; online at *www.sourceoecd.org*).
REMIT Consultants (1991), *Impediments to Parallel Trade in Pharmaceuticals within the European Community*, report to DG IV of the European Commission.
Scherer, F. M. and Jayashree Watal (2001), 'Post-TRIPS Options for Access to Patented Medicines in Developing Countries', paper prepared for Working Group 4 of the Commission for Macroeconomics and Health of the World Health Organization.
World Bank (2000), *World Development Report: 1999–2000*. (New York: Oxford University Press).

4 FATAL SIDE EFFECTS: MEDICINE PATENTS UNDER THE MICROSCOPE

Oxfam

INTRODUCTION

Every week, 250,000 people die of infectious diseases, the great majority of them women, men and children living in poverty in the developing world.[1] Global patent rules agreed at the World Trade Organization (WTO) in 1994 are deepening this public health crisis by increasing the cost of medicines. In this paper, Oxfam argues that governments must change the rules in order to ensure that impoverished people have access to the medicines they so desperately need, at prices they can afford. This demand has been at the heart of a campaign launched by Oxfam in February 2001. The paper on which this chapter is based was written before the WTO Ministerial Conference in Doha, Qatar on 9–14 November 2001, at which a special declaration on global patent rules and access to medicines was approved.[2] The impact of the WTO Agreement on Trade-Related Aspects of Intellectual Property Rights (TRIPS) on the price of medicines, and what governments can do about it, was the most prominent issue of debate. This high-profile debate, coming on top of worldwide public concern about access to AIDS drugs in Africa, makes it politically harder for industrialized countries and large pharmaceutical companies to continue to insist on the sanctity of drug patents in developing countries. Moreover, the unambiguous endorsement by the Ministerial Conference of a pro-public health interpretation of the WTO rules enables developing countries to produce cheaper generic versions of patented medicines with less fear of damaging trade disputes or costly litigation.

---

[1] This figure is calculated from statistics in the WHO's *World Health Report* (Geneva: World Health Organization, 2000).
[2] Oxfam's campaign reports and policy papers can be found at *www.oxfam.org.uk/cutthecost/*. Oxfam's briefing paper *Priced out of Reach*, prepared in advance of the Doha conference, and the joint press statement issued by Oxfam, Médecins Sans Frontières and other NGOs after the event are also available at this web address.

> Two million children die every year from pneumonia, almost all of them in developing countries. The US-based company Pfizer's best-selling antibiotic azithromycin (Zithromax) is particularly good for treating child pneumonia. It is under patent in Kenya, where it costs as much as in Norway. But Kenya spends only $17 per head every year on health care, while Norway spends $2,300. Kenya is not allowed to import the generic equivalent of azithromycin, which is available in India at one-fifth of the price in Norway and Kenya. Indian companies manufacture azithromycin because the government has not yet implemented medicine patenting. If TRIPS-compliant rules had come in earlier, its manufacture would have been impossible.[a]
>
> [a] 'Formula for Fairness: Patient Rights before Patent Rights', *Oxfam Briefing on Pfizer*, 2001.

Although Doha represents an important step forward in the battle for affordable medicines, Oxfam still believes that the TRIPS Agreement should be amended in the review scheduled for 2002. Developing countries should be allowed the flexibility to reduce the length and scope of pharmaceutical patenting, and the transition to higher levels of intellectual property protection should depend on development milestones rather than arbitrary dates.

The WTO rules, laid down in the Agreement on Trade-Related Aspects of Intellectual Property Rights,[3] were introduced after sustained lobbying by transnational corporations (TNCs).[4] The agreement obliges the member countries to grant at least 20-year patent protection in all fields of technology, including medicines. This enables already powerful Northern pharmaceutical TNCs to consolidate their market domination on a global scale. Longer patent periods will delay the appearance of the low-cost generic equivalents that traditionally supply developing-country needs – only the expensive, patented version of a new medicine will be available. At a time when millions of people are already unable to afford essential medicines and when public health is threatened by a combination of new diseases and drug-resistant variants of old killers, the WTO rules will further reduce access to modern medicines for poor people and lead to unnecessary death and suffering.

In 1999, the world's attention was drawn to the patenting issue by the controversy surrounding the high price of HIV–AIDS drugs in Southern Africa. In 2001, the legal action brought by international pharmaceutical companies

[3] Text available on the WTO website: *www.wto.org*.
[4] P. Drahos, 'Global property rights in information: the story of TRIPS at the GATT', *Prometheus*, vol. 13, no. 1, June 1995.

against the government of South Africa over its Medicines Act and the trade dispute initiated by the United States against Brazil over its Industrial Property Law dramatically increased public anxiety about the effects of patenting.[5] Fortunately, world opinion forced the companies and the United States to withdraw in these two cases, but the issue did not go away. The strength of international concern encouraged developing countries to seek a formal debate on TRIPS at the WTO, despite opposition from the industrialized countries. Regrettably, developing-country requests for clarification and reaffirmation of the public health safeguards in TRIPS were stonewalled by the United States, Switzerland, Japan and Canada at special sessions in June and September 2001.

The international controversy reignited shortly afterwards when the United States and Canada threatened to override patents in order to secure adequate supplies of anti-anthrax drugs at reasonable prices. As this was a policy option they were systematically seeking to deny to developing countries, they were widely accused of hypocrisy and double standards. By the eve of the Fourth WTO Ministerial Conference, in Doha, it had become clear that a major row was brewing over TRIPS.

This chapter explains how the WTO patent rules work and how they will affect the price of medicines in developing countries in the context of the deepening health crisis. Next it assesses the 'flexibility' in the TRIPS agreement that supposedly enables governments to ensure access to affordable medicines and examines the problem of the 'TRIPS plus' patent regimes imposed by the United States. It then considers the issue of whether high levels of patent protection will stimulate pharmaceutical research and development (R&D) relevant to developing countries, and it is argued that the TRIPS Agreement as a whole is anti-developmental. The relationship between TRIPS and the problem of bio-piracy in the pharmaceuticals field is addressed next. It is followed by a look at what socially responsible companies should be doing in developing countries. The chapter concludes with a presentation of Oxfam's policy recommendations. These focus on TRIPS reform and on the need for rich countries and TNCs to stop harassing developing countries on patent issues. They also cover the necessity for public funding for research into new medicines and the role that industry could play in making medicines affordable.

THE HEALTH CRISIS

Medicine prices will rise in the context of a growing health crisis. Although there have been improvements in health indicators in many developing countries, 14 million people, the great majority of them poor, die every year from infectious

---

[5] Oxfam briefings on the South Africa and Brazil cases can be found at *www.oxfam.org.uk/cutthecost/*.

diseases. AIDS claims three million of these lives, tuberculosis two million and malaria one million.[6] This human tragedy is compounded by the economic consequences of ill health, which destroys opportunities for poverty reduction. Africa's gross domestic product (GDP), for example, would be one-third higher if malaria had been eliminated 35 years ago.[7] Drug-resistant strains of many common diseases such as pneumonia are spreading fast, making existing medicines redundant and posing a threat to public health in the industrialized world as well. In addition, developing countries face a rising incidence of 'First World' illnesses such as heart conditions, cancer and diabetes. The HIV–AIDS epidemic now infecting up to 25 million people in sub-Saharan Africa demonstrates the huge risk posed by previously unknown diseases.[8] All the new or improved drugs developed to face these challenges will be under patent for at least 20 years and, unless something is done, they will be too expensive for people living in poverty.

The causes of public health crises are complex. One in five of the world's population does not have access to health services. Poor nutrition, inadequate water supply and sanitation and the low quality of education are major contributory factors to ill health. Underlying these failures is the lack of equitable economic growth, itself a product of both national and international factors and the lukewarm commitment to poverty-reduction policies by many governments. Where governments have done their best, they have been seriously constrained by public expenditure cuts caused by debt obligations and the structural adjustment packages prescribed by international creditors over the past two decades. Developing-country governments could do more to make medicines accessible to the poor. Many continue to spend far less on public health than on other priorities, such as military budgets. The impact of inadequate overall spending is compounded by inequitable patterns of spending. All too often, tertiary-level services used mainly by better-off groups absorb a disproportionately large part of the health budget, while primary health care is chronically underfunded.

Although the achievement of public health goals depends fundamentally on equitable economic development and appropriate social policies, as well as on intensified interventions in the health field, one key policy is to ensure the supply of effective, affordable medicines. Access to medicines is particularly sensitive to price, as most poor people in developing countries pay out of their own pockets. Price is related to the presence of monopoly, or market exclusivity, in pharmaceutical markets, and this is now greatly extended by the TRIPS Agreement – a point commonly ignored until very recently in Northern government discussions.

[6] WHO, *World Health Report on Infectious Diseases* (Geneva, 1999).
[7] WHO, 'Economic costs of malaria are many times higher than previously estimated', Press Release (2000), *www.who/inf-pr-2000/en/pr2000-28.html.*
[8] UNAIDS, *Report on Global HIV/AIDS Epidemic*, June 2000.

> 'Many – even very poor people – can afford to buy drugs when the need is urgent and they are desperate. Our parents are just like all parents anywhere in the world. If a child is sick, they will do everything they can to help that child. They will borrow money. They will sell a cow. They will sell the tin from their roof. I see this every day.'
>
> Dr Zafrullah Chowdhury, health activist in Bangladesh

The health crisis and the related question of access to medicines are now on the political agenda in rich countries. In 2000, the rising death toll from killer diseases prompted the G-8 to support global action to reduce the number of HIV–AIDS-infected young people by 25 per cent and to halve the cases of death and sickness caused by tuberculosis (TB) and malaria. In the same year, the European Commission launched its strategy to help combat major infectious diseases. And in April 2001, the UN agreed to establish a Global Health Fund in order to support medical research, investments in infrastructure and purchase of medicines. Although these are all very positive initiatives, the financial commitments that convert rhetoric to reality have been disappointingly small to date. Another step forward in 2001 was the start of a major debate at the WTO about the potential impact of TRIPS on drug prices – a topic the rich countries could no longer avoid, owing to growing pressure from developing countries and public opinion.

HOW MUCH WILL THE NEW PATENT RULES INCREASE PRICES?

The WTO-mandated introduction of industrialized-world intellectual property (IP) rights in developing countries means that, at a conservative estimate, new patented products could have a market monopoly lasting nine or ten years longer than in the past. In other words, poor people could have to wait an *extra ten years* before they can buy low-cost generic equivalents of new or improved drugs on the market.

During this extended period, pharmaceutical TNCs will continue to charge high prices for patented medicines – prices that may be even higher in developing countries than in rich countries. Poor people and under-resourced health services will find themselves paying *at least three times* what they would otherwise have paid, particularly for the life-saving medicines for which there are no closely equivalent, off-patent substitutes.[9] This figure is likely to be an

---

[9] It is impossible to calculate how much patented products will cost in comparison with non-existent generic rivals, but rough estimates can be made. Watal, for example, calculates that prices in India could rise by 250 per cent, and globally by 200–300 per cent. (Jayashree Watal, 'Access to Essential Medicines in Developing Countries: Does the WTO TRIPS Agreement Hinder It?' Harvard University, Center for International Development, 2000;

> In the past, after a new, patented medicine appeared in an industrialized country, it took an Indian drug company about four years to develop an equivalent generic product.[a] It then took a year or two for this equivalent to establish a foothold in markets. This meant that the TNC originator had an effective monopoly of *five to six years* in countries with low levels of IP protection, such as India. Under TRIPS, the worldwide patent term is at least 20 years, but as the originator spends the first five to ten years after filing the patent on research, trials and obtaining regulatory approval, the effective monopoly on the market is *10 to 15 years*. Because product development and regulatory approval have been getting faster, the average period of effective monopoly is now probably closer to *15 years*. This double bonus for pharmaceutical TNCs underlines how the extension of patent periods in TRIPS has little to do with social benefit and everything to do with corporate gain.
>
> [a] B.K. Keayla, *New Patent Regime: Implications for Domestic Industry, Research and Development and Consumers* (New Delhi: Centre for Study of GATT Issues, 1996).

underestimate – for some products, prices could be 10 or 20 times higher. But of course many sick people will simply do without, making TRIPS a prescription for a public health disaster. The European Commission, in a frank moment, accepted that the problem had already arrived: 'Several key products to prevent, diagnose and treat HIV/AIDS, malaria and tuberculosis, largely produced in industrialized countries, under patent, are still too expensive for the poor.'[10]

Until recently, many developing countries excluded products such as medicines or plants from patentability, or had short patent periods in order to keep prices down and encourage local industry. Up to 50 countries, including Brazil and Argentina,[11] did not grant patents on pharmaceuticals. Some, such as India and Egypt, granted only process patents. In about 12 developing countries, most notably India, national pharmaceutical industries emerged capable of developing, manufacturing and exporting inexpensive equivalents of the

and, by the same author, 'Pharmaceutical prices and welfare losses: Policy options for India under the TRIPS agreement', *World Economy*, vol. 23 (2000), pp. 733–52.) Average prescription costs in the United Kingdom and the United States are three to four times higher when the medicines are patented.

[10] *Accelerated Action Targeted at Major Communicable Diseases within the Context of Poverty Reduction*, Communication of the European Commission to the Council and the European Parliament, September 2000.

[11] R. Weissman, 'A long strange Trips: the pharmaceutical industry drive to harmonize global intellectual property rules and the remaining WTO-legal alternatives available to Third World Countries', *Journal of International Economic Law*, University of Pennsylvania (Winter 1996).

> *'Price increases shall be a regular feature, and not an accident, with the introduction and/or strengthening of patent protection in developing countries. One outstanding example is the case of pharmaceuticals. There is an uncontested and solid set of studies, undertaken in developed and developing countries and in institutions such as the World Bank and the International Monetary Fund, that consistently indicate that developing countries are going to suffer from substantial price increases and other costs.'*[a]
>
> Prof. Carlos Correa, academic and TRIPS negotiator for Argentina during the Uruguay Round
>
> [a] C. Correa, *Intellectual Property Rights, the WTO and Developing Countries* (London and Penang: Zed Books/Third World Network, 2000).

patented products appearing in industrialized countries.[12] Egypt was able to cover over 90 per cent of its drugs needs and to supply neighbouring countries through domestic generic manufacture.[13] Under TRIPS, every member of the WTO must introduce a comprehensive IP protection system, with a minimum 20-year term for all patents, including medicines, or face costly disputes that could lead to trade sanctions. WTO rules thus treat patents on life-saving drugs and patents on ice-cream machines in exactly the same way.

There are three different deadlines for poor countries to bring their national patent laws into line with TRIPS. The 49 least developed countries (LDCs) have until 2006, with the possibility of further extensions. Of the rest, some countries, including India, have until 2005, but the majority had to be TRIPS-compliant by January 2000. Even before becoming compliant, countries are obliged to offer 'market exclusivity' – in effect, a provisional patent – for new medicines. Moreover, countries have been under considerable pressure from industrialized countries to become TRIPS-compliant before the deadlines. Brazil, for example, was persuaded to introduce a new patent law in 1996, nine years before it needed to. The fact that many European countries, including Switzerland, resisted providing pharmaceutical product patents until their industries had reached a certain level of development demonstrates the double standards of the rich world. France introduced product patents in 1960, Germany in 1968, Japan in 1976, Switzerland in 1977 and Italy and Sweden in 1978.[14]

[12] R. Balance, J. Pogany and H. Forsteiner, *The World's Pharmaceutical Industries: An International Perspective on Innovation, Competition and Policy* (UNIDO, 1991).
[13] A. A. Abouellenein, *Trade-Related Aspects of Intellectual Property Rights and the Pharmaceutical Industry in Egypt* (Cairo: Federation of Egyptian Industry, 1996).
[14] Consumers International, *Health and Pharmaceuticals* (1999), www.consumersinternational.org/roap/health/balapapers/wto_trips/main.htm.

TRIPS already affects many developing countries, creating monopolies for new drugs, some of which are already on the market, such as Roche's and Merck's anti-retrovirals, GlaxoSmithKline's new triple therapy for HIV–AIDS and a new class of broad-based antibiotics known as fluoroquinolones, which work well with drug-resistant infections. But this is just the tip of the iceberg. Any new or improved medicines for treating TB and HIV–AIDS, for example, or for drug-resistant pneumonia, meningitis and gonorrhoea will be patented worldwide. Advances in biomedical science hold out hope for novel medicines able to treat existing or new infectious diseases as well as traditionally 'First World' diseases. Oxfam fears that these medicines will also be surrounded by patents and priced out of reach of developing-country health services and individual families. Where there is widespread drug resistance, the established, cheap treatments are becoming ineffective, but people will not be able to afford the substitutes, or will suffer even greater economic hardship in their effort to pay. Women will be deterred more than men from buying medicines for themselves because of financial austerity or lack of control over family resources. Higher prices also exacerbate the problem of people not completing courses of treatment or taking the right doses, which contributes to the spread of drug resistance.

Some industrialized countries claim that the patenting issue is not crucial for public health in developing countries because 'only' five per cent of the current WHO (World Health Organization) Model List of Essential Drugs is under patent (see Chapter 1 by Lippert in this volume). However, one criterion for inclusion in the list, which helps developing countries to decide which medicines they must give priority to in the face of severe resource constraints, is price. This rules out a number of vital but expensive products, such as important anti-HIV–AIDS drugs. With the spread of drug resistance and with new or improved drugs appearing, the number of essential, patented products will grow. And as one developing country trade official put it to Oxfam, 'When people's lives are at stake, five per cent is five per cent too many.' For this reason, some Third World governments argue that drugs on the WHO list or comparable national lists should be exempted from patenting in developing countries.

IS TRIPS 'FLEXIBLE' ENOUGH, AND ARE THE PUBLIC HEALTH SAFEGUARDS ADEQUATE?

The TRIPS Agreement is a mixture of rules and principles that countries have to incorporate into their national legislation (see Chapter 2 by Scherer and Watal in this volume). As it is not a detailed law, there can be widely different interpretations. According to the industrialized countries, TRIPS grants a government the leeway to strike an appropriate balance among the inventor's interests, the public interest in innovation and the public good. This leeway includes the freedom to incorporate in national legislation public health safeguards such as the ability to override a patent and license local manufacture of a medicine. Faced with growing concern about the negative development impact of TRIPS, including the threat to public health, some industrialized-country governments such as Holland and Norway now accept a more liberal application of the agreement. Oxfam welcomes this shift, but argues that the value of this 'flexibility' should not be overstated and that the agreement remains seriously flawed. The problems stem, first, from the terms of the agreement itself and, second, from the political reality in which it is being implemented.

With regard to its terms, the simple fact is that TRIPS gives countries no choice about important aspects of their national IP law or about the huge extension of patent protection for all products and processes, including medicines. Moreover, the safeguards to protect public health are hedged with conditions that make them difficult to operate, especially for the poorer countries:

1. Article 8 of TRIPS allows countries to adopt measures necessary to protect public health but then qualifies the principle by requiring that measures be 'consistent with' the agreement. Oxfam believes that TRIPS should be amended to include a stronger statement on the primacy of public health needs, similar to the 'general exception' clauses found in other WTO agreements.
2. Article 31 of TRIPS allows compulsory licensing, i.e. government authorization of the production of a patented product by another manufacturer on public interest grounds, without the permission of the patent-holder. This is an important safeguard in the event of abusive pricing or failure to supply a market. Yet most developing countries cannot derive advantage from this measure because they do not have the capacity to copy and manufacture medicines. They cannot import from elsewhere because Article 31 contains the requirement that production be 'predominantly' for domestic needs, and thus prevents production for export. The WTO needs to agree that production for export to a country where a compulsory licence has been issued is acceptable. Even if this is done, the procedures required for compulsory licensing create opportunities for companies with deep pockets to start expensive litigation, e.g. over compensation or over the duration of the licence.
3. Even if potential legal impediments facing a government wishing to issue a compulsory licence for a medicine are reduced, the market for the medicine may well be too small to allow low-cost production. A market consisting of a single developing country, or even a group of them that have issued a compulsory licence, will generally not offer the sales volume necessary to bring the price down below that of the patented product. If a country such as India or Brazil has started low-cost production under a compulsory

licence, the picture is different, but a country's access to cheaper equivalents of patented drugs should not depend on what a handful of other governments might or might not have done.

4. Article 6 of TRIPS also allows a country to pass laws which enable it to import a patented product from wherever it is sold most cheaply, whatever the wishes of the patent-holder. This 'parallel importing' is an effective restraint on the most abusive pricing, especially if there is a country with effective price controls from which medicines can be obtained. However, with the extension of 20-year patenting worldwide and the resulting lack of generic competition, the tendency will be for patent-holders to set higher prices everywhere, and there may be less 'parallel' differential. TNCs and the US government have been pressing vigorously for national laws to prohibit parallel importing, which Oxfam believes should be resisted. If TRIPS were consistent with the WTO's ostensible trade liberalization philosophy, it would outlaw these prohibitions (see Chapter 3 by Maskus and Ganslandt in this volume for a different view).

5. Finally, as defenders of TRIPS like to point out, developing countries have a longer period for compliance with the agreement. However, for all least developed countries and most developing countries, this right is empty of content because there will be nowhere to buy generic versions at reasonable prices (unless one of the biggest developing countries has already initiated domestic production under a compulsory licence). For this reason, Oxfam argues that the timing of TRIPS compliance should depend on a country's level of development, not on an arbitrary date.

Workable compulsory licensing is a necessary last resort for governments, but the associated legal and practical difficulties mean that it cannot be the 'normal' way of ensuring affordable medicines in developing countries. Oxfam believes that the solution lies in greater competition. In other words, vital medicines in developing countries should have shorter patent periods, or be exempted altogether, thereby allowing generic production to kick in sooner and bring down prices. This can be done either by amending TRIPS or by allowing all developing countries longer times for compliance.

'TRIPS PLUS'

The problems with the terms of the TRIPS Agreement are compounded by the political realities. To date, the United States and the pharmaceutical TNCs have been using the 'flexibility' of TRIPS to their advantage, imposing their interpretations of the grey areas of the agreement on developing countries. Countries are bullied into passing national laws based on the most restrictive interpretation of TRIPS, purged of the original safeguards and often containing

> In April 2001, the Dominican Republic was put on the United States' 'priority watch list' for alleged IP violations – a process that can lead to sanctions under the US Trade Act. In June, the United States Pharmaceutical Manufacturers Association (PhRMA) sought a review of the trade preferences granted to the Dominican Republic. If these were withdrawn, the effects on income and employment, especially for women working in the textile sector, would be devastating. PhRMA also wanted the US government to initiate a formal dispute process at the WTO. PhRMA complains that Dominican patent law has too many exclusions from patentability, too much scope for compulsory licensing, too little protection of clinical trial data presented to regulatory authorities and an unacceptable requirement that patented products be manufactured in-country.[15] The real 'problem' is that the Dominican Republic is trying to preserve the local pharmaceutical industry, which grew up before the country was forced to introduce drug patenting. This industry is now starting production of anti-retrovirals so as to meet the country's pressing need for affordable treatment for HIV–AIDS.

levels of IP protection that go beyond anything mandated by TRIPS. Until recently, the European Union was also overtly pressing for strict interpretations of the agreement.

The aim of the US government is simply to provide the longest possible period of effective IP protection for its corporations. The leverage over developing countries is the threat of trade sanctions, which can be authorized either by Section 301 of the US Trade Act or by a WTO Dispute Settlement panel in the event of a TRIPS violation. Countries such as South Africa, Brazil, Argentina, the Dominican Republic and Thailand have all been threatened with sanctions by the United States if they do not bring laws governing pharmaceuticals into line with what the TNCs want. Many developing countries do not have the political strength, economic resources or technical expertise to resist these pressures. These realities underline the pressing need for the WHO to provide independent data and technical assistance to poor countries, but they also call further into question the nature of TRIPS itself.

The US government also uses the negotiation of bilateral and regional trade agreements to induce countries into accepting the patent rules sought by US

---

[15] The list of countries accused by the Office of the US Trade Representative (USTR) of not respecting the property rights of US companies can be found in reports available at *www.ustr.gov*. The detailed complaints of the US pharmaceutical industry about alleged TRIPS violations, which form the basis of the USTR reports, can be found at *www.phrma.org*.

companies, and then binds them to those commitments.[16] Even the Africa Growth and Opportunity Act (2000), heralded by the United States as a generous response to poverty in the poorest region of the world, requires the US government to take account of a country's record on IP when deciding whether to grant preferential trade terms. The recently ratified United States–Jordan free trade agreement, for example, has four provisions that threaten public health in Jordan:

1. 'parallel importing' is prohibited: Jordan cannot import patented medicines from the cheapest international source;
2. the grounds for compulsory licensing are restricted to national emergencies;
3. patent periods must be extended if there is delay in regulatory approval; and
4. an existing Jordanian rule, which makes granting a patent conditional on the holder marketing an adequate supply of the product at a reasonable price, has been abolished.

The United States' IP policy contrasts with a substantial body of informed public and even business opinion in America and throughout the world which recognizes that there are problems with the current excesses of the patent system, North and South. Leading members of the liberal establishment, including commentators in the *Financial Times* and *The Economist*, and renowned free-traders such as Professor Jagdish Bhagwati[17] of Columbia University, have publicly expressed concern about the economic inefficiency and social costs associated with IP monopolies. In addition, public health experts, medical associations, trade unions and other civil society organizations are actively voicing their concern. Some have even suggested that IP protection, which is anti-competitive by nature, has no place in the WTO. Now that many developing-country governments have taken up the issue, the pressure for changes in the policy of the United States and other pharmaceuticals-exporting countries such as Britain, Germany and Switzerland will become hard to resist.

WILL PATENTING IN DEVELOPING COUNTRIES STIMULATE RESEARCH INTO THE DISEASES OF POVERTY?

The main argument offered in support of TRIPS is that increased TNC revenues from patents will translate into greater pharmaceutical R&D. However, Oxfam believes that little of the extra profit derived from developing countries will be spent on R&D relevant to the diseases of poverty; it argues instead for large-scale public funding.

---

[16] See Oxfam's briefing paper, *Priced out of Reach* (October 2001), which draws on research by Peter Drahos.
[17] *Financial Times*, 14 February 2001.

One aspect of the deepening global 'health divide' between rich and poor is the tragic failure of the pharmaceutical industry to meet the need for medicines in the developing world. Only 10 per cent of health research targets the illnesses that make up 90 per cent of the global disease burden. A miserly 0.2 per cent of research effort is directed to diarrhoea, pneumonia and TB, which cause 18 per cent of all illness.[18] Instead, TNCs are geared to manufacturing medicines of commercial interest, which means producing for the consumers in the industrialized world who make up 85 per cent of their market. Because, for example, poor women do not have the money to become a 'market', there is little investment in the development of vaginal microbicides effective against sexually transmitted diseases, including HIV.[19]

Advocates of a high level of patent protection in developing countries argue that it will stimulate research into the diseases from which poor people suffer. For diseases common to rich and poor countries, the argument is false. As most developing-country markets will remain relatively small for the foreseeable future, the extra revenue for companies will make no perceptible difference to R&D investment decisions. The lucrative markets will be the better-off households in economies such as Argentina, Brazil, India and China – the prizes sought by TNCs through the worldwide extension of IP protection. But the pattern of illness among the middle classes in the developing world is similar to that in the industrialized world, so their demand does not stimulate research into the diseases common among low-income families. For these diseases, the purchasing power of 1.2 billion people living on one dollar a day simply does not constitute a commercial incentive to R&D investment – a reality admitted by companies themselves. Spending on drugs by health ministries is also not large enough to act as a significant stimulus. Sixty-one countries have public drug expenditure of less than $10 per capita.[20]

Drugs TNCs justify patent protection by the large sums needed for R&D. However, what matters from a business perspective is not that R&D is costly but whether there is an adequate return on the investment. In the case of the pharmaceutical industry, returns are among the highest of any sector. According to a US Senate report, not only does the pharmaceutical industry perennially lead all others in size of profits in relation to sales but it also has the highest rate of return on capital and on shareholder equity. The 1999 pre-tax profits of Merck's global pharmaceutical business were comfortably over 30 per cent of

---

[18] UNDP, *Human Development Report* (New York, 1999).
[19] *Accelerated Action Targeted at Major Communicable Diseases within the Context of Poverty Reduction*, Communication of the Commission to the Council and the European Parliament, September 2000.
[20] WHO, *WHO Medicine Strategy 2000-2003* (Geneva, 2000).

sales, while its R&D expenditure was only about 12 per cent of sales. Glaxo Wellcome's figures were 30 per cent and 15 per cent respectively.

Although patents in Northern markets do generate huge resources for companies, only a relatively small part is allocated to therapeutically valuable research – indeed, marketing costs are often double expenditure on R&D. Annual drug-industry advertising in the United States alone costs more than Africa spends on all medicines in a year.[21] Marketing costs in developing countries can also be up to 30 per cent of sales, and these costs are passed on to patients.

Company figures for R&D spending are frequently exaggerated by including the opportunity cost of the capital employed at high discount rates; by relating total R&D spending only to 'new molecular entities' and not to new combinations and formulations, thus inflating the 'cost per new drug'; and by including marketing costs. Moreover, a great deal of research goes into non-essential drugs, into prolonging the life of money-spinning patented products by changing a dosage or formulation or into producing equivalents of the patented 'blockbusters' marketed by rivals. For example, Eli Lilly is researching an impotency drug to compete with Pfizer's lucrative Viagra (sildenafil); this could reduce prices, but is not therapeutically productive. Much socially useful research is funded by governments and charities and, through fiscal incentives, by the taxpayer, although the resulting financial benefits accrue primarily to the patent-holder.[22]

Because the market fails hundreds of millions of people living in poverty, there is an overwhelming case for major investments by governments in R&D, as well as in health care delivery systems, and in subsidizing access to treatment for those who cannot pay. Oxfam believes that increased public funding is the most effective and efficient way of generating the appropriate research. This effort should harness the strengths and resources of industry, North and South. In order to maximize the benefits to people in poverty, governments should exercise due control over financial returns to the private sector. Oxfam has called for the creation of an international fund for research into medicines and vaccines, supported by governments worldwide in proportion to their means. Operating under the auspices of the WHO, this mechanism could help to fill the gaps in funding and overcome the fragmentation of current research efforts and public–private partnerships. Regrettably, the current proposal for a Global Health Fund does not include significant investment in research.

---

[21] NIHCM, *Prescription Drugs and Intellectual Property Protection*, NIHCM Foundation Issue Brief (Washington, DC, August 2000).
[22] A. Story, unpublished research commissioned by Oxfam in 2000.

IS TRIPS GOOD FOR DEVELOPMENT AND POVERTY REDUCTION?

Patents can benefit society by encouraging innovation, but the rules must strike a balance between the interests of the innovator and the public good. In multilateral agreements, a balance must also be struck between the commercial interests of the advanced industrial states and the development needs of poorer countries. Oxfam believes that TRIPS and associated national legislation in the pipeline are extremely unbalanced on both counts. The enforcement of excessive IP protection will put a brake on economic development in poorer countries by raising the cost of the technology and knowledge-intensive products they need.

Industrialization usually relies on reproducing the technologies of the more advanced economies – patenting becomes of interest to a country only when it can innovate too.[23] But even if patenting does have a pro-innovation effect in some sectors, prolonged patent duration across-the-board is a blunt instrument for achieving it. Nor is there any necessity for patent periods to be globally uniform, as the socially optimal trade-offs will differ among countries.

Advocates of the TRIPS Agreement argue that TNCs, including pharmaceutical companies, are reluctant to manufacture products in developing countries where patent protection is weak. It is claimed that because local manufacture makes it easier for competitors to obtain a TNC's know-how, a TNC will prefer to export finished products. Strong IP protection therefore increases licensing and direct investment by TNCs, and this in turn will stimulate R&D. There is some evidence that pharmaceutical TNCs are encouraged to invest because of the reduced damage caused by know-how 'leakage', but it is unlikely to be the most important factor in their decision. A report commissioned by the WHO says that despite claims that TRIPS will encourage the transfer of technology for drug development, the reality has been a lack of technology transfer, with the multinational companies maintaining control in industrialized countries, and that their response has primarily involved opening local distribution centres whose activities are restricted to the final stages of production – finishing and distribution.[24]

Oxfam's view is that, overall, the TRIPS Agreement will hinder the achievement of the 2015 international development targets agreed by the OECD, to which the British government and others are committed. These include the reduction of child mortality by two-thirds. By depriving developing countries of a policy instrument for promoting national development that they themselves have used, the rich countries are effectively 'pulling up the ladder'.

---

[23] C. S. Mayer, 'The Brazilian pharmaceutical industry goes walking from Ipanema to prosperity: will the new intellectual property law spur domestic investment?', *Temple International and Comparative Law Journal* (Autumn 1998).

[24] See S. O. Schweitzer, *Pharmaceutical Economics and Policy* (Oxford: Oxford University Press, 1997), pp. 126–32.

Further, TRIPS lacks a credible development rationale, and many developing countries had little idea what the agreement would commit them to in reality and little choice about signing it, as it was an integral part of the Final Act of the Uruguay Round. Oxfam thus believes that there should be a far-reaching review of the public health and development impact of TRIPS; this would reopen discussion on the appropriate length and scope of IP protection for poor countries. The TRIPS review now scheduled for 2002 offers an excellent starting point.

As noted above, TRIPS established different deadlines for country compliance. This provision, based on the practical recognition that it takes time to set up IP-protection systems, follows the 'one-size-fits-all' approach, and Oxfam disagrees with it. There is a strong case for linking transition periods to changes in development indicators rather than to arbitrary dates. A developing country could introduce higher levels of patent protection earlier for product areas where it has achieved international competitiveness, for example India in software. A delay in implementation would also help the many countries currently facing the huge administrative and financial burden of instituting complex IP systems.

THE IP THAT TRIPS DOES NOT PROTECT

Paradoxically for an agreement designed to protect property rights, TRIPS is silent about the appropriation from the South of traditional knowledge about medicinal plants, an IP 'crime' motivated by the desire of Northern companies to find new pharmaceutical products. First, TRIPS is unconcerned about the means by which a patent-holder has obtained the knowledge needed for the 'invention' and about the identity of the legitimate owners or originators of that knowledge. Second, the agreement requires countries to allow patenting of microorganisms and microbiological processes. This, combined with loose interpretation of 'inventiveness' in national patent offices, accelerates the patenting of genetic resources and stimulates Northern companies' appropriation of developing countries' biological assets. If a two per cent royalty were levied on genetic resources, the North would owe the South more than $5 billion in royalties for medicinal plants alone.[25] Many developing countries want TRIPS amended so as to require patent applicants to disclose the origin of the resources or knowledge they are using, to obtain the prior informed consent of the original knowledge-holders and to share the benefits with them. A tight definition of 'inventiveness' and 'novelty' in national law would exclude applications whose subject matter is not a real invention or whose knowledge is already in the public domain.

[25] UNDP, *Human Development Report* (New York, 1999).

Bitter gourd. Thailand faces a major AIDS problem. Its scientists have been researching many ways to relieve suffering and perhaps even to develop a medicine that can prevent infection by the virus. One research team has focused on bitter gourd (*Momordica spp.*), which was found to contain compounds that work against HIV. To its dismay, it recently learned that American scientists had not only copied its research agenda but had patented, in the United States, the active ap-30 protein from a native strain of Thai bitter gourd. The variety is called 'bird droppings gourd' because of its small size. The Thai scientists feel that their work has been pirated and that their country's indigenous biodiversity has been stolen as well.

Neem. A better-known example of bio-piracy is the patent granted by the European Patent Office to the multinational company W. R. Grace on a process for extracting oil from the Indian neem tree for use as a fungicide. The European Patent Office revoked the patent in May 2000 after a legal challenge by a coalition of NGOs on the grounds that the fungicidal effects of the seed extracts were widely known and had been used for centuries in India.

CORPORATE SOCIAL RESPONSIBILITY

Oxfam believes that the pharmaceuticals TNCs can play a more positive role in public health in the developing world by adopting fairer pricing polices and research priorities, although this should complement rather than substitute for the reform of WTO patent rules and national IP systems. The industry's greatest responsibility, arguably, is to give due weight to the public good when lobbying for legislation, and not to pursue commercial interest above all else.

TNCs should reduce the price of key drugs in developing countries, within the framework of a standardised, transparent global system of equitable pricing. Medicines marketed in LDCs should be priced as low as possible, with marginal unit cost as a guideline and with appropriate safeguards against re-export. This is affordable because these countries probably constitute less than 0.25 per cent of the world market. During 2001, a number of companies made well-publicized reductions in the price of AIDS drugs in Africa, partly owing to potential competition from Indian generic manufacturers, but these concessions are ad hoc, reversible and limited.

If companies disregard the fate of millions of poor people, they risk public criticism and the consequent threat to sales and investor confidence, as well as the greater likelihood of regulatory action by governments. Some companies appear to have taken note of this, and are making a greater effort to respond to their critics. For example, in June 2001 GlaxoSmithKline published a policy on

> Pfizer, which recorded profits of $13 billion in 2000, has long been in the firing line for refusing to drop the price of its anti-fungal drug fluconazole (Diflucan), which is vital for treating meningitis and thrush infections in people with HIV. In Kenya, thanks to patenting, Diflucan costs 30 times the price of generic equivalents produced elsewhere. After long public campaigns, Pfizer has finally agreed to donate Diflucan to Africa, but this is only for a brief time before the patent expires. The question now is what Pfizer will charge for its improved version, Vfend, which will soon reach the market protected by patents spread throughout the world by TRIPS.

access to medicines in developing countries which commits the company to offer certain medicines to the poorer developing countries at lower prices and which outlines the research undertaken on diseases of poverty. But Pfizer, the largest pharmaceutical company in the world, which claims 'to enhance life worldwide', appears to have done nothing on equitable pricing, although it does have two large-scale donations programmes. More importantly, it has been the industry's leader in the design and stringent enforcement of high levels of IP protection throughout the world.

Although an equitable pricing system would make drugs more affordable in developing countries, it should be seen as a complement to the strategy of maintaining a low level of patent protection on medicines in poor countries and letting generic competition reduce prices. However, equitable pricing does pose a significant administrative challenge, which does not arise with the market-based approach. Moreover, with TRIPS untouched, many generic manufacturers will go out of business, and developing countries will become increasingly dependent for drug supplies on a handful of Northern transnational corporations. In contrast, the kind of patent regime for medicines many developing countries had before TRIPS indicates that there is scope to develop the local industry and greater pharmaceutical self-sufficiency, with corresponding benefits for livelihoods and 'health security'. For these reasons, Oxfam not only calls for fairer TNC pricing but also stresses the need for the reform of WTO rules for intellectual property. As the UK is the world's second-largest exporter of pharmaceuticals and Europe as a whole supplies 75 per cent of the branded drugs imported by developing countries, European companies and governments have a major responsibility to act urgently on both these fronts.

OXFAM'S PRINCIPAL RECOMMENDATIONS

1. TRIPS should become the means for limiting the headlong advance of excessive protection and the threat it poses to public health and economic efficiency, rather than acting as its springboard. WTO member states should use the review scheduled in 2002 to amend TRIPS so that poor countries retain the right to make or import low-cost generic equivalents of the key medicines they vitally need. Existing public health safeguards need to be strengthened now so that countries can limit or override patent protection on medicines without facing the threat of trade sanctions. Any legal impediment to a manufacturer exporting a generic equivalent of a patented drug to a country that has issued a compulsory licence should be removed immediately.
2. The industrialized countries should substantially increase funding for research into new medicines and vaccines for infectious diseases plaguing poor countries. Resulting patents should be held as public goods, and prices controlled, in order to ensure full benefit to people living in poverty. Funding should also be increased for primary health services and drugs purchases in LDCs.
3. Rich countries, above all the United States, should stop using global trade rules and the threat of trade sanctions to force developing countries to introduce the excessively strong national patent laws sought by the pharmaceutical TNCs. IP should not be the subject of regional or bilateral economic agreements with developing countries, and coercive measures such as Section 301 of the US Trade Act should be repealed.
4. Developing countries should ensure that their national patent regimes take full advantage of TRIPS safeguards and are not fettered by bilateral economic agreements, while working for changes to the TRIPS Agreement. Governments should also pursue a rational drugs policy that includes promotion of a national pharmaceuticals industry, the use of generics and price regulation.
5. TNCs should reduce the price of key medicines in developing countries in order to improve poor people's access to them and reduce pressures on overstretched health service budgets. Prices should be determined within the framework of a standardized, transparent system of equitable pricing that would offer drastically reduced prices to the poorest countries. Companies should also accept rather than block the introduction of strong public health safeguards into patent laws.

5 PATENTS, PATIENTS AND DEVELOPING COUNTRIES: ACCESS, INNOVATION AND THE POLITICAL DIMENSIONS OF TRADE POLICY

Harvey E. Bale Jr

INTRODUCTION

The Secretary-General, CEOs and United Nations officials agreed that prices of medicines and diagnostics are an important component of efforts to increase access to care, but – on their own – reduced prices are not sufficient to catalyze the scaling up that is needed. Additional resources are required, together with the political will and skills to spend them effectively.

UN Press Release, 4 October 2001

In December 1999, the United Nations Secretary General Kofi Annan called African health leaders and representatives of the international pharmaceutical industry, international health institutions and NGOs together in New York to signal a new, multi-party effort to address the serious threat of HIV–AIDS to Africa. In response, Dr Gro Harlem Brundtland, Director General of the World Health Organization (WHO), has stepped up international efforts to treat and find cures for malaria and tuberculosis (TB) and has helped to implement Mr Annan's initiative against the AIDS pandemic.

A number of research-based pharmaceutical companies[1] foresaw in early 2000 that possibly a new time had arrived in which national governments were raising AIDS to a higher level on their national agenda, and some of them began to consider what initiatives they could take as part of a coordinated global effort against the most serious infectious diseases. In 2000, donation programmes, long established for diseases such as river blindness, polio and trachoma, were expanded to include AIDS. Specific programmes were created for opportunistic infections and mother-to-child transmission (MTCT) of the HIV virus. For example, Boehringer Ingelheim launched a programme in June 2000 to donate its new drug Viramune to all developing countries until at least 2005, and Pfizer

---

[1] References in this chapter to 'industry', 'companies' or 'producer(s)' are to international pharmaceutical manufacturers doing research into innovative drugs or vaccines.

initiated a programme to donate its drug Diflucan for AIDS-related infections to all of the UN's least developed countries. On 11 May 2000 five companies, Boehringer Ingelheim, Bristol-Myers Squibb, GlaxoSmithKline, Merck and Co. and Roche, joined with UN agencies and the World Bank to launch a new coordinated effort – the Accelerated Access Initiative – to expand access to AIDS treatments, while the companies also continued with research and development (R&D) efforts on new therapies and vaccines. For instance, GlaxoSmithKline announced publicly that it would offer a price of $2 per day for anti-retroviral therapy, a price less than 15 per cent of that charged in many OECD countries.

In July 2001 the G-8 leaders announced in Genoa the creation of the Global Fund to Fight AIDS, Tuberculosis and Malaria (GFFATM) to address the spread of HIV–AIDS, malaria and TB. Its primary source of funding would be public agencies in donor countries, although private donations would also be welcomed. Unfortunately, this fund has only $1.5 billion in non-renewable commitments from all sources, and it is not yet in place. Furthermore, local infrastructure in many developing countries is inadequate to treat hundreds of millions of affected people, thus limiting the scope of the expansion of treatment.

By summer 2000, as major international companies announced their individual plans and negotiations were begun with a number of countries, the issue of price as a barrier to expanded access to AIDS medicines became practically a non-issue. The prices made available were competitive with prices offered later in 2000 from Indian 'generic' companies that had copied the original products. Thus, in autumn 2000 the government of Senegal publicly announced that prices from international innovative companies were as low as or lower than prices of copycat products from India and elsewhere, even though the copycat producers incur no R&D costs and do not provide the same capacity and product support.

Despite the deep price reductions initiated by research-based companies, which have been followed and extended by some smaller developing-country generic producers, the number of people being treated for AIDS in Africa today is still limited to a population size in the range of 10,000 to 30,000, according to WHO and industry information sources. This limited access is attributable not to patents but to funding and infrastructure limitations. This fact has been recognized by Kofi Annan and senior representatives of the Joint United Nations Programme on AIDS (UNAIDS) and the WHO.[2]

---

[2] See UN press releases following discussions with industry leaders after these sessions: SG/SM/7764/AIDS/3/5 April 2001 and SG/SM/7982/AIDS/34/4 October 2001. (See quotation at the beginning of this chapter.)

THE ROLE OF INDUSTRY AND OF INTELLECTUAL PROPERTY RIGHTS

> If you wish to encourage an activity, reward it. If you wish to discourage it, punish it.
>
> Aristotle, *Ethics*

I am convinced that the access issue is not one of patents or prices. Instead, the challenge is to generate substantial additional global funding, to install needed infrastructure to diagnose, treat and counsel patients and to encourage all parties to work together to implement effective programmes. This point has been made in a recent peer-reviewed article published in the *Journal of the American Medical Association*. In this article, Dr Amir Attaran analyses actual patenting activity by companies in the AIDS drugs field. He finds that patents cover only about 20 per cent of the cases of patentable antiviral AIDS drugs in Africa.[3] Even if many more patents existed for AIDS drugs in Africa, they would be effectively irrelevant to the access problem in view of the major price reductions and donations offered by originating companies.

Nevertheless, some would like to make prices – and patents – the main issue. This is puzzling because, as noted, originator companies, committed to R&D in AIDS, where there is still no vaccine or cure, initiated programmes in early 2000 (before generic copiers from India appeared) that reduced the price of existing therapies very substantially below prices charged in developed countries. If patents are made the main political issue, then a serious question arises: will companies continue to have the appropriate intellectual property incentives to do important R&D or will they be harassed by compulsory licensing threats? Compulsory licensing is mainly for the benefit of some generic producers, which contribute nothing to research, and only marginally to improved access, but which can make a large profit from taking others' inventions.

Industry's primary roles are to discover and develop new therapies and vaccines that are effective against diseases and acceptably safe to use, and to manufacture these according to the highest international standards. Its goal is to find those molecules among the estimated 10^{18} possibly effective molecules (i.e., a billion billion molecules) that are effective against diseases. Millions of molecules are in company libraries, and most are unpatented yet because their utility is not yet determined. Meanwhile, the competing private and public human genome projects are increasing the number of potential receptor targets from the few hundred that have been identified up to several thousand. As molecules are investigated for efficacy against diseases, industry must assume the risks and costs of demonstrating their efficacy and the safety and quality of

---

[3] Amir Attaran, 'Do Patents for Antiretroviral Drugs Constrain Access to AIDS Treatment in Africa?', *Journal of the American Medical Association*, Vol. 286, No. 15 (17 October 2001), pp. 1886–92.

their manufacture to regulators on a global scale. Drug development costs are on average in the range of more than $500 million (counting drugs failures and the opportunity costs of tying up capital for the decade or more required finally to bring a molecule to patients).

Thus, patent and other elements of intellectual property protection are critically important. Looking at India, one is not surprised that it lacks R&D in new medicines, given the lack of intellectual property protection for pharmaceuticals. Although India has strong, 'world-class' film and software industries – because of good copyright protection given to them – it does nothing to develop new drugs, even for the range of infectious diseases (TB, malaria, AIDS, etc.) that burden its own society; and this is despite its relatively strong scientific tradition and its knowledge of biochemistry manufacturing techniques. Its potential to develop its pharmaceutical and biotechnology potential lacks the most important element – patent protection and related forms of intellectual property protection. 'The statistical average figure for R&D expenditure as a percentage of sales income in India is about 2 percent, but a number of leading companies are spending around 4 to 6 percent and seeking to push the ratio higher, but as they do, they become increasingly conscious of the uncertainties in government policies that also preoccupy MNC investors regarding patent protection.'[4] Also, as is pointed out by Dr Anjit Reddy, the chairman of one of India's most important companies, which is seeking to become a major R&D company too, 'Indian firms need patent protection to develop cheap drugs that suit our [national] profile.'

The undermining effect of the lack of patent protection works in a number of important ways. Innovative Indian scientists are more likely to move to countries where their creativity is better rewarded. It may be no coincidence that, as recently reported in the journal *Nature*, Indian scientific journals have a remarkably low impact. What is clear is the negative conditioning effect of the relative lack of patent protection, which results in low levels of patenting by Indians in India.

China, Brazil, Argentina, Egypt and other developing countries also have the capability to contribute to therapeutic advances and to profit locally in keeping needed talent at home and building commercial supporting enterprises. But the development of this capability will depend on whether they seriously undertake patent reform or whether they decide that it is easier, if only in the short term, to take (or, in the view of the innovator, steal) technology through systematic compulsory licensing or other 'gimmicks' such as parallel trade.

The latter course would not augur favourably for patients worldwide, and will certainly not contribute economically in the longer term. Fewer than 10

---

[4] Europe Economics (UK), special report, 'Medicines Access and Innovation in Developing Countries' (September 2001), p. 58.

per cent of TB and malaria patients in Brazil and India receive curative drugs, although both diseases are treatable effectively and cheaply in terms of drug costs. Access to medicines does not depend mainly on patents and their enforceability, but drug development does, as suggested by the fact that in its 80-year history, the Soviet Union never produced an important new drug for common infectious diseases. Intellectual property rights are an extension of physical property rights, and the Soviet Union had neither.

Today there are more than 1,000 drugs and vaccines in industry's global development pipeline for various infectious diseases, including approximately 170 compounds for HIV–AIDS. Interestingly, there are over 1,000 biotechnology-based drugs and vaccines in development. These products come both from large pharmaceutical companies and from small, newly formed biotechnology companies. The nature of the latter source suggests an opportunity for developing countries to found new enterprises under an effective patent system, as biotechnology companies rely heavily on ideas and know-how and look to funds coming from outside sources.

DEVELOPING COUNTRIES AND TRIPS – THE ROLE OF PATENTS

The global intellectual property system is one of global standards and applicability, after a transition period of between 5 and 10 years to allow developing countries to adapt their legislation to conform to the TRIPS rules. What are the developing countries' interests in it, and what is their interest in TRIPS? Of course there is the interest that follows from additional incentives for investment in R&D that might provide a cure or a vaccine for HIV–AIDS, TB or malaria. This interest is informed by two (questionable) assumptions, however: that these drugs and vaccines will all originate in the developed world, and that there is little 'producer' interest in developing countries. There is also concern that there are heavy net costs for patents for many developing countries.

Actually, the issue of developing countries' interests in patents is more complex, and I believe that developing countries form three groups relevant to this issue. One group contains countries, such as China, India, Korea and Singapore, that can evolve relatively quickly from being drug-copiers to innovators. In the second group are countries such as Egypt, Malaysia and Brazil that have the potential to take advantage of TRIPS but need to build further infrastructure and privatize more. The third group of countries, the least developed, has need of economic assistance. For this group, TRIPS can produce new medicines that can be delivered to patients, but only if financial aid and health care infrastructure are developed. People in these countries can afford neither generic nor patented medicines – both sets of medicines are out of reach, and the issue is neither price nor patents.

When the WHO states that one-third or more of the world's population, about two billion people, lacks regular access to essential drugs, let us keep in mind two facts: approximately 35 million have the HIV virus, and many of them need treatment largely with patented drugs (although I believe that few companies have patents in Africa, where most AIDS victims live). But what types of drug do the other 98 per cent of the people who lack access need? They need drugs mainly for malaria, TB, acute respiratory infections, diarrhoeal diseases, yellow fever, measles, leprosy and polio. In fact, all of the vaccines and drugs needed are off-patent, and what we actually face now is a massive global public policy failure to treat people with medicines that can cure these diseases relatively inexpensively. Further, in view of the fact that we have not solved the problem of access to older treatments, we are in danger of repeating history in the AIDS crisis unless we focus on the main barriers to access: insufficient political commitment, financing and infrastructure, and political instability, wars, civil strife and corruption. Are patents an issue? Yes, but mainly insofar as they are essential to create and develop the new therapies needed to cure and prevent AIDS and overcome resistance to existing anti-infectives. Are prices an issue? Not if governments and international institutions do what is necessary to supplement the earnings of people who have incomes of less than a few dollars a day and who cannot afford any medicines, patented or generic. If funds are available on a sustainable basis and if health care capacity exists, companies will find ways to get medicines to the people who need them. Companies are doing so in a variety of disease areas already.

International pharmaceutical companies have made drug donations totalling almost $2 billion over the past few years, and gave more than $500 million in 2001. I sometimes hear from a few NGOs that the world does not need 'charity'. They say that donations are not 'sustainable'. This is very odd, as these comments come from NGOs that are themselves involved in charitable activities. How can anyone doubt the sustainability of the Merck and Co.'s Mectizan donation programme that reaches 25 million people a year – and has been going since 1987? Or of Novartis' commitment to help eliminate leprosy through donations and partnership over the next six years? Or of the commitment of two international companies to help eliminate lymphatic filariasis over the next 20 years through the donation of over $1 billion in drugs? Moreover, as noted by Harvard economists J. Sachs and A. Attaran in *The Lancet*: 'the private sector ... is in many cases more generous than governments.'[5] Thus, if companies had not taken the initiative,[6] how much worse off would global public health be? A great deal.

[5] J. Sachs and A. Attaran, *The Lancet*, Vol. 357, No. 9249 (January 2001), p. 59.
[6] See the IFPMA website *www.ifpma.org* for information on various programmes.

In the October 2001 issue of *Foreign Affairs* Professor Ethan Kapstein of INSEAD notes in his article 'The Corporate Ethics Crusade' that 'The starting point for a global discussion on AIDS should not be a unilateral demand for cheap drugs but a search for the most effective way to end the epidemic.'[7] He also argues that the demand that industry bear the main part of the heavy cost of subsidizing drugs deliveries to developing countries represents 'cynical posturing and cheap talk on the part of the world's politicians and activists. The public health policies of many developing countries are a shameful mess, and industrialized nations put up no more than a pittance to help them.'[8] Professor Kapstein could have added that this cynicism extends further to those whose advocacy of breaking down patent protection 'coincidentally' reflects the interest of certain copycat and state-owned companies. These companies hope to profit from the expropriation of innovators' rights to their inventions – with minimal marginal cost savings to patients but with potentially great damage to finding a future cure and vaccines for AIDS, TB and malaria.

WEAKENING PATENT RULES VERSUS ACCESS PARTNERSHIPS

One has to wonder what is the real purpose of some of the advocacy of compulsory licensing and parallel trade, as it seems to have little relevance to improving access to medicines. In spring 2001, activists lobbied the Kenyan government to introduce legislation encouraging the use of compulsory licensing and parallel trade; they considered that this legislation would greatly improve access to AIDS drugs and save lives. On 5 June, Médecins Sans Frontières issued a statement boldly claiming that 'Every Day Parliament Delays Passing IP Bill, 700 More Die of AIDS in Kenya'.[9] It asserted that if the bill were passed, there would be a rapid change in access, the assumption being that patents were the main barrier. This claim was made despite the fact that more than half of all anti-retrovirals for HIV–AIDS in Kenya are not even subject to patent protection[10] and thus that generic drugs could already be imported without enactment of the bill. Naturally, MSF was among those who praised the passing of the bill on 13 June 2001.[11] But three months after the passage of the legislation, the Kenyan government realized that the law had done nothing to increase access to AIDS drugs significantly: 'The [Kenyan] government yesterday announced it does not have funds to purchase ... despite the recent passing by Parliament of

---

[7] Ethan Kapstein, 'The Corporate Ethics Crusade', *Foreign Affairs* (September/October 2001), p. 111.
[8] Ibid., p. 112.
[9] See *www.accessmed-msf.org/prod/publications*, press release, 6 June 2001.
[10] Attaran, 'Do Patents for Antiretroviral Drugs ...?', p. 1888.
[11] 'The battle for affordable medicines has been won in Parliament ...', press release, 14 June 2001, MSF website.

the Industrial Property Rights Act ... The revelation dealt a big blow to people living with AIDS who had hoped that the passing of the bill would make drugs more accessible ...'[12] The lessons of the Kenyan case are that, first, patents are not a critical issue in access to drugs in developing countries, especially AIDS drugs; second, infrastructure and funding are critical barriers which, if addressed, will allow discounted 'brand name' (or generic) medicines to be utilized more widely; and, third, focusing on the weakening of patents not only is irrelevant to the access issues but also costs time and, more importantly, lives (700 per day in Kenya according MSF's own estimates).

In contrast to the approach of seeking to expand access by weakening patent rules, there is the partnership founded in May 2000 involving UN agencies, coordinated by UNAIDS, and a number of pharmaceutical companies. According to UNAIDS,

> Accelerating Access represents a redoubling of efforts by UNAIDS to assist countries in implementing comprehensive packages of care for their citizens living with HIV–AIDS ... and involves 'fast track' support for those developing countries ...

With the involvement of UNAIDS, 18 of these countries have reached agreement with manufacturers on significantly reduced drug prices in the context of national plans. These countries include Barbados, Benin, Burkina Faso, Burundi, Cameroon, Chile, Congo, Côte d'Ivoire, Gabon, Honduras, Jamaica, Mali, Morocco, Romania, Rwanda, Senegal, Trinidad and Tobago and Uganda. UNAIDS reports further that 78 countries have 'indicated their interest in collaborating ...'[13] In reviewing UNAIDS' analysis we can see that a rather large number of countries have opted for collaboration rather than for legalistic patent modifications as the main way to address the problem of the AIDS pandemic.

In sum, the weakening patents approach argues that patents are a key barrier to access and derides the use of discounted pricing by companies as a form of 'charity' not to be relied upon.[14] In contrast, the collaborative approach does not see intellectual property rights as a significant barrier; it links them with company discounts (and appropriate donations) and UN coordinated assistance for the building of needed health care infrastructure and international funding for prevention and treatment. Indeed, the collaborative approach sees 'continued investment in research and development by the pharmaceutical industry' as critical, and this R&D depends on adequate and effective intellectual property

---

[12] *The East Africa Standard*, 13 September 2001.
[13] See *www.unaids.org/acc_access/index.html*, also *www.unaids.org/acc_access/AAcountries220302.doc*
[14] See the MSF's statement on Kenya: 'Kenya cannot afford to rely on the charity of profit making companies for its future.' *www.accessmed-msf.org/prod/publications*, press release, 5 June 2001.

rules. Further, the UN and a number of companies see the issue of discounted pricing not as 'charity' but instead as part of a sustainable solution that takes into account vastly different levels of economic performance, especially those of the least developed countries. Other companies and the UN see donations as another part of the longer-term solution.

SHOULD INCREASED R&D INTO AIDS AND OTHER INFECTIOUS DISEASES BE ENCOURAGED?

As experiments in weakening patent protection will be unlikely to have much effect on access, should we be concerned about the future of research and development? Some activists have begun to raise this issue. In view of the controversy about the potential harmful impact of weakening intellectual property rules on investment in R&D, there are interesting but disconcerting survey data on drug compounds in the industry pipeline (see Figure 5.1). These data suggest that after a substantial rise in most of the past decade in the number of anti-retroviral drug compounds in preclinical and clinical development for the treatment and possible cure of HIV–AIDS, there has been a decline in this number for the past three years – during the period of growing attacks on intellectual property rights issues linked to AIDS medicines. The current level of approximately 170 compounds is down, probably for several complex reasons, by about one-third from the levels in 1994 and 1998. This lower level of compound development suggests that, first, there remains a strong commitment to AIDS R&D by major companies now in this important field of drug and vaccine development and that, second, there are no new entries of major pharmaceutical companies into this area of research. In contrast, the corresponding data for non-HIV antivirals and overall anti-infective compounds in development show not a decline but an increase in recent years (see Figure 5.2 for a comparison of trends since 1997, when comparisons became possible).

Figure 5.1: HIV anti-retroviral compounds in development, 1990–2001

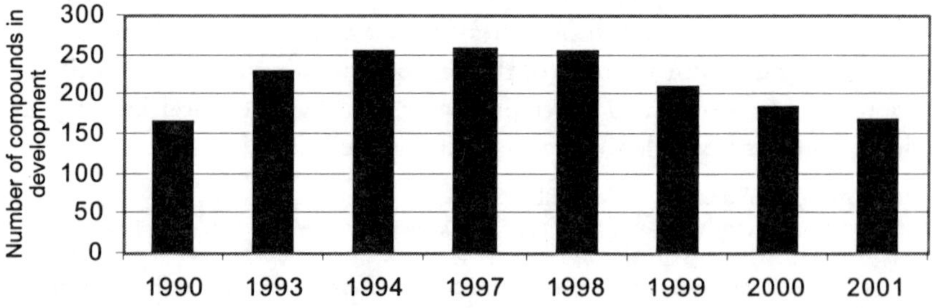

Source: Pharmaprojects (PJB Publications, UK).

Figure 5.2: Trends in anti-infective R&D

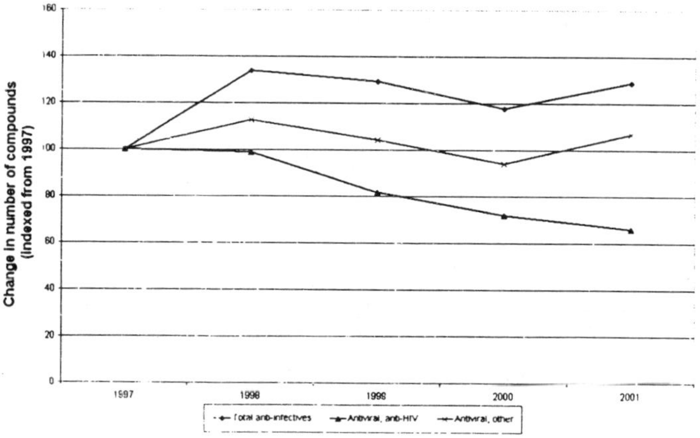

Source: Pharmaprojects (PJB Publications, UK).

Recently, some AIDS activists have become increasingly concerned that the attacks against the industry, including the intellectual property basis of its drugs development investments, threaten to discourage investment in new AIDS treatments by some companies. Whether or not the changes in Figure 5.1 reflect only in part the disincentive effect of attacks against the intellectual property status of AIDS compounds, we would be concerned if this trend accelerated in the future along with further threats to intellectual property rights. Today, we still lack cures and vaccines. Further, the level of resistance to existing AIDS compounds is rising in developed countries. Current R&D will lead to more effective drugs and vaccines for the global AIDS community, so we should encourage R&D, not urge the weakening of intellectual property incentives.

Indeed, in September 2000, at a high-level roundtable on AIDS organized in Brussels by the European Commission, two of industry's executive leaders stated that if enthusiasm for compulsory licensing of patented pharmaceuticals becomes too great, there will soon be no more patents on AIDS drugs to license compulsorily: new product development in this critical field will decline dramatically.

What positive steps can be taken that reflect the concern to encourage biomedical research in AIDS and other important infectious diseases while expanding access to health care and treatments for those in need? I list briefly actions that I believe meet short- and medium-term 'access' concerns as well as providing longer-term research capacity and incentives.

1. Provide much additional major international assistance to help in the prevention and treatment of infectious diseases, especially HIV–AIDS, TB and malaria in the poorest countries. The announced Global Fund needs to

be implemented quickly and augmented many times over in order to address the infrastructure and treatment needs of the poorest countries.
2. Encourage companies, through national actions and the sustained existence of the Global Fund, to negotiate on expanded access terms where feasible and appropriate. Companies will try to expand access (including the offer of discounts) where they think the effort will succeed, has local political support and national and international backing and is sustainable. There are many current examples of this.[15]
3. Protect intellectual property, which is vital to ensuring a long-term industry R&D commitment. Avoid liberal use of the escapist compulsory licensing approach that is simply an industrial subsidy to copycat companies to continue to sell products without contributing to research and development. The largest costs of any weakening of TRIPS rules or enforcement will be borne by the developing countries most heavily burdened by infectious diseases. As expressed in one of the press releases by the UN Secretary General's office referred to above, 'intellectual property protection is key to bringing forward new medicines, vaccines and diagnostics urgently needed for the health of the world's poorest people. The United Nations fully supports the TRIPS agreement, including the safeguards incorporated within it.'[16]
4. Avoid formulaic 'tiered pricing systems'. Any theoretical global scheme linking competitive, market-driven prices to a ranking of countries will be unstable because of macroeconomic changes. It will also be inequitable among populations within and across countries. Further, it will probably result in underinvestment in needed drugs development and, in any case, raise difficult legal issues involving many countries' competition policies.
5. Avoid harmful trade policies, including high tariffs and anti-dumping duties on medicinal imports. There are many cases of both, and these actions tend to raise substantially the final costs to patients. In recent years, India and South Africa have actually raised tariffs or imposed anti-dumping duties because medicines were being imported at prices that were deemed to be too low. Local wholesale and retail margins may also artificially inflate drug costs, as may local indirect taxes. Parallel trade is more of a cost than a benefit to countries, especially to low-income low-price countries, and tends also to expose patients to trade in counterfeit drugs. Thus, parallel trade (i.e., product diversion) is not a measure to embrace.[17]

[15] See *www.ifpma.org*.
[16] UN press release SG/SM/7764/AIDS/3/5 April 2001.
[17] See H. Bale, 'The Conflicts Between Parallel Trade and Product Access and Innovation: The Case of Pharmaceuticals,' *Journal of International Economic Law*, Vol. 1, No. 4 (December 1998), pp. 637–53.

6. Encourage public–private partnerships to address intractable access and drugs development issues. The UN's Accelerating Access Initiative, the Global Alliance for Vaccines and Immunization (GAVI) and the Medicines for Malaria Venture are three such partnerships launched in recent years that are already having a positive impact on present and future health outcomes. Donations are also a form of partnership that can yield sustainable positive public health outcomes, and they are part of the strategy to help overcome the failure of public policy in past decades to address the health status of poorer countries.
7. In general, raise the national political commitment in developing countries to better health. As long as countries place health towards the bottom of national political and financial priorities, no global strategic plans will succeed in the medium to long term. From what I observe, unless additional political commitment is secured, the search will continue for the 'scapegoat' for the failure of public policy. And, predictably, the consequences will be disastrous – far more for public health than for industry, which will tend to shift its efforts away from policy-created public health disaster areas.

In conclusion, neither TRIPS nor patents have any significant bearing on the issue of access to health care. Poor people earning less than $2 a day and spending less than $20 a year on health can afford neither patented nor non-patented drugs. But with much assistance for infrastructure and financing, conditions can be greatly improved, and the private-sector drugs access programmes launched in 2000 will be in a position to be made more effective. Treatment and discounted prices 'follow' funding and infrastructure, as the GAVI experience has shown – they do not 'dictate' access.

Poor AIDS, TB and malaria patients, current and future, need R&D to find cures and vaccines. The pre-TRIPS world (which we are still in) has failed patients dismally in many ways. Most notably, it has allowed major countries with large populations and sizeable disease burdens and with significant scientific resources and chemistry know-how to get away with pirating patents instead of contributing to the global R&D effort to deliver new cures. A number of countries are still trying to roll back TRIPS provisions and keep to 'business as usual'. And although some countries' representatives sympathize with calls for new 'flexibility' in applying TRIPS, by seeking to undermine 'commercial interests' by weakening intellectual property protection at home, they are actually harming the interests of victims of serious and as yet incurable diseases, such as AIDS.

A BRIEF COMMENT ON THE DOHA WTO MINISTERIAL MEETING

> Scientists must recognize that the old academic maxim 'publish or perish' should be replaced for the new millennium by one of 'patent and profit'.
>
> Dr R. A. Mashelkar, Director General, Council for Scientific and Industrial Research (India), Address, New Delhi, 28 March 2001

At the meeting of trade ministers in Doha, Qatar from 9 to 14 November 2001, efforts to introduce a basic change in the nature of the relationship between TRIPS and the WTO were rebuffed. Language proposed for the 'Declaration on the TRIPS Agreement and Public Health' that would have removed TRIPS' restriction on all actions taken in the name of 'public health' was rejected in favour of language that reasserted all members' commitments to TRIPS and clarified existing TRIPS flexibilities (relating to compulsory licensing, parallel trade etc.).[18]

Whatever NGOs or industry may claim about the balance of the textual message, three realities remain: first, 'fixing TRIPS' will have no durable impact on the accessibility of HIV–AIDS medicines; second, we have to ensure that India, China and other developing countries join in exploiting the potential of TRIPS as an engine of R&D for major diseases; and, third, we must ensure that existing R&D is not threatened by the efforts of copycat generic companies to put their commercial interests above the need for more biomedical innovation. The TRIPS language agreed in Doha appears to reflect a reaffirmation of every WTO member state's commitments to TRIPS, but how the Doha agreement is actually implemented will determine whether the WTO ministers have made progress.

---

[18] All texts from the Doha meeting are available at the WTO website: *www.wto.org*.

PART II
STATE RESPONSES

6 DEVELOPING STATES' RESPONSES TO THE PHARMACEUTICAL IMPERATIVES OF THE TRIPS AGREEMENT

Jillian Clare Cohen

Few industries have suffered more from success – at least in lost public esteem – than the drug industry. We have become a pill-happy society, expecting a capsule for everything from heart disease to hair loss. One minute we applaud the drug companies for their medical breakthroughs. The next, we condemn them for high prices and profits.

Daniel S. Greenberg[1]

INTRODUCTION

The Uruguay Round (1986–94) was a path-breaking trade round. It was the first under the General Agreement on Tariffs and Trade (GATT) to include developing states as active participants; over three-quarters of its members were developing states. It was ambitious in scope, addressing a range of issues, including new ones such as intellectual property rights, that had not been covered by previous rounds. And, ultimately, it transformed the architecture of the global trade environment by creating the World Trade Organization (WTO). The WTO has become a key institution of global governance: the Final Act of the Uruguay Round established it as an international institution recognized by international law.

For the developing states, the Uruguay Round not only defined new rules of the game for the multilateral trading system but also aimed to level the playing field in trade issues between advanced states and developing states. The trade package that resulted from the Uruguay Round benefited developing states in particular by improving their market access in important export areas such as agriculture and textiles, and by clarifying anti-dumping rules and establishing countervailing measures. Overall, it made the rules for international trade more

---

The views, findings, interpretations and conclusions expressed in this paper are entirely those of the author.
[1] Daniel S. Greenberg, *The Washington Post*, 22 February 2000.

equal by establishing a permanent dispute settlement mechanism within the WTO. The particular needs of the developing states were formally acknowledged as well. The preamble of the Agreement Establishing the World Trade Organization confers a distinct status on developing countries. It suggests that their specific needs would be taken into account in the new trading system: 'There is a need for positive efforts designed to ensure that developing countries, and especially the least developed among them, secure a share in the growth of international trade commensurate with the needs of their economic development.'[2] But in addition to these expressed safeguards and trade gains for developing states, the WTO trade package included provisions that impose new burdens on them. One of the most salient of these is the pharmaceutical provisions of the Agreement on Trade-Related Aspects of Intellectual Property Rights (TRIPS).

The TRIPS Agreement is included in the Agreement Establishing the World Trade Organization and thus is subject to the WTO dispute settlement system. TRIPS covers a range of intellectual property issues besides patents, such as trade marks, industrial designs and copyright.[3] It incorporates by reference most of the provisions of the international agreements on the protection of intellectual property rights,[4] and it requires each member state to maintain sufficient procedures and remedies within its domestic law to ensure the protection of intellectual property. These procedures and remedies must also be made available to foreign right-holders.

TRIPS provides minimum standards for intellectual property law and for procedures and remedies, so that right-holders can enforce their rights effectively. It includes in Part I the general provisions, in Part II the specialist patent provisions and in Part III the enforcement provisions. The transitional arrangements are defined in Part IV. TRIPS's main rule for patents is that they should be available for any invention, whether product or process, in all fields of technology without discrimination. Inventions covered under patent law have to meet the criteria of novelty, 'inventive step' and industrial applicability. Member states are required to make the granting of a patent dependent on adequate disclosure of the invention.

More exactly, the minimum legal obligations concerning pharmaceuticals are that, first, pharmaceutical products and micro-organisms are patentable for up to 20 years from the date the inventor files for patent application. Second, discrimination against patent rights for imported products is not permitted. Third, exclusive marketing rights are granted until patent expiry. Fourth, there

---

[2] *http://www.wto.org*, June 2000.
[3] This chapter discusses only patent protection for pharmaceuticals.
[4] Jeffrey J. Schott (ed.), *The WTO After Seattle* (Washington, DC: Institute for International Economics, 2000), p. 115.

is a transitional period of one year, which can be extended to up to 10 years, for developing countries without pharmaceutical product patents.[5]

Many developing states opposed the inclusion of pharmaceutical patents because they had local firms that benefited from copying drugs patented elsewhere and could anticipate the economic and political costs associated in a significant reform of intellectual property law. To address some of the opposition to the inclusion of pharmaceutical intellectual property rights in the trade package from developing countries, the agreement provides a degree of freedom to member states, which can deny patent protection for specific inventions (Articles 27(2) and 27(3)). The most significant of these are 'diagnostic, therapeutic and surgical methods for the treatment of humans or animals' and plants and animals (other than micro-organisms) and the biological processes (other than microbiological ones) for their production.[6] Furthermore, 'invention' and 'discovery' are not defined in the agreement. How member states choose to define them could have important consequences for innovation in biotechnology.[7] The agreement also provides governments with the authority to issue a compulsory licence for a pharmaceutical without the permission of the patent-owner when it can be justified as in the public interest, such as for public health.[8] Proponents of compulsory licensing stress that consumer price benefits arise from, in effect, abrogating the patent's market exclusivity.

The TRIPS Agreement does not prohibit the parallel importing of drug products. Parallel trade refers to the act of purchasing a drug product that is lower-priced in another country and importing it for resale in a country where the same product is higher-priced. The international pharmaceutical industry strongly opposes parallel trade because it is a significant threat to its rent extraction. It argues that 'parallel traders "free-ride" on market development and quality-control efforts of manufacturers and their authorized distributors, thereby increasing risks to manufacturers and consumers, impeding entry into markets and raising the cost of distribution.'[9]

The agreement allows developing countries a general transition period of up to five years to amend their patent legislation so that it is in accordance with WTO standards. As noted above, a longer time, up to 10 years, is allowed for developing countries that have not provided product patent protection for

---

[5] Heinz Redwood, *Brazil: The Future Impact of Pharmaceutical Patents* (Felixstowe, Suffolk: Oldwicks Press, 1995).
[6] Schott, *The WTO After Seattle*, p. 118.
[7] WHO, 'Globalization and Access to Drugs: Perspectives on the WTO/TRIPS Agreement', Health Economics and Drugs, DAP Series No. 7 (Geneva: World Health Organization, 1999), p. 4.
[8] Ibid., p. 41.
[9] International Federation of Pharmaceutical Manufacturers Association (IFPMA), 'The Question of Patents: The Key to Medical Progress and Industrial Development' (Geneva: IFPMA Publications, 1998), p. 50.

pharmaceuticals, i.e. countries that have 'process' patents in place but no protection for the final product. Least developed countries were originally given up to 11 years (until 2006) to implement the agreement, with the possibility of extending that period in order to harmonize their regulations with international standards. This deadline has recently been extended to 2016.[10]

The imperatives outlined above for pharmaceuticals in the TRIPS Agreement present costs and benefits for developing states as well as a measure of flexibility concerning how the agreement is implemented. Two basic responses to TRIPS are available to the developing states: they can accept it and make a commitment to it or they can shirk it.[11] If a state shirks the agreement, it risks losing economic gains made during the Uruguay Round in sectors such as agriculture, services and textiles. Its leadership would confront domestic political opposition; and even though it might be able to contain this opposition, it might have to deal with sanctions imposed by the WTO. A state would thus risk a significant degree of isolation from the global economy. Conversely, acceptance could mean general benefits in select areas of the economy but could impose costs on the pharmaceutical and health sectors.

How developing states have responded to the imperatives of the TRIPS Agreement as it affects their pharmaceuticals policy is the subject of this chapter. The costs and benefits of observing TRIPS are discussed and the WTO mechanisms for ensuring its observance are outlined. An optimum policy response to TRIPS is suggested and there follows a comparison of how, that is with what degree of commitment, Romania, Brazil and India have actually responded to the agreement.

COSTS AND BENEFITS OF INTELLECTUAL PROPERTY PROTECTION

Intellectual property protection is a positive government intervention insofar as it can prevent others' exploitation of a patent without cost and the attendant 'congestion problem', which is particularly acute when intellectual assets are easy to copy. (This applies to the pharmaceutical sector, as the reverse engineering of patented drugs is not technically demanding.) The argument here is that new knowledge may suffer from overuse in the absence of intellectual property rights because access to it would not be costly. At face value, this in itself is not undesirable, but its effects are. This is because the overuse of knowledge could minimize the economic value of an innovation and limit incentives for others

---

[10] This information is based on WHO, 'Globalization and Access to Drugs', p. 20.
[11] I define 'shirk' as the capacity of a government to disengage itself from the international imperatives of the TRIPS Agreement to meet local imperatives. This disengagement can be both legal and non-legal action pursuant to the terms of the Agreement.

to pursue advances in knowledge.[12] Intellectual property rights thus protect against the tendency to take free advantage of a patent by limiting intellectual access. These rights also provide inventors with some degree of certainty that they can secure sufficient rent for their innovation efforts by preventing 'congestion'. In simple terms, intellectual property rights encourage the pursuit of new knowledge.

It should follow from this general argument that pharmaceutical patents ought to provide incentives for firms to invest resources in the research and development (R&D) of new drug therapies. New drug therapies are desirable if we assume that they can help to cure or prevent diseases and improve the health of the population, which in turn can lead to economic growth.[13] The protection of pharmaceutical patents should thus encourage firms to invest in the R&D of new drug therapies specific to the disease burden of developing states which had not previously protected pharmaceutical patents.

Currently, the research and development of new drug therapies is concentrated heavily in advanced industrial economies. According to WHO's Ad Hoc Committee on Health Research Relating to Future Intervention Options, seven countries – in decreasing order of importance the United States, Japan, the United Kingdom, Germany, Switzerland, France and Italy – conducted 97 per cent of all worldwide pharmaceutical R&D in 1992. Private pharmaceutical industry investments in R&D exceeded the corresponding public expenditure in four of these countries (France, Japan, Switzerland and the United Kingdom) in that year.[14]

In all other countries, pharmaceutical industry investments in R&D were less than 0.4 per cent of one per cent of total global pharmaceuticals research and development expenditure. Few pharmaceutical companies registered in low- and middle-income countries conducted R&D, and outside the advanced industrial economies only a few of the largest such companies spent even a small amount of research and development budgets.[15] Thus, before the TRIPS Agreement the pattern of R&D did not make it rational for developing states to honour pharmaceutical patents. They calculated that they could gain more by permitting local

---

[12] Keith E. Maskus, 'The International Regulation of Intellectual Property', paper prepared for the IESG Conference on International Trade and Investment, Nottingham, 12–14 September 1997, p. 3.
[13] A World Bank document on health sector strategy notes that 'no country can secure sustainable economic growth or poverty reduction without a healthy, well nourished, and educated population'. World Bank, 'Health, Nutrition, and Population Sector Strategy Paper' (Washington, DC: World Bank Group, 1997), p. 10.
[14] Catherine Michaud and Christopher J. L. Murray, 'Resources for Health Research and Development in 1992: A Global Overview', Annex 5 of World Health Organization, *Investing in Health Research and Development: Report of the Ad Hoc Committee on Health Research Relating to Future Intervention Options* (Geneva: WHO Publications,1996), p. 224.
[15] Ibid.

'rogue' pharmaceuticals firms to copy and imitate the products of innovating firms. This strategy would help economic development (by supporting local firms) and ensure the supply of essential medicines at affordable prices.

The TRIPS Agreement, as mentioned above, imposes minimum standards for pharmaceutical patents on members of the WTO. For most developed states, including those with relatively mature production and innovation systems, compliance did not demand significant changes in existing standards and institutions.[16] However, the pharmaceutical patent regime of developing states was, for the most part, considerably below the minimum criteria of TRIPS. From the standpoint of innovating drugs firms in the advanced economies, the TRIPS Agreement corrects deficiencies in that patent regime that lead to the copying of products and ultimately to loss of rent. These deficiencies include the absence of patents for pharmaceutical products, the issuing of compulsory licences for products without adequately compensating the firm that created an innovating product, and a weak or poorly defined system of rules to protect trade secrets.[17]

Intellectual property protection for pharmaceuticals could also maintain or aggravate the North–South divide in product research and development, thus limiting the type of drug therapies available to treat diseases of the poor. Patents can impede progress in technology by precluding other firms from learning from and building on the original innovation. Patents produce a loss or 'deadweight burden' insofar as the benefits of the new knowledge to society would have been greater in the absence of a patent regime, and they reduce the ability of other firms to exploit the knowledge on a competitive basis.[18]

Further, the protection of a pharmaceutical patent could result in a greater concentration of production in advanced economies. International drugs firms will be free to export finished or semi-finished products instead of transferring technology. As a result, foreign direct investment may be reduced.[19] Another anticipated cost of the TRIPS Agreement is that it gives pharmaceutical firms scope for price discrimination, a rational move for profit-maximizing firms but potentially exploitative to persons in developing countries.[20] In addition to the

---

[16] Claudio R. Frischtak, 'Harmonization versus Differentiation in Intellectual Property Rights Regimes', in Mitchel B. Wallerstein, Mary Ellen Mogee and Roberta A. Schoen (eds), *The Global Dimensions of Intellectual Property Rights in Science and Technology: A Conference* (Washington, DC: National Academy Press, 1993. p. 99.
[17] Maskus, 'The International Regulation of Intellectual Property', p. 3.
[18] Ibid., p 34.
[19] WHO, 'Globalization, TRIPS and Access to Pharmaceuticals', WHO Policy Perspectives on Medicines (Geneva: WHO, March 2001).
[20] Joseph Stiglitz, 'Two Principles for the Next Round: Or How to Bring Developing Countries in from the Cold', paper prepared for the WTO/World Bank Conference on Developing Countries in a Millennium Round, WTO Secretariat, Geneva, 20–21 September 1999. p. 34. Stiglitz argues further that in the next round of trade negotiations, efforts should be made to explore ways to ensure that developing countries achieve 'most favoured pricing' status.

obvious implications of an increase in drugs prices for public health, there could be politically disastrous consequences for many politicians in developing states, who are already under pressure from their constituents to improve access to medicines and to lower prices for pharmaceuticals. Referring to TRIPS, a recent WHO publication notes, 'Such a monopoly situation could lead to an increase in drug prices.'[21] This could mean the poor have even less access to essential medicines. As the director of WHO reported, 'At the beginning of the 21st century, one-third of the world's population still lacks access to the essential drugs it needs for good health. In the poorest parts of Africa and Asia, over 50% of the population do not have access to the most vital drugs.'[22] Pricing, although not exclusively responsible for the poor's lack of access of to medicines, is one of the main determinants.[23]

Although the innovating sector of the pharmaceutical industry emphasizes the importance of patents as an incentive for research and development and although the economic arguments presented earlier in this chapter support this argument, there are powerful economic arguments that counter them. Arrow argues, for example, that the entrenched patent monopolist has weaker incentives than a 'would-be' entry firm to initiate an R&D programme that would produce substitutes, even superior-quality ones, than to produce goods that were already generating profit.[24] This, in turn, results in sub-optimal outcomes for social welfare.[25] This argument can be discredited in the main for pharmaceutical products, where there is often a race to the market between leading research and development firms. As a result, new products are regularly introduced. The majority of these products are not new chemical entities but combinations and duplicates of drugs already developed ('me-too' products).[26]

The TRIPS Agreement is designed to reward innovators. It rewards innovation by pharmaceutical firms by guaranteeing them a product market monopoly for 20 years and by imposing sanctions on states whose firms breach international

---

[21] WHO, 'Globalization and Access to Drugs: Perspectives on the WTO/TRIPS Agreement' (revised) (Geneva: WHO, 1999), p. 25.
[22] G. H. Brundtland, speech to the WHO–Public Interest NGO Pharmaceuticals Roundtable, Third Meeting, WHO, Geneva, 1 May 2000.
[23] Others are poor health infrastructure, mismanagement of drug supplies and inefficient and/or corrupt purchasing methods.
[24] Kenneth J. Arrow, 'Economic Welfare and the Allocation of Resources for Invention', in *The Rate and Direction of Inventive Activity: Economic and Social Factors* (Princeton, NJ: National Bureau of Economic Research, 1962), pp. 609–25, as quoted in Paul A. David, 'Intellectual Property Institutions', in Wallerstein, Mogee and Schoen, *The Global Dimensions of Intellectual Property Rights*, p. 4.
[25] Wallerstein, Mogee and Schoen, *The Global Dimensions of Intellectual Property Rights*, p. 3.
[26] Peter Davis, *For Health or Profit: Medicine, the Pharmaceutical Industry, and the State in New Zealand* (Auckland: Oxford University Press, 1992), p. 3.

standards for pharmaceutical patents.[27] This increases the likelihood that a state will commit itself to the agreement by tying the protection of pharmaceutical patents to other economic issues – what Keohane and Nye term 'complex interdependence'.[28]

In responding to the pharmaceutical imperatives of the TRIPS Agreement, politicians in developing states face difficult choices. Although it could be costly for them to shirk the Agreement, it is also costly for them to honour it. This raises two questions: which choice is more costly and, given the costs, what is the best strategy to pursue *vis-à-vis* the TRIPS Agreement? Resolving these questions demands some understanding of how the WTO, which governs TRIPS, functions institutionally, as well as of the costs politicians may face if they honour the terms of the treaty.

THE WTO

The international relations literature stresses that states have little incentive to cooperate because in the absence of a central authority – an enforcer – the prevailing principle of the international system is anarchy. The establishment of an international regime such as the WTO fills this lacuna in the sphere of trade by changing the incentives affecting states' behaviour. International regimes can be defined as sets of implicit or explicit principles, norms, rules and decision-making procedures around which actors' expectations converge in an area of international relations.[29] Proponents of international regimes emphasize benefits such as improved information-sharing, burden-sharing and the coordination of state behaviour in achieving an outcome in an issue area.[30]

The Agreement Establishing the World Trade Organization calls for a single institutional framework encompassing GATT, as modified by the Uruguay Round, and all agreements and arrangements concluded during the round. The WTO has the same principles as GATT but a wider scope. Equally important, the WTO has the power to impose sanctions on member states that deviate from their commitments. In 2000, the WTO had more than 134 members, over 75 per cent of which were developing states; its members accounted for over 90 per cent of world trade. More than 30 others are negotiating membership.[31]

---

[27] In its 1998 report to the Office of the US Trade Representative, the Pharmaceutical Research and Manufacturers of America (PhRMA) estimated that trade barriers, particularly the lack of adequate and effective intellectual property protection for pharmaceuticals and market-restricting price controls, cost US drugs firms more than $9 billion a year.

[28] Robert O. Keohane and Joseph S. Nye, *Power and Interdependence: World Politics in Transition* (Boston: Little Brown and Company, 1977).

[29] Stephen D. Krasner (ed.), *International Regimes* (Ithaca: Cornell University Press, 1983), p. 28.

[30] Robert M. Axelrod, *The Evolution of Cooperation* (New York: Basic Books, 1984).

[31] http://www.wto.org.

All member states participate in decision-making, usually by consensus. A majority vote is also possible; but it has never been used in the WTO, and was used infrequently under GATT.

The WTO's highest-level decision-making body is the Ministerial Conference, which meets at least once every two years. Below this is the General Council. It oversees the operations of the WTO between meetings, acts as a dispute settlement body (DSB) (which is composed of all members of the WTO) and administers the Trade Policy Review Mechanism. The DSB establishes a unified system for settling disputes arising from agreements that the WTO oversees. The General Council has three subsidiary bodies: the Council for TRIPS, the Council for Trade in Goods and the Council for Trade in Services.

The WTO Treaty states that 'membership in the WTO entails accepting all the results of the Round, without exception.'[32] Its 'Understanding on Rules and Procedures Governing the Settlement of Disputes' provides a limited timeframe and an automatic mechanism for the settlement of disputes. It stipulates a 'negative consensus' rule for the establishment of dispute settlement panels, the adoption of their reports and the authorization of retaliatory measures. This rule means that the panel process will be instituted if at least one state is in favour of it. Stricter procedural disciplines, including time limits and deadlines for each process, were also adopted, and a standing appellate body was set up. As a result of these changes, many observers believed that smaller countries would be able to raise disputes more easily and that these countries would be treated more fairly.[33] The provisions and the dispute-settlement enforcement rules of the TRIPS Agreement can be used by developing countries in bilateral trade disputes with more powerful developed countries, which creates a more level playing field in international trade.[34] The adoption of the 'Understanding on Rules and Procedures Governing the Settlement of Disputes' also means that unilateral actions, such as action under section 301 of the US Trade Act, cannot be imposed before the DSB has verified the existence of a case of non-compliance and authorized retaliatory action. Any unilateral action taken before or outside this procedure would be illegal under the WTO treaty.[35]

The WTO has institutional mechanisms for helping to deter states from 'cheating' on their commitments. There is, as noted above, the Council for TRIPS; this is composed of representatives from the member states of the WTO. Its

---

[32] See the Agreement Establishing the World Trade Organization.
[33] Bernard M. Hoekman and Petros C. Mavroidis, 'Enforcing Multilateral Commitments: Dispute Settlement and Developing Countries', paper prepared for the WTO/World Bank Conference on Developing Countries in a Millennium Round, WTO Secretariat, Geneva, 20–21 September 1999, p. 1.
[34] Oxford Analytica Brief, WTO, 27 September 1999.
[35] http://www.southcentre.org/publications/TRIPs.

members can raise any issue relating to compliance by other parties. Alternatively, there is the notification and review of the national legislation of member countries. The Council for TRIPS has set up procedures for the notification and distribution to members of implementing legislation by each member once its transition period expires.[36] The review of intellectual property legislation is performed by peer groups. The legislation is studied by the notifying country's trading partners, who can pose questions through the TRIPS Council; it responds to questions from the floor of the council and in writing. These questions and answers are available to the public through the WTO's website (*www.wto.org*). The reason for these standards of scrutiny is that there is a belief that unless there is very careful review of compliance with international commitments, they will be worthless. Another reason for these standards is that they serve as a check on state commitment to the terms of the treaty. Further, the review mechanism is seen as a way to avoid disputes.[37] Most disputes are settled by the two parties without a formal invocation of the dispute settlement mechanism, but the knowledge that this is available possibly facilitates their resolution.[38]

TO ACCEPT OR TO SHIRK? THE COSTS AND BENEFITS OF TRIPS

The objectives of the TRIPS Agreement and its anticipated impact were points of conflict between developing states and developed states during the Uruguay Round. Politicians in developing states generally perceived that the agreement would be costly for them in the short term. (For politicians, longer-term benefits are usually less important than more immediate ones owing to the frequency of elections in democratic states.) And although TRIPS was eventually endorsed by all member states, its endorsement did not necessarily mean agreement: most politicians felt compelled by short-term trade considerations to accept the conditions of the agreement as they pertained to pharmaceuticals.

Opinion on the costs and benefits of the agreement remains sharply divided. Those in favour of TRIPS argue that its implementation will stimulate greater technology transfer, foreign direct investment, and research and development for cures for diseases of the poor.[39] Critics of the agreement argue that it will result in higher prices for drugs, exacerbate existing imbalances in the R&D of drug therapies between developed states and developing states and threaten the

---

[36] Adrian Otten, 'Implementation of the TRIPS Agreement and Prospects for Its Further Development', *Journal of International Economic Law* (1998), Vol. 1, No. 4, pp. 523–36.
[37] Ibid., p. 525.
[38] Ibid., p. 527.
[39] See, for example, Richard P. Rozek and Ruth Berkowitz, 'The Effects of Patent Protection on the Prices of Pharmaceutical Products – Is Intellectual Property Protection Raising the Drug Bill in Developing Countries?', *Journal of World Intellectual Property*, Vol. 1, No. 2 (March 1998), pp. 179–244.

viability of local industry.[40] To date, an evaluation of the real health and economic impacts of the agreement has been limited because there is insufficient empirical evidence.

However, the political consequences of TRIPS can be evaluated. My contention is that politicians in developing states *will* incur political costs from the agreement. Those politicians reasonably perceived that TRIPS would be more costly for them given the marked differences in the protection of pharmaceutical patents that exist between developed states and developing states. Politicians from the former would have to enact minimal reforms, if any, in order to ensure standards for pharmaceutical patents as prescribed by the agreement. But politicians from developing states would be obliged to initiate substantial reforms so as to bring local standards up to international ones. The political cost of these reforms will vary, depending on market structure, trade imperatives and the strength of special interest groups in the pharmaceutical sector. For example, politicians with constituents who have benefited from manufacturing medicines under patent or who have gained from consuming locally produced 'free-rider' drugs will have more to lose from the application of the agreement than others who do not have these types of constituent.

Before TRIPS, many developing states had adopted an explicit policy to disregard intellectual property protection for pharmaceuticals, to attempt to be self-sufficient in the production of basic medicines and, as in the case of India, to develop a competitive local industry. Domestic producers, both private and public, could then supply their populations with basic medicines at prices often considerably lower than those of the research-based pharmaceutical industry and learn by doing. The state of the global pharmaceutical market in the past supported many politicians' choice to pursue no patent protection for the sector's products. During the 1960s and 1970s, the vast majority of the 'miracle' drugs from the 1935–60 discovery period remained under patent.[41] However, the situation is starkly different today: about 95 per cent of WHO's essential drugs are off-patent.

Different trade imperatives and state industrial policies can account for the sometimes acute divergence of patent systems. Developing states did not, for the most part, support the protection of pharmaceutical patents because they needed to develop their pharmaceutical industry and to enhance competition in the market. Many developing states' economic and health development policies have been based on imitation and expropriation of the intellectual property of pharmaceutical firms based in industrialized states. Quite a few, notably India,

---

[40] Note, for instance, Carlos Correa, *Integrating Public Health Concerns into Patent Legislation in Developing Countries* (Geneva: South Centre, 2000), p. 2.
[41] Redwood, *Brazil: The Future Impact of Pharmaceutical Patents*, p. 33.

have achieved a level of success through learning by doing.[42] The TRIPS Agreement requires their politicians to reform the national drugs policy, and one of the most critical reforms is limiting the drugs portfolios of local firms. The potential impacts of this are more costly pharmaceuticals and/or the population's limited access to essential medicines. Developed states, by comparison, have tended to support the protection of pharmaceutical patents in order to protect revenue streams from their established innovative pharmaceutical industry and to promote investment in technological innovation.[43]

If a state contravenes a trade agreement, under the WTO other states have the right to turn to the dispute settlement mechanism for a resolution and, potentially, to impose economic sanctions on the contravening state. The TRIPS Agreement has thus changed the rules of the game by tying the protection of pharmaceutical patents to other trade issues and making contravention more costly for developing countries. The agreement may be unfair to developing states because it imposes standards that are more in line with those of advanced industrialized states. This application of patent protection for pharmaceuticals, which does not adequately reflect the economic and health needs of developing states, seems unjust at best. States such as Italy, Japan and Korea waited until they had reached a comfortable level of economic development before they implemented a patent system for pharmaceuticals in the 1970s. Why should the case be different for other states?

Despite the apparent costs of shirking the TRIPS Agreement, as a general rule 'rational actor' developing states should seek to honour its terms as little as possible and to shirk its terms as much as possible. However, this 'rational' behaviour requires politicians to play a complex game between the international and domestic levels of politics. Many politicians favoured making a commitment to the WTO and all of its conditions because it could help them to move their country more rapidly towards the economic liberalization that many had initiated before the Uruguay Round, and for the economic payoffs in the Agreement from which select groups in their countries could benefit. Their WTO obligations effectively 'bound' politicians to market reforms and helped them to override those special interest groups opposed to liberalization of the economy.[44] A GATT report in 1991 noted that trade liberalization had been initiated by 30 developing countries since the beginning of the Uruguay Round.[45]

---

[42] Ibid., p. 13.
[43] Correa, *Integrating Public Health Concerns*, p. 5.
[44] For further arguments about countries' decision to 'tie their hands' to international institutions, see James Vreeland, 'The IMF: Lender of Last Resort or Scapegoat?', draft paper prepared for the Midwest Political Science Association Annual Meeting, Chicago, 15–17 April 1999.
[45] John Croome, *Reshaping the World Trading System: A History of the Uruguay Round* (Geneva: World Trade Organization, 1995), p. 289.

The perceived costs of liberalizing may well be higher in developing countries than in developed countries. But the costs of not liberalizing are even higher: poor countries simply cannot afford either the costs associated with inefficient resource allocation that result from protection or the costs that protectionism incurs when it reduces the flow of investment and ideas from outside.[46] Accepting the TRIPS Agreement was thus a necessary concession for politicians in developing states in return for the greater benefits of moving more rapidly towards economic reform, making trading gains in key economic sectors and having the force and utility of the WTO in support of them. Still, resistance to TRIPS with regard to pharmaceutical products continues, because of its perceived costs. This resistance is manifest in the sluggish passage of legislation in conformity with TRIPS standards, in the use of the agreement's exceptional provisions and in public campaigns emphasizing its harsh effects on the health of the poor.

THE OPTIMAL POLICY CHOICE

In view of the above analysis, I argue that the best approach for a developing state to take towards the TRIPS Agreement is to make a minimum commitment to it and to shirk it as much as possible. (It should be kept in mind that the inclusion of an intellectual property agreement in the Uruguay Round had been opposed by the G-77 states[47] and that a compromise was reached to allow intellectual property issues to remain under national jurisdiction.[48])

States can shirk commitment to TRIPS by delaying the passage of legislation in line with pharmaceutical patents, as in the case of India (see below). They can also neglect to allocate sufficient resources for the infrastructure, institutions and personnel needed to implement and monitor the agreement. This strategy is of course potentially costly, as it risks WTO sanctions in other areas of the economy.

The less risky policy would be to minimize the reach of the agreement while keeping within the bounds of its conditions. A state could, for example, become a champion opponent of the TRIPS Agreement, arguing against the imposition of standards supporting international corporations instead of local firms and calling attention to the agreement's potentially adverse impact on public health. This policy would be supported by public health advocates, who have contended that TRIPS may widen the world health divide, enhancing rich populations'

---

[46] Ibid., p. 13.
[47] The G-77 is a coalition of developing states that was created in 1964. This coalition (currently representing some 133 states) provides the means for these states to communicate common economic interests to the United Nations system and to promote economic and technical cooperation among themselves.
[48] Health Action International, 'Power, Patents, and Pills: An Examination of GATT/WTO and Essential Drug Policies', Seminar Report, Amsterdam, November 1997, p. 17.

access to essential vaccines and medicines but depriving the more needy.[49] On a more practical level, the leadership of a state could actively erode the reach of the agreement by interpreting its exceptional provisions broadly and applying the requisite legal and regulatory support.

COUNTRY COMPARISONS: THE SPECTRUM OF COMMITMENT

To illustrate my arguments empirically, I compare three developing countries: Brazil, Romania and India (see Table 6.1).[50] (Making comparisons among this small number of states does not constitute scientific proof, but it can provide insights into states' commitment to TRIPS.) This comparison is based on a much deeper analysis I have made for a separate research project, but only its main findings will be referred to here.[51] Each of the developing-country cases fulfils four criteria. First, each state represents a significant market for the international industry and has a local pharmaceutical industry. Second, each state, particularly Brazil and India, has firms that have benefited from copying patented drugs without cost and thus constituents who opposed the TRIPS Agreement during the Uruguay Round. Third, each state is a member of the WTO and is obliged to harmonize its drugs legislation and regulations with TRIPS. Finally, each state is a democracy; its politicians must stand for office in elections on a regular basis.

Despite these similarities, the manufacturing capacities of Brazil, India and Romania differ, and those differences may explain some of the differences in their implementation of the TRIPS Agreement. A focus on domestic imperatives helps to illuminate the reasons why states may choose to make a commitment to or defect from international agreements.

These states' responses to the TRIPS Agreement range from high commitment to low commitment. Romania has a high commitment to TRIPS. It has expressed commitment to the patent law by harmonizing its domestic legislation and regulations with international standards. Brazil is in the middle of the commitment spectrum: it has passed legislation (the Industrial Property Act 1996) in line with TRIPS but has also interpreted its obligations widely, so that

---

[49] Elen Jakubowski and Henry W. Wyes, 'Global Trade Liberalisation: Challenges and Opportunities for World Health', *EuroHealth*, Vol. 6, No. 4 (2000), p. 17.

[50] The World Bank divides economies according to Gross National Income per capita for 2000, calculated using the World Bank Atlas method. The groups are: low income, $755 or less; lower middle income, $756–2,995; upper middle income, $2,996–9,265; and high income, $9,266 or more. Brazil is an upper-middle-income economy; Romania is a lower-middle-income economy; and India is a low-income economy.

[51] See Jillian Clare Cohen, 'Pharmaceutical Napsters? A Comparative Study of State Response to the Pharmaceutical Imperatives of the Agreement on Trade Related Aspects of Intellectual Property Rights', PhD Dissertation, New York University, 2001.

Table 6.1: Comparative commitment to TRIPS: Brazil, Romania and India

Country	Value of pharmaceutical market ($ bn)	Viability of pharmaceutical industry	TRIPS-compliant legislation	Commitment to the TRIPS Agreement
Brazil	6.3*	Medium	Industrial Property Act (1996)	Medium
Romania	0.390*	Weak	Patent Law No. 64 (1991)	High
India**	7.2*	Strong	Amendments to the Patent Act (1970)	Low

*1999. **2000.
Sources: IMS Health and World Bank internal documents.

there is room to manipulate the terms of the agreement in the light of domestic realities. A recent dispute brought to the WTO's dispute settlement mechanism between Brazil and the United States about Brazil's local working requirements refers to the sections of the new law which sanctions patent-owners who do not 'work' their patented inventions within Brazil (e.g. manufacture the product locally). The discriminatory aspects of the law, in effect, do not permit patent rights in Brazil unless companies relocate their manufacturing facilities into Brazil. Coupled with the growing popular antagonism in Brazil to the research-based pharmaceutical industry, this could in time move Brazil towards a lower commitment level.

India has been sluggish in moving towards international standards for pharmaceutical patents. It indicated its intention to use the full transition period permissible under the TRIPS Agreement (January 2006 originally and recently extended to 2016) and only began the legislative process to amend its pharmaceuticals patent law in November 2000, two months before the initial deadline of 1 January 2000. India's Parliamentary Patent Select Committee delayed the reform process by creating additional legislative processes, such as a series of consultations, that had to be completed before the patent law could be reformed.

The extent to which these (and other) states have made a commitment to the TRIPS Agreement can be explained in large part by two factors: the capacity of the local industry to supply drugs to the population, and trade imperatives. But other considerations must be taken into account too. Thus, Romania's greater commitment may be a result of its economic and political transitions, which may present a greater possibility for policy reform. Expanded pluralism and less stable government rule may explain why there has been policy gridlock in India, whereas in Brazil the Cardoso administration has maintained consistent control of the government since 1994. This warrants much further study, which goes beyond the scope of this chapter

Romania

Compared with Brazil and India, Romania has shown a strong degree of commitment to the TRIPS Agreement. This commitment is corroborated by the fact that the 2001 submission by the Pharmaceutical Research and Manufacturers of America (PhRMA) to the US Trade Representative at the WTO does not include Romania on its extensive list of 'watch countries'.[52] Romanian politicians have not expressed an intention to use the language of TRIPS to shirk the patent law for pharmaceuticals, despite compelling public health reasons – the rise of HIV–AIDs – to do so. Romania's commitment is strongly motivated by economic reasons – primarily, its interest in becoming a member of the European Union (EU). By harmonizing its pharmaceutical patent law with that of the EU, Romania is demonstrating it can commit to regional standards and has the potential to harmonize other laws and regulations to standards set by the trade body.

Another factor that can help illuminate why Romania is committing to the TRIPS Agreement is the state of its local industry. By way of background, the Romanian pharmaceutical market was valued at $390 million in 2000. Total expenditure (public and private) on pharmaceuticals in 1997 was $402 million or $18 per capita.[53] This was about one-sixth of the value of the per capita consumption of pharmaceuticals in other states in eastern Europe, such as the Czech Republic and Hungary. Romania's domestic pharmaceutical industry does not have innovative capabilities, but it produces both therapeutic ingredients and finished products.[54] In other words, local firms do not invest in the development of new drug therapies, and some do little more than produce the finished product from imported inputs. These firms may be locally owned subsidiaries of multinational drugs companies or joint ventures between local firms and international companies.[55]

Romania's domestic pharmaceutical industry is not robust enough to justify the risks Romania would have to assume if its leadership shirked the TRIPS

---

[52] Brazil and India are both listed.
[53] Ramesh Govindaraj and Klaus Imbeck, 'Assessment of the Romanian Pharmaceutical Sector – An Update', mimeo, World Bank, 1998.
[54] Robert Ballance, Janos Pogany and Helmut Forstner, *The World's Pharmaceutical Industries: An International Perspective on Innovation, Competition and Policy* (Aldershot and Brookfield: Edward Elgar Publishing, 1992), p. 9.
[55] Ibid., p. 10.

Agreement to some extent. It is incapable of providing sufficient quantities of medicines for the population. The poor state of the industry was noted in an assessment of the state of public drugs-producers in Romania in 1993. Although this study is now out of date, its findings are valuable, as they well describe the conditions of the local pharmaceutical industry. For example, the report noted that the primary production facilities of the domestic producers needed upgrading. Secondary production facilities were seen to be of mixed age and quality. The production of drugs was inefficient and labour-intensive. The report also emphasized that the packaging plant and materials were below international standards, that some practices, such as no provision for solid waste and no effective water treatment facilities, were environmentally hazardous and that quality control was unacceptable as a result of poor equipment and outdated production lines.[56]

Brazil

Brazil perceived a moderate commitment to the TRIPS Agreement to be beneficial for resolving trade disputes between itself and the United States in other economic sectors.[57] Some commitment could help to make it a more attractive market for foreign direct investment and technology transfer. Also, American trade sanctions for earlier breaches of pharmaceutical patents had proved to be costly. In August 1988, the Reagan administration passed the Omnibus Trade and Competitiveness Act. This act created two provisions, Super 301 and Special 301, which effectively strengthened the ability of the United States Trade Representative to retaliate against countries for inadequate intellectual property protection and for practices that discriminated against American commerce. On 30 October 1988, the American government imposed a punitive tariff of 100 per cent on $390 million of Brazilian goods in retaliation for Brazil's refusal to grant patent protection to pharmaceuticals and other information-intensive technologies.[58]

But the Brazilian government has sought to modify the terms of the TRIPS Agreement to Brazilian political realities by issuing a Presidential Decree (6 October 1999) which regulates the implementation of Article 71 of the Law and allows for the granting of a compulsory licence during national emergency situations. In December 1999, the government also issued 'Medidas Provisorias'

---

[56] PA Consulting Group, 'Romanian Pharmaceutical Industry Restructuring and Strategic Plan: Industry Restructuring', draft, June 1993.
[57] Oxford Analytica Brief, 'Brazil: Pharmaceutical Patents', 3 June 1996.
[58] Edgardo Buscaglia and Clarissa Long, 'U.S. Foreign Policy and Intellectual Property Rights in Latin America', Hoover Institution, Essays in Public Policy, Stanford, CA, September 2000. p. 21.

(Temporary Measures) whereby under a revised Article 229-C, the new drug regulatory agency, the Agencia Nacional de Vigilancia de Sanitaria (ANVS), has the authority to approve all patent applications related to pharmaceutical products or processes. PhRMA argues that this is inconsistent with the anti-discrimination clause of TRIPS Article 27.1 and that any review of applications other than for the criteria of patents is not consistent with the TRIPS Agreement. The US industry argues that the Institut National de la Propriété Industrielle (INPI) and not the ANVS should be the agency in charge of patent applications.

Finally, Brazil continues to manufacture drugs needed to treat HIV–AIDS by making a case for the use of a legal loophole in the TRIPS Agreement that allows for the manufacture of drugs in the case of a national emergency. Brazilian politicians and public health activists have argued that the HIV–AIDS crisis in Brazil is a national emergency; an estimated 580,000 persons[59] are HIV-positive. Brazil has put the international pharmaceutical industry on notice that unless they lower the prices of the remaining anti-retroviral drugs still under patent, the government will break patent licences.

At the time of writing, public manufacturers in Brazil are making generic copies of eight out of twelve anti-retroviral drugs used in for the treatment of HIV-positive persons. The Brazilian approach has been to import the generic raw materials and use their public manufacturing facilities, such as FURP and Farmaguinhos to locally manufacture finished products, and this is being lauded by public health activists as a model for other states to emulate or benefit from. Developing states such as Burkina Faso, Cambodia, South Africa and Uganda have approached Brazilian (and Indian) manufacturers for their discounted HIV–AIDS pharmaceuticals. Brazil has also been discussing technology transfer with other developing states, so that they can begin producing pharmaceuticals.[60] All of these drugs were registered prior to the implementation of the Industrial Property Law in 1997. The research-based pharmaceutical industry has argued that Brazil is in violation of the WTO regulations and initiated a case against Brazil with the WTO Dispute Settlement Body. It opposes the way in which Brazil uses a provision in the TRIPS Agreement (to manufacture generic drugs in the case of national emergency) to manufacture brand-name, US-made HIV–AIDS drugs as well as locally produced generics.[61]

In time, this power may widen because of pressure on the WTO to provide 'breathing space' or selective disengagement for developing states, particularly

---

[59] Author's interview with World Bank AIDS I Project Manager Sandra Rosenhouse, Washington, DC, September 2000.
[60] Médecins Sans Frontières, 'Six-Month Report Card: Have AIDS Drugs Prices for the Poor Been Slashed?', press release, Geneva, 1 December 2000, *http://www.accessmed-msf.org*.
[61] Stephen Buckley, 'Brazil Becomes Model in Fight against AIDS', *The Washington Post*, 17 September 2000, p. A22.

in view of the Doha Declaration on the TRIPS Agreement and Public Health (November 2001). The Declaration calls for recognition of the importance of public health priorities over and above intellectual property protection. This pressure has partially come from the international alliance of health activists that has coalesced around the issue of drugs prices in developing states and has successfully negotiated lower prices for HIV–AIDS drugs with some of the research-based pharmaceutical industry.[62] The pressure for wide interpretation of the TRIPS Agreement has also been brought to the fore by the media's attention on the profit-seeking motives of this industry.

India

India's low level of commitment (defined primarily by what it has not done) suggests its politicians perceive that implementing the TRIPS Agreement could entail very high domestic costs, even though local firms are already pursuing unsophisticated research and development themselves. A few of the leading Indian firms that have benefited from copying patented drugs, such as Dr Reddy's Laboratories and Ranbaxy Laboratories, are beginning to invest in research and development of drugs themselves. The amounts they are investing are small and the types of R&D they are undertaking are not complex; they are making innovations in drug delivery systems and are using similar molecules in their research and development efforts. Ranbaxy has licensed the Novel Drug Delivery System (NDDS) to Bayer for the product ciprofloxacin.[63] Dr Reddy's Laboratories has licensed two anti-diabetic new chemical entities (NCEs) to the major international firm Novo Nordisk for clinical trials and further research and development.[64] India's pharmaceutical companies may stand to lose the most from the TRIPS Agreement when compared to firms in Brazil or Romania because they have been tremendously successful in producing pharmaceuticals under patents. Within three to five years of the entry into the market of a patented drug in an advanced industrial state, its industry has been able to produce a copy for sale in the local market as well as for export.[65] PhRMA's annual submission to the United States Trade Representative noted that 'India is the fourth

---

[62] This alliance includes Oxfam, Health Action International, ACT UP, the World Health Organization and Consumers Project on Health Technology.
[63] The recent anthrax scares in the aftermath of the 11 September 2000 terrorist attacks created an unprecedented increase in the demand for the drug ciprofloxacin and further demonstrates the complexities of the costs of protecting pharmaceutical patents when public health demands are compelling.
[64] Ramesh Govindaraj, G. Chellaraj, with Jillian Clare Cohen, G.N.V. Ramana and Ngan Le, 'The Pharmaceutical Sector in India: Issues and Options', mimeo (Washington, DC: World Bank, 2000).
[65] See Chapter 4 by Oxfam in this volume, esp. pp. 86–7.

leading supplier of bulk pharmaceutical products and active ingredients, but expends precious little of its profits on basic research and/or original product development.'

The Indian pharmaceutical industry has captured the majority of its domestic market by making copies of pharmaceuticals and selling them at lower prices (thanks to small R&D costs) in the Indian market.[66] Indian firms have consolidated their position by manufacturing new but unpatentable active ingredients for pharmaceuticals, which international research-based pharmaceutical firms have refused to do as there is no patent protection.[67] The local industry has been helped to grow by government policies such as tax relief and the imposition of hefty import duties (as high as 80 per cent) on products from international drugs firms. In 1999, the Indian market was valued at $7.2 billion or 1.1 per cent of the global pharmaceutical market. In terms of volume, it is third globally.[68]

The pharmaceutical industry grew at about 10 per cent annually from 1990 to 2000, well above India's general industrial growth rate.[69] India was the most rapidly growing market of the top 15 pharmaceutical markets in the world. The projected value of this market in 2006 will exceed $13 billion.[70] Formulations account for 82 per cent of the market and bulk drugs account for the remaining 18 per cent. The industry has a fragmented structure, with about 300 firms operating in the organized sector and as many as 24,000 small-scale 'backyard' firms. The government reported in 1999 that India is now capable of meeting 70 per cent of the country's requirements for bulk drugs (chemicals which have therapeutic value and are used for the production of formulations) and almost all of the local demand for formulations.

India is taking the full transition period for product patent protection, which has recently been extended from 1 January 2006 to 1 January 2016. Moreover, it has been slow to implement preparatory measures for the TRIPS Agreement. It was required by Article 70(8(a)) of the agreement to set up a mechanism (known as the 'mailbox') that allows inventions to be notified to the patent officials so that the invention can be established as 'new'. Nor did India put into place the measure establishing exclusive marketing rights, whereby if a government allows a new drug to be marketed, the firm that invented it has the right to market it exclusively for a time.

The application of the TRIPS Agreement in India is, not surprisingly, highly controversial. For example, the proposed amendments to the Patent Act of 1970 were contested not only by the local pharmaceutical industry but also by its

---

[66] This also applies to exported drugs.
[67] Redwood, *Brazil: The Future Impact of Pharmaceutical Patents*, p. 25.
[68] Govindaraj and Chelleraj et al., 'The Pharmaceutical Sector in India'.
[69] Ibid.
[70] Ibid.

international counterpart. On the one hand, the ruling government was accused of selling out to the international research-based pharmaceutical industry and on the other hand, the government was accused of not doing enough to ensure that the intellectual property law in India was up to international standards.

The American industry association, PhRMA, argues that the new Indian law, if enacted as proposed, will continue the discrimination against patent-holders who manufacture products outside India. It will prevent full enjoyment of patent rights unless companies relocate their manufacturing facilities to India, despite Article 27(1) of the TRIPS Agreement, which states that local working as a requirement for full enjoyment of patent rights is prohibited.[71] Furthermore, extensive authority will remain available to the Indian government to use patented technology without the consent of the patent-holder. PhRMA argues that the new law attempts to provide the government with ample opportunities to mitigate the law by way of declaring a national emergency, situations of extreme urgency, and public non-commercial use. Third parties will continue to have the right to harass and challenge applicants for patents and patent-owners, and numerous other grounds are provided for opposing, cancelling and seeking revocation of patents on grounds not permitted under the TRIPS Agreement.

CONCLUSIONS

The TRIPS Agreement presents complex policy choices between international and domestic imperatives for politicians in developing states. This chapter is not intended to be hard science but rather a suggestive framework for understanding how a state may respond to the imperatives of an international treaty so that prevailing domestic norms and institutions are not eroded entirely. The dilemma of meeting local economic and public health needs while creating incentives for pharmaceutical innovation is complex, and finding a balance between these two objectives demands thoughtful policy-making.

What I have attempted to illustrate is that although the TRIPS Agreement requires the harmonization of pharmaceutical patent law for all member countries of the WTO, its application is not uniform. The treaty allows developing states some room for selective disengagement, such as through the use of compulsory licences and local working requirements. My explanations for what can account for the differences in state responses to the international treaty have focused on two variables – the robustness of the local pharmaceutical industry and economic incentives and their interaction. Although India has a mature and competitive local industry, it has shown resistance to pharmaceutical patent

[71] See *http://www.phrma.org/intenatl/intellprop*.

protection. Brazil also has a strong local industry but a more open economy, and particularly a harsh experience of past economic sanctions from the United States. It has implemented the agreement but interpreted its application in a way that does not pose a complete threat to local economic and public health interests. Finally, the case of Romania reveals how a state with a weak domestic pharmaceutical industry and an expressed commitment to become a member of the European Union has shown little effort to disengage itself selectively from the commitments of the TRIPS Agreement.

7 THE PHARMACEUTICAL SECTOR: THE GENERICS DEVELOPMENT TRAJECTORY

Brigitte Granville and Carol Scott Leonard

INTRODUCTION

This chapter is about the impact of the trade in and production of pharmaceuticals on local learning in less developed countries. It examines mainly countries where intellectual property (IP) is not adequately protected and where generic drugs are the primary product, as distinct from those where protection for IP is adequate and where the research branch of the pharmaceutical sector has evolved. Although the production of generics does not lead to the most profitable research activities, it does generate learning effects that can nevertheless be significant.[1] For example, the learning effects resulting from the greater involvement in export markets of countries where generic drugs are the primary product are well known.

The first objective of this chapter is to provide a summary of evidence that will permit a determination of how pharmaceutical production has spread in the developing world and of roughly to what extent Trade-Related Aspects of Intellectual Property Rights (TRIPS) are enforced there. The second objective is to try to answer this question: with changes in pharmaceutical markets, is the balance of benefits also changing? IP protection fosters investment in research and innovation in pharmaceuticals. However, with the expansion of market share of generic drugs, as in Asia and Latin America, and with the expiry of key patents, the development significance of generic drugs production for local learning may also be expanding. We note local pharmaceutical industries' responses to the international trade and production of drugs and assess the contribution of these responses to their competitiveness.

This paper draws on material from 'The Digital Divide, Local Learning and Innovation in the Developing World: The Remarkable Case of Pharmaceuticals', a paper delivered at the Tokyo Club in Paris on 24–5 January 2002.
[1] See particularly Gambardella (1995) and Pisano (1996).

The chapter has four parts. The first reviews the increase in developing countries of pharmaceutical production and trade. The second part describes the spread of pharmaceutical production to countries where there is adequate protection of IP and where there is not. The third part suggests the nature of learning effects through response to trade where TRIPS may not be well enforced or officially protected and where production is primarily of imitative generics. We also underscore the importance for on- and off-patent drug production of collaboration between researchers and firms of all kinds and sizes. The conclusion focuses on policy implications.

PHARMACEUTICAL DEVELOPMENT ACROSS REGIONS

As the other chapters in this volume have shown, the developing world is a beneficiary of pharmaceutical production even when it is not involved in innovation. Among the passive benefits countries receive are cost reductions and the availability of drugs, which improve the health of the populace. More active participation in pharmaceutical production and trade improves export revenues and, sometimes, learning effects in drug discovery, and it always improves the marketing of generic drugs in domestic and global networks.[2]

To be sure, the production and sales of R&D-based pharmaceuticals (brand products) are, as Table 7.1 shows, geographically concentrated mostly in the advanced Western economies, where there is a high level of per capita income and technological development. Of these countries, the United States has a particularly large share. According to IMS Health data, 57 per cent of sales of new medicines marketed since 1995 are in the US market, compared with 25 per cent in the European market, 5 per cent in Japan and only 13 per cent in other countries. In biotechnology, US firms are dominant in the patenting of innovations. Of the 150 genetic engineering health care patents issued by the United States Patent and Trademark Office in 1995, 122 were granted to US applicants. On a per capita basis, spending on drugs is highest in the United States, with France the next highest.[3] The leading pharmaceutical markets, as identified by IMS, are all in developed countries. Japan is the world's second-largest market (after the United States) for pharmaceuticals.

This geographical concentration is well known to be a result of the high and growing costs of the technology-intensive process and product development of pharmaceuticals. The costs and increasing sophistication of products are reflected in the increasing average time and expense required for the production

---

[2] For example, beginning in 2000 Brazil and India held talks on cooperative agreements to foster in both countries public–private partnerships in pharmaceutical developments and to enhance reciprocal trade through the WTO.
[3] PhRMA International (2001).

Table 7.1: Ten leading global pharmaceutical markets – projected pharmaceutical sales and growth rates to 2005

Country	Annual sales,* 2000 ($ bn)	Projected sales,* 2005 ($ bn)	Projected compound annual growth rate, 2000–5 (%)	Projected 10-country market share, 2005 (%)
Australia	3	5	9.3	1.1
Belgium	2	3	5.6	0.7
Canada	6	10	10.7	2.4
France	16	22	6.0	5.0
Germany	17	24	7.5	5.6
Italy	11	16	8.2	3.6
Japan	58	66	2.3	15.1
Spain	6	10	9.9	2.3
UK	11	16	8.3	3.7
US	150	263	11.8	60.5
Total	281	434	9.1	100

* Sales cover direct and indirect pharmaceutical channel purchases from pharmaceutical wholesalers and manufacturers in 10 key international markets. Figures include prescription and certain over-the-counter data, and represent manufacturers' prices.
Source: IMS Health, *Pharma-Prognosis International, 2001–2005*.

process. In the early 1990s, it typically took 10 years and $100 million in R&D to take a new drug from the laboratory to the marketing phase.[4] DiMasi has estimated that the average cost of innovation in 1997 was $312 million and that the average production time for turning a newly synthesized active substance into a marketable medicinal product was 12 to 13 years.[5] In aggregate numbers, research-based pharmaceutical companies invested $30.5 billion in R&D in 2001. This represents an 18.7 per cent increase over expenditures in 2000 and more than triple the investment in 1990. As a percentage of sales in the research-based industry, allocations to R&D increased from 11.4 per cent in 1970 to 17.4 per cent in 1999, and for 2001 the estimate is 18.5 per cent.[6] Corporate tax data for the United States show that pharmaceutical manufacturers invest a higher percentage of sales revenue in R&D than does any other industry, including high-tech industries such as electronics, aerospace, computers and automobiles. The pharmaceutical industry's percentage of sales revenue in R&D far exceeds that of the oil and gas sector, which devotes only 0.7 per cent of turnover to R&D.

[4] UNIDO (1997), p. 188.
[5] Research report cited in PhRMA International (2001).
[6] Ibid.

Table 7.2: Top 10 pharmaceutical companies by sales, 1999

Company by rank	Sales ($ bn)
Glaxo SmithKline	22.2
Pfizer (Warner-Lambert)	20.2
Merck	15.5
AstraZeneca	14.8
Aventis	13.1
Bristol-Myers Squibb	12.0
Novartis	11.6
Roche	11.0
J&J	10.7
Lilly	9.3
Pharmacia	9.3

Source: Philing (2000), p. 92.

Table 7.3: Top 10 pharmaceutical companies by revenue, 1980 and 1990

Company	Position in 1990	Position in 1980
Merck	1	4
Bristol-Myers Squibb	2	8
Glaxo	3	Not in first 10
SmithKline Beecham	4	10
Hoechst	5	1
Ciba-Geigy	6	3
Johnson & Johnson	7	Not in first 10
American Home Products	8	6
Sandoz	9	7
Eli Lilly	10	Not in first 10

Source: quoted in Beesley (1997), Table 23.3, p. 460.

Part of the high cost is because of strict controls and rules to ensure that the products are safe and that they have the advertised effect: entire divisions in government health departments manage the regulatory process, which can consist of thousands of tests. There are large amounts of data, drawn on laboratory experiments on the basic chemicals for reaction changes (indicating toxicity or therapeutic action), trials on animals to monitor the effect of the product and clinical trials on patients when the drug has been declared non-toxic.[7] Only

---

[7] Government intervention practised outside the United States includes (1) de-listing, which disallows reimbursement for over-the-counter products that otherwise could be prescribed and reimbursed or which forces switching of prescription drugs to over-the-counter status;

when these stages of the process have been completed can the drug be licensed so that doctors can prescribe it, or so that pharmacists can stock those drugs not requiring a prescription, and the public can purchase it.[8] Also, in most European countries and Japan the government is the largest purchaser of drugs, so it can negotiate directly or indirectly to control prices of pharmaceutical products. With differing kinds of control, the general effect is a lower profit margin, keeping the cost of drug development high.

Within the industry, concentration at the firm level in the mid-1990s was relatively low: only the three largest firms had more than a four per cent share of the world market, and none had more than 20 per cent of any major national market.[9] However, intense competition led to mergers.[10] Ballance, Pogány and Forstner, in their typology of pharmaceutical producers, emphasize that the multinationals are large, integrated corporations engaged in all three stages of production (research, manufacture and distribution); they give high priority to product development, generating the new molecular entities (NMEs) upon which their R&D is based.[11] Table 7.2 lists the top 10 companies by sales.

---

and (2) local performance requirements to stimulate private investment in own markets, requiring companies to manufacture products locally, conduct R&D locally, co-market or co-develop products with a local partner and/or license their products to a local manufacturer (PhRMA International (2001)).

[8] The development and testing of drugs, conducted primarily by pharmaceutical companies in company and university laboratories, includes clinical trials, dosage testing and research to determine information that should be included in product labelling. Human clinical trials take up roughly one-third of the R&D budget in the United States; the first-, second- and third-phase trials, required for drug approval, account for 29.1 per cent, and an additional 11.7 per cent is allocated to trials that occur after a product has been approved by the FDA. In addition, 8.3 per cent of R&D is for process-development and quality-control functions required to meet stringent manufacturing standards. Companies allocate approximately 36 per cent of R&D expenditure to pre-clinical functions. Ten per cent is spent on synthesizing and extracting compounds for evaluation; 14.2 per cent is for biological screening and pharmacological testing, in which thousands of compounds are evaluated for every one that continues in the development process; 4.5 per cent is for continuous testing in the areas of toxicology and safety; and 7.3 per cent is spent for dosage formulation and stability testing. Only 3 of 10 drugs introduced after 1980 had higher than cost of R&D returns (PhRMA International (2001)).

[9] Tarabusi and Vickery (1997), p. 71.

[10] Saxenian (1994), p. 9: 'As a rule, drugs newly developed by innovative companies are patented and sold by them under their own brand name at prices sufficient to recuperate research costs and finance further innovation. When patents expire, the same drugs may be marketed by other firms, which will often sell them under "generic" (non-proprietary) names at a lower price since they need make no allowance for research expenses. Until recently, most companies specialised either in research based innovative products or in generics. Since the late 1980s, the distinction has become blurred, with many firms engaging directly or through subsidiaries in both types of activities. Since 1980, a large concentration trend has led to the take-over of most large western manufacturers of generic drugs by multinational research-based pharmaceutical companies.'

[11] Ballance, Pogány and Forstner (1992).

There is substantial continuity in the market share of these firms over the past two decades, as Table 7.3 demonstrates. However, even with the growth of intra-industry concentration, new entries of other kinds of firms, innovative companies and reproductive firms, have multiplied. Innovative companies tend to be small in size, but they have sufficient capacity to produce patent-expired drugs, and they discover and develop NMEs and export them in significant quantities. Reproductive firms tend to be family-owned enterprises or publicly owned companies of medium size. They grow by accessing the technological knowledge developed by the larger firms and manufacture products sold under brand names or low-cost generics.

In the development trajectory of pharmaceuticals, niche producers and other specialists, known for research or marketing strength or for the particular drugs that they produce, grow in number as large companies disperse their activities.[12] The industry is not a global one in the way that textiles, food processing, clothing and steel are, but it is increasing in size rapidly, with many of the developing countries achieving and holding on to roughly a one per cent share of the export market, despite the growing dominance of American and European producers. The larger Latin American and central and eastern European countries have substantial innovative capabilities, and many of the smaller and less developed countries produce finished products. Establishing a strong base after the Second World War, by the early 1990s the drug industry had reached at least $100 million in nearly 60 countries.[13] The distinguishing feature of the industry is the great variety of products, with about 20,000 drugs in large markets such the United States and Japan and more than 10,000 in leading developing countries such as Brazil, Mexico, Algeria and the Republic of Korea and in smaller developing countries.[14]

The rapid growth of pharmaceuticals was initially and remains largely a result of on-patent drugs sold only by prescription. These drugs have high profit margins as well as high fixed costs, as emphasized above. They tend to be marketed and to spread in places where they are registered, that is in the country where the patent-holder has the legitimate right to market them exclusively.[15]

---

[12] Ibid., p. 2.
[13] Ibid., p. 22.
[14] Ibid., p. 4.
[15] This prerogative is incorporated in the TRIPS Agreement (1995) governing the rights of patent-holders and minimum standards of intellectual property protection for WTO members. See Chapter 1 by Lippert and Chapter 2 by Scherer and Watal in this volume for analysis of and details on TRIPS. There is a heated debate about parallel trade: developing countries claimed parallel imports are clearly allowed under Article 6 and that it is essential to ensure prices are as low as possible. The EU, US and Switzerland warned that this could undermine 'differential pricing' (companies selling at lower prices in poorer markets) if cheaper products flow into developed countries' markets. (For the debate see Chapter 3 by Maskus and Ganslandt and Chapter 11 by WHO–WTO in this volume.)

More recently, off-patent generic and multi-source drugs, also sold by prescription under their original patented brand names or generic names, have provided a large source of growth. Generics production has low profit margins, like over-the-counter (OTC) drug production, with high advertising and low R&D costs. But generics received a boost in sales following the passage of the Drug Price Competition and Patent Term Restoration Act of 1984 in the United States. The Waxman–Hatch Act made entry into the market easier by lowering testing requirements. The law created the Abbreviated New Drug Application (ANDA), which required a generic product only to be 'bioequivalent' to an innovator drug for approval when the patent expired.[16] The lenient new acts, coupled with the expiry of the patents of many widely sold drugs in the mid-1980s, resulted in the transformation of the competitive dynamics of drugs markets in the 1990s.[17]

The share of generics in the drugs market differs widely among countries. In the late 1980s it was roughly 14 per cent of all drugs, and OTCs were 16 per cent. By the early 1990s, generics had grown to about 20 per cent of the US market, but were only six per cent of the European market.[18] The share of generic drugs sold by prescription in pharmacies more than doubled in the 1980s, from 18.5 per cent at the end of 1984 to 47 per cent in 1990,[19] and the large number of innovator products due to lose patent protection over the next 10 years will foster an even greater expansion of generics.

In Brazil, for example, the market has recently experienced a transformation. Both generic and brand products were hampered by a centralized distribution system and by the requirement that all medicines be licensed by the Ministry of Health. In 1996, original and licensed brands had a market share of about 58 per cent; generics had about 42 per cent. However, a law in 1999 facilitating generic production and also liberalizing the OTC markets,[20] as medicines could

---

[16] PhRMA International (2001).

[17] Competitive market forces are constrained in most parts of the world. In most European countries and Japan, the government is the largest purchaser of pharmaceuticals and negotiates directly to control the prices of drugs. The methods of price-control systems differ, but price controls everywhere tend to undermine the innovation and vitality of the European and Japanese pharmaceutical industries. (See also Chapter 8 by Reekie in this volume for a view on price controls.)

[18] Tarabusi and Vickery (1997), pp. 70–72.

[19] Frank and Salkever (1995).

[20] The Generic Law of January 1999 allows a 40–45 per cent reduction of pharmaceutical prices, in view of the income constraint on drug purchases, and provides incentives for manufacturers of generic drugs. The legislation makes it mandatory for the generic name to be included on all product packs (at least half the size of the brand name) and requires that under the government system all prescriptions be written by their generic name and that generic drugs be used in all purchasing proposals and contracts. Industry sources estimate that the market for these products should increase by 40 per cent over the next two years.

Table 7.4: World pharmaceutical market growth by region, 1999–2003

Region	Compound annual growth rate (%)
North America	8.6
Europe	5.3
Japan	–0.2
Latin America	7.2
Southeast Asia and China	11.1
Eastern Europe	9.4
Middle East	10.4
Africa	3.2
Indian sub-continent	7.9
Australasia	9.2
CIS	6.1
Total world market	6.6

Source: IMS Health Global Services Forecasts.

not previously be sold in supermarkets, assisted the industry in overcoming those obstacles, with a resulting expansion of the production of generics in Brazil.

As estimated by the IMS, generics, along with patented products, will be increasingly responsible for expanding markets in the pharmaceutical sector over the next three years. Regions that are particularly fast-growing in combined generics and patented products are Southeast Asia, including China, at 11 per cent; the Middle East, at 10 per cent; and North America, at nine per cent (see Table 7.4).

Sales growth in seven key Latin American pharmaceutical markets (Mexico, Venezuela, Peru, Colombia, Brazil, Chile, Argentina) is estimated to be at a compound average rate of 7.8 per cent in constant dollars for the five years to 2005 (see Table 7.5). Sales in Mexico and Venezuela grew at a compound average rate of 5.6 per cent between 1995 and 2000. Total pharmaceutical sales in the seven Latin American countries featured in the IMS Health *Pharma-Prognosis* to 2005 are expected to exceed $29.6 billion in 2005, up more than 45 per cent from the $20.4 billion in sales recorded in 2000. Mexico is the most dynamic pharmaceutical market in Latin America, with a 13 per cent annual growth rate forecast to 2005. The IMS expects sales in Mexico to reach $11 billion annually by 2005, when Mexico will account for more than 37 per cent of total Latin American sales and supplant Brazil as the region's top market. The IMS forecasts a 11 per cent annual growth rate in Venezuela, which is expected to account for an estimated $2.5 billion in annual pharmaceutical sales and 8.4 per cent of the total Latin American market by 2005. Sales in Brazil, whose market share declined from 44 per cent in 1995 to 33 per cent in 1999 owing to economic conditions there and to the strong performance of Mexico and Venezuela, are

Table 7.5: Projected Latin American pharmaceuticals sales and growth rates to 2005

Country	Projected annual sales, 2005 ($bn)	Projected compound annual growth rate, 2000–5 (%)	Projected regional market share, 2005 (%)
Mexico	11.0	13.0	37.4
Venezuela	2.5	11.0	8.4
Peru	0.5	7.0	1.8
Colombia	1.7	6.0	5.8
Brazil	8.4	5.0	28.4
Chile	0.9	4.0	2.9
Argentina	4.5	4.0	15.3
Total	29.6	7.8	100.0

Source: IMS Health, *Pharma-Prognosis Latin America, 2001–2005.*

forecast to grow by five per cent a year during this period. Robust annual growth for Peru and Colombia of seven per cent and six per cent respectively is expected. Pharmaceuticals in both Chile and Argentina are predicted to grow by four per cent annually to 2005. Argentina is projected to have a 15.3 per cent regional market share in 2005, down from its 18.4 per cent market share in 1995–2000, as shown in Table 7.5.

PHARMACEUTICAL PRODUCTION AND IP PROTECTION

It is important to note that where off-patent production of drugs is the mainstay of the industry, property rights laws, however strong, may not have much overall effect.[21] The importance of property rights is usually held to be in setting conditions favourable for research-based production, where much of the profit lies. However, a lengthy period of development of generics may make property rights difficult to implement, even where they are protected. Those countries with strong property rights in the past two decades are those that have achieved the most benefit from IP protection.

---

[21] Stiglitz (1999), pp. 314–15: 'The stance sometimes taken by producers of knowledge, that we need "strong" intellectual property rights, masks this underlying debate. Strong, in this context, becomes equivalent to "good", with the implication that the "stronger" the better. But [...] stronger, in the sense of "tighter" protection, could not only have large distributive consequences (between, say, developed countries and less developed countries) but also large efficiency consequences, with the pace of innovation actually impeded and living standards in less developed countries diminished.'

The introduction of patent protection, for example, has had a striking effect on the Italian industry. Strong patent protection, beginning in 1978, led to the quadrupling of investment in local pharmaceutical R&D. In Canada, patent protection was recently under pressure from the World Trade Organization (WTO). When it was strengthened, investment in R&D grew dramatically, from 2.7 per cent of pharmaceutical sales in 1979 to 15.7 per cent by 1997 according to the Pharmaceutical Manufacturers Association of Canada. Although Canada still fails to provide an effective period of exclusivity for the commercially valuable and confidential clinical test data generated for gaining approval to market pharmaceutical products, legal reforms have brought its generic products into compliance after a ruling by a WTO panel that its manufactures prior to patent expiration violated the TRIPS Agreement.

Of the larger emerging markets, Korea and Mexico introduced strong patent protection in the early 1990s and experienced significant increases in R&D. Brazil enacted strong intellectual property protection for pharmaceuticals in May 1996, and since then it has become a major recipient of multinational investment and domestic development.[22] However, new petitions for exclusions suggest that the enforcement of IP protection in Brazil may be difficult.

Emerging-market countries that lack strong patent protection are numerous. On the whole, those countries without IP protection are less developed in pharmaceuticals. But there are exceptions. India adopted a patent law in 1970, but it disallowed product patents and permitted only seven years of process patent protection from the date of filing or five years from the date of granting a patent (by comparison with 16–20 years from the date of filing in Europe and 17 years from the date of granting a patent in the United States).[23] Indian regulations are in conflict with the TRIPS Agreement, whose patent term is 20 years from the time of filing and a period of exclusivity for the confidential and commercially valuable clinical data generated in the course of research and development of pharmaceutical products.[24] Argentina has implemented only very weak product-patent protection, and only in 2000 through a new industrial property law that does not meet many TRIPS standards. It has a case before the WTO. Egypt recognizes its TRIPS requirements in the areas of exclusive marketing rights and data exclusivity, but it also has approved marketing applications for illegal copies of the patented products of foreign companies and generally has failed to meet minimum international standards for protection of intellectual property for pharmaceutical products. Hungary has never had effective data protection, and remains in violation of TRIPS requirements; it acknowledges its obligations but fails to meet them. Israel has disregarded intellectual property protection of

---

[22] PhRMA International (2001).
[23] Acharya (1999), pp. 87–8.
[24] PhRMA International (2001).

THE GENERICS DEVELOPMENT TRAJECTORY   147

pharmaceutical products by curtailing the effective patent term, limiting exclusive rights for patent-holders and allowing parallel importation. In Taiwan, the 1993 patent law failed to provide a WTO-consistent 20-year term for all patents, curtailing by five years patent terms for applications filed before 1994. China's 'administrative protective' regime for pharmaceutical products, part of its pending TRIPS obligations, are unenforceable; the counterfeiting of pharmaceutical products is so widespread that it poses a serious public health threat.

We shall now focus more closely on just three of these countries, to distinguish the course of recent developments that, despite the lack of adequate patent protection, give some sense of the importance of the as yet not well-identified learning processes.

India

Pharmaceuticals development in India has taken place under a protective regime whose purposes are to provide low-cost health care and to encourage innovation in the industry. Thus there is *de facto* minimal patent protection and, in addition, a cap on royalties from bulk sales – four per cent of the sales price, in contrast to the 30–45 per cent maximum imposed in Europe. The result has been a significant increase in the number of large and small firms and substantial domestic production. India became a net exporter in 1979, and is now the fourth-largest exporter of bulk pharmaceutical products worldwide. India has a natural advantage in its large pool of low-cost skilled professionals and an abundance of low-priced chemical raw materials, making the cost of setting up a plant as much as 40 per cent lower than in the developed countries and bringing down the comparative cost of bulk drug production by 60 per cent. The high annual growth of the production of pharmaceuticals and of exports reached 14.6 per cent and 16 per cent respectively between 1998 and 2001.[25] Larger firms attained success in imitating patented products and processes, and small service-oriented firms multiplied and acquired experience in exports. To be sure, another result has been low levels of R&D in comparison with the industry in advanced countries: India conducts only 0.001 per cent of global pharmaceutical research, but this is not a negligible figure for a developing country.

Brazil[26]

Brazil is the most industrialized economy in Latin America. In 1998, it was the eighth-largest GDP in the world and the sixth-largest market for pharma-

---

[25] Confederation of Indian Industry (July 2000; Sept 2001).
[26] See also Chapter 9 by Bermudez in this volume.

Table 7.6: Brazilian pharmaceuticals – market, production and trade ($bn)

	1997	1998	1999*	2000*
Total market size	12.7	10.3	11.0	11.5
Local production	11.6	9.5	10.0	10.3
Imports	1.2	1.0	1.3	1.5
Exports	0.1	0.2	0.3	0.3
Imports from the United States	0.2	0.2	0.2	0.2

*Estimate.
Sources: SECEX (Brazilian Government Statistics) and ABIFARMA (Brazilian Association of Pharmaceutical Industries).

ceutical products, representing three per cent of total sales worldwide. Much as in India, pharmaceuticals grew up in a protective environment. The non-patentability of pharmaceutical products was designed initially to promote public health, but it became a means of protecting local industry. Until 1992, prices were allowed to increase only at a rate below inflation. After 1992, the regime 'loosened' to a state characterized by the World Health Organization as 'monitored freedom', with voluntary price controls arranged between the government and the pharmaceutical industry. The market for generic products is growing in Brazil, especially after the passing of the Generics Law in January 1999, which resulted in a 40 to 45 per cent reduction of pharmaceutical prices. There has been a policy trend favouring the manufacturers of generic drugs: the generic name is required on all product packs; prescriptions must be written by generic name; and generic drugs must be used in all purchasing proposals and contracts. One problem is the lack of access of at least 40 per cent of the population to needed pharmaceutical drugs. The generic drug programme is designed to avoid the unfortunate trade-off between the promotion of innovation and of public health. The data in Table 7.6 show that the impact of the new patent laws has not shrunk domestic production or damaged exports of Brazilian pharmaceuticals.

China

By extensive regulation and protection, China too has become a large producer, generating almost 40 per cent of Southeast Asian pharmaceuticals sales. The incentive for government intervention is the same as elsewhere in the developing world: the urgent price–cost problem whereby pharmaceuticals account for an estimated 60 per cent of all health care-related costs in China (compared to 8 per cent and 12 per cent in the United States and Germany respectively). More than 50 per cent of this cost is directly related to expensive foreign-produced drugs.[27] The Chinese government has instituted reforms, including price caps, and passed strict marketing and advertisement laws. State-owned enterprises, selling primarily generic drugs, have been reorganized so as to be more competitive with foreign companies. China's support of patents generally conforms to TRIPS requirements. However, the registration of foreign-produced drugs takes roughly two years, while domestic drugs are not subject to the same approval process. For all these reasons, sales of foreign-produced drugs have stagnated.

The reason why the lack of adequate IP protection has not stopped China from becoming a major producer and recipient of foreign investment and technology is probably unique to China. Foreign multinationals are able to market their products through former health care professionals (doctors, pharmacists) by directly approaching hospitals, pharmacies and wholesalers and consumer distribution companies. Funded by drug sales, hospitals have an incentive to sell Western-produced products. The opening of the OTC market has been another factor encouraging foreign investment to continue. Most of the world's largest pharmaceutical producers have an established presence in China; they claim that this investment leads to better relationships with the bureaucracy responsible for the sale of pharmaceuticals in China.[28]

In summary, the experience of these three major producers suggests that despite the disadvantages of protectionist laws and weakly enforced patent laws, particular environments, characterized by sales of foreign brand products, can be attractive to investors for region-specific factors. And even where such factors inhibit high levels of investment, there is sufficient low-level spillover of knowledge from the multinationals to ensure the hardy growth of pharmaceuticals, as Table 7.7 shows.

THE LEARNING AND FEEDBACK MECHANISMS IN PHARMACEUTICAL PRODUCTION AND TRADE

Pharmaceuticals are thus demonstrably an area of production in which developing countries can become competitive in value-added manufacturing and derive some benefit through experience in export markets, even without research-based production. In contrast to older models, based on price and cost factors in export markets, industrial competitiveness is now based on export potential for high-technology products. This kind of competitiveness does not depend on labour costs, which have greatly declined as a value-added factor in manufacturing.

[27] Quinn (1998).
[28] Ibid.

Table 7.7: Selected emerging markets and developing countries: net trade balance ($000), 1993–8

Origin/destination	1993	1994	1995	1996	1997	1998	Average annual percentage rate of growth of trade balance 1993–8
World	7,566,953	8,674,908	10,081,710	11,030,102	13,668,828	15,437,626	6
G7	-187,859	19,985	-44,421	-866,959	-49,849	1,229,336	2
OPEC	1,486,285	1,524,884	1,688,629	1,449,999	1,699,039	1,869,929	6
CIS	404,728	490,024	533,323	711,302	996,586	770,952	9
MERCOSUR	339,126	488,056	591,735	722,771	892,312	932,644	9
ASEAN	495,030	571,140	703,632	793,521	923,520	711,108	3
OECD	844,171	1,174,013	1,092,732	1,457,839	3,224,459	4,747,448	15
NAFTA	29,558	371,213	623,767	22,803	929,691	2,304,111	38
Korea	122,843	156,887	165,915	191,692	194,454	167,624	3
Czech Republic	123,171	215,756	283,036	340,884	373,378	422,724	11
Hungary	176,155	226,379	267,519	265,625	299,976	357,614	6
Poland	347,202	396,109	540,044	638,014	772,842	895,334	8
Turkey	193,556	192,089	309,726	363,286	469,492	562,515	9
Russian Federation	257,404	376,305	378,738	557,751	746,442	566,910	7
Slovak Republic	24,937	45,967	82,857	101,533	118,609	128,420	14
Slovenia	47,926	57,149	72,897	78,481	87,328	109,669	7
Other Former Yugoslavia	28,719	53,365	85,497	95,523	97,268	120,988	12
Baltic states	15,099	29,794	60,949	95,745	137,186	165,072	21
Algeria	320,097	448,353	451,020	229,930	348,297	458,631	3
Egypt	120,759	145,072	178,732	182,587	215,266	262,919	7
South Africa	198,411	250,789	303,798	331,915	403,419	409,444	6
Colombia	53,036	79,111	94,354	102,083	117,505	137,988	8
Brazil	166,024	282,795	371,109	478,135	589,428	562,431	11
Argentina	146,133	176,743	184,908	209,431	245,940	298,420	6
Saudi Arabia	527,964	467,584	467,102	497,565	539,271	571,490	1
India	42,286	63,553	50,460	66,422	110,534	135,828	10
Singapore	101,563	116,209	131,502	172,835	199,194	174,388	5
China	-70,453	-112,180	-119,555	-28,126	-79,282	-148,601	-6
Taipei	163,950	183,395	203,998	245,926	267,425	292,542	5

Source: OECD, *Foreign Trade by Commodities 1993–1998*, Vol. 5, p. 354.

The critical component is quality standards. In the past, competitiveness in developing countries was restricted to a narrow range of non-traded goods. Now developing countries must trade in more goods and compete in a world where high technology is the main basis for competitiveness. Product life cycles are short, sometimes no longer than three years, and the demand for commodity exports is falling. In the area of pharmaceuticals, developing countries are adapting to these requirements in global trade with particular success because universalized standards are effectively diffused via collaborative global research in drugs, are accessible through university research and are widely shared between countries.

The diversity of pharmaceutical exports, stimulated by large demand in the 1990s, provides an incentive for adaptive learning. Countries taking advantage of the demand for diversity achieve tangible growth of output as well as of export earnings. The literature notes the rise of non-traditional exports of all kinds, for example the garment industry in Bangladesh, fish processing in East Africa or the expansion of tourism, the most important service export of developing countries. To this group of products can be added most developing countries' universities, where classical education in chemistry provides sufficient basis for the growth of some expertise in the imitative production of pharmaceuticals, and thus competitiveness in the production of high-value products.

Developing countries generate pharmaceutical exports from their markets for fine chemicals. In 1991, 44 per cent of the application areas for fine chemicals was for pharmaceuticals. The drugs industry tends to produce its own fine chemicals; the largest drugs companies are also dominant in fine chemicals production. The growing interest in substituting cheap generic drugs for their branded equivalents after medicines are off-patent will not only make certain common analgesics and heart medicines more available at lower cost but also require the production in large volume of fine chemicals as specific intermediates used in the final product.[29]

The production of generic drugs based on off-patent products requires little investment in R&D.[30] For developing countries, the technical part of the process will lie in the imitation or development of known technologies that are widely available in scientific digital databases or from networked science.[31] It is well known that imitation can be of advantage in development, as in Japan and East Asia. (However, the degree of advantage is a matter of guesswork. The empirical research that would be required for further generalization has not been done.[32]) The advantage is that the feedback provided from the first imitative steps may be powerful. It is clear that in the developing countries, there is

[29] Ibid., p. 188.
[30] Barro and Sala-i-Martin (1995).
[31] Caselli and Coleman (2001).
[32] Coe, Helpman and Hoffmaister (1997).

not only imitative work but also some considerable advancement of R&D-based pharmaceuticals.[33]

The technologies used in distributing and sharing knowledge about pharmaceutical production are inherently the same as those used to advance corporate management across the sector, and they have spillovers into health management and resource development. These technologies are:

1. computer-aided design and computer-aided manufacturing, to generate flexibility in response to changing design requirements and production tasks;
2. information and communications technologies for finance and accounting, personnel and marketing, which have solid benefits for efficiency;
3. quality management, to aid firms in gaining contracts with developed countries; and
4. biotechnology, with implications for health and waste management and for the substitution of engineered for more expensive natural products.[34]

Firms that gain experience in pharmaceuticals, in which sector innovation and cost savings depend upon updated information, acquire skills in maintaining technology partnerships, strategic alliances and acquisitions. An important informal benefit is the mobility of scientists and engineers, who participate in international trade or communicate at conferences and social meetings.[35] Technology transfer in pharmaceuticals has, in other words, too often been limited in scholarly discussion to R&D-based industrial development. The rapid development of new products, generic or patented, can be viewed as a consequence of knowledge transfer, and it is certainly a demonstration of local learning in the developing world.

In Third World countries, rarely are resources available for integrating all phases of process and production development in pharmaceuticals. Depending upon the kind of IP regime and health policy in those countries, domestic production may move in a more or less research-oriented direction, and in all likelihood will specialize in the imitative production of generic drugs. It is important to underscore, however, that even this kind of technology transfer via digitalized resources will improve the efficiency of drug supplies in developing countries and thus benefit doctor, patient and development itself, as Wartensieben has observed:

> Any reduction of outright losses and/or extra costs incurred in a poorly operated system would immediately make more resources available both for health in general and for drug procurement in particular, whether domestically or by way of imports. In the long run, strengthening the pharmaceutical sector in

---

[33] Barba Navaretti and Carraro (1996), p. 239; Barba Navaretti and Carraro (1999).
[34] UNIDO (1993/1994), p. 240.
[35] Deeds, Decarolis and Coombs (2000).

developing countries at increasing levels of employment, productivity and income connected with the industrial and technological capacity opens up promising new dimensions for both public and private commercial intercountry cooperation, independently of whether drug supplies in developing countries follow more or less centralised organizational schemes.[36]

Learning as an economic good is not easily measurable. Most measurements are of capacity for learning, and thus are indirect. Inputs to learning are gauged by years of schooling, outputs by various indicators of innovation, including the composition of exports and R&D (university research and patents).[37] Because knowledge is a public good, with the use of it non-rivalrous,[38] it is also generally a non-excludable good, in that preventing its unauthorized use is difficult. In the drugs industry, patent protection has been the focus of much international and national policy discussion as virtually the only way to ensure the viability of the pharmaceuticals industry. In the industry, however, patent laws can be difficult to enforce. That IP is difficult to enforce is both a stimulus to production and a source of spillovers from advanced to less advanced countries. Moreover, it is the cause of regulatory responses, which also affect the production and consumption costs of drugs.

The stock of knowledge has to be increased continuously for productivity growth to be self-sustaining.[39] Developing countries tend to 'imitate' imported technologies, at least initially, rather than develop their own R&D-based industry.[40] The best-known mechanisms for information spillovers and technology transfer between developed and developing countries are foreign direct investment through multinationals, which transfer staff, equipment and communications networks from the home firm to the locally based affiliate, and learning in outward processing industries.[41] But the stock of knowledge accumulates too through all kinds of cross-border acquisitions and mergers and collaborative alliances in R&D. Thus, although pharmaceutical R&D remains highly centralized in the advanced countries, the joining of large firms with small biotechnology firms through risk- and cost-sharing and the expansion of markets is productive for both sides. The large companies recover R&D expenditure, and in the developing world the small innovative firms import intermediary goods and the pharmaceutical service-deliverers and generics-producers also benefit. Tarabusi and Vickery explain how critical local services and production are in this process:

[36] Wartensieben (1983), p. 170.
[37] Barba Navaretti and Tarr (2000).
[38] Arrow (1962).
[39] Romer (1990), 258.
[40] Caselli, Esquivel and Lefort (1996) and Klenow and Rodrigues (1997).
[41] Eichengreen and Kohl (1998).

International trade is not as important as in many other industries, reflecting the multi-country pattern of globalisation, high penetration of foreign firms, and the necessity to produce finished products in final markets. Intermediates make up a fairly high share of pharmaceutical trade (40 per cent), as international firms ship active ingredients for formulation in final markets, but overall the ratio of imported to domestic sourcing is still lower than for many other industries, reflecting strategies and requirements to produce locally.[42]

The incentives for international collaboration and learning are powerful at both ends: shorter product life cycles, cost-containment pressures and the need for diverse research skills and knowledge dictate cost-sharing. Multinationals form strategic alliances, whose number grew from 121 in 1986 to 712 in 1998.[43] Collaboration at the international level involves small and large companies, biotechnology firms, university research centres and contract research organizations. Strategic alliances allow companies to bring products to market more rapidly and to market drugs more effectively and quickly between licensing and patent expiry. For example, to gain venture capital, experience in dealing with regulations or reputation, a small biotechnology firm may form a strategic alliance with a larger pharmaceuticals company in order to develop a drug, while another specialized firm advertises and markets in an ever-expanding global community. Their experience underscores intra-sectoral spillovers from networked knowledge groups.[44]

Within industries and across entire economies, the contribution of knowledge-based production or research-based innovation enhances local activity.[45] The gradual expansion of pharmaceutical production from the 1930s to the 1950s began with highly specialized, integrated manufacturing firms drawing mainly on their own R&D rather than on outside research. But there are now pressures, because of the diversity required for continuous innovation, for offshoots of parent companies to spread in new urban markets across the developing world,

---

[42] Tarabusi and Vickery (1997), p. 71.
[43] See Deeds and Hill (1996); Della Valle and Gambardella (1993); Nightingale (1999); Grabowski and Vernon (1990).
[44] PhRMA International (2001).
[45] In the environment of revolutionary health discoveries, incentives exist for spillovers from scientists to consumers, who thus affect the spread of that scientific knowledge. From 71 interviews conducted with representatives of the media, specialist medical societies, special consumer interest groups, the Australian Red Cross Blood Service (ARCBS), government, private health insurers, technology manufacturers, prominent clinicians in the area and a sample of clinicians drawn from hospitals with variable use of blood-saving technologies, Treloar et al. (2001) identified the source of technical advances. The main influence on the decrease in the use of allogeneic blood transfusion in the past decade, for example, was 'enthusiasts', i.e. consumers (doctors or others), who became involved in educating, negotiating, finding new resources for and maintaining the use of a technology (Treloar et al. 2001).

and thus learning effects are increasingly rapid as the industry becomes more diversified and localized.

To be sure, the capacity for learning and using transferred technology or information depends upon local regulations and the elasticity of domestic demand for new drugs. In pharmaceutical markets the two kinds of competitive structure – branded substitutes, which typically have unique chemical compounds as well as patent protection, and generic versions of new and existing products – have entirely different pricing and demand conditions. For branded competitors, the differentiated products initially face inelastic demand owing to the power of physicians to influence choice of product and to the impact of patent protection. Once a firm registers a patent for a new product, it has the exclusive right to market the product anywhere. Because of the small number of firms in the industry, an R&D-based firm exercises power over the production of specific products and prices as a monopoly supplier until the expiry of the patent. Patent expiry promises future returns, and intellectual property rights do not allow the spread of information about products, including their composition and testing, whatever the regulatory regime.

With increasing competition after the expiry of patents, demand is more elastic and opportunities for developing countries are large. For off-patent brand and generic drugs, then, the competition is entirely price-based. In the year of a patent's expiry, for example, a branded drug's sales may fall by up to 20 per cent while its price remains high or even increases, and the product's life cycle may soon end. This will have a particular effect on development in that it provides opportunities for new entrants with generic products even as profit margins shrink.[46] With the patent expiries of the 1980s and those of two of the best-selling brand drugs in 2002, generics markets will maintain a powerful expansionary momentum.[47]

CONCLUSION

This chapter has examined the synergy between characteristics of pharmaceutical production, process development and marketing strategies, and the needs of the developing world. This synergy enhances the possibility of increased domestic production of pharmaceuticals, primarily generics. This has obvious benefits for health when countries take measures to control costs; and although these measures are a barrier to investment, the unique conditions of some emerging markets, such as China, can retain foreign interest and investment.

---

[46] Caves, Whinston and Hurwitz (1991); Lu and Comanor (1998), p. 110.
[47] See Chapter 3 by Maskus and Ganslandt in this volume for a discussion on demand elasticity in the context of parallel trade and differentiated prices.

Neither trade liberalization nor TRIPS requirements are likely to suppress the spread of research and innovation and of generics production, which are a result of knowledge distribution and spillovers as well as property rights protection. The factor most responsible for enabling and encouraging information spillovers by multinationals is their cooperation in domestic and export markets with local producers, who are in contact with local researchers. Collaboration is effective in every phase of the complex process development and marketing and for every kind of firm in the marketing of brand and generic products. Communication steadily improves among researchers of different countries and research environments.[48] From their research on Mulford, Sharp & Dohme and Merck, Galambos and Sturchio have shown that although large multinational firms are highly competitive in the development of serum antitoxins and vaccines, their scientists collaborate with government researchers and local officials, with university scientists and, at times, with other pharmaceutical firms. Not only are spillovers unavoidable, they are desirable. Firms that were successful as innovators maintained close links among industry, academe and government.

Another factor promoting the spread of the pharmaceutical industry and the diversity of its firms in the 1980s was the generic sector itself, despite its early negative impact on innovation in developing countries. An example can be drawn from Canada. Prior to 1993, compulsory licensing of brand-name pharmaceuticals allowed generic producers to copy and sell drugs still under patent in return for a royalty fee, generally set at four per cent of sales. At the provincial level, the government encouraged substitution of lower-priced drugs, usually generics. In 1996, the generic sector accounted for 39.8 per cent of the total number of prescriptions filled in Canada and 17.4 per cent of their value.

Generic production may also have the indirect effect of helping to foster research on tropical diseases. The usual view of IP is that it discourages the search for drug treatments that are most needed in the area of tropical diseases because most of the resources for drugs research are located in the developing world, where tropical diseases are not of major concern. However, Lanjouw and Cockburn have found that it is probably too early for more than a preliminary judgment, that TRIPS, concluded in 1995, did not decrease research on malaria and that research on other tropical diseases has increased.[49] With greater diversity in drugs production in the developing world, opportunities for research and applications through collaboration between countries remain important. But the lack of a market for high-priced treatments may still influence research decisions, even in the developing world.[50] For example, it is commonly feared that once India is fully TRIPS-compliant on patent protection and its

[48] Galambos and Sturchio (1997).
[49] Lanjouw and Cockburn (2001).
[50] Government of the UK, Performance and Innovation Unit (2001), Annex 3, p. 27.

pharmaceutical industry is more R&D-based, research will be diverted towards developed-world diseases, such as heart disease and obesity, for which there is a guaranteed and profitable market, and away from more urgent research on anti-infectives. Indeed, only about 10 per cent of global pharmaceutical R&D activity actually focuses on the 'diseases of poverty'. The challenge of the research, the uncertain prospects of success and the long timescale required for developing effective new products, combined with the absence of effective markets, are expected to discourage innovative research where it is especially needed. This chapter argues, however, that this pessimistic conclusion for the future may not be borne out.

In the early 1980s, when the drugs question became a vital public health issue in the developing world, ways were sought to reduce the cost of imported drugs and to increase the local production of pharmaceuticals.[51] There is a substantial literature attesting to the tendency of manufacturing performance to improve with cumulative production experience,[52] and the evidence is overwhelming that learning by doing is required in productivity improvement. Learning by doing is a self-sustaining process which may lead naturally from imitative and generic production of pharmaceuticals to the development of a capacity for innovation or at least to diversification. The incentives for this development come from a number of sources: collaborative research, experience in export markets, the ease of entry of a variety of firm types and progress from imitation to innovation – and not only from fully adequate IP protection, which is difficult to achieve in developing countries.

This conclusion does not imply that intellectual property protection policies for developing countries should be based on those of India and China, or Israel. It suggests that although IP protection is important for R&D development in pharmaceuticals, it is increasingly not the only means for assisting the spread of pharmaceutical companies and some of the more profit-making research in emerging markets. The changing dynamics of the pharmaceutical industry should be considered carefully in applying policy. Where adequate enforcement of IPRs is inconceivable, policies can focus on relaxing restrictions on generics, assistance that concentrates on learning capacity in firms, and especially on communications facilities for local university chemists.

As noted above, the knowledge and skills required for the development of new drugs could be found, at least until very recently, in the classical education of chemists, which is part of research education across the developing world. To be sure, where, as in high-income countries, public expenditure on education is higher (5.4 per cent of GDP in 1997), the number of skilled chemists is larger.

---

[51] Patel (1983), p. 165.
[52] Pisano (1996); Stobaugh and Townsend (1975); Adler and Clark (1991).

In middle-income countries, spending reached 4.8 per cent of GDP, but in low-income countries it averaged only 3.3 per cent.[53] India ranks even lower than sub-Saharan Africa in the level of government expenditure on education, but is marginally higher in this category than other Asian countries. Although this has not stopped India from becoming a major domestic producer of pharmaceuticals, it may have a bearing, along with the lack of patent protection, on the relatively low level of R&D investment as a percentage of sales.[54]

The main cause of the spread of pharmaceutical production in most of the developing world will remain multinational corporate investment. Many multinationals now have generic divisions or close ties with generic companies. Generic companies in the developing countries can make arrangements with multinationals that take advantage of the former's local distribution capabilities. In reducing barriers to such collaboration, TRIPS will help to spread pharmaceutical production of all kinds further into developing regions, especially Latin America and Asia. For 10 years, the United States, Europe and Japan have coordinated the International Conference on Harmonization, to modify and harmonize requirements for drug development and approval. In 1997, the United States and the European Union negotiated the pharmaceutical Mutual Recognition Agreement (MRA), whose intentions are to eliminate regulatory barriers and to promote trade between the two regions. Once the MRA is fully implemented, each region will recognize the other's inspections of manufacturing facilities for human drugs and biologics in its own region. This sort of collaboration should speed up the clinical and administrative phases of drug development and reduce costs, which are the main barrier to entry into this lucrative field. This benefit may, in turn, assist entry by firms from developing countries.

REFERENCES

Acharya, R. (1999), 'Bio-Pharmaceuticals in Chinese Taipei and India', in L.K Mytelka (ed.), *Competition, Innovation and Competitiveness in Developing Countries* (Paris: OECD), 77–114.
Adler, P. and K. Clark (1991), 'Behind the Learning Curve', *Management Science*, 37, 267–81.
Arrow, K. J. (1962), 'The Implications of Learning by Doing', *Review of Economic Studies*, 29, 155–73.
Ballance, R., J. Pogány and H. Forstner (1992), *The World's Pharmaceutical Industries: An International Perspective on Innovation, Competition and Policy* (Cheltenham: Edward Elgar).
Barba Navaretti, G., and C. Carraro (1996), 'From Learning to Partnership: Multinational R&D Cooperation in Developing Countries' (Milan: Fondazione Eni Enrico Mattei and Centro Studi Luca d'Agliano).

---

[53] World Bank (2001), Table 6, p. 285.
[54] However, Acharya (1999) points out that the approximately 1.5 per cent of sales invested in R&D by Indian companies, although much lower than the average of 15.8 per cent by multinationals globally, is well above the norm for developing countries (p. 88).

Barba Navaretti, G. and C. Carraro (1999), 'From Learning to Partnership: Multinational R&D Cooperation in Developing Countries', *Economics of Innovation and New Technologies*, 8, 137–73.
Barba Navaretti, G. and D.G. Tarr (2000), 'International Knowledge Flows and Economic Performance: A Review of the Evidence', *The World Bank Review*, 14, 1–15.
Barro, R. and X. Sala-i-Martin (1995), *Economic Growth* (New York: McGraw-Hill).
Beesley, M. E. (1997), 'Schumpeter and UK Pharmaceuticals', in M.E. Beesley (ed.), *Privatization, Regulation and Deregulation* (London: Routledge), 452–88.
Caselli, F. and W. J. Coleman II (2001), 'Cross-Country Technology Diffusion: The Case of Computers', *The American Economic Review*, 91, 328–35.
Caselli, F., G. Esquivel and F. Lefort (1996), 'Reopening the Convergence Debate: A New Look at Cross Country Growth Empirics', *Journal of Economic Growth*, 1, 366–89.
Caves, R. E., M. D. Whinston and M. A. Hurwitz (1991), 'Patent Expiration, Entry, and Competition in the United States Pharmaceutical Industry' (Washington, DC: Brookings Institution), 1–48.
Coe, D., E. Helpman and W. Hoffmaister (1997), 'North South R&D Spillovers', *The Economic Journal*, 107, 134–149.
Confederation of Indian Industry (July 2000, September 2001), Press Releases, http://www.ciionline.org/index.html.
Deeds, D. L., D. Decarolis and J. Coombs (2000), 'Dynamic Capabilities and New Product Development in High Technology Ventures', *Journal of Business Venturing*, 15, 211–29.
Deeds, D. L. and C. W. L. Hill (1996), 'Strategic Alliances, Complementary Assets and New Product Development: An Empirical Study of Entrepreneurial Biotechnology Firms', *Journal of Business Venturing*, 11, 41–55.
Della Valle, F. and A. Gambardella (1993), 'Biological Revolution and Strategies for Innovation in Pharmaceutical Companies', *R&D Management*, 23, 287–302.
Eichengreen, B. and R. Kohl (1998), *The External Sector, The State and Development in Eastern Europe* (London: Centre for Economic Policy Research).
Frank, R. G. and D. S. Salkever (1995), 'Generic Entry and the Pricing of Pharmaceuticals' (Cambridge, MA: National Bureau of Economic Research).
Galambos, L. and J. L. Sturchio (1997), 'The Transformation of the Pharmaceutical Industry in the Twentieth Century', in J. Krige and D. Pestre (eds), *Science in the Twentieth Century* (Paris, France: Harwood Academic Publishers), 227–52.
Gambardella, A. (1995), *Science and Innovation: The United States Pharmaceutical Industry during the 1980s* (Cambridge: Cambridge University Press).
Government of the UK Performance and Innovation Unit (2001), 'Tackling the Diseases of Poverty, Meeting the Okinawa Millennium Targets for HIV/AIDS, Tuberculosis and Malaria' (London: Cabinet Office, Performance and Innovation Unit).
Grabowski, H. and J. Vernon (1990), 'A New Look at the Returns and Risks to Pharmaceuticals R&D', *Management Science*, 36, 804–21.
Klenow, P. and A. Rodrigues (1997), 'The Neo-Classical Revival in Growth Economics: Has It Gone Too Far?' in B. Bernanke and J. Rosenberg (eds), *Macroeconomics Annual* (Cambridge: MIT Press), 73–102.
Lanjouw, J. O. and I. Cockburn (2001), 'New Pills for Poor People? Empirical Evidence after GATT', *World Development*, 29 (2), 265–89.
Lu, Z. J. and W. S. Comanor (1998), 'Strategic Pricing of New Pharmaceuticals', *Review of Economics and Statistics*, 80, 108–18.
Mytelka, L. K. (1999), *Competition, Innovation and Competitiveness in Developing Countries* (Paris: OECD).
Nightingale, P. (1999), 'Knowledge Management in the Changing Pharmaceutical Innovation Process', paper at conference on 'Global Knowledge Partnerships: Creating Value for the 21st Century', Austin, TX.

Patel, S. J. (1983), 'Editor's Introduction: Pharmaceuticals and Health in the Third World', *World Development*, 11, 165–67.
Philing, D. (2000), 'Pharmacy in the 21st Century', International Pharmaceutical Federation.
PhRMA International (2001), 'The Pharmaceutical Industry Profile 2001', *http://www.phrma.org /publications/industrydata/*.
Pisano, G. P. (1996), 'Learning-Before-Doing in the Development of New Process Technology', *Research Policy*, 25, 1097–1119.
Quinn, B. M. (1998), 'China: Drugs and Pharmaceuticals', US & Foreign Commercial Service and US Department of State.
Romer, P. M. (1990), 'Endogenous technological change', *Journal of Political Economy* (October): S71–S102.
Saxenian, H. (1994), 'Getting the Most out of Pharmaceutical Expenditures', Human Resources Development and Operations Policy (HRO).
Spar, D. L. (1999), 'The Public Face of Cyberspace', in I. Kaul, I. Grunberg and M. A. Stern (eds), *Global Public Goods: International Cooperation in the Twenty-First Century* (New York and Oxford: Oxford University Press for the United Nations Development Programme), 344–62.
Stiglitz, J. (1999), 'Knowledge as a Public Good', in I. Kaul, I. Grunberg and M. A. Stern (eds), *Global Public Goods: International Cooperation in the Twenty-First Century* (New York/Oxford: Oxford University Press for the United Nations Development Programme), 308–25.
Stobaugh, R. and P. Townsend (1975), 'Price Forecasting and Strategic Planning: The Case of Petrochemicals', *Journal of Marketing Research*, 12, 19–29.
Tarabusi, C.-C., and G. Vickery (1997), 'Globalisation in the Pharmaceutical Industry', in *Globalisation of Industry: Overview and Sector Reports* (Paris: OECD), 69–108.
Treloar, C. J. et al. (2001), 'Factors Influencing the Uptake of Technologies to Minimize Perioperative Allogeneic Blood Transfusion: An Interview Study of National and Institutional Stakeholders', *Internal Medicine Journal*, 31 (7).
United Nations Industrial Development Organization (UNIDO) (various years), *Industrial Development: Global Report 1997* (Oxford: Oxford University Press).
Wartensieben, A. V. (1983), 'Major Issues Concerning Pharmaceutical Policies in the Third World', *World Development*, 11, 169–76.
World Bank (2001), *World Development Report 2000/2001: Attacking Poverty* (Washington, DC: World Bank).

8 THE DEVELOPMENT TRILEMMA AND THE SOUTH AFRICAN RESPONSE

W. Duncan Reekie

THE DEVELOPMENT TRILEMMA: PATENTS, PRICE DISCRIMINATION AND PARALLEL IMPORTS

There is a three-horned policy dilemma (or trilemma) underlying the supply of medicines to poorer markets. According to the *World Development Report*, 'intellectual property rights are important for encouraging innovation, particularly in such areas as medicine and agriculture. When creators of knowledge do not retain exclusive rights of ownership for a period of time, there is far less incentive to produce new knowledge.'[1] The problem then is that the presence of patents can hamper distribution of goods to poorer consumers who 'can seldom afford the prices charged by patent owners'.[2] So 'developing countries have responded ... by proposing safeguards [such as] ensuring of access to essential medicines at reasonable cost'.[3] But if this implies lower prices for poorer markets today it can, through arbitrage, translate into lower prices elsewhere and so less innovation for all markets tomorrow. Commissioner Lamy of the European Commission stated that then 'there must be barriers to re-export' to wealthier markets.[4]

Patents

Economic development requires the protection of private property and the application of the rule of law. As even these minimal requirements are lacking in many developing countries, perhaps it seems rather irrelevant to discuss the protection of intellectual property (IP). After all, if the average citizen is unable

---

This paper is drawn in part from J. Morris, R. Mowatt and W. D. Reekie, *Ideal Matter: Globalisation and the Intellectual Property Debate* (London: Institute of Economic Affairs, forthcoming).

[1] *World Development Report*, 2000/2001, p. 184.
[2] Idem.
[3] Ibid., p. 185.
[4] From a statement made by Commissioner Lamy at Brussels roundtable, 28 September 2000.

Table 8.1: Per capita GNP, R&D employment, technology exports and patents filed: international comparisons

Country	Per capita GNP ($) (1999)	R&D scientists and engineers per million people	High-technology exports as percentage manufacturing exports (1998)	Patents filed (1997)	
				Residents	Non-residents
Brazil	4,420	168	9	2,655*	31,947
India	450	149	5	10,155	6,632*
South Africa	3,160	1,031	9	n.a.	n.a.
United States	30,600	3,676	33	125,808	110,884

*For 1996.
Source: *World Development Report*, 2000–2001 (Washington, DC: World Bank, 2000).

to protect even his or her own land or to enforce contracts in a court of law, of what use is the hypothetical ability to protect intellectual property? Actually, it turns out to be of much use. A recent survey found that many inventors from developing countries patent their inventions in the United States. This suggests that there is considerable demand for patent protection in those countries. If they had a cheap and reliable system of patent protection, it seems reasonable to suppose that there would be more invention. The benefits for the wider community in developing countries would be twofold: a more vibrant local industry and products that are more relevant to the desires of the local people.

Moreover, better patent protection would encourage innovators from developed countries to engage in joint projects. Rather than surviving on the leftovers from the research and development (R&D) of developed countries and producing chemicals and pharmaceuticals invented by others, firms in developing countries would become not only inventors but also the legitimate partners of developed country inventors, engaging in complementary R&D.

Countries such as Brazil have in their hinterlands large numbers of as yet unscreened plants, vegetables and other sources of substances that may have therapeutic potential. There are stocks of untapped knowledge about some of these substances existing in the minds of 'traditional healers' and in oral folklore. But without incentives to capitalize on these assets, they may remain untapped or – particularly in the case of folk traditions – be lost altogether if the small, local and often tribal communities in which they are embedded become submerged in the larger, anonymous nation-state.

South Africa has a similar potential, along with large existing clinical research assets of both physical and human capital. Pharmaceutical firms have for decades carried out disproportionate amounts of clinical trial activity there. The country has a large tertiary medical sector and clinical access to both First World and Third World diseases. Yet another country with complementary R&D potential is India. Sharing some of the characteristics of Brazil and South Africa, it also has a large, sophisticated and well-developed manufacturing sector that could readily exploit chemical and pharmaceutical inventions and discoveries.

In sum, patent protection in developing countries would lead to a larger R&D-based local industry, which in turn would lead to economic growth. Table 8.1 provides some basic data comparing patents and technology in Brazil, South Africa and India with similar figures for the United States.

Critics argue that, as with intellectual property in developed countries, introducing stronger IP protection in developing countries is likely to lead to higher prices for the protected products. This concern is heightened by the importance of some of those products to people in developing countries, specifically the drugs used to combat deadly diseases such as malaria and AIDS. However, the reality is that if patent-holders are able to price-discriminate, they will be willing to sell those drugs at whatever price the buyers are willing to pay as long as their costs are covered. Moreover, as we know in general, without patent protection, potential inventors have less incentive to develop their ideas.

Price discrimination

What is this ability to price-discriminate? The word is technical, and has no pejorative meaning. It simply indicates that a product is being sold at different (non-marginal cost-related) prices. This can be justified on welfare grounds in that it enables a firm to appropriate to itself 'consumers' surplus' and thus increase producer profits. This is economically desirable where marginal production costs are very low (as in pharmaceuticals) or close to zero (as in providing for the crossing of a river on an already constructed bridge).

Consider Figure 8.1. DE represents the demand curve for a medicine. Assume zero marginal production cost. There are three different market segments with differing levels of willingness or ability to pay. These different segments each have the same volume potential, say a million units. The profit-maximizing price and output level for the firm is to sell 2Q units at £0.5 per unit. Sales and profits (as there are no costs) would be equal to the area ABCO. Provided this area exceeded the expected innovative costs of product development, the firm would conduct R&D and produce and sell the product as described. Consumers would also receive, 'free' as it were, welfare benefits equal to the consumers' surplus (triangle ABD).

There are two welfare defects in this situation, however. First, if the innovative costs exceed ABCO (i.e., £1 million) the product would not be

Figure 8.1: A simple price discrimination model

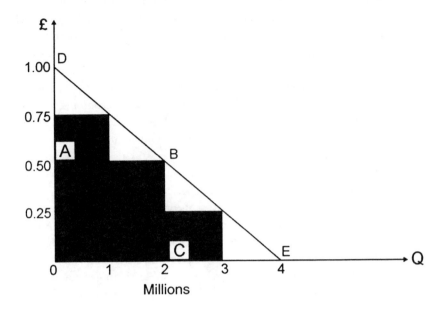

developed at all, despite the fact that at output level C total welfare (producer's revenue plus consumers' surplus) equals ODBC, i.e. £1.5 million. Second, total possible gross consumer welfare is not restricted to ODBC; it is equal to the whole area under the demand curve (ODE), i.e. £2 million. A single uniform price of £0.5 would result in a 'deadweight-loss' of BCE. But no firm would produce three million units to avoid this. To sell these extra units, the firm would have to reduce the price to £0.25, and it would realize an income of only £0.75 million.

The firm *would* invest up to £2 million in R&D, however, if it could practise price discrimination. This is because it would sell one million units to the least price-sensitive segment at £0.75, a similar number to the next segment at £0.5 and another one million units at £0.25 to the most price-conscious market. It would then earn revenues equal to the shaded area in the figure, a number approaching £2 million.

In short, price discrimination enables the firm to service people who otherwise could not afford to purchase. It enables it to expand its output beyond the physical level it would select if limited to choosing a uniform, profit-maximizing price; and as the discriminatory alternative is more profitable, it brings into the firm's realm of choice R&D projects that it would otherwise not consider.

The British Office of Fair Trading describes the process as follows:

> There are many areas of business where [price discrimination] is a usual and legitimate commercial practice. For example ... in industries where there are large fixed costs and low marginal costs (the cost of supplying each additional unit of output is very small compared to the initial investment to set up the business). In most markets undertakings are normally expected to set prices equal to their marginal cost but in industries with high fixed costs an undertaking which did so might never be able to recover its fixed costs. It may therefore be more efficient to set higher prices to customers with a higher willingness to pay. In general price discrimination will not be an abuse in such industries if it leads to higher levels of output than an undertaking could achieve by charging every customer the same price.[5]

Thus price discrimination benefits all. Poorer people less able or unable to pay the normal, uniform profit-maximizing price gain access to a product that they would not otherwise have. Today's medicines, for example, can be made available more cheaply. Producers reap greater profits, which give an incentive to engage in further research in order to develop tomorrow's medicines more quickly. And a portion of these additional profits comes from the better-off, who have the most obvious desire to purchase innovations (as indicated by their willingness to pay) and who tend (sometimes, but not always) to have altruistic feelings towards the poor and less privileged.

The ability to practise price discrimination depends, of course, on the preservation of market segments as distinct markets. This requires, in markets subject to innovation, the presence of a degree of monopoly protected by patent or other legal arrangements. In our simple example, with zero marginal costs the price would be driven to zero by competition in an unprotected environment. And it would be driven to zero in each segment. By extension, the ability to practise discriminatory pricing also depends on a lack of arbitrage or leakage between segments. A firm can charge different prices in the segments only if it is not possible for a third party to come along and buy cheap in one segment and sell dear in another (but at a lower price than the existing firm is currently charging).

The truth of the matter is that patent protection combined with price discrimination enables higher rates of economic development through the encouragement of an R&D-based industry as well as low prices for essential medicines. But the twist in the tail for developing countries attempting to achieve these dual benefits is the threat of parallel imports. Without some means of preventing parallel imports, it will not be possible to price-discriminate effectively.[6]

---

[5] Office of Fair Trading (1999), para. 4.15.
[6] For a full discussion pertinent to pharmaceuticals, see US International Trade Commission (2000).

Preventing parallel imports

Parallel trade is the exporting or importing of a product through channels other than those authorized by the owner of a patent. It occurs if no compulsory licence is granted in the country of importation but imports continue all the same. One remedy open to the patent-owner is to ask the government in the importing country to enforce the patent in the import market. Another, less clear-cut remedy is for the patent-owner in the exporting country (often the same firm or a firm associated with the one being commercially damaged by the imports) to challenge the right of the exporter to resell to the importing country. (The exporter will presumably have obtained legitimate legal title to the goods through, for example, their purchase in the exporting country.) This involves challenging the principle that the product, if legally acquired by the exporter in the country of origin, can be legally resold in the importing country. This belief, that international resale is legitimate everywhere and always, is the doctrine of international patent exhaustion. And here the World Trade Organization's (WTO) Agreement on the Trade-Related Aspects of Intellectual Property Rights (TRIPS) is of no assistance. Article 6 of TRIPS states that for 'the purpose of dispute settlement ... nothing in this Agreement shall be used to address the exhaustion of intellectual property rights'.

The issue is contentious and unresolved. Some argue that parallel importation is a normal competitive practice arbitraging away price differentials and therefore that governments in importing countries should ignore the practice. They argue that local laws, in either the importing or the exporting state, which deny the principle of exhaustion are equivalent to protectionist trade barriers. This argument can be supported by the 'first-sale doctrine', according to which once ownership has been transferred, the patent-holder has already received full value for the patent. Resale is of no concern to it. The patent-holder has 'alienated' or 'exhausted' its exclusive rights to control distribution of the product once it has placed it in the stream of commerce. The counter-arguments are, *inter alia*, that Article 28 of TRIPS specifically recognizes the right of patent-holders to prevent the unauthorized sale of both domestically produced and imported versions of their products. A bar on parallel imports of identical products acquired from a sister company is simply a logical application of the patent-holder's right to be the exclusive importer or domestic producer.

Economists cannot adjudicate on these legal issues. They can, however, argue about when and why conditions exist that should or should not favour price arbitrage. Conversely, they can argue about when and why immediate, as opposed to gradual, convergence of price on marginal cost is or is not optimal. For example, we know that much of the sound and fury in the debate on parallel trade of medicines within the European Union (EU) is misplaced. The arbitrage process there – trading within the EU – is due in the first place to artificially induced price differences brought about by varying national price control regimes existing side-by-side within a legally defined single international market.

Parallel trade within the EU is thus easy to explain, if not necessarily to condone. It is perverse to have different price controls within one (allegedly single European) market. It is the individual controls resulting from each member state wishing to direct its own social and health policies that are the problem, not the pricing behaviour of the manufacturers or the marketing behaviour of the wholesalers doing the international trading. An economist, then, would condemn not parallel trade within Europe but the price controls that give rise artificially to arbitrage. These price controls have nothing to do with the spontaneous price discrimination and intellectual property issues with which this chapter is concerned.

Parallel importation or trade in the rest of the world is more difficult. Most countries are economically segmented from one another in a way that member states are not in the politically determined, so-called common market of the EU. The market conditions that affect price determination do indeed vary between non-EU countries. However, and this applies to European markets too, it can be difficult initially to understand that market conditions also vary within countries.

In South Africa, for example, the government is essentially a monopsony (single) purchaser for the bulk of the pharmaceuticals market (some two-thirds by volume but only one-quarter by value). Table 8.2 shows the sectoral distribution. Patent-holders practise price discrimination within the total national market in order to recover the proportion of development overheads attributable to that market mainly from the much wealthier private sector. Only patent protection, backed by Article 28 of TRIPS and coupled with the identifiability of more than one market segment (government and private) with different price sensitivities, enables this to be done. In short, the absence of parallel importation, combined with patent protection, facilitates disproportionately large purchases by the government on behalf of poorer members of the population. Table 8.3 shows South Africa's per capita income relative to other countries. It shows how South Africa can be regarded commercially as having two distinct market segments, gauged by income and thus presumably by ability to pay. The income of the top quintile exceeds the per capita GNP in high-income countries.

One example of successful price discrimination of this sort is for bronchodilators. The public sector benefits quite clearly from domestic price discrimination. About 80 per cent of South Africa's population relies on (mostly unpriced) care through the government sector, while the remaining 20 per cent relies on a private sector system much like that of the United States. The price discrimination between these sectors works to the advantage of low-income patients. Prices are higher in the low-volume private sector and lower in the high-volume public sector. Government purchases account for 66 per cent of

Table 8.2: South African pharmaceuticals, percentage sales by sector at manufacturers' prices, 1999

Sector	(%)
Retail pharmacy (ethical)	46.8
Retail pharmacy (unscheduled medicines)	3.0
Public sector	25.3
Dispensing doctors	12.2
Private hospitals and clinics	12.7

Source: Pharmaceutical Manufacturers Association of South Africa, *Annual Economic Report* (2000), Midrand, South Africa.

Table 8.3: Per capita GNP at purchasing power parity, 1999: an international comparison

Country	$
South Africa	27,699*
United States	30,600
High-income countries	24,430
Middle-income countries	4,880
Low-income countries	1,790

*Top 20 per cent of income-earners.
Source: *World Development Report*, 2000/2001.

industry volume but only one quarter of revenues, while the private sector generates volumes and values of turnover close to a reversal of these proportions. For example, in the late 1990s the South African private sector paid R28.99 for the asthma inhalant Ventolin, while the state sector paid R5.66. The world average price was R22.86. Aid organizations such as the International Dispensary Association (IDA) could not beat the South African public-sector price (Table 8.4).

The price discrimination system that has evolved spontaneously in South Africa (a middle-income country) illustrates the resolution of the patents–price discrimination–parallel imports trilemma. Price discrimination depends on patent protection and on the absence of illegal imitation, of parallel importation from countries where third parties can buy and import to the higher-priced segment from abroad, and of resale from the state sector into the private market. These conditions have been met. By contrast, in the EU the artificial presence of

Table 8.4: Selected drugs prices (R) in the South African and other markets, 1997

Product	Ventolin (out of patent)	Zantac (still in patent)
SA private sector	28.99	205
SA government sector	5.66	28
SA weighted price (by volume)	9.05	109.97
United Kingdom price	15.73	169.34
World average price	22.86	161.04
Product sourced via IDA*	8.45	On patent (n.a.)
Lowest-priced source identified by IDPIG**	8.34	On patent (n.a.)

* International Dispensary Association.
** International Drug Price Indicator Guide.
Source: Company sources and price lists cited in Reekie (2000).

differentiated national price controls demonstrates the trilemma at its worst. The movement of goods is free within the EU area and WTO obligations are unambiguously met, but artificially induced price differences result in parallel imports. In the rest of the world, the resolution of the trilemma requires the enforcement of TRIPS and the application of non-exhaustion of patent protection at the international level. The South African example above shows how patents, properly protected from parallel imports, can help to alleviate poverty. But the trilemma is not always so easily resolved. For example, governments may refuse to purchase medications even when they are available at a lower price than exists elsewhere in a national market. This has been the case with AIDS drugs in South Africa. Alternatively, manufacturers may refuse to launch products in countries without patent protection.[7]

AIDS IN SOUTH AFRICA

AIDS in South Africa is one area where IP, prices and parallel imports in the context of poverty have created a major political debate. South Africa is mired in a health crisis. There were 4.2 million people at the end of 1999 who were HIV-positive there. This figure exceeds that of any other country.[8] The rate of HIV infection has reached 22 per cent of adults, including more than one in five

---
[7] Sir Richard Sykes of Glaxosmithkline remarked in the Indian magazine *Business Today* (3 February 2002, p. 68) that his company had no intention of launching new drugs on the Indian market in the near future since they would quickly be copied and the prices undercut; whereas if they were sold in India at a lower price they would be bought by third parties and resold in other countries.
[8] UNAIDS (2000).

pregnant women. According to UNAIDS an estimated 500,000 AIDS-related deaths have already occurred, with the current annual toll of 200,000 expected to peak at 600,000 by 2006. The current figure represents 40 per cent of all deaths. For political reasons AIDS is not a notifiable disease, so these figures are open to dispute. Nevertheless, the immensity of the problem seems to be generally accepted now. The crisis is expensive. Drug treatment costs for AIDS range from $15,000 to $20,000 per year in the United States. The per capita income in South Africa is only $6,990.

What can be done? Government spending on health is actually budgeted to decrease by 2003–4, from 11.1 per cent to 10.8 per cent of total expenditure. The private sector is clearly expected to increase its share of the burden. One technique the private sector can apply is appropriate use of spontaneous price discrimination. Ironically, this approach, stemming from enlightened self-interest by medicines manufacturers, is often misunderstood against the emotional backdrop of a health crisis on the scale of the South African epidemic.

In recent months, the South African government and non-governmental organizations (NGOs) such as the Treatment Action Campaign have accused manufacturers of AIDS drugs of price gouging. In truth, South Africans already pay some of the lowest prices found anywhere in the world (see Table 8.5). Within South Africa, public-sector drugs prices are a fraction of those the private sector pays. Moreover, in many ways the government is exacerbating the crisis by threatening price controls and permitting a pharmacy 'cartel' that keeps retail drugs prices far above competitive levels.[9]

South Africa benefits not only from domestic price discrimination (see earlier discussion) but also from international price discrimination. South African prices for AIDS drugs have long been well below those in the United States and other developed countries. For example, in 2000, while US consumers paid $10.12 for AZT, the South African government paid $2.16 (although for policy reasons the quantities it purchased at that price were tiny). For Didanosine, it was $7.25 and $2.80 respectively. South Africa also paid less for both drugs than Côte d'Ivoire, another sub-Saharan country: Ivorians paid $3.48 for Didanosine and South Africans paid $2.80. The respective prices for AZT were $2.43 and $2.16. The $2.43 was the UNAIDS negotiated figure for Côte d'Ivoire; the $2.16 was the tender price made to win the small South African government purchase order.[10] (It is reasonable to assume that a still lower price would have been offered by the manufacturer for a higher-volume purchase.)

Even at these prices, the South African government could not afford to treat more than a small fraction of all those affected by AIDS. In response,

---

[9] See Reekie (1997).
[10] Ibid.

Table 8.5: International prices of AZT (600 mg), 2000

Country	$
United States[a]	10.12
Côte d'Ivoire[b]	2.43
South African state sector[c]	2.16

[a] Paid by patients to low-price mail order pharmacies.
[b] UNAIDS price.
[c] Successful Glaxo Wellcome price in bidding for a (small) state tender.
Source: *Financial Mail* (Johannesburg), 21 July 2000.

pharmaceutical companies offered to reduce their prices or even to give away their drugs, as long as the medications were distributed in a controlled manner. (Control is necessary for economic and medical reasons.[11] Price discrimination, we know, requires segmenting in order to inhibit sales from outside to inside the segment.) Glaxo Wellcome offered the drug Retrovir, which lowers mother-to-child transmission of HIV, at a preferential price; it also offered several thousand treatments free of charge. Bristol-Myers Squibb committed $100 million to women and children with HIV–AIDS in five Southern African countries, including South Africa. Pfizer and Boehringer Ingelheim (Germany) offered to donate AIDS medications.

These and several other similar offers were rebuffed by the South African government. Until very recently, it has refused or been ambivalent about accepting gifts of AIDS drugs, arguing that acceptance would divert resources from other disease areas. The health minister stated that even if anti-AIDS drugs were available at marginal cost, her department could not afford the delivery mechanisms, testing procedures and medications for maintenance of the lives 'saved'.[12] The specific reasons for rejecting the pharmaceutical companies' offers were that the Boehringer offer was 'only' for five years and that Pfizer's offer had a 'time limit'. These rebuffs raised the question of whether the government has either the power or the will to treat AIDS. President Mbeki's prolonged policy uncertainty about the linkages between AIDS and HIV were certainly puzzling

---

[11] As a corollary, the growing AIDS epidemic in sub-Saharan Africa could be worsened by giving the medications in an uncontrolled fashion. In areas with inadequate health care infrastructure to monitor precise distribution and dosage, there are serious compliance problems. There are dangers in indiscriminate distribution of HIV–AIDS drugs. The US Center for Disease Control (CDC) recently found that 75 per cent of participants in the United Nations AIDS programme in Uganda had drug-resistant HIV strains. By contrast, in the US – with good monitoring – only about 10 per cent of patients harbour HIV strains resistant to AZT. If the drugs are dumped into an unsupervised setting without vigilant monitoring, virulent, drug-resistant strains of HIV could emerge and threaten AIDS patients worldwide.

[12] *The Citizen* (Johannesburg), May 2000.

to many. And of course, it has been policy over the past few years for the public sector to expand primary care and cut back on expensive, curative medicine. AIDS is apparently no exception.

There are other ways to practise price discrimination that involve private-sector buyers, not the government. Several drugs firms in South Africa now offer their anti-AIDS medicines to large employers such as the mining companies, which have large labour forces at high levels of risk. These companies could purchase drugs at price levels close to those offered to, and previously rejected by, the government. They have the necessary clinical infrastructure to monitor and administer medicine consumption and the incentive as employers to minimize their health care costs. This incentive includes avoiding the indirect cost of losing labour through illness or death, with ensuing recruitment and training costs. Selling at rock-bottom prices to large employers avoids the problem of undesirable intersegmental arbitrage and clinical misuse of medicines. But otherwise, there is no reason why individual South Africans of an income or wealth level equal to that of a rich European or American should pay substantially less for medicines than they do (unless the costs of managing the price differences exceed the benefits).

THE TRILEMMA IN SOUTH AFRICA

Controls on the supply of medicines are also necessary in order to prevent parallel importing. This consideration highlights the patents–price discrimination–parallel imports trilemma that has existed in South Africa for a number of years. In 1997 the Medicines and Related Substances Act was passed. Under that act the minister of health was empowered to authorize the importation of particular branded products sourced overseas without the authorization of the holder of the South African patent and/or trademark. The international and local pharmaceutical industries challenged the act's validity, and a legal battle about the meaning of the wording of the act went on for four years, until the case was settled out of court in April 2001.

The essence of the debate centred, first, on whether the act merely endorsed the right of the government to overrule IP protection in states of national emergency and, second, on whether the act referred to compulsory licensing or to parallel importation. The right to overrule patent-holder privileges already existed in cases of national emergency. An additional piece of legislation relating exclusively to medicines appeared to the manufacturers to be unnecessary. If it referred to compulsory licensing, then that too is provided for elsewhere in the country's legislation: the Patents Act provides for the issuing of a compulsory licence on a case-by-case basis. (Indeed, the large Indian manufacturer Cipla recently asked the patent authorities for permission to supply the country with eight low-cost generic copies of patented anti-retroviral drugs.[13] This request for the compulsory licences was made on the grounds of 'patent abuse' and that the patent-holders had failed to supply the relevant products on 'reasonable terms'.) In other words, the Medicines and Related Substances Act was redundant as far as either a state of emergency or compulsory licensing was concerned. Thus it was opposed by the plaintiffs. It was also opposed on the grounds that it could be interpreted as permitting parallel importation of patented products purchased more cheaply elsewhere and resold in South Africa. Commercially this was not a major issue for the industry: as already pointed out, the bulk of the drugs sold in the country, including AIDS medications, are already sold at world-best prices.

Why then was there this long legal battle in South Africa that was followed all round the world? The answer lies in the power of precedent. If the disputed act referred to parallel importation and was implemented, then a TRIPS signatory (South Africa), while ostensibly recognizing its IP obligations under TRIPS Article 28, would be acting explicitly on the failure of Article 6 to define what is meant by patent exhaustion. South Africa's argument would be that after initial sale by a patent-holder, the patent-holder's rights are exhausted. If that view were to be upheld, then international price discrimination would become almost impossible to practise. Other countries would follow the South African precedent. If price discrimination became impossible to practise, then the funds for R&D could fall, at worst, catastrophically close to zero or, at best, be held at the (smaller) level permitted by uniform, profit-maximizing pricing. (In Figure 8.1, this level would be at price level B.) The South African case was therefore crucial for the global pharmaceutical industry and, by extension, for all who depend on it for the flow of future innovations.

Why did the South African government fight so hard if it had little to gain in terms of prices paid? One can only speculate. Possible reasons include, first, the policy ambivalence of President Mbeki, who doubted the HIV–AIDS linkage. There was, second, a long-standing lack of trust between the pharmaceutical industry and the Department of Health (which led to a successful appeal in 1997 to the ombudsman (the Office of the Public Protector) by the industry, which claimed that the then minister, Dr Zuma, had made several 'misleading statements' about its pricing policies). Third, the government was aware that it could not finance the delivery and monitoring of clinical delivery and patient compliance even if medications were made available at zero cost. Thus the industry was possibly useful in diverting public attention away from the government's inability to deliver.

The international pharmaceutical industry withdrew from the case in April 2001 in exchange for the opportunity to be consulted on the drawing up of the

---

[13] See *Wall Street Journal*, 9 March 2001.

174 STATE RESPONSES

rules and regulations through which the act will be interpreted. These have still to be finalized and will no doubt evolve over time and in practice. Other health care providers have also now become actively involved in this process of preparing for the implementation of what is regarded by all, including government, as an imperfectly drafted act. Certainly, in the context of the trilemma, government claims that it intends to stick to its TRIPS obligations; but, as noted, these obligations are ambiguous.

PROMOTING ACCESS FOR THE DEVELOPING WORLD

There are problems in marketing anti-retroviral drugs for use in HIV–AIDS treatments in poor countries. But at least the medicines are there and research continues. The R&D continues, of course, because there is a market in richer countries.[14] Biotechnological research into improving plant productivity and resistance to disease and pests also proceeds apace – because there is a market in richer countries. The poor certainly may benefit, but transferring the technology does have its problems. Let us restrict ourselves here to examining access to pharmaceutical products.

Access to products boils down to price. And if price (generated from all segments of the market) fails to cover innovation costs, we shall certainly get today's medicines more cheaply. But the stark reality then is that we may not get tomorrow's medicines at all. There are three main groups of pricing proposals available: first, compulsory licensing and the principle of international patent exhaustion and hence parallel importation;[15] second, 'tiered pricing';[16] and, third, discriminatory pricing. Compulsory licensing (without attendant parallel importation) has been most overtly threatened by Brazil, where some local manufacturers have been awarded compulsory licences to manufacture products in Brazil against the wishes of the patentee domiciled elsewhere. The granting of such licences appears to be in accord with Brazilian patent law, but inconsistent with TRIPS provisions. Of particular importance to pharmaceuticals is Article 27(1) of TRIPS. It talks of patent rights as 'enjoyable without discrimination as to the place of the invention, the field of technology and whether products are

---

[14] The International Federation of Pharmaceutical Manufacturers cites survey data compiled by *Pharmaprojects* (PJB Publications, UK). In 1990, over 150 HIV anti-retroviral compounds were under development in the industry worldwide. This figure rose to over 250 in the years to 1998. The numbers have since steadily fallen year-on-year to just over 150 in 2001. By contrast, anti-infective compounds in general, currently under investigation in the industry 'pipeline' and not subject to negative public perceptions, have risen by 30 per cent.
[15] This policy is proposed by Médecins Sans Frontières' Campaign for Access to Essential Medicines (2001).
[16] See the definition of, for example, Oxfam's Policy Department in Oxfam, Great Britain (2001).

imported or locally produced'. This effectively bans the granting by national patent authorities of compulsory licences for local manufacturers where requirements for local sale can be met by imports (i.e., the patent is not being abused and it is being 'worked', even if there is no local manufacture).

Most governments agree with this interpretation of Article 27(1), although Brazil did not, and this failure to agree lay at the heart of America's complaint about Brazil to the WTO Dispute Resolution Panel. In essence the Brazilian defence was that Article 68 of Brazilian patent law requires patent-holders to manufacture locally, in default of which compulsory licences may be awarded. The US Trade Representative at the WTO, Robert Zolleic, wrote in his 2001 'Special 301 Report' that 'Article 68 is unrelated to health or access to drugs, but instead is discriminating against all imported products in favor of locally produced products. In short, Article 68 is a protectionist measure intended to create jobs for Brazilian nationals'. The Brazilian health ministry rejected this criticism, and in an attempt to bolster its government's stance on compulsory licensing at the WTO it took the argument to another forum, the World Health Organization. But at the WHO's Annual Assembly in Geneva on 21 May 2001, the Brazilians failed to gain support for their position on Article 68. South Africa provided no support for the Brazilians on that occasion. In the meantime the US government has withdrawn its objection to the WTO Dispute Resolution Panel. This may be a direct consequence of the earlier industry withdrawal from the Pretoria case.

The Brazilian and South African precedents threaten – even if only at the margin – the minimum standards of patent protection mandated by TRIPS. Legal clarity and stronger international consensus on the interpretation of TRIPS are required in order to avoid further erosion. Meanwhile, as contention continues subsequent to the WTO Doha meeting, participants in the debate need to understand better the economic and social benefits of spontaneity in price discrimination.

The spontaneous and free application of discriminatory pricing made possible by patent protection in the absence of parallel importation has been discussed above. However, a middle way between discriminatory pricing and compulsory licensing may be tiered pricing. Oxfam defines tiered pricing to involve countries or groups of countries calling for tenders for medicines for use in their state health care agencies. To avoid reimportation of the purchased medicines into markets in richer countries, differential packaging or formulations would be encouraged. Rich countries' copyright laws or regulatory agencies would then be used to prevent parallel importation.[17]

Tiered pricing appears to be merely a planned alternative to spontaneous, market-driven price discrimination. What are the differences? Tiered pricing

[17] Ibid.

would impose uniformity among countries in pricing and in product availability (only products called for on tender would be available). Spontaneous discrimination allows for different prices between richer and poorer patients within a country – according to the health care provision system of the patient's choice. Moreover, it allows for a choice of products within and between countries. If groups of countries are involved, then national health care policies are also subordinated to the group, just as individual patient and doctor choices would be diminished if the system were country-specific. South Africa is a good example of spontaneous discrimination. All therapies are available. For the poor, the state sector can provide at world-best prices; in the richer, private sector, downward price pressures are exerted competitively by insurers. A variety of competitive methods exists too. These range from total freedom of choice by patient and prescriber to restricted but voluntarily adopted formularies or insurance cost containment schemes such as limits, co-insurance, co-payments and insurable thresholds or limits.

A tiered pricing system, on the other hand, precludes this operational flexibility, and would be cumbersome and insensitive to demand-side variations by time or place. Private tendering and negotiation between patients (and their agents, such as insurers, doctors, hospitals and local health administrators) is more likely to be equitable between richer and poorer patients. It will avoid the political gridlock that can occur about which therapies to 'allow' for tender and which to preclude for the country or countries participating in an official constructed tiered price system. In contrast to spontaneous price discrimination, which of course depends on the international legal framework of patents, a tiered price system would overthrow the value of patent protection. This is because there would be no sales of patented products to protect for those products that did not make it into the politically determined list for which tenders were called.

CONCLUSIONS

Only spontaneous price discrimination, coupled with patent protection and not undermined by the presence of parallel importation, can resolve the economic development trilemma involving patents, price discrimination and parallel imports. This resolution provides simultaneously today's medicines more cheaply and tomorrow's medicines more rapidly.

At a fundamental level the WTO should ensure that already negotiated quid pro quos are carried out.[18] There remains a perceived unfairness in the Uruguay

---

[18] Trade negotiations tend historically to be conducted in bargaining fashion. National negotiators are thus under pressure from domestic vested interests not to give something away without a compensating benefit in return.

Round trade negotiations that led to the creation of TRIPS. The negotiations began in 1984, when the HIV–AIDS epidemic and the sale of patented medicines in controlling its spread had hardly been discussed. Oloko-Onyango and Udagama (2000) note that the clear trade-off in the Uruguay Round was that the developed countries 'got TRIPS' in exchange for granting the developing countries access to rich world markets, particularly for textiles and agricultural products. Since most countries in the developed world still have not implemented their side of the bargain, it is understandable that trade ministers in countries such as Brazil, India and South Africa and others find it difficult to persuade their fellow politicians of the urgency of implementing their TRIPS commitments. But without that implementation, spontaneous price discrimination will be impossible.

Both the economic and physical health of populations in the developing world require a greater understanding of how a revised, clarified and unambiguous TRIPS agreement can exploit and not hamper spontaneous price discrimination. It may be more than coincidence that since hostile attacks on patents and TRIPS began, particularly on the HIV–AIDS sector, research into HIV anti-retrovirals has fallen. Tomorrow's medicines could drift out of reach if we fail to resolve the trilemma.

REFERENCES

Edelman, M. (2001), *Inventors, Innovation and Intellectual Property* (Fairfax, VA: Hispanic American Center for Economic Research).

Médecins Sans Frontières' Campaign for Access to Essential Medicines (2001), 'Recommendations to the European Commission for Discussion at the June 2001 TRIPS Council on Health and Access to Medicines', 27 May 2001.

Office of Fair Trading (1999), *The Chapter II Prohibition of the Competition Act 1998*, London, Office of Fair Trading, 402, March.

Office of the Public Protector (1997), *Report on the Propriety of the Conduct of Members of the Ministry and Department of Health Relating to Statements in Connection with the Prices of Medicines and Utilisation of Generic Medicines in South Africa*, Pretoria, South Africa.

Oloko-Onyango, J. and Udagama, D. (2000), *The Realisation of Economic, Social and Cultural Rights: Globalisation and its Impact on the Full Enjoyment of Human Rights*, UN Economic and Social Council.

Oxfam, Great Britain (2001), 'Tiered Pricing and Access to Medicines: Some Critical Questions', May.

Reekie, W. D. (1997), 'Cartels, Spontaneous Price Discrimination and International Pharmacy Retailing, *International Journal of Economics and Business*, Vol. 4.

Reekie, W. D. (2000), *South Africa's Battle with AIDS and Drug Prices*, Brief 334, National Center for Policy Analysis, Dallas, Texas.

UNAIDS (2000), *Report on the Global HIV–AIDS Epidemic*, Report of UNAIDS and WHO, Geneva.

US International Trade Commission (2000), *Pricing of Prescription Drugs*, Investigation No. 332-419, Publication 3333, Washington, DC.

9 EXPANDING ACCESS TO ESSENTIAL MEDICINES IN BRAZIL: RECENT ECONOMIC REGULATION, POLICY-MAKING AND LESSONS LEARNT

Jorge Bermudez

> Yet at the beginning of the 21st century inequities in terms of access to essential drugs, quality and rational use remain widespread in many parts of the world. An estimated one-third of the world population lacks regular access to essential drugs, with this figure rising to over 50 per cent in the poorest regions of Africa and Asia. The reasons often include inadequate financing and poor health care delivery. And even if drugs are available, weak drug regulation may mean that they are substandard or counterfeit. Irrational use – for example, high rates of antibiotic prescription, very short dispensing times and incorrect drug use by patients – is of great public health concern too.
>
> WHO Medicines Strategy: 2000–2003[1]

INTRODUCTION

Worldwide, many people have little or no access to essential medicines. According to the World Health Organization (WHO), probably almost one-third of the world's population lacks regular access to medicines and more than 50 per cent lack access in the poorest parts of Africa and Asia.[2] This situation is serious in developing countries, where there are great differences in access, which are characteristic of the inequity globalization promotes. Economic pressures make this problem worse, and in some areas in the least developed countries it is critical. Governments face severe difficulties in applying scarce resources to social programmes. The struggle between economic and social programmes is a worldwide problem for which no single approach is appropriate. Instead, there must be differentiated strategies that consider the individual circumstances and the development of each country's own national health systems and procurement practices.

---

[1] *WHO Policy Perspectives on Medicines*, No. 1 (December 2000).
[2] WHO (2000a, 2000b).

Moreover, the global pharmaceutical market is unbalanced: North America and Europe consume nearly 70 per cent of medicines, despite the inverse proportion of the distribution of the world's population. This imbalance has long been recognized: in 1976, it was estimated that 75 per cent of medicines produced were consumed by the 27 per cent of the world's population living in the developed countries.[3]

It is thus clear that access to medicines must be treated as a priority in all health forums and in all international initiatives now being implemented. According to Management Sciences for Health,[4] besides accessible health services and qualified staff as necessary components of health care, medicines are important, for the following reasons:

- Drugs save lives and improve health;
- Drugs promote trust and participation in health services;
- Drugs are costly;
- Drugs are different from other consumer products;
- Substantive improvements in the supply and use of drugs are possible.

The recommendations and guidelines strongly advocated by the WHO stipulate access to essential drugs as one of four fundamental objectives, the others being support for countries' efforts to formulate, implement and monitor national drug policies; ensuring global standards for drug quality and safety; and promoting rational use of medicines.[5]

Pharmaceutical markets in developing countries have special characteristics, notably unequal supply and demand, exacerbated marketing practices and imperfect competition. Competition is imperfect as it is not regulated in equal situations by price. Rather, brand loyalty is exacerbated and creates an unequal monopoly, because the totality of marketing practices is directed towards highlighting the advantages (not necessarily real) that one brand has over the rest in a specific market. These issues have made it possible for population groups to have a clearer perception that has been stressed by media coverage, as has recently been observed in Brazil. Failures in general pharmaceutical markets may include asymmetry and asynchrony of information, limited competition motivated by brand loyalty, patent protection and market concentration, besides the unclear roles represented by the actors involved in the prescription, dispensing and use of medicines.[6] Latin America has interesting figures: whereas the annual revenues with medicines may come to $29 per capita, they may reach 50 per cent of overall costs with health care; an additional problem is that 83 per

---
[3] WHO (1998).
[4] Management Sciences for Health (1997).
[5] WHO (2000b, 2000c, 2000d, 2001a, 2001b).
[6] Fundación Isalud (1999).

cent of this represents consumption in the private sector, being paid by patients.[7]

Access is difficult to define clearly. On the one hand, the importance of access in national drug policies is stressed as one of the main issues for policymakers in discussions of the effects of health programmes and policies. On the other hand, availability and acceptability are often considered to be synonymous with access.[8] Access, according to Perchansky and Thomas,[9] is a concept which considers a group of dimensions that measure the compatibility between the patient and the health care system and that include availability, accessibility, accommodation, affordability and acceptability.

BRAZIL: A PROFILE

Brazil, a continental South American country of 8.5 million square kilometres, is a federal republic, with 26 states and the federal district which include 5,508 municipalities. It is a country of enormous contrasts, economic as well as geographical, as a relatively high economic growth rate coexists with one of the worst income distributions in the world.[10] Thus, the richest 10 per cent of Brazilians have an average income nearly 30 times that of the poorest 40 per cent. This compares with a disparity of nearly 10 times in other countries.[11]

Until the early 1990s, the Brazilian economy had unstable growth and a high rate of inflation. These resulted in the failure of the policy that had prevailed since the 1950s, of industrialization and import substitution with a heavy public-sector presence in various industries. The 1994 economic stabilization plan, known as the Real Plan, pegged the Brazilian currency to the dollar, with apparent gains in terms of the poorer population's share of the national income and an increase in the gross domestic product (GDP) from US$662 billion to US$711 billion between 1994 and 1996.[12] More recent developments have included an increasing review of the priority core activities and a consequent reduction in the state's role, deregulation of the economy, privatization, 'flexibilization' of social rights, including unification of the negotiating powers of different professional categories, minimum or zero increases in incomes in spite of losses through inflation, cooperativism and other indirect contractual alternatives, as well as financial asphyxia, especially in social expenditure.[13]

---

[7] Madrid, Velasquez and Fefer (1998).
[8] Perchansky and Thomas (1981), Aday and Anderson (1992) and Frenk (1992).
[9] Perchansky and Thomas (1981).
[10] OPAS (1998) and Schilling (1994).
[11] OPAS (1998).
[12] Ibid. These figures have been discussed in a previous paper (Bermudez, Epsztejn, Oliveira and Hasenclever (2000)).
[13] Feghali (1998).

Table 9.1: Brazil: selected mortality indicators

Mortality indicators (1997)	Overall rate
Infant mortality rate (estimated number of infant deaths per 1,000 live births)	37.4
Early neonatal mortality rate (estimated number of deaths from zero to six days per 1,000 live births)	17.7
Late neonatal mortality rate (estimated number of deaths from seven to 27 days per 1,000 live births).	4.7
Post-neonatal mortality rate (estimated number of deaths from 28 to 364 days per 1,000 live births).	14.9
Perinatal mortality rate (estimated number of deaths during the perinatal period per 1,000 live births).	29.4
Maternal mortality rate (reported number of deaths owing to maternal causes per 1,000 live births)	59.1
Proportional mortality owing to ill-defined causes (per cent of reported deaths)	14.7
Proportional mortality owing to acute diarrhoeic disease in children under five years of age (per cent of reported deaths)	5.7
Proportional mortality owing to acute respiratory infection in children under five years of age (per cent of reported deaths)	6.8

Source: MS (1998).

Recent demographic indicators in Brazil estimate a total population of 159,636,000 inhabitants, with an annual growth rate of 1.4 per cent. Some 78 per cent of the population live in urban areas. The total fertility rate (the mean number of live births per woman) is 2.4, and the overall birth rate (number of live births per 1,000 inhabitants) is 21.7. The overall death rate is 7.1 per 1,000 inhabitants; life expectancy at birth is 64 years for men and 72 years for women.[14]

As for socioeconomic indicators, the literacy rate (the percentage of the population 15 years old and over that can read and write) is some 85 per cent for both sexes. The aggregate income of the wealthiest 20 per cent of Brazilians is 18.9 times that of the poorest 20 per cent.[15] Some 28 per cent of the population live on a per capita family income less than or equal to one-half of the monthly minimum wage,[16] which is far from sufficient to cover minimum basic needs.

Mortality indicators for Brazil are shown in Table 9.1. Note that there are sharp differences among the various regions of the country and that the breakdown of proportional mortality indicators for specific causes has not been included.

---

[14] MS (1998).
[15] This indicator is known as income ratio, according to the Basic Health Data Indicators. MS (1998).
[16] The minimum wage in Brazil is set at R$180 a month (the exchange rate is currently at approximately R$2.44/ US$1 as of February 2002).

As for morbidity indicators and risk factors, the figures for 1997 were as follows for vaccine-preventable diseases: 53,664 confirmed cases of measles; 103 of neonatal tetanus and 897 of non-neonatal tetanus; 120 of diphtheria; three of yellow fever; 7,621 of hepatitis B; 25 of human rabies; and 1,883 reported cases of whooping cough.

The incidence rates for transmissible diseases include 11.8 AIDS cases per 100,000 inhabitants. In addition to diseases such as tuberculosis, dengue fever, American tegumentary leishmaniasis and leprosy, Brazil has health problems typical of the industrial development process.

With regard to Brazil's disease control strategies, in the early twentieth century its health practices emphasized large-scale campaigns to combat diseases such as yellow fever, bubonic plague, smallpox and malaria. Until the 1950s this emphasis tended to strengthen centralized policies emphasizing health campaigns which focused on controlling those diseases that were economically more important, therefore ensuring the necessary exchanges with developed countries. From the 1950s on, during its developmentalist period, Brazil incorporated the issue of health care in its social security programmes and pension funds. Despite this adverse context, which was strongly directed to recovery of individuals' health as a factor in reducing absenteeism at work, advances have been made since the approval of the new Constitution in 1988. Its chapter dealing with social security has progressively established a broad social protection system, merging health, social security and social care and guaranteeing the universal right to health.[17]

The Brazilian pharmaceutical market has very peculiar characteristics.[18] Its sales, values and units make it one of the main world markets, valued at nearly $7.6 billion per year. Transnational companies are responsible for over 75 per cent of this market, and self-medication is increasing rapidly. The sales vendors in most retail services that by law must have a pharmacist change prescriptions on a very irresponsible basis. Specific laws regarding the prescription and dispensing of certain pharmacological groups are not enforced in Brazil, so that there is little or no monitoring of retail units. This leaves a totally unregulated market, with income growing each year, as shown in Table 9.2. (We consider the mean price of drugs to be an inadequate indicator, as discussed in a previous paper on that issue, in the context of the need to establish comparative price surveys for medicines in Latin American countries.[19])

---

[17] Feghali (1998) and Bermudez, Epsztejn, Oliveira and Hasenclever (2000).
[18] See Bermudez (1992, 1994, 1995, 2001), Bermudez and Possas (1995) and Bermudez and Bonfim (1999).
[19] Bermudez and Reis (1999).

Table 9.2: The Brazilian pharmaceuticals market: trends in revenue, units sold and mean drug prices, 1995–8

Year	1995	1996	1997	1998
Annual revenue (US$ 1,000)	6,291,784	7,257,070	7,693,757	7,781,097
Number of units sold (x 1,000)	1,454,640	1,464,368	1,391,680	1,332,606
Mean price (US$)	4.33	4.96	5.53	5.84

Source: Data from IMS, *Profile of the Brazilian Pharmaceutical Market* (1999).

ACCESS TO MEDICINES: THE ESSENTIAL BACKGROUND

Brazil is implementing a broad range of initiatives to expand access to medicines, and these are providing potential approaches that other developing countries could use. Of special interest is the universal access to anti-retroviral drugs (ARVs) that the Ministry of Health has established in recent years, which will be discussed below. These initiatives must be considered not as isolated actions but as a sequence of steps that have enabled Brazil's national health system to make advances.[20] I shall describe briefly and comment on the most important ones, establishing the link between them as a possible model that other developing countries could apply in the light of their circumstances.

The most important initiative in recent years in Brazil has been the Federal Constitution, updated in 1988. Its chapter on social security stipulates the right to health as a citizenship right and therefore as a duty of the state. Drawing up this chapter was an arduous process that involved mobilizing civil society, congressmen, professional organizations, politicians and the public and private sectors. The chapter is considered to be a very modern and advanced proposal for public health. Following from the Constitution, Brazil's national health system is defined in specific laws (Laws 8,080 and 8,142) as a coordinated health system with three levels of management (federal, state and municipal). The health system comprises, under one authority, the public, the private not-for-profit and the private for-profit health sectors, and there is a trend towards decentralization and evaluation of actions within the system. As the health system is responsible for the procurement and distribution of a great number of medicines throughout Brazil, the provision of access to pharmaceutical care has to be considered in the light of recent trends in this system.

[20] See Bermudez, Epsztejn, Oliveira and Hasenclever (2000), and Bermudez (2001).

RECENT REGULATION RELATED TO ACCESS TO MEDICINES

The absence of a specific government policy to protect domestic industry, its greater vulnerability in the 1940s and economic measures in the 1950s favouring the entry of foreign capital in Brazil led to a denationalization process that was acute in the 1970s.[21]

Even though there was authoritarian rule after the 1964 military *coup d'état* and although costs were cut in public health programmes in favour of greater individual medical care, a government initiative in 1971 created an enterprise intended to be responsible for all aspects of medicines policy: the Central de Medicamentos (CEME).[22] Its initial functions were defined as regulating the production and distribution of drugs by the pharmaceutical manufacturers subordinated or linked to the various government levels. In fact, CEME was a catalyst for the conflicts between the public and private sectors in pharmaceutical production because it centralized the procurement of medicines.

CEME was decommissioned in 1997. Its activities had dwindled mainly to the buying of large quantities of medicines from the private sector, and its involvement in research, technological development and the coordination of a national quality assurance system had declined. At a time of crisis for CEME that jeopardized all its initial activities and that also involved scandals and alleged corruption, its activities were reallocated within various organs of the Ministry of Health.[23] The decommissioning of CEME created the need for an explicit national drugs policy in the Ministry of Health, and was a first step towards establishing the current priorities regarding access to medicines.

Following WHO guidelines and other countries' experience and having evaluated its past experience of drugs provision, the Ministry of Health has issued Ruling No. 3,916/98. This approved the National Drug Policy and laid down the guidelines for activities to be implemented, linking actions among the health provision sectors.[24] The essential guidelines and priorities of the National Drug Policy were defined as follows:

Guidelines:
(a) Adoption of a list of essential drugs;
(b) Health-related regulation of drugs;
(c) Reorientation of pharmaceutical care;
(d) Promotion of rational use of drugs;
(e) Scientific and technological development;

---

[21] See Bermudez, Epsztejn, Oliveira and Hasenclever (2000).
[22] The specific aspects and flaws of this enterprise's performance have been discussed by Bermudez (1992, 1995) and by Bermudez and Possas (1995).
[23] Wilken and Bermudez (1999).
[24] MS (1999) and Yunes (1999).

(f) Promotion of national capacity for drug manufacturing;
(g) Safety, efficacy and quality assurance;
(h) Development and training of human resources.

Priorities:

(a) Permanent review of the National List of Essential Drugs;
(b) Pharmaceutical care;
(c) Promotion of rational use of drugs;
(d) Organization of drug-related health surveillance or monitoring activities.

Following the approval of the National Drug Policy, the National List of Essential Drugs was reviewed – the last updating had been in 1982. The revision was based mainly on the WHO's Model List for Essential Drugs and on evidence-based backgrounds, mainly a broad revision of publications on meta-analysis or clinical trials. It was officially adopted as Ministry of Health Ruling No. 597/99, and has been distributed throughout the health system. States and municipalities are being encouraged to use similar lists at their own level. In 2001, the Ministry of Health set up a national commission that is responsible for the standing revision of the National List of Essential Drugs.

The current essential drugs list in Brazil comprises 312 items with 561 presentations. Of these, 43.1 per cent are injectables (including all the vaccines and sera), and 24.6 per cent of all the medicines are intended for hospital use. The classification of all the medicines on the list was made in accordance with the proposals of the WHO Model List in order to make it easier to use by health system professionals, mainly the prescription in health services, including general guidelines for treatment of the principal manifestations of disease as well as the medicines used for treatment of systemic organic diseases. The process of determining whether to include or exclude a medicine from the essential drug list was strongly supported by evidence-based criteria. Following from the National List of Essential Drugs, a therapeutic formulary, including guidelines and evidence-based information for the essential drugs, has also been developed. It is meant to be a guide for rational prescription within the health services, and not to be restricted to the public sector.

The general health budget in Brazil, as related to the GNP, varied from 1980 to 1990, with a maximum value of 3.3 per cent in 1989. This amounted to nearly R$20 billion per year. The Ministry of Health has an annual budget of about R$1.3 billion (nearly US$600 million) allocated to procurement of drugs, as classified in Table 9.3. The federal government allocates funds directly to programmes or transfers them to the state or local governments, and they also allocate their own funds to meet specific demands or to supplement the funds received from the federal government.

Table 9.3: Drugs procurement funds (R$000*) for distribution by Ministry of Health programmes

Programmes	1999	2000
Incentives for basic pharmaceutical care (decentralized to the state and local levels)	163,947	164,200
Drugs dispensed infrequently (high cost) (decentralized, with partial federal funding)	296,357	316,000
Essential drugs for mental health (decentralized to the state level)	22,178	26,800
Strategic Ministry of Health programmes (leprosy, tuberculosis, AIDS, diabetes, blood products and endemic disease control) (centralized)	908,500	806,047
Total	1,390,982	1,313,047

* R$2.44 = US$1 as of February 2002.
Source: Brazil, Ministry of Health.

Table 9.3 shows that Brazil has centralized the procurement of medicines destined for strategic programmes, which include leprosy, tuberculosis, ARV drugs for AIDS, diabetes (exclusively insulin), blood products (coagulation factors) and endemic diseases, mainly malaria and phylariasis.

The decentralization of medicines for basic pharmaceutical care being implemented in Brazil is based on the experience of a previous centralized procurement programme called Basic Pharmacy. It was established in 1997 and aimed to supply a group of 40 essential medicines to small counties throughout Brazil.[25] Decentralized basic pharmaceutical care is a shared programme, which involves the federal, state and municipal governments in funding the procurement of medicines that are settled individually by each state.

The procurement of drugs dispensed infrequently because of their high cost is decentralized to the states, which arrange for them to be dispensed to registered patients. The programme for this small number of medicines accounts for a relatively large share of financial resources. These medicines are crucial for chronic renal patients. The medicines used most are Erythropoietin (recombinant) and Ciclosporin; they take up 43 per cent of the Ministry of Health's allocation for high-cost drugs. Growth hormones and the interferons (alpha and beta) also take up a large amount of this allocation (see Table 9.3).

The definition of high-cost drugs was officially adopted by the Ministry of Health in 1982, after it had considered drugs purchased by the government on individual bases and with financial resources different from those used for drugs included in the Essential Drugs List. The ruling that established the initial

[25] MS (1997) and Cosendey (2000).

authorization for procurement and defined the high-cost drugs in 1982 also determined that the total funding for these drugs could not exceed 15 per cent of expenditure on essential drugs.[26] The values that states pay as reference prices for the high-cost drugs have been updated constantly and have been established as Ministry of Health rulings.

STRENGTHENING REGULATORY CAPACITY AND GENERIC DRUGS POLICY

Brazil's National Regulatory Agency has been created as a special agency, along the lines of the American Food and Drug Administration model, for regulating health-related products and services. It operates within the structure of the Ministry of Health but has administrative and financial autonomy. It was created by Law 9.782/99 in 1999, and replaced the previous body in the Ministry of Health with that responsibility.

An additional law, Law 9.787/99, was enacted in October 1999. It amends a former law that dealt with various aspects of licensing and inspecting products and that established the basic framework and concepts that introduced generic drugs to the Brazilian market. Supplementary regulatory measures issued by the National Regulatory Agency complement the regulation for implementing a generic drugs policy in Brazil. They establish technical standards and norms and define the concepts of bio-availability and bio-equivalence and also those of generic, innovative, reference and similar drugs. This is not the first time that attempts at definition have been made, but these measures are certainly the first effective legal act.

Law 9.787/99 has led to domestic manufacturers replacing branded products from transnational companies, thus provoking media campaigns by those companies in an effort not to lose the hegemony of brand-name drugs in the national market. Data available from the National Regulatory Agency on their web page (*http://www.anvisa.gov.br/mercado/monitora/genericos/index.htm*), show that the market share of generic medicines within the total market has risen from 0.62% to 3.2% in the period from June 2000 to August 2001. Within the generic market share, anti-hypertensives, antibiotics and anti-ulcer products are the leading drugs. Examples of market increase include amoxycillin (generic products account for 9.81% of total amoxycillin sales), ranitidine (7.48%), cefalexin (6.96%), captopril (6.95%) and enalapril (6.07%). Moreover, the National Regulatory Agency has prohibited the use of generic denomination for branded products, which has been a common recent practice in Brazil, unless there is proven compliance with the bio-equivalence regulation.

---

[26] Silva (2000).

The first drug licences in Brazil for generic drugs were issued in February 2000; and two years later, more than 400 products are available as generics. The National Regulatory Agency is also aware of the differences in the price of new products coming onto the Brazilian market, as it would not be acceptable to have more expensive drugs being introduced to the public. For this reason, generic products need to be nearly 40 per cent cheaper than the reference products, which are mostly brand products from big transnational companies whose patent protection has expired.

Nearly all pharmacological groups of drugs have had generic products licensed in Brazil, including those for hospitals and out-patient use. No strict controls on licensed products are being implemented, but the Ministry of Health has proposed two reference lists of products that would be strongly encouraged to have generic drugs. These lists are based on the WHO's Model List for Essential Drugs, on Brazil's Essential Drugs List, on basic health care lists of drugs in the Brazilian health system and on considerations of the market share of medicines. These two lists have had a positive reaction from manufacturers, and requests to license generic drugs on the lists have been granted.[27]

The monitoring of prices, another aspect of economic regulation related to the pharmaceutical sector in Brazil that has been addressed in the past few years, is being implemented by the National Regulatory Agency. The identification of increases in prices led to a protocol of understanding between the Ministry of Health and the pharmaceutical companies that froze prices for one year in 2000. After that time expired, a parametric formula for the readjustment of prices was issued as a Provisional Measure by the President and later issued as a Law (Law 10.213/2001), and the federal government has nominated the Medicines Chamber, with representatives from different ministries. The parametric formula considers the mean evolutions of prices for each company for the period between August 1999 and November 2000 and an Index, in order to determine the maximum value for price readjustments. The Medicines Chamber is responsible for monitoring compliance with different regulations and for proposing measures in the event of infractions. The Ministry of Health has also proposed and issued a list of continuous-use medicines that have received exemption from payment of federal and state taxes at commercialization.

The Ministry of Health has established a database of procurement of medicines by health centres, hospitals and state or federal governments that can be accessed on a web page. The setting up of a similar database for six regional countries (Brazil, Argentina, Uruguay, Paraguay, Chile and Bolivia) has been agreed by their respective ministers of health and is being implemented.

---

[27] Bermudez, Epsztejn, Oliveira and Hasenclever (2000) and Bermudez (2001).

HEALTH ISSUES INVOLVING INTELLECTUAL PROPERTY AND TRADE

Recently the United States has complained to the World Trade Organization's (WTO) Dispute Settlement Body (DSB) that copies of branded medicines in Brazil do not comply with recent trade agreements, especially the WTO Agreement on Trade-Related Aspects of Intellectual Property Rights (TRIPS), in spite of Brazil's Industrial Property Law passed in 1996. On 8 January 2001 the United States sent the WTO a request for a panel. It focused mainly on the provisions in the Brazilian IPR Law establishing 'local working' requirements and no importation in order to ensure patent protection within the Section of Compulsory Licensing, arguing that these provisions would not be consistent with Brazil's compliance with the TRIPS Agreement. This complaint focused worldwide attention on measures the Brazilian federal government has been implementing to ensure universal access to anti-retroviral drugs. This complaint to the DSB may be regarded as an initiative by pharmaceutical manufacturers with the US government's backing. It represents the interests of manufacturers of patented drugs that have been challenged by the lower, more affordable prices of medicines being produced in Brazil.[28] The United States argues that, besides the excessive price control measures, local production does not respect patent protection rights on medicines used for treatment of HIV–AIDS. It is clear that the market share is changing with the initiatives being implemented by the Ministry of Health, as we have shown before discussing the generic products that have been introduced in Brazil. Even so, the threat of trade sanctions has been a feature of relations between Brazil and the United States for many years; and, along with strong pressure from the United States Trade Representative at the WTO, it led to the passing of Brazil's Intellectual Property Law in 1996.

In response to a worldwide mobilization in support of Brazil's AIDS programme, which the United Nations has judged to be the most effective in the developing world, the United States withdrew its complaint from the DSB. In a joint press release, both governments agreed to discuss future initiatives by Brazil, such as compulsory licensing or similar TRIPS Agreement safeguards, to ensure access to medicines. The full joint communication made by Brazil and the United States on 25 June 2001 is as follows:

> In the spirit of the efforts of Brazil and the U.S. to find a mutually satisfactory solution to the dispute about the compatibility of Article 68 of Brazil's Industrial Property Law (Law 9.279/96) with the TRIPS Agreement, the two countries agreed on the following.
>
> Without prejudice of the U.S. and Brazil's different interpretations of the consistency of Article 68 with the TRIPS Agreement, the U.S. Government will

---

[28] Oxfam (2001a).

withdraw the WTO panel against Brazil concerning the issue, and the Brazilian Government will agree, in the event it deems necessary to apply Article 68 to grant compulsory license on patents held by U.S. companies, to hold prior talks on the matter with the U.S. These talks would be held within the scope of the U.S.–Brazil Consultative Mechanism, in a special session scheduled to discuss the subject.

Brazil and the U.S. consider that this agreement is an important step towards greater cooperation between the two countries regarding our shared goals of fighting AIDS and protecting intellectual property rights.

World trade rules, and particularly the TRIPS Agreement, have been criticized severely by Brazil and other developing countries and by non-governmental organizations for not benefiting the poor populations or countries but being heavily biased in favour of the industrialized economies. Besides introducing a minimum 20-year patent term for all products, thereby delaying cheaper generic products and creating monopolies, developed countries are pressuring developing countries to enact laws that, on the basis of a very restrictive interpretation of TRIPS, jeopardize the implementation of public health safeguards.[29] Of specific interest for increasing access to medicines are the TRIPS Agreement's provisions for compulsory licensing, patent law exceptions, bolar provision (also better known as early working, included in the exceptions to rights which facilitate prompt marketing of generic medicines, as long as such exceptions do not conflict with normal exploitation and legitimate interests of the patent-owner) and parallel importing. They are recognized as necessary to allow low-cost, legally approved versions of patented medicines.[30]

In view of the progress with regulation related to providing access to medicines and on universal access to ARV drugs within the HIV–AIDS control programme, the Brazilian delegation, headed by the Ministers of Foreign Affairs and Health, played a prominent role during the WTO Ministerial Conference in Doha, Qatar, from 9 to 14 November 2001. It reaffirmed that Brazil promoted and upheld intellectual property rights, but would not hesitate to make full use of the flexibility afforded by the TRIPS Agreement to safeguard the health of its citizens.

The approved Declaration on the TRIPS Agreement and Public Health, adopted in 14 November, states (item 4):

> We agree that the TRIPS Agreement does not and should not prevent Members from taking measures to protect public health. Accordingly, while reiterating our commitment to the TRIPS Agreement, we affirm that the Agreement can and should be interpreted and implemented in a manner supportive of WTO

---

[29] See Oxfam (2001b) and Chapter 4 in this volume.
[30] VSO (2000) and WHO (2001b).

Members' right to protect public health and, in particular, to promote access to medicines for all.

In this connection, we reaffirm the right of WTO Members to use, to the full, the provisions in the TRIPS Agreement, which provide flexibility for this purpose.

A previous analysis[31] has demonstrated clearly that the greatest beneficiaries of recent changes in Brazilian legislation and of the implementation of the TRIPS Agreement have been not Brazilian companies but transnational corporations, which enjoy hegemony in the Brazilian market. During the period 1992–8, a total of 1,301 chemical product patent claims were filed by the international pharmaceutical industry in Brazil. Of this total, the greatest number by far were filed by the United States. Switzerland, Germany, Great Britain, Canada and Sweden also made claims for Brazilian recognition of their intellectual property rights. The analysis shows that the three countries that benefited most from the pipeline mechanism in Brazil were the United States, with 46 per cent of the claims filed; Great Britain, with 13 per cent; and Germany, with 10 per cent. In comparison, the number of Brazilian patent claims filed was negligible – 17, only 1.4 per cent of the total of 1,182 applications. A similar situation arises in the field of biotechnology. Thus, the analysis proposes in-depth sectoral studies in order to establish alternatives and strategies for the effective implementation of social policies in developing countries.

MAIN HIGHLIGHTS OF THE HIV–AIDS CONTROL PROGRAMME

Universal access to anti-retroviral medicines in Brazil cannot be analysed in isolation. It must be seen as one of the key elements of a global programme that has been implemented on a step-by-step basis over the years. The conditions set up for pharmaceutical care in Brazil's health service, are, as described above, conducive to enabling measures that improve the health of people living with HIV–AIDS.

From 1980 to December 2000, some 203,353 cases of AIDS were reported to the Ministry of Health, leading to the estimate that 536,000 Brazilians were infected with HIV. Other countries in the Americas have much worse figures. In Brazil, the Ministry of Health's policy and guidelines for the care of people living with HIV–AIDS has the necessary legal support. In addition to the regulations of the Constitution and the health system, Law 9.113/96, passed in 1996, guarantees every patient free access to all medication required for treatment. Standard treatment guidelines are set forth and reviewed at least once a year under the sponsorship of the Ministry of Health.[32]

[31] Bermudez, Epsztejn, Oliveira and Hasenclever (2000).
[32] MS (2001).

Brazil's infrastructure for distributing low-cost, locally produced medicines, mainly anti-retrovirals, comprises 362 accredited hospitals, 148 specialized care services, 69 day hospitals and 52 home therapeutic care projects. The health service has also set up a network of 70 laboratories with the capacity to perform TCD4+ lymphocytes counts and 63 laboratories for viral load quantification.[33]

Brazil's epidemiological surveillance of HIV–AIDS is a broad programme that includes HIV-infection monitoring as well as notification of cases. Research and studies are encouraged about users of health facilities for sexually transmitted diseases, emergency hospitals and public maternity wards. HIV seroprevalence among recruits to the Brazilian Army is monitored, and surveillance of infected pregnant women and children is also a part of the monitoring programmes.[34]

From its launch in 1992 until 1995, the provision of access to HIV–AIDS treatment in Brazil was limited because of the insufficient supply and availability of medicines in the public health network. In 1996, intensive media coverage of available new technologies, as well as the availability of new efficacy-proven protease inhibitors and the proposal for the combined use of medicines, led to a more comprehensive approach and to the creation of Ministry of Health guidelines. From 1996, the Ministry of Health ensured an increased supply of drugs, and the first Brazilian consensus on the use of ARV therapy and Technical Advisory Groups was established. A logistic system was developed for purchase, storage and distribution of medicines while Law 9.313/96 established the right to receive free medication, as noted above.

According to the Ministry of Health,[35] the principles of universality and equality ensure that 100 per cent of patients with HIV–AIDS will receive the necessary treatment. The results have been dramatic. Two studies carried out in São Paulo and Rio de Janeiro show a reduction of 48 per cent and 49 per cent respectively in the death rate of patients. There has been a considerable reduction in hospital admissions since 1997. It has been estimated that approximately 234,000 AIDS-related hospital admissions were prevented in the period 1997–2000, representing an overall saving of US$677 million for the health system.[36]

Currently, the Ministry of Health is responsible for the supply of 13 ARV drugs, including five nucleoside analogue reverse transcriptase inhibitors, three non-nucleoside analogue reverse transcriptase inhibitors and five protease inhibitors, and comprising in total 27 pharmaceutical presentations. The medicines are distributed throughout 424 pharmacies of HIV–AIDS out-patient

[33] MS (2000a, 2000b, 2001).
[34] MS (2001).
[35] MS (2000b).
[36] MS (2000a, 2001).

services.[37] State governments are responsible for providing medicines for HIV-associated opportunistic infections.

There exist one federal manufacturer and five state-owned manufacturers of ARV drugs in Brazil.[38] The federal manufacturer, Far-Manguinhos, is responsible for developing the manufacturing process for the final products, and supplies nearly 30 per cent of the AIDS medicines used in Brazil. In strategic support of Ministry of Health policy, it is also responsible for reverse-engineering the technology for developing the raw materials and the medicines. All of the products produced by the public manufacturers undergo bio-equivalence tests, in accordance with the Generics Law. Quality control includes compliance with good manufacturing practices, certification by inspection by the National Regulatory Agency, monitoring of the first batches and double-checking with university laboratories accredited by the Ministry of Health.[39]

ARV prices in Brazil have fallen in recent years owing to negotiation and centralized procurement with international pharmaceutical companies and to the promotion of state manufacturing. Recent patent protection law includes the safeguard of compulsory licensing on behalf of public health, in compliance with the TRIPS Agreement. According to data from the Ministry of Health,[40] domestic production has reduced prices by 78 per cent, negotiation based on differentiated prices with international companies has reduced them by 70 per cent, and prices of imported products have been reduced by 25 per cent of the initial cost. A cost-benefit analysis finds that, even considering the resources that are being spent on ARV therapy, the savings in hospitalization, welfare and years of life gained are clear. Government support for the AIDS treatment programme has been sustained by pressure from a coalition of social forces, by the good design of the programme and by the worldwide importance given to AIDS.[41]

A decrease in the frequency of the most common opportunistic infections has also been reported in Brazil – at a mean reduction rate of 60 to 80 per cent, including cryptococcosis (60 per cent), CMV infection (54 per cent) and Kaposi's sarcoma (38 per cent) – in major centres that receive severe immunodeficiency patients. New cases of tuberculosis in HIV+ patients also have decreased.[42]

---

[37] MS (2001).
[38] Besides Far-Manguinhos, which is a federal manufacturer linked to the Ministry of Health, other state manufacturers producing ARV drugs whose products are being submitted to bio-equivalence assays include Fundação para o Remédio Popular (São Paulo); Laboratório Farmacêutico do Estado de Pernambuco (Recife); Indústria Química do Estado de Goiás (Goiânia); Fundação Ezequiel Dias (Belo Horizonte); and Instituto Vital Brazil (Rio de Janeiro).
[39] MS (2001).
[40] MS (2001).
[41] MS (2000a).
[42] MS (2001).

Further evidence of the positive aspects of providing universal access to ARV drugs is provided by the partial immunological reconstruction that is being promoted by treatment. This has been shown by the progressive rise of the main TCD4+ count after 18 months of treatment. This improvement seems to reduce the frequency and severity of opportunistic infections and gives a better quality of life.[43] All of this evidence is a response to the criticisms that have frequently been made regarding the poor quality of domestic state production in Brazil, mainly regarding intellectual property rights and the domestic production of ARV drugs in Brazil, publicized at recent forums.

Ensuring and monitoring adherence to treatment is a priority for the Brazilian Ministry of Health, and efforts are being directed at providing more comfortable presentations of the ARV medicines that are being supplied within the health system. Current studies support the findings of other international studies, showing that adherence to treatment in Brazil is similar to that in other countries. Risk factors for non-adherence, such as low levels of education and income, are being addressed in several studies.[44]

Other, mainly African, developing countries are seeking cooperation with Brazil, since its expertise in AIDS-related medicines has been offered to such countries, particularly during the XIII International AIDS Conference held in Durban, South Africa, in July 2000. The Brazilian Ministry of Health has stated that it can promote the transfer of the technology for establishing production facilities, and it has agreed to discuss with several countries different approaches to creating comprehensive AIDS programmes. The Brazilian government has indicated that it does not intend to export its products or to promote worldwide acceptance of them. On the contrary, it is seeking technical cooperation that may enhance local production in other developing countries.

LESSONS LEARNT AND THE WAY FORWARD

There is no doubt that the issue of access to medicines is a priority for health policy-makers worldwide. The WHO's medicines strategy and its main objectives are well established, and they should be emphasized as necessary to developing countries as they implement their public health programmes. Formulating, implementing and monitoring national drugs policies must be mandatory for national health authorities, and the WHO must give the necessary guidance, directly or indirectly, upon request, utilizing the collaborating centres specified for that purpose.

---

[43] MS (2001).
[44] See Vitoria (2002).

All countries must consider a developed regulatory capacity as a necessary framework for setting up and implementing general policies, and national authorities must seek the appropriate commitment and cooperation towards this end from all relevant sectors.

It is important to realize that the developing world must find its own way to implement public health programmes and that an effective way for some regions is not necessarily suitable for the rest of the world. It is necessary to create alliances where possible and to use developing countries' experiences as possible models for implementing public health policies. A public health approach must be undertaken whenever we discuss access to medicines.

In recent discussions[45] and in view of the updating of the WHO's Model List for Essential Drugs, Brazil has proposed six evidence-based guidelines as following a systematic and transparent process for revision of the essential drugs lists, ensuring that it may really be a participative process, but maintaining the necessary technical background for the following:

- Guideline development with wide professional representation;
- Careful consideration of conflicts of interests (of special importance for industrial lobbying in developing countries);
- Systematic computer search for evidence;
- Evaluation of strength of evidence and systematic comparative cost-effectiveness analysis;
- Evaluation of public health considerations;
- External review and a consensus of expert opinion where there is insufficient evidence.

Brazil's recent experience has shown that the process of formulating guidelines for national drug policies and the revision of country lists of essential drugs can be very conflictual processes if not correctly implemented, and that evidence-based revision must rely strongly on randomized clinical trials and meta-analysis of different therapeutic groups of medicines.

A strong capacity for the domestic pharmaceuticals industry may be a delicate question in least developed countries that receive drugs donations from international companies or that are involved in price reduction negotiations, but it may also be a sensitive issue in developed countries that have to struggle with conflicting interests.

Access to medicines must be considered to be a fundamental human right, as UN institutions such as the Human Rights Commission maintain. This right strengthens the commitment to provide access to medicines. Brazil's representatives

---

[45] Presentation by Hans Hogerzeil/HTP and Tessa Tan Torres Edejer/EIP), HTP Cluster Meeting of Interested Parties, Geneva, 26–27 June 2001.

at recent annual meetings of the World Health Assembly have stressed this view and proposed resolutions that will promote the provision of access.

REFERENCES

Aday, L. and R. Andersen (1992), 'Marco Teórico para el estudio del acceso a la Atención Médica', in K.L. White (ed.), *Investigaciones sobre servicios de salud*. Washington, DC: Organización Panamericana de la Salud (OPS), pp. 604–13.
Bermudez, J. A. Z. (1992), *Remédios: Saúde ou Indústria. A produção de medicamentos no Brasil*. Rio de Janeiro: Relume-Dumará.
Bermudez, J. (1994), 'Medicamentos Genéricos: uma alternativa para o mercado brasileiro', *Cadernos de Saúde Pública*, 10 (3), 368–78.
Bermudez, J. A. Z. (1995), *Indústria Farmacêutica, Estado e Sociedade*. São Paulo: Hucitec/Sobravime.
Bermudez, J. A. Z. (2001), 'Ao Brésil, le triomphe dês génériques', *Biofutur* (Paris), 210, 40–42.
Bermudez, J. A. Z. and J. R. A. Bonfim (Org.) (1999), *Medicamentos e a Reforma do Setor Saúde*. São Paulo: Hucitec/Sobravime.
Bermudez, J. A. Z., R. Epsztejn, M. A. Oliveira and L. Hasenclever (2000), *The WTO TRIPS Agreement and Patent Protection in Brazil: Recent Changes and Implications for Local Production and Access to Medicines*. Rio de Janeiro: Oswaldo Cruz Foundation.
Bermudez, J. A. Z. and C. A. Possas (1995), 'Análisis crítico de la política de medicamentos en el Brasil', *Boletín de la Oficina Sanitaria Panamericana*, 119 (3), 270–7.
Bermudez, J. A. Z. and A. L. A. Reis (1999), 'A necessidade de se comparar preços nos mercados farmacêuticos', in J. A. Z. Bermudez and J. R. A. Bonfim, *Medicamentos e a Reforma do Setor Saúde*. São Paulo: Hucitec/Sobravime.
Cosendey, M. A. E. (2000), 'Análise da implantação do Programa Farmácia Básica: um estudo multicêntrico em cinco estados do Brasil'. Rio de Janeiro: ENSP/ FIOCRUZ (Tese de Doutorado).
Feghali, J. (1998), *Saúde: uma questão estratégica*. Brasília: Câmara dos Deputados.
Frenk, J. (1992), 'El concepto y la medición de Accesibilidad', in K.L. White (ed.), *Investigaciones sobre servicios de salud*. Washington, DC: OPS, pp. 929–43.
Fundación Isalud (1999), *El Mercado de Medicamentos em la Argentina. Estudios de la Economía Real*. Buenos Aires: Centro de Estudios de la Producción, Ministerio de Economia y Obras y Servicios Públicos.
Madrid, I., G. Velásquez and E. Fefer (1998), *Reforma del Sector Farmacéutico y del Sector Salud en las Américas: Una Perspectiva Económica*. Washington, DC: OPS.
Management Sciences for Health (1997), *Managing Drug Supply*, second edition, revised and expanded. Connecticut: Kumarian Press.
MS (Ministério da Saúde) (1997), *Farmácia Básica: Programa 1997–98*. Brasília: Ministry of Health.
MS (Ministério da Saúde) (1998), *IDB 98, Brasil. Indicadores e dados básicos para a Saúde* (Rede Interagencial de Informações para a Saúde – RIPSA). Brasília: Ministry of Health.
MS (Ministério da Saúde) (1999), *Política Nacional de Medicamentos*. Brasília: Ministry of Health.
MS (Ministério da Saúde) (2000a), *The Brazilian Response to HIV–AIDS: Best Practices*. Brasília: Ministry of Health.
MS (Ministério da Saúde) (2000b), *Programa Brasileiro de DST e AIDS / The Brazilian STD and AIDS Programme / Programa Brasileño de ETS y SIDA*. Brasília: Ministry of Health.
MS (Ministério da Saúde) (2001), *National AIDS Drug Policy*. Brasília: Ministry of Health.
OPAS (Organização Pan-Americana da Saúde) (1998), *A Saúde no Brasil*. Brasília: OPAS.
Oxfam (2001a), *Drug Companies vs. Brazil: The Threat to Public Health* (mimeo). Oxford: Oxfam.

Oxfam (2001b), *Cut the Cost. Fatal Side Effects: Medicine Patents Under the Microscope.* Oxford: Oxfam.
Perchansky, D. and J. Thomas (1981), 'The Concept of Access: Definition and Relationship to Consumer Satisfaction', *Medical Care*, 20 (2), 127–40.
Schilling, P. R. (1994), *Brasil: a pior distribuição de renda do planeta: os excluídos.* São Paulo: Cedi/Koinonia.
Silva, R. C. S. (2000), 'Medicamentos Excepcionais no Âmbito da Assistência Farmacêutica no Brasil'. Dissertação de Mestrado. Rio de Janeiro: Escola Nacional de Saúde Pública.
Vitoria, M.A.V. (2002). Conceitos e recomendações básicas para melhorar a adesão ao tratamento anti-retroviral. *http://www.aids.gov.br/assistencia/Adesao.arv.html* (accessed 19 February 2002).
VSO (2000), *Drug Deals: Medicines, Development and HIV–AIDS* (VSO Position Paper). London: VSO Books.
WHO (1998), *Globalization and Access to Drugs: Perspectives on the WTO/TRIPS Agreement.* Health Economics and Drugs DAP Series No. 7, revised. Geneva: WHO (WHO/DAP/ 98.9).
WHO (2000a), *Guidelines for Developing National Drug Policies*, second edition (draft, March 2000). Geneva: WHO.
WHO (2000b), *Progress in Essential Drugs and Medicines Policy 1998–1999.* Geneva: WHO (WHO/EDM/2000.2).
WHO (2000c), *WHO Medicines Strategy: Framework for Action in Essential Drugs and Medicines Policy, 2000–2003.* Geneva: WHO (WHO/EDM/2000.1).
WHO (2000d), *WHO Medicines Strategy: 2000–2003.* Geneva: WHO (WHO/EDM/2000.4).
WHO (2001a), *Highlights of the Year 2000 in Essential Drugs and Medicines Policy.* Geneva: WHO (WHO/EDM/2001.4).
WHO (2001b), *Globalization, TRIPS and Access to Pharmaceuticals.* Geneva: WHO (WHO/ EDM/2001.2).
Wilken, P. R. C. and J. A. Z. Bermudez (1999), *A Farmácia no Hospital: como avaliar? Estudo de caso nos hospitais federais do Rio de Janeiro.* Rio de Janeiro: Editora Ágora da Ilha.
Yunes, J. (1999), 'Promoting essential drugs, rational drug use and generics: Brazil's National Drug Policy leads the way', *WHO Essential Drugs Monitor*, 27, 22–3.

10 CHALLENGES IN WIDENING ACCESS TO HIV–AIDS-RELATED DRUGS AND CARE IN UGANDA

Dorothy Ochola

INTRODUCTION

Uganda is located in East Africa and has a total area of 241,039 sq. km, of which 43,942 sq. km are water and swamps. The major economic activity is agriculture. The population is estimated to be 22.4 million people, with an annual growth rate of 2.5 per cent. A low-income country, Uganda has an average per capita GDP of $300. Its annual per capita public health expenditure remains low, at $4. This cannot finance the essential health care package as recommended by the World Bank and the World Health Organization, which specifies $12 per capita. Forty-six per cent of the population live below the absolute poverty line.[1]

The purpose of this chapter is to outline and discuss the challenges that exist in widening access to HIV–AIDS-related drugs in a low-income developing country like Uganda. The themes that will be discussed include the health status of the population, the health care delivery system, essential medicines, the UNAIDS/Ministry of Health drug access initiative – a pilot project – challenges and lessons learned and conclusions.

HEALTH STATUS

Although there has been an improvement in the health status of the Ugandan population in general, improvement in health indicators remains slow (see Table 10.1). Infant mortality rates improved from 127 to 97 per 1,000 live births between 1991 and 1995, indicating the need for further improvement in the access to and availability and quality of health care.

The demand for health care continues to increase owing to the high population growth rate and to the HIV–AIDS pandemic, both of which pose a challenge to the health care system and the limited national resources. External resources

---

[1] Uganda Poverty Status Report (preliminary draft), 2001.

Table 10.1: Uganda: various health indicators

Indicator	Status
Infant mortality rate per 1,000 live births, 1998	84
Under-five mortality rate per 1,000 live births, 1995	134
Life expectancy (years) at birth, 1996	40
Probability of death before five years (%)	14.3
Total fertility rate,* 1998	6.9
Total expenditure on health as a percentage of total government expenditure, 1998–9	6.7
Percentage access to health facility within five km, 1996	55
Population per doctor, 1997	187,000

Source: UNDP, *Uganda Human Development Report* (2000), p. 8.
*Total fertility rate = the number of children a woman would have from age 15–49 years if she were to bear children at the prevailing age-specific rates.

have been predominant in financing health service delivery, and this raises important questions about sustainability and affordability. The major funding agencies in recent years have been the International Development Agency (IDA), which makes the highest contribution (19 per cent), followed by the United States Agency for International Development (USAID) (16 per cent), the United Nations Children's Fund (UNICEF) (11 per cent), and the African Development Fund and others.[2]

According to the Burden of Disease report for Uganda,[3] over 75 per cent of the life years lost because of premature death were due to 10 preventable diseases. Perinatal and maternal conditions (20.4 per cent), malaria (15.4 per cent), acute lower respiratory tract infections (10.5 per cent), AIDS (9.1 per cent) and diarrhoea (8.4 per cent) account for over 60 per cent of the total national death burden. Others at the top of the list include tuberculosis, malnutrition, trauma and accidents.

HIV–AIDS situation

Since the first HIV–AIDS case was reported in Uganda in 1982, approximately 2,276,000 people have been infected. An estimated 1,448,000 are living with the infection as of December 1999; 838,000 have died.[4] The main mode of transmission is heterosexual intercourse (75–80 per cent), followed by mother-

[2] National Health Accounts for Uganda, June 2000.
[3] Ugandan Ministry of Health, Burden of Disease Report, 1995.
[4] Ugandan Ministry of Health, NACP quarterly report, 2000.

to-child transmission (15–25 per cent) and infected blood and blood products, which account for two per cent of transmission.

The current average HIV–AIDS prevalence rate in the general population is about seven per cent. Prevalence rates have declined dramatically, from 33 per cent in 1992 to 10 per cent in 2000 in urban areas and from 15 per cent in 1992 to five per cent in 2000 in rural areas.[5] Uganda is reported to be the first country in sub-Saharan Africa to report declining trends for this devastating epidemic.[6]

Major interventions for HIV–AIDS

The major interventions to combat the epidemic employed in the country include:
- Information, education and communication, and advocacy;
- Sexually transmitted diseases (STD) diagnosis and management;
- Effective blood transfusion services;
- Care and support of people living with HIV–AIDS;
- Epidemiological surveillance;
- Involvement in AIDS research, the perinatal transmission study, the Nevirapine study and vaccine trials;
- Participation in various pilot interventions: the UNAIDS Drug Access initiative and prevention of mother-to-child intervention.

A spirit of collective effort, openness, strong political commitment and support has characterized the response to the epidemic.

HEALTH CARE DELIVERY

The minimum health care package

According to Uganda's national health policy, the government shall implement a minimum health care package that will consist of interventions that address the major causes of the burden of disease and shall be the cardinal reference in determining the allocation of public funds and other essential inputs. The government shall allocate the greater proportion of its budget to the package in such a manner that health spending gradually matches the magnitude of the priorities within the burden of disease.[7]

The Uganda National Minimum Health Care Package consists of control of communicable diseases such as malaria, STD and HIV–AIDS and tuberculosis; integrated management of childhood illnesses; sexual and reproductive health and rights and essential antenatal and obstetric care; family planning; adolescent

[5] National HIV–AIDS Sentinel Surveillance Report, 2000.
[6] UNAIDS Report, 1999.
[7] Uganda National Health Policy, September 1999.

Table 10.2: Recurrent budget out-turn, 1999–2000*

Department	Approved ($)	Released ($)	Released/approved (%)
Ministry of Health	7,306,931	6,229,937	85
Butabika Hospital	865,945	718,132	83
Mulago Hospital	7,687,027	6,845,542	89
Districts	20,177,335	18,495,891	92
Total	36,037,242	32,289,503	90

* As of 31 May 2000. All figures in dollar equivalents ($1 = UGSh1,750).

reproductive health; addressing violence against women; and other public health interventions, including immunization, environmental health, health education and promotion. This package is an essential focus of the new Health Policy and Health Sector Strategic Plan.[8] To ensure greater access of the population to the Minimum Health Care Package, a larger proportion of new resources have been directed to delivery activities for district services. Support to NGO services has been increased considerably in order that they are used to full advantage and help as much as possible in delivering the national health care package. In addition, some of this support is to be extended to a few non-facilities-based NGOs.

The provisional budget out-turns for 1999–2000 show that expenditure of $32.3 million (90 per cent) of the allocated $36 million was for recurrent expenditure on NGO and primary health care, district primary health care, district medical services, district referral hospitals, district hospitals and district and hospital lunch allowances. Table 10.2 shows a summary of recurrent expenditure return.

ESSENTIAL MEDICINES

Essential drugs are required for the management of the common conditions that affect the majority of the population. 'Essential drugs are those drugs which satisfy the needs of the majority of the population and should therefore be in adequate amounts and appropriate dosage forms.'[9] The Essential Drugs List indicates those essential drugs considered to be most appropriate for use in the Ugandan public health system. The criteria for selection include efficacy, safety, quality, cost-effectiveness and appropriateness. Most but not all of the drugs required for the management of common conditions associated with HIV–AIDS are on the list. The government heavily subsidizes drugs for tuberculosis and STD. Anti-retroviral drugs are not included on this list.

[8] Uganda Health Sector Strategic Plan, 2001–5.
[9] Essential Drugs List for Uganda, 2001.

The UNAIDS–Ministry of Health HIV–AIDS Drug Access Initiative

In 1998 UNAIDS, in collaboration with four pharmaceutical companies and the Ugandan Ministry of Health, began the UNAIDS HIV–AIDS Drug Access Initiative as a pilot programme with the goal of widening access to HIV-related drugs and care. Three other countries were involved in this project: Côte d'Ivoire, Chile and Vietnam.

A non-profit company known as Medical Access Uganda Limited was established with the help of four participating pharmaceutical companies (Glaxo Wellcome, Bristol-Myers Squibb, Hoffman-La Roche and Merck Sharp and Dohme). Its role was to ensure the timely procurement, storage and distribution of relevant HIV-related drugs, mainly anti-retrovirals, at a reduced price.

Specific treatment centres were selected for providing the drugs to patients after procuring them from Medical Access Uganda. The selection criteria included the availability of adequate clinical expertise in the management of HIV–AIDS, adequate laboratory services, psychosocial support and follow-up, adequate management of opportunistic infections and an adequate and efficient drugs storage and dispensing system.

Negotiations with the pharmaceuticals companies for reduced prices for anti-retroviral drugs were carried out at the international level by UNAIDS and at the national level by the Ugandan government. In Uganda, patients meet the full cost of anti-retroviral treatment, including consultation and laboratory fees. Between August 1998 and June 2000, price reductions on various products were achieved that ranged from 5 to 49 per cent compared with international prices, and in the following year (June 2000–June 2001) the price reductions were as much as 80 per cent (see Table 10.3).

These reductions were partly a result of the announcement in May 2000 by five pharmaceutical companies (Glaxo Wellcome, Bristol-Myers Squibb, Hoffman-La Roche, Merck Sharp and Dohme, and Boehringer Ingelheim) and five UN agencies (UNAIDS, the World Health Organization, the World Bank, UNICEF and the United Nations Fund for Population Activities (UNFPA)) that they would work towards achieving as many price reductions for developing countries as possible. At the same time, one of the Ugandan treatment centres started importing generic anti-retrovirals (ARVs) from India from a company called Cipla.

After these reductions, there was an increase in patient enrolment, and, more importantly, the number of patients enrolling for triple-therapy highly active anti-retroviral therapy increased compared with those on dual-drug combinations.

A number of important observations were made during the implementation of the pilot project. Mainly because of the high price of drugs at the initiation of the project, most patients tended to report when in advanced stages of the disease. Although the medical recommendation was to start treatment on patients with

Table 10.3: Comparison of drug supply prices ($), 1 October– 30 November 2000

Product	Measure	Unit pack	Old price*	New price	% price decrease
Combivir (a combination of two drugs in one tablet)	tabs 300/150 mg	60s	213.	68.82	67.79
Epivir (3TC)	tabs 150 mg	60s	95.482	20.904	78.11
Hydrea	caps 500 mg	100s	16.416	15.552	5.26
Videx (ddi)	tabs 25 mg	60s	19.159	9.72	49.27
Videx (ddi)	tabs 100 mg	60s	76.594	39.528	48.39
Viramune (Nevirapine)	tabs 200 mg	60s	265.77	132.885	50.00
Viramune (Nevirapine)	suspension	240 ml	68.931	34.466	50.0
Zerit (d4t)	caps 20 mg	56s	155.52	108.259	30.3
Zerit (d4t)	caps 40 mg	56s	168.372	114.091	32.2
Zerit (d4t)	syrup 200 ml	200 ml	39.96	27.886	30.22

*Wholesale prices from Medical Access Uganda.

CD4 counts of less than 350 cells per ml^3 and viral load greater than 10,000 copies per ml, more than 80 per cent of patients reported for treatment with CD4 cell counts of less than 200 cells per ml^3 and viral load of more than 100,000 copies per ml.

This made therapy even more complex and expensive, as a patient with multiple opportunistic infections was likely to respond more slowly to therapy. Most patients started on two drug combinations because that is what they could afford. When the price of drugs fluctuated owing to the depreciation of the Ugandan shilling against the major currencies, some patients dropped one drug or stopped treatment altogether. This affected the number of patients remaining in care over a period of time.

Patient survival was found to be 79 per cent at six months of follow-up, 71 per cent at 12 months and 68 per cent at 15 months.[10]

CHALLENGES AND LESSONS LEARNT

Poverty is the underlying cause of most health problems in developing countries. Low-income countries have a multitude of health problems, and the major challenge is to establish priorities for limited resources in order to be able to offer a minimum package of health care that will benefit the majority of the population.

[10] UNAIDS–Ugandan Ministry of Health, HIV–AIDS Drug Access Initiative, quarterly reports, 2000.

At the same time, the governments of these countries have to acknowledge and address emerging and hazardous epidemics such as HIV–AIDS that pose a major threat to their people.

The provision of high-cost medicines such as ARVs remains a challenge that has to be dealt with no matter the circumstances. Even though Uganda was one of the first countries to benefit from debt relief, it still has an outstanding external debt burden of $300 billion. Uganda's debt service obligation in 1997–8 was 9.6 per cent of total government expenditure. This was much more than the total expenditure on health, which was 6.7 per cent of total government expenditure in 1998–9.[11]

Competing demands for health care

Other health conditions such as malaria and diarrhoea aside, the provision of comprehensive care for HIV–AIDS patients in Uganda remains a challenge, even without including treatment with anti-retrovirals. It must take in voluntary testing and counselling, basic drugs for treatment of opportunistic infections, palliative care and symptom relief, and psychosocial support. Basic care is provided for the majority of the population, and those who have access to ARVs pay from their own pocket until the price is low enough to be affordable by the state. The result is that although ARVs are now readily available in the country and prices are lower, only a few patients can afford them. The overall benefit is for only a small proportion of those that need them unless a practical mechanism for ensuring adequate access and efficient use of the drugs is put in place.

Even when drugs are provided free, e.g. Nevirapine for prevention of mother-to-child intervention, the cost of their procurement and distribution within a weak health infrastructure may far exceed the cost of the drug. Providing wider access to drugs and care requires:

- adequate infrastructure;
- personnel with the right knowledge and skills (capacity-building);
- an adequate and responsive drugs distribution system;
- availability of other services such as voluntary counselling, testing and follow-up;
- adequate laboratory systems.

This requires heavy investment, especially if the intervention is to be scaled up to the rest of the country. There is a need for more coordination of funding strategies (public and private) in order to enhance health care infrastructure and to subsidize further drugs costs.

[11] UNDP, *Uganda Human Development Report, 2000*.

Price of drugs

The cost of ARVs is only one aspect of the total cost of providing HIV–AIDS care. Pharmaceuticals companies, the international development and medical communities and bilateral agencies have played significant roles in bringing about the reduction of the price of HIV-related drugs, especially ARVs, in developing countries. Much more still needs to be done, however, in order to have a tangible impact. There is a need to find mechanisms that can ensure effective and sustained international support for increased access to HIV-related drugs and care in developing countries.

CONCLUSION

Uganda is a low-income country with a high population growth rate and a wide range of competing health problems. A high level of strategic planning is necessary in order to set priorities that will adequately address the increasing demand for health care while taking into account aspects of equity, affordability and sustainability. The government has endeavoured to address this need by developing a minimum health care package whereby the country's limited resources can be channelled to meet the needs of the majority of the population. Owing to Uganda's limited resources, health financing is highly donor-dependent, which raises questions of sustainability.

Despite all the existing challenges, patients with HIV–AIDS in Uganda and other developing countries are in dire need of proper access to drugs and care. Solutions are being sought at all levels; and whatever effort, however small, is made to support access to HIV–AIDS care is of great benefit to patients in the developing world.

PART III
DELIVERING EFFECTIVE HEALTH

11 DIFFERENTIAL PRICING AND THE FINANCING OF ESSENTIAL DRUGS

WHO–WTO

INTRODUCTION

This chapter is based on, and follows the structure of, the report of a workshop jointly convened by the World Health Organization and the World Trade Organization Secretariats on 8–11 April 2001 in Høsbjør, Norway. It summarizes the principal issues identified and points made at the workshop about two topics: differential pricing and the financing of essential drugs.[1] First, it proposes that differential pricing could, and should, play an important role in ensuring access to existing essential drugs at affordable prices, especially in poor countries, while allowing the patent system to continue to play its role of providing incentives for research and development into new drugs. Second, it proposes that although affordable prices are important, actually getting drugs, whether patented or generic, to the people in poor countries who need them will require a major financing effort, both to buy the drugs and to reinforce health care supply systems. For these countries, most of the additional financing will have to come from the international community.

Access to essential drugs

There is a wide range of obstacles to adequate access to essential drugs in poor countries, including issues of financing, pricing, supply, selection and distribution.

[1] The workshop was hosted and financially supported by the Norwegian Ministry of Foreign Affairs, co-financed by the Netherlands Ministry of Foreign Affairs and organized and planned with the assistance of the Global Health Council. The workshop brought experts together to explore the complex questions involved in ensuring both access to essential drugs at prices affordable in poor countries and adequate financing for this purpose while providing sufficient incentives for R&D into new drugs. Besides the views of individual academic, legal and consultancy experts, the perspectives of governments, pharmaceutical manufacturers (research-based and generic), non-governmental organizations concerned with health, and intergovernmental organizations were heard in presentations and discussions. Background papers for the workshop are available from the World Health Organization at *http://www.who.int/medicines/docs/par/equitable_pricing.doc* and from the World Trade Organization at *http://www.wto.org/english/tratop_e/trips_e/wto_background_e.doc*.

The price of drugs alone does not determine who gets access to health care. Nevertheless, the health expenditure of the world's poor is devoted largely to buying drugs, often through private outlets. So the price of essential drugs matters to poor people and to poor countries. However, low-priced drugs, or even those made available free of charge, are often not sufficiently used. Locally available health services, adequately staffed, equipped, managed and financed, and oriented to local needs and priorities, as well as efficient distribution systems and tariff- and tax-free treatment for drugs, are some of the other factors that play an important role in enabling access on the basis of medical need. The individual factors influencing access to care have differing importance, and the whole access puzzle is complex and variable from one setting to another.

Financing health care and essential drugs

Even with low prices, expanding access to essential medicines substantially will require additional domestic and international financing for the purchase of essential drugs and for building effective health and supply systems. This is important not only for newer drugs, such as the anti-retrovirals, but also for essential generic drugs such as many of those for treating tuberculosis, malaria, diarrhoeal disease and respiratory infections. The mobilization of domestic resources in middle-income developing countries is an important way of improving access, but in poor countries financing needs will have to be met primarily by the international community. This chapter does not attempt to estimate what these needs are or to explore the most suitable modalities for meeting them, but it recognizes that there is a need for a massive upward shift in the level of international health aid.

Differential pricing is necessary and feasible

By differential pricing is meant the adaptation of prices charged by the seller to the purchasing power of governments and households in different countries. More widespread and sustainable differential pricing can be feasible provided the right legal, technical and political environment can be secured.

Economic feasibility

Differential pricing can be feasible where there are substantial fixed costs and variable or marginal costs of production are relatively low. Although there is perhaps greater scope where patented products are concerned, because of the high level of sunk research and development (R&D) costs, differential pricing can also be feasible for non-patented products. Differential pricing can be in the interests of both consumers in poor countries and manufacturers, while not adversely affecting consumers in richer countries, provided markets can be segmented effectively. This entails preventing the diversion of low-priced products into high-income markets (a technical issue) and a readiness on the part of consumers in these markets to accept sustained price differences (a political issue). Differential pricing can help to reconcile the twin objectives of affordability of existing essential drugs and providing incentives for research and development into new drugs, as support for R&D costs is shared according to ability to pay.

Differential pricing is already practised, in a limited manner

Several manufacturers already offer heavily discounted prices and donations to certain poor countries for selected drugs. Experience with vaccines, contraceptives and drugs for tuberculosis shows that low prices can be made available for poor countries, for both patented and non-patented products. Reductions of 90 per cent or more below developed country prices have been achieved through bulk purchasing, competitive tenders and skilful negotiation. Generic competition has also been shown to bring prices down.

Ways of giving effect to differential pricing

There are a variety of options for carrying forward differential pricing. These include creating the right conditions and leaving it to the market, the bilateral negotiation of price discounts between companies and governments, the use of regional or global bulk purchasing, the impact of moral suasion, the role of voluntary and, where necessary, compulsory licensing and the establishment of a flexible, global differential pricing system. Donations are also a possibility. These approaches have various pros and cons. For example, a global mechanism could be difficult to manage and could have undesirable, unintended consequences. And relying on individual initiatives that focus on a limited number of drugs and countries may not be sufficient. There is a need for greater international cooperation to support differential pricing.

More than one of the modalities mentioned above may need to be used, depending on the circumstances. Their possible use raises the issues of the role of competition in reducing prices, for example through voluntary licensing, and the relation of this to intellectual property regimes, the scope for incentives by developed countries for differential pricing and donations, and the constraints that competition law in many countries places on arrangements involving concerted action among companies concerning how they compete with one another.

Achieving favourable prices

Essential drugs should be made available to poor countries at the most favourable price, which is a marginal cost or not-for-profit price, but how this price should be determined is uncertain. This question is considered to be important not only by developing-country buyers but also by developed-country donors, who are concerned that if large amounts of development funding were to be allocated for financing the purchase of essential drugs, the products would indeed be bought at the lowest possible price. Among the approaches for achieving the lowest price are negotiation, perhaps aided by local cost-of-production calculations and large-volume purchases; increased competition through voluntary licensing or eventually compulsory licensing or its possibility; and the development of target prices relating to therapeutic value through economic analysis.

Maintaining separate markets and preventing diversion

Markets for differentially priced drugs need to be tightly segmented in order to prevent leakage of differentially priced drugs to higher-income markets. Among the mechanisms that can be used for this purpose are marketing strategies by manufacturers relating to the use of different trademarks and the presentation of products, stricter supply-chain management by purchasing entities, the role of the drug regulatory authorities in high-income countries and export controls in poor countries, and intellectual property-based rights for preventing parallel imports into high-income countries. These issues will require further study, but the available techniques, used in combination with each other with responsibility shared between the low-income and high-income ends, could ensure the degree of market separation necessary for differential pricing to be feasible.

Political feasibility

Preferential prices in developing counties should not be a factor in pricing in developed countries. Differential pricing policies hinge critically on the political acceptability of lower prices in poor countries. In a climate of increasing international scrutiny of prices and growing direct and indirect reference-pricing schemes, the industrialized countries may need to undertake not to use differential prices meant only for poor countries as benchmarks for their own price regulation systems or policies. A more difficult matter is how to forestall differential prices being used in the political process in these countries. This would seem to require political leadership, advocacy efforts and public education, and there will be the need to reassure public opinion that lower prices in poor countries do not mean higher prices in rich ones or a greater burden on national health budgets. Also, consideration must be given to whether differentially priced products may be seen as a form of unfair competition by local industries in developing countries, which may seek anti-dumping relief.

Middle-income countries and well-to-do populations in poor countries

The questions of middle-income countries paying prices proportionate to their income level and of the possible prohibition of parallel trade between low- and middle-income countries are difficult to resolve. There are further thorny questions: would the eligibility of the well-to-do segments in poor countries for differential prices significantly affect the implementation of price differentiation; and, if so, would it be feasible to separate the market for the well-to-do from that for the poor in those countries? One possibility is that differential prices would not be restricted to the public sector but would also cover not-for-profit providers and large employers.

The role of intellectual property rights

The differential pricing of essential drugs is fully compatible with the TRIPS Agreement and should not require countries to forgo any flexibility they have under it. There is a need to find an appropriate balance in intellectual property rights systems between providing incentives for the development of new drugs and facilitating access to existing ones. It is important to respect the balance found in the negotiation of the TRIPS Agreement and the rights of developing countries to use the flexibility in it, particularly compulsory licensing and parallel imports, to respond to health concerns. There is as yet relatively little experience with the use of these safeguard mechanisms, and external pressure on countries to limit the use of these options is a matter of concern. However, there are important reassurances on this issue. The TRIPS Agreement does not prohibit countries from aiding market segmentation through the prohibition of parallel imports, for example from poor countries to high-income countries. The patent system, although a necessary condition for much R&D, is not a sufficient one for securing adequate R&D into the neglected diseases of the poor. Additional measures of support for such R&D are necessary. There are possible negative effects on local and global innovation from excessive resort to TRIPS safeguard provisions.

Differential pricing and greater international funding

Many issues concerning differential pricing and the financing of essential drugs require in-depth analysis and discussion, and are developed further in the remainder of this chapter. They include:

- The international funding required for ensuring effective access to essential medicines in poor countries and the most appropriate mechanisms for the mobilization and distribution of these funds.
- The most appropriate ways in which differential pricing can be given effect. Linked with this are questions of how the differential price at which products will be sold in poor countries can be determined, including how negotiation and competition should contribute, in ways compatible with international agreements, to achieving the most favourable prices; what constraints are imposed by competition law; and how to develop incentives for differential pricing.
- How politically to insulate pricing in developed countries from differential pricing in poor countries, particularly the use of reference pricing. Also, the best ways of securing effective separation of markets and preventing trade diversion while taking into account international trade rules.
- How to treat middle-income developing countries and well-to-do populations in poor countries under differential pricing.

ACCESS TO ESSENTIAL DRUGS IN DEVELOPING COUNTRIES

The World Health Organization, UNAIDS and several other UN agencies identify four components of an 'access framework', each of which is felt to be necessary for ensuring access to essential drugs in developing countries: rational selection; affordable prices; sustainable and adequate financing; and reliable health care and supply systems.

Any effort to expand and assure access to essential drugs should ensure that all four of its principal aspects are adequately addressed. They includes the provision of local health services, adequately staffed, equipped, managed and financed, and oriented to local needs and priorities, in addition to efficient and tariff- and tax-free distribution systems. As was also noted above, the individual factors influencing access to care are of varying importance and the complex access puzzle differs from one setting to another. Countries' health and drugs supply systems, public, NGO and private, need to offer services of reasonable quality that respond to local needs. And priorities need to be considered carefully – between health and other demands, within the health sector and among competing demands for drugs. The WHO's essential drugs concept is widely used by countries in order to set evidence-based priorities for cost-effective.

The price of essential drugs does matter, especially to poor people and to poor countries. At the same time, the price of drugs alone does not determine who gets access to health care; in the words of one speaker, 'price is a necessary but not sufficient condition' for improving access to essential drugs in poor countries. Nevertheless, private purchases of drugs dominate household spending for health care in developing countries. The private sector there, which includes NGOs and 'quality health centres' as well as 'quacks', provides from 50 per cent to 90 per cent of drugs by value, paid for from the patient's pocket.

Effective drugs exist to combat the principal components of the global burden of disease: HIV–AIDS, tuberculosis, malaria and depression and suicide. But in many poor countries, expenditure to meet basic drugs needs falls short of the earlier WHO recommendation of at least $2 per head per year. With personal incomes frequently less than $2 a day, half the world's population is too poor to pay for many of the drugs it needs from its own resources, even at the lowest possible prices. Organized, sustainable health financing is required from domestic public health and social security budgets, where national resources are adequate, with reinforcement in poor countries by international assistance.

Although this chapter is not specifically about HIV–AIDS, the situation regarding access to drugs to treat this condition commands attention in view of the scale of the pandemic and the extent of the gap between the price of drugs and the means to pay for them in poor countries. In 2000–1, a combination of corporate responsiveness, domestic production and competition led to substantial reductions in the price of HIV–AIDS drugs (see Figure 11.1). This renders them more affordable for both domestic and international procurement, thus making mobilization of additional financial assistance the principal limiting factor to improved access to treatment.

Figure 11.1: The decline in anti-retroviral prices

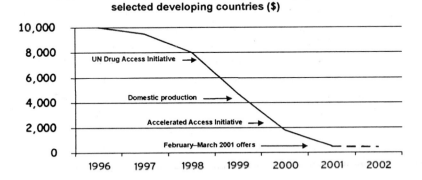

Source: Presentation by Dr J. Quick.

Even at these low prices, many developing-country governments and most of the world's poor cannot afford the HIV–AIDS drugs and the related health care services. The scaling up of the number of HIV–AIDS sufferers treated in poor countries from thousands to millions is a major challenge.

Even with reduced prices, the rates of uptake of the relevant drugs have sometimes been low. There are several possible reasons for this: low levels of discount, the recent date of the offer, under-recognition of the role of NGOs and the private sector in drugs supply and constraints on human and financial capacity in the health system. In many poor countries, the sometimes 'leaky safety net' of public health care systems provides less first-contact care than networks of private for-profit, not-for-profit or employer-based care. For this reason, differential prices could be extended from the public sector to not-for-profit providers and employers of large numbers of low-income workers.

The problems of under-utilization of existing essential drugs can be seen for many relatively inexpensive generic products. Most essential drugs are not under patent protection anywhere. Important exceptions are anti-retrovirals for HIV–AIDS and drugs for resistant tuberculosis.

As for governments' role in health care, regulations and standards need to be set for all components of a country's health system, both public and private. Governments have a special role in relation to essential drugs in view of the unusual character of demand and supply in the drugs market. Public purchasing of essential drugs is necessary on behalf of poor populations. To achieve public health objectives in developing countries, essential drugs have to be made available to individuals by public health authorities or NGOs on the basis of need, not ability to pay.

Some components of the retail price of drugs in developing countries are local. Tariffs, taxes and local distribution costs in particular, can double the manufacturers' selling price. So lower prices call for action by government, distributors and manufacturers. Although customs tariffs in most developing countries are low or moderate, below 20 per cent, developing countries have not committed themselves in the WTO to zero duties on pharmaceuticals, as most OECD countries have done. OECD states have drawn attention to harmful trade policies in some developing countries, which have affected price. An example is an anti-dumping action taken against generic imports on the grounds that low prices harm domestic industry.

One problem of access is that in some countries some essential drugs have not been approved by the local drug regulatory authorities and therefore cannot be imported and marketed. Problems can arise where local approval depends on prior approval of a drug in a major market in which the drug has not yet been submitted for approval. It may be that production and process standards required in developed countries are at times unnecessarily strict when applied in a developing-country context and lead to higher costs than necessary.

The pattern of stakeholder interests in the debate on improving access is as complex as the parties to the debate are numerous – developing- and developed-country governments, international organizations, NGOs, manufacturers of both generic and patented drugs and experts in trade and health policy.

THE ROLE OF FINANCING IN ENSURING ACCESS TO ESSENTIAL DRUGS

Even with lower prices, substantially expanding access to anti-retrovirals and other essential medicines will require additional domestic and international financing for the purchase of essential drugs and also a significant investment in building effective health and supply systems.

The mobilization of domestic resources is an important way of improving access to essential medicines. For this to be done more effectively, greater priority must be given to health in the developing countries' budgets. Some countries would benefit from diverting expenditure from defence for this purpose.

Brazil and Thailand demonstrate the impressive results that can be obtained through domestic mobilization. Between 1995 and 2000 Brazil implemented a programme of free and universal anti-retroviral treatment, which increased access to 92,000 patients, achieved a 40–70 per cent reduction in mortality and a 60 to 80 per cent reduction in morbidity and avoided 234,000 hospitalizations. The average price of locally made anti-retrovirals fell by 72 per cent over a five-year period. This programme was cost-effective, given the savings of costs that would otherwise have been incurred.

In Thailand, user fees constitute one-third to one-half of public expenditure on drugs, while the balance is taken from tax revenues. Over 80 per cent of Thailand's population has some degree of health insurance protection against the full costs of needed care. In many middle-income countries, more effective mobilization of domestic resources, combined with the untying of aid, differential pricing and, in the case of patented products, the use of the flexibility in the TRIPS Agreement, may prove to be sufficient.

For poor countries, however, the mobilization of domestic resources is limited by the level of economic growth and incomes, and a debate confined to ways of mobilizing domestic resources alone would be misdirected. Health systems are underfinanced in poor countries; many of them have a per capita public health expenditure of less than two per cent of their gross domestic products, or $6 per person per year. Even with differential pricing and the strongest political commitment to increase public health expenditure, external assistance is critical for these countries to improve access to essential medicines.

To tackle only the three major communicable diseases (HIV–AIDS, malaria and tuberculosis) massive increases in external assistance to poor countries are needed. This assistance would have to cover health system development requirements as well as treatment costs. The rough estimates for this aid range from $4.5 billion per year to $12–15 billion per year. These figures were compared with the existing, rather modest flows of official development assistance devoted to public health ($6 billion).[2]

It may be that the estimated financial requirements for TB drugs or HIV–AIDS drugs are too high, for example because HIV-positive persons have been shown to benefit from anti-retroviral treatment only later in the illness. But some consider that not enough has been set aside for developing the necessary health system capacity. The requirements for financing R&D of drugs for neglected diseases in situations where the patent system would not by itself provide adequate incentives are also important. More detailed work is needed in order to obtain better estimates of the external financial assistance required for tackling the health crisis in poor countries.

A massive increase in the level of international health aid is necessary. This might be the best investment that could be made in the future of poor countries, especially those in sub-Saharan Africa. Now that prices of HIV–AIDS drugs have been reduced to a fraction of their previous levels, the main constraint to getting the drugs to HIV–AIDS patients is finance. Without finance, price discounts will benefit a small number of people relative to the number in need.

There are plans on the part of some countries or regional groupings to increase their commitment to this form of aid. However, there must be a greater degree of international cooperation and coordination, both in order to maximize the usefulness of the aid and in order to ensure proper burden-sharing among donor countries. Concerning the latter point, possibly account should also be taken of differing degrees of public support in donor countries for medical research, especially that of relevance to tropical diseases. There are various ideas for increasing commitment to international health aid, including the creation of a global trust fund and expanding the role of bodies such as the UN, the WHO, UNAIDS, the World Bank and UNICEF.

DIFFERENTIAL PRICING

As indicated above, by differential pricing is meant the adaptation of prices charged by the seller to the purchasing power in different countries. Differential pricing can and should play an important role in ensuring access to existing essential drugs at affordable prices, especially in poor countries. In doing so, it could help to reconcile affordability with incentives for research and development. The general objective of differential pricing should be to obtain the best possible prices for essential drugs in poor countries. This is both desirable and feasible.

[2] Commission on Macroeconomics and Health, 2001.

The economic feasibility of differential pricing

Given the right conditions, differential pricing can be in the interest of both consumers in poor countries and manufacturers, while not adversely affecting consumers in richer countries and maintaining incentives for research and development. In theory it would be in the interests of producers to relate prices inversely to price sensitivity in each market, provided the markets can be separated. As prices in developed-country markets are generally already set at what the market will bear or by government, a move towards differential pricing involving lower prices in developing countries should have no adverse effects on prices in developed-country markets. On the other hand, differential pricing should, as a general rule, lead to lower prices in poor countries in view of the greater price sensitivity of consumers in those markets. The alternative to differential pricing is the setting of internationally uniform or nearly uniform prices (to the extent that government regulation permits), which probably would be established at the level the market can bear in the rich countries and thus be much higher than the optimal price in poor countries. This pricing is neither equitable nor efficient.

Poor countries collectively represent a very small share of the global pharmaceutical market (see Figure 11.2). In practice, therefore, a large part of the R&D and other fixed costs are already allocated mostly to high- and middle-income countries – another reason why differential pricing should be feasible.

A number of conditions have to be in place in order for differential pricing to be feasible. One is that the producer's fixed costs have to be substantial in relation to marginal production costs, and the producer must have the necessary degree of market power to be able to allocate those fixed costs differentially among different consumers. Fixed costs include R&D costs, many marketing and administration costs and fixed production costs (see Figure 11.3). What is a fixed cost and what is a marginal cost – and therefore the degree of differential pricing that is feasible – depends to some extent on whether additional demand can be met through existing unused capacity or whether it requires investment in new capacity. Although the scope for differential pricing is generally greater where patented products are concerned because of the high sunk R&D costs, the importance of other fixed costs means that differential pricing may also be feasible for non-patented products.

A second condition is that differential pricing requires market segmentation. This requires the prevention of leakage of low-priced products into high-priced markets (a technical issue) and a readiness by consumers in high-income markets to accept sustained price differences (a political issue). The way in which these conditions can be met are explored further later in this chapter.

Global bulk purchasing schemes exist that are able to offer prices to developing countries well below those in industrialized countries. UNFPA, the largest public-sector purchaser of contraceptives, obtains reductions of up to 99 per

Figure 11.2: The world pharmaceutical market by value

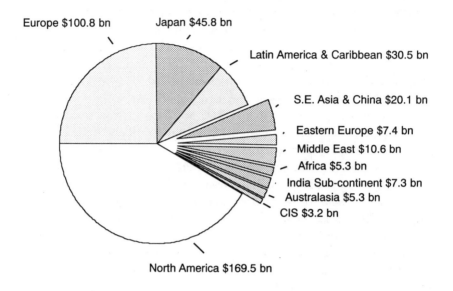

Source: www.ims-global.com/insight/report/global/report.htm.

cent of the US market price for some contraceptives and sells at a standard low price to developing countries (see Table 11.1).

UNICEF's supply division also obtains major price reductions through extensive volume-purchasing. Competitive bidding and direct negotiation with suppliers for long-term agreements are other ways to achieve lower prices. For manufacturers, concessionary pricing has sometimes opened access to markets that were not previously considered and has enhanced their public image. Regional bulk purchasing funds such as those of the Gulf Cooperation Council and ACAME (African Association of Central Medical Stores) have also negotiated price reductions of up to 30 per cent on some drugs.

Lower prices have also resulted from several pharmaceutical companies negotiating discounts on a product-by-product and country-by-country basis. More recently, some of these negotiations have been opened to groups of countries. One company planned the anti-malarial product Coartem/Riamet from early in its life to be packaged, branded, registered and priced differently in low- and high-income markets. The life of this product may suggest some important steps that companies can take to prevent the backflow of products from low- to high-income markets. Among the kinds of corporate donation, some involve open-ended commitments of time and quantities of drugs.

Figure 11.3: Differential pricing is economically feasible because of the nature of pharmaceutical cost structures

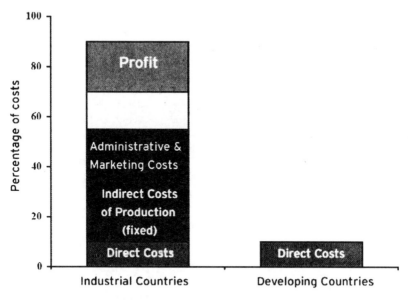

Source: Presentation by Dr J.-F. Martin.

The success of the mechanisms for achieving lower pricing, in particular donations, depends importantly on the drug companies' effective partnership with the public authorities in developing countries, on those authorities' political will, on the availability of dependable local distribution and health care systems and on the education of providers and patients. The rate of uptake of the drugs offered at substantially lower prices or free of cost was sometimes low, reflecting factors such as the lack of adequate financing, constraints on the capacity of the health system, lack of up-to-date information on those offers and underutilization of private-sector or NGO health systems.

On the pros and cons of donations, one view is that donations have the disadvantage that they are not always sustainable or generally available. They could come with conditions that reflect an imbalance of negotiating power between donors and recipients. Another view is that in situations where even a low price is too high, donations are to be preferred where possible. The notion that donations are unacceptable because they reflect an imbalance of power would, if carried to its logical conclusion, rule out philanthropic activity in general.

On the issue of conditionalities, there are differences of view about the extent to which conditions are attached to existing programmes, for example for HIV–AIDS drugs. One suggestion is that if any conditions are to be attached to

Table 11.1: Contraceptive price reductions through UNFPA procurement practices

Item	Unit	UNFPA price	US price	Reduction (%)
Oral contraceptives – generic (off-patent)	Cycle	0.175	30.00	99.4
Oral contraceptive – single-source (on-patent)*	Cycle	0.364	34.00	98.9
Condom	Piece	0.025	0.50	95.0
Intrauterine device	Piece	0.430	350.00	99.9
Injectable contraceptives	Dose	0.675	65.00	99.0
Spermicides	Table	0.060	1.20	95.0
Hormonal contraceptive implants	Set	23.000	393.00	94.1

* Example of third-generation oral contraceptive.
Source: Presentation by Mr C. Saunders.

the supply of differentially priced products, they should be minimal and worked out openly with the participation of all stakeholders.

Among the factors that influence the extent to which reduced prices can be obtained under existing programmes are the volume, duration and standardization of purchases; the patent status of the product; its importance in high-income markets; competitive pressure on the supply side; the buyer's monopsony power; the use of transparent, competitive and corruption-free procurement procedures; negotiating expertise; and the existence of technical or legal obstacles to trade diversion. More widespread and sustainable differential pricing is economically, legally and technically feasible with the right combination of consistent and mutually supportive strategies.

Giving effect to differential pricing

There are a variety of ways, discussed here, for giving effect to differential pricing. Each has its pros and cons and each has implications for securing favourable prices. The effect should be that essential drugs are made available to poor countries at the most favourable price, which is a marginal cost or not-for-profit price.

Leaving it to the market If the right conditions are created, according to one view, market forces will by themselves result in differential pricing by sellers, as this would be in their own interest. According to another view, however, this approach reflects unproved theory: there is no evidence that differential pricing in favour of developing countries takes place systematically, despite the absence of serious risks of trade diversion. And there is doubt about whether market forces by themselves will result in the lowest possible prices for poor countries.

Bilateral negotiated discounts   In one view, experience demonstrates discounted prices negotiated bilaterally between individual companies and countries to be a practical and feasible way of implementing differential pricing. The supplying companies themselves are the best judges of the maximum discounts that can be offered, as this assessment depends on confidential data on product mix, profitability and costing. Another view maintains that given the unequal bargaining power and access to information between the government of a poor country and a pharmaceutical company, unfair conditionalities could be imposed, and there is no way of verifying that the product is being offered on a not-for-profit basis or at the lowest possible price.

There are various ways in which a perceived imbalance of negotiating power can be addressed. One is the use of monopsony purchasing power, especially where a large volume is at stake. One concern is that just because a country is small, prices should not be less favourable than for large countries. There is also the view that there should be no discrimination between equivalently placed developing countries in the provision of differentially priced products.

Possibly, intergovernmental agencies can play a useful mediating role in negotiations and, together with civil society groups, exert influence by way of moral suasion. Also, a country's negotiating position might be improved by the use of local or other, generic companies to assess the cost of production. This technique has been used successfully in a number of cases.

The pharmacoeconomic approach to price determination is another way in which to respond to the imbalance of negotiating power. This brings together evidence of a new drug's likely cost and clinical effectiveness relative to the existing treatment alternatives. Product-specific information on R&D or production costs is not required in this approach. 'Value for money' prices can be identified, and the method adapts easily to low- or middle-income country contexts. An example was presented illustrating how pharmacoeconomic analysis could establish a target price using data on the performance of a drug (drawn from clinical and epidemiological evidence of effectiveness) and information on GNP per capita (see Table 11.2).

Regional or global bulk purchasing   For certain diseases and products, regional or global procurement and distribution systems can be effective in implementing differential pricing. For contraceptives, vaccines, first-line drugs for tuberculosis and most other essential drugs, competition is among off-patent generic equivalents, and it can be effective in lowering prices. Competition may also occur when there are several on-patent alternatives for the same therapeutic indication.

Table 11.2: Example of indicative target monthly prices for a specific cardiovascular therapy, based on drug performance and GNP per capita

Country	GNP ($) per capita	Target monthly price ($)
Armenia	500	0.20
Australia	20,511	8.07
Bangladesh	359	0.14
Belgium	24,088	9.47
Brazil	4,541	1.79
Canada	20,000	7.87
China	826	0.32
India	461	0.18
South Africa	3,112	1.22
USA	31,880	12.54

Source: Presentation by Dr D. Henry.

Table 11.1 above shows savings of over 95 per cent for an on-patent oral contraceptive subject to therapeutic competition. Although regional or global bulk purchasing can help to redress perceived imbalances of negotiating power and provide a channel for the use of international funding, it could harm local manufacturing capacity if products were bought only from large global producers.

Voluntary licences Wherever feasible, local production under voluntary licensing could be the most effective way of implementing differential pricing while enabling the patent-owner to be adequately compensated. It is advantageous because it could promote competition, especially if applied on a non-exclusive basis, take advantage of potentially lower manufacturing costs in poor countries, help to reinforce local production capacity and facilitate the transfer of technology. It could also help to avoid trade diversion, as products manufactured in poor countries could more easily be differentiated from products on sale in developed countries and would require separate regulatory approvals for importation into those countries. But this would be feasible only where there was a sufficient local manufacturing capacity and market. The question arises as to the readiness of originator companies to engage in more widespread voluntary licensing and to emphasize its voluntary nature and the importance of a strong and effective intellectual property rights regime for the transfer of technology. It is questionable whether voluntary licensing would necessarily lead to lower prices than would direct supply of the market. Normally, companies would prefer to supply the market and only license to third parties in situations where direct supply was not feasible. Other concerns are the possible liability of originator companies for the quality of products manufactured under licence, and the potential for parallel imports.

Compulsory licences An important incentive for differential pricing, which could be relevant to any of the approaches set out above, is the credible possibility of the grant of a compulsory licence. Subject to certain conditions, compulsory licensing, and also government use without the authorization of the right-holder, is permitted under the TRIPS Agreement. There could be difficulty in meeting the procedural requirements of these authorizations, and problems with the technical feasibility of local production in some developing countries. Under the TRIPS Agreement, compulsory licences could also be given for importation in situations where local production is not feasible. However, the availability of supply might be constrained by the limitation in TRIPS that compulsory licensing should be principally for the supply of the local market. There could be negative effects as a result of excessive resort to TRIPS safeguard provisions on local and global innovation. There needs to be a trade-off between access to drugs today and access to newer and better drugs tomorrow.

Flexible global systems The present approach towards differential pricing is a patchwork of individual initiatives focused on a limited number of drugs and countries. It may not be adequate, and there is a need for a more coherent global framework. This framework would facilitate the mobilization of the funds necessary to ensure that differential pricing actually contributes to meeting the needs of the poor for access to essential drugs. A global mechanism could be difficult to manage and have undesirable, unintended consequences, but relying on individual initiatives focusing on a limited number of drugs and countries is insufficient.

Intellectual property rights Another modality for differential pricing consists of arrangements for the allocation of intellectual property rights under IAVI (the International AIDS Vaccine Initiative). This provides for public–private partnership arrangements under which private partners in the development of HIV vaccines retain full intellectual property rights in the OECD countries and IAVI retains march-in rights for HIV vaccines in developing countries in the event that the company partner is unable or unwilling to produce and distribute the vaccines to the developing world at accessible prices.

There is no single solution to achieving differential prices. A combination of mutually supportive strategies, adjusted to the circumstances of individual countries, is needed.

With regard to the impact of competition or antitrust law on ways of implementing differential pricing, agreements between companies on how they compete are an offence, often criminal in nature, under the national competition laws of many jurisdictions. In many of these jurisdictions, it is not a defence that the purpose of an agreement is to promote the public good. This would be a barrier to companies engaging in differential pricing through concerted action (i.e. an agreement between competitors). On the other hand, competition law does not generally stand in the way of firms engaging in international price differentiation through actions that are independent of their competitors and that are not a part of a concerted arrangement to lessen competition. Issues might still arise under competition law provisions relating to predatory pricing or abuse of dominant position if the tests applicable under these provisions are met. Nor do competition laws prevent legitimate discussion of public policy issues or government actions authorized by legislatures.

Local generic production *vis-à-vis* that by the patent-owner could have a valuable part in giving effect to differential pricing. According to one view, provided that a product is made available at an appropriate price, the patent-owner should, wherever possible, retain control over supply. Control would optimize the balance between affordable access and incentives to research and development. Another view is that local production, for example under voluntary licences, could make an important contribution to the sustainability of differential pricing and could, by generating competition, lead to more favourable prices.

Generic companies in developing countries may have reason for concern about possible damaging competition from differentially priced products supplied by large foreign companies, especially if those products are financed through international funds. Imports of those products from high-income markets could be liable to anti-dumping action if they caused or threatened material injury to the local industry. Local generic companies should be able to benefit from international funding for the purchase of essential drugs. What was important to developing countries was the price at which products could be made available rather than where they were produced. There are cases where developing countries have used the threat of local production to secure more favourable import prices.

It is important to find ways of ensuring that products are supplied to the poor at the most favourable price possible, not only from the perspective of the needs of poor countries but also from the perspective of donor countries. If donor countries are to be ready to mobilize substantial resources to finance the purchase and distribution of essential drugs, they need to be sure that these drugs are being purchased at the most favourable price. A related point is the scope for donor countries to provide incentives to companies for donations or for supply at heavily discounted prices. This needs further study, and may require international cooperation.

Maintaining separate markets and preventing diversion

Markets for differentially priced drugs need to be tightly segmented in order to prevent leakage of differentially priced drugs to high-income markets. This is important not only for manufacturers but also for the recipients in the poor countries, because otherwise a differentially priced product would not reach the people for which it is intended. Manufacturers, governments, including regulatory authorities, and purchasers all have a role in minimizing leakages out of the intended markets.

There are at least six ways of achieving market segmentation:

- *Manufacturers' marketing strategies.* These strategies concern the use of different trademarks and the presentation of products. Marketing could be helpful in preventing trade diversion and could also make price comparisons between countries more difficult. However, it may not always be appropriate to use more than one trademark, and repackaging may still be worthwhile where price differences are large.
- *Strict supply chain management by purchasing entities.* A number of companies have indicated the importance they attach to effective supply chain management, which could ensure that a differentially priced product is not diverted to persons other than those for which it is intended. The supply chain for vaccines has special features, and when it comes to anti-retrovirals, an assessment of supply chain security has to be made on a case-by-case basis. With the use of batch numbers, bar coding and dating methods, the flow of drugs through distribution channels can be effectively tracked and many forms of diversion can be minimized. These arrangements require a sufficient degree of organization and accountability.
- *The role of drug regulatory authorities.* Essential drugs produced in developing countries and sold at differential prices, for example under voluntary licensing arrangements, can be imported into developed-country markets only if they obtain authorization from the drug regulatory authorities in those countries. This would be granted only if an application were made and the relevant production standards were met. A condition for granting a voluntary licence could be to undertake not to make an application.
- *Import controls by the customs authorities.* High-income countries may need additional legal authority in order to prevent the import of products marketed elsewhere at differential prices. Customs authorities have developed special expertise in preventing the import of counterfeit and other illicit products, and full use should be made of this. However, border controls are frequently less than fully effective even in the wealthiest countries, which have the most resources to devote to them. Additional responsibilities for regulating parallel imports, for example, might require a major increase in the resources devoted to border control.
- *Export controls.* It is uncertain whether export controls implemented by the customs authorities of the countries receiving differentially priced products

can be an effective means of preventing diversion. Further study is necessary in order to assess the extent to which they can be a credible mechanism in poor countries. Account would have to be taken of the burdens entailed, the extent to which customs authorities in developing countries already have the necessary legal authority and whether there are any international trade rule implications that need attention.

- *The use of intellectual property rights to restrict parallel imports.* Some consider that in order to provide the right conditions for differential pricing, it is important to have effective means for preventing parallel imports into developed-country markets and also into middle-income country markets. To some extent, patent law already gives the patent-owner such rights in developed-country markets, and this does not raise problems under the provisions of the TRIPS Agreement. There are variations in the extent to which public authorities such as the drug regulatory authorities and the customs administration can play a role in the enforcement of restrictions on parallel trade. At least in some jurisdictions, the powers of the customs authorities to prevent imports of infringing goods do not extend to parallel imports. Differential pricing requires restrictions on parallel imports into high-income countries and possibly into intermediate-income countries, but poor countries should be left free to engage in parallel importing where it would help secure best-value products.

The above mechanisms could effectively prevent diversion of differentially priced products, but further study is necessary into the legal and technical issues involved. If there is agreement on the principle of preventing diversion, the international community and national governments should be able to work out how this could be done in practice. More than one mechanism would be necessary, and the low-income and high-income countries should share the burden of preventing diversion. If the same differential prices could be offered in large, contiguous geographical areas, the problem of diversion would be reduced.

Political feasibility

As mentioned above, preferential prices in developing counties should not be a pricing factor in the developed countries. Differential pricing policies hinge critically on the political acceptability of lower prices in poor countries. There are two aspects to this issue. One is the issue of price interdependency, which results from the use of third-country prices for the calculation of permissible domestic prices (usually referred to as reference pricing). The other is the less tangible way in which prices in one country can affect the acceptability of prices in another country, for example as mediated through the political process.

Figure 11.4: The 'web' of countries using formal international price comparisons or price referencing

Source: Presentation by Dr E. Schoonveld.

With regard to reference pricing, market separability is breaking down in some parts of the world. The price regulation of pharmaceuticals is increasingly based, either formally or informally, on international price comparisons, and it is increasingly including, either directly or indirectly, developing-country prices. Figure 11.4 show the 'web' of countries which either use international price comparisons in their negotiations with manufacturers or are countries of reference for price purposes; much of this web has developed over the past five years.

Developing-country prices should not be used, either directly or indirectly, as references in developed countries' reference-pricing systems. Indeed, the more widespread use of differential pricing may call for some kind of international agreement among developed countries to desist from those forms of reference pricing for the products involved.

A more difficult point is how to forestall differential prices being exploited in the political process in developed countries. This difficulty arose a few years ago when concern was expressed in the legislature of a major developed country about tiered prices for vaccines. Some feel that political leadership, advocacy efforts and public education would be essential in preventing exploitation. Part of this effort would need to be directed at reassuring public opinion that lower prices in poor countries do not mean higher prices in rich ones or a greater burden on national health budgets. Others feel that without a vigorous campaign and the understanding and support of industrialized-country purchasers and consumers and civil society organizations, any transparent scheme of lower prices for poor countries may be taken as setting price benchmarks for negotiations in better-off markets. Uncertainty regarding future pricing policy can itself be a considerable disincentive to investment in R&D.

Middle-income countries and well-to-do populations in poor countries

The question of middle-income developing countries paying prices proportionate to their income levels is important. These countries should not be excluded from differential pricing, especially as many have large numbers of poor people. But they could be expected to pay a price somewhat higher than that in poor countries. The Human Development Index developed by the United Nations Development Programme could be used as a reference point for this purpose. There would need to be measures in place to prevent the diversion of the lowest-priced product intended for poor countries to middle-income developing countries. The mechanisms discussed earlier for this purpose would need to be examined.

As for the treatment of the well-to-do in poor countries, one view is that if they too benefit from differential pricing, this would be a significant disincentive to differential pricing; it could also aggravate any political repercussions in the high-income markets. Another view is that it would be difficult to segment a country's health system into separate parts for this purpose. A related issue that would have to be addressed is whether the supply of differentially priced products should be limited to the public sector, should also be supplied to non-governmental organizations and possibly large employers or should be made generally available in recipient countries.

THE ROLE OF INTELLECTUAL PROPERTY RIGHTS

The need to maintain and, if possible, enhance incentives for research and development into new drugs is widely recognized, as is the importance of the intellectual property system for this purpose. This system needs to find an appropriate balance between providing incentives for the development of new drugs and facilitating access to existing ones. Although the patent system is necessary for much R&D, it is not sufficient for securing adequate R&D into the neglected diseases of the poor. Additional measures of support are necessary, and available. There is concern about the implementation of the existing patent system and the extent to which it is open to abuse, for example in regard to the grant of weak patents and the 'evergreening' of pharmaceutical patents so as to delay generic competition.

Differential pricing of essential drugs is fully compatible with the TRIPS Agreement, and should not require countries to forgo any flexibility they have under it. Respecting the balance reached in the negotiation of this agreement and the rights of developing countries to use the flexibility it provides is quite important. As indicated above, the rules of the TRIPS Agreement provide for compulsory licensing and parallel imports, but there is as yet relatively little experience with the use of these safeguard mechanisms. There is concern about external pressures on countries not to incorporate them into their national legislation or to use them if they are already in national legislation. Developing countries may need technical assistance so that they can effectively implement compulsory licensing and parallel imports as well as other parts of the TRIPS Agreement. The decision of the Council for TRIPS to launch a debate on the relation between TRIPS and health needs is welcome.

CONCLUSION

The aim of this chapter has been to contribute to a better understanding of a number of key issues about differential pricing and the financing of essential drugs. However, many points require further in-depth analysis and discussion. They include:

- The international funding required for ensuring effective access to essential medicines in poor countries and the most appropriate mechanisms for the mobilization and distribution of that funding.
- The most appropriate ways in which differential pricing can be given effect. Linked with this are questions of how the differential price at which products will be sold in poor countries can be determined; how negotiation and competition should contribute, in ways compatible with international agreements, to achieving the most favourable prices; and how to develop incentives for differential pricing. There is also the issue of what restrictions are imposed on differential pricing by competition law.
- How politically to insulate pricing, and also reference-pricing systems, in developed countries from differential pricing in poor countries. Also, the best ways of securing effective separation of markets and preventing trade diversion while taking into account international trade rules.
- How to treat middle-income developing countries and the well-to-do in poor countries under differential pricing.

12 THE INTERNATIONAL EFFORT FOR ANTI-RETROVIRALS: POLITICS OR PUBLIC HEALTH?

Louisiana Lush

INTRODUCTION

The number of people living with the human immunodeficiency virus (HIV) or its associated acquired immunodeficiency syndrome (AIDS) rose to over 36 million globally in 2000. Of these, three million died, bringing the cumulative number of deaths from AIDS to 26 million since the beginning of the epidemic.[1] The vast majority of these deaths take place in developing countries; and most are premature, as sufferers rarely gain access to life-prolonging treatment and care. Poor access is determined partly by the price of drugs[2] and partly by weak public health systems for preventing and treating HIV–AIDS.[3]

Sub-Saharan Africa has suffered from a widespread HIV–AIDS epidemic and from few resources with which to address it. It is by far the worst affected region in the world: an estimated 25 million Africans were living with HIV at the end of 2000.[4] Two million more women than men carry HIV, and some 12 million children have lost their mother or both parents to the epidemic. By the end of 2000, over a million children were living with HIV, largely owing to mother-to-child transmission. Uganda remains the only African country to have turned the epidemic around, with adult HIV prevalence down from about 14 per cent in the early 1990s to eight per cent in 2000. Elsewhere in East Africa, prevalence rates are still in double digits. In several Southern African countries, at least one in five adults is HIV positive. In West Africa, rates are lower, but they are growing in some countries. Meanwhile, most countries spend less than $100 per capita annually on health care. By contrast, a year's treatment with anti-retroviral drugs costs $15,000 per head in the West,[5] and although drugs prices have dropped, much of the cost lies in the infrastructure needed to ensure high-quality care.

---

[1] UNAIDS (2000a).
[2] UNAIDS–UNICEF (2000).
[3] Stover and Johnston (1999).
[4] UNAIDS (2001).

Managing patients with HIV and AIDS includes a range of complex health services: voluntary counselling and testing (VCT) for the presence of the virus; monitoring progression of the disease; prevention, diagnosis and treatment of the opportunistic infections that attack those with HIV; delaying reproduction of the virus with anti-retroviral (ARV) drug therapy; managing the side effects of these drugs; preventing transmission of virus from mothers to their children during labour and through breast milk; and providing psychological and moral support to both patients and their carers.[6] However, health care systems in many poor countries are overstretched, underfunded and unable to deliver these services. As a result, policy-makers have neglected treatment and care issues and focused instead on preventing the spread of HIV.

Recently, however, one aspect of treatment and care policy has received substantial attention: access to ARVs. International media headlines, from the *Washington Post* ('As drug testing spreads, profits and lives hang in balance'[7]) and the *Guardian* ('At the mercy of the drug giants'[8]), attacked high drugs prices. Others, such as the *New York Times* ('Drug companies are vincible. The world's AIDS crisis is solvable'[9]), offered accounts of potential solutions to AIDS. Media reports have been accompanied by a rapid expansion in activity among non-governmental organizations (NGOs) at international and national levels.[10] Using ARVs as a highly symbolic and emotive issue, they have highlighted ethical problems concerning the role of international pharmaceutical companies, drugs prices and the effects of new rules under the World Trade Organization (WTO) and its agreement on Trade-Related Intellectual Property Rights (TRIPS).

ARVs are thus at a level on the political agenda rarely achieved by health problems. A special session of the United Nations on AIDS (UNGASS) in June 2001 was dedicated almost entirely to enhancing access to care. Summit meetings of the G-8 group of rich countries in October 2000 and July 2001 paid unprecedented attention to health in poor countries. At the Doha meeting of the WTO in November 2001, drugs access proved to be a major sticking point between an increasingly vocal developing-country lobby and rich-country trade representatives. Perhaps most importantly, the new Global Fund to Fight AIDS, Tuberculosis and Malaria (GFFATM) could mobilize large sums of money for purchasing and delivering ARVs, although to date the $1.7 billion forthcoming of a total $10 billion requested is disappointing.[11]

[5] Schieppati et al. (2001).
[6] WHO (1998) and WHO–UNAIDS (2000).
[7] Stephens (2000).
[8] Boseley (2001).
[9] Rosenberg (2001).
[10] Lurie (1999); International HIV–AIDS Alliance (2000); VSO (2000); Oxfam (2001a); Oxfam (2001b); Oxfam (2001c); and Treatment Access Forum (various dates).
[11] Brugha and Walt (2001).

As this resource gap demonstrates, there is a risk that as political enthusiasm wanes in the face of practical problems of service delivery, ARVs will fall from the agenda as quickly as they rose onto it. For policy-makers, the quandary is how to balance three elements of public interest: first, the universal human right to life and health through equal access to care (the main concern of NGOs); second, maximum efficiency in prioritizing and delivering health care, including HIV–AIDS prevention and treatment; and, third, maintaining incentives for research and devlopment of new drugs and vaccines through intellectual property protection. The answer lies in careful use of the political resources generated by the issue of ARVs in order to improve the health systems needed to deliver those drugs.

ACCESS TO ARVS: INTERNATIONAL POLITICAL DEVELOPMENTS

A number of international political developments formed the background to the recent agenda for access to ARVs. First, during the late 1990s global partnerships between governments or international agencies and private companies proliferated. For example: the International AIDS Vaccine Initiative (IAVI) started in 1996;[12] the French Fond de Solidarité Thérapeutique Internationale (FSTI) was established in 1997 in order to improve supplies of ARVs; and, from 1998, the Joint UN Programme on HIV–AIDS (UNAIDS) Drugs Access Initiative negotiated reduced prices with five pharmaceutical companies for ARVs for developing countries.[13] UNAIDS specifically highlights the potential for partnerships to increase funds for HIV–AIDS-related activities,[14] and it is likely that these initiatives will proliferate both for product development (drugs and vaccines) and for enhancing access for the poor.

Second, there was an unprecedented involvement of NGOs. Taking the lead from the vocal AIDS lobby in the United States, grass-roots representatives of people with HIV–AIDS in developing countries demanded access to treatments similar to those for their counterparts in rich countries. These representatives included international partners of ACT UP (AIDS Coalition to Unleash Power) (for example, in francophone West Africa) as well as smaller, local NGOs, such as the Treatment Action Campaign in South Africa or patient rights representatives in India, and church groups. Northern NGOs, such as Oxfam, Médecins Sans Frontières, Voluntary Service Overseas, the International AIDS Alliance and the Save the Children Fund, also put pressure on their home governments

[12] International AIDS Vaccine Initiative (2000).
[13] UNAIDS (1997); UNAIDS (1998); République de Côte d'Ivoire Ministère de la Santé: (2000); Uganda Ministry of Health (2000); UNAIDS (2000b, c and d).
[14] UNAIDS (1997).

to cancel debts and to increase investment for promoting access to drugs. The Consumer Project on Technology, based in Washington, DC, was a further vocal proponent of reducing patent protection of monopoly prices on essential HIV–AIDS medicines.

Third, in 1994 the WTO was formed with the explicit aim of standardizing global trade rules. The TRIPS Agreement lays down new, stricter minimum standards of intellectual property protection as a condition of WTO membership and 'aims to strike a balance between inventor's interests, public interest in innovation and public good'.[15] By 2000, many developing countries had to have passed national legislation guaranteeing product and process patent protection for 20 years, although some of the poorest countries had until 2006. Limited safeguards are available in Article 31 of TRIPS, which allows governments to override a patent by issuing a compulsory licence in the public interest under conditions of 'national emergency'.[16] However, these conditions are poorly defined legally and strongly resisted by the international pharmaceutical industry, which is allied with those rich-country governments it can persuade to lobby on its behalf.

Fourth, the pressure of negative public opinion and 'ethical investors' on the pharmaceutical industry increased, fuelled by reports of shareholders benefiting from high profits while the global majority had little access to drugs. Most agree that the economics of research and development are highly complex and that the cost of bringing a new drug to market is high. However, the lack of financial transparency in this area enhances the perception of shocking global inequity coexisting with vast profit. For example, in 1999 GlaxoSmithKline's $245 million operating profits for just one of its drugs, Combivir, were $89 million more than the $156 million combined health expenditure of all the members of the African Regional Industrial Property Organization.[17] Other criticism has highlighted the pharmaceutical industry's piggy-backing on scientific developments that actually took place in the public sector.

Finally, pressure on rich-country governments also increased as debt relief and anti globalization campaigns joined the fray. Development economists such as Jeffrey Sachs and colleagues at the Commission on Macroeconomics and Health emphasized the importance of health care as a development investment. They suggested that the costs of treating HIV–AIDS, at about $10 billion, could be relatively easily met through existing aid channels if macroeconomic conditions were suitable.[18] These developments, although controversial in their simplification of complex issues, led the US government to double its spending

[15] Oxfam (2001a), p. 3.
[16] World Trade Organization (1994).
[17] Oxfam (2001b).
[18] Attaran and Sachs (2001).

on HIV–AIDS in 1999[19] and to donate $200 million to the Global Fund to Fight AIDS, Tuberculosis and Malaria.

Problems of high politics lead to solutions of high politics: calls for and the subsequent establishment of a global fund for purchasing and delivering drugs;[20] drugs donations and price reductions by pharmaceutical companies; and demands for access to drugs by politicians in developing countries.[21] These quick-fix solutions make for good public relations and therefore are popular with politicians and company chief executives. However, these solutions are often formulated by the international community, in which developing countries have little representation. For example, at a joint WTO–WHO meeting in April 2001 on the pricing of essential medicines, of about 80 participants, fewer than 10 represented developing-country governments.[22] By contrast, there were 16 pharmaceutical industry representatives, and the remainder came from rich-country aid programmes or from international organizations and NGOs. Similarly, at the November 2001 WTO meeting in Doha, observer places were heavily restricted, and favoured pharmaceuticals lobbyists over developing-country representatives. As a result, complex issues of how to deliver treatment and care for people with HIV–AIDS in a context of extreme underinvestment in health care are neglected, and the balance of public interest in intellectual property protection versus that in public health remains heavily weighted towards the former.

NEGLECT OF PRACTICALITIES AT THE NATIONAL LEVEL

Although international effort raised additional funds for HIV–AIDS, questions remain over whether purchasing ARV drugs is actually the best use of new resources. Even with lower drugs prices, central drugs administrations are often under-regulated, out of date and weakly monitored. Peripheral drug distribution systems rarely function efficiently enough to ensure regular commodity supplies.[23] Providing ARVs also requires intensive monitoring of viral load or immune system status and the development of drug resistance or severe side effects. Sensitive and confidential VCT is clearly a precondition, as is substantial improvement in clinical capacity through training, supervision and technical support. Decisions over whether to integrate these services with existing care or to establish dedicated AIDS treatment centres are intertwined with concerns about quality and equity.

---

[19] The White House, Office of the Press Secretary (2000).
[20] Attaran and Sachs (2001) and Brugha and Walt (2001).
[21] Organization of African Unity (2001).
[22] Consumer Project on Technology (2001).
[23] Forsythe and Gilks (1998).

These improvements are difficult and likely to draw funds away from other important preventive and treatment activities. Economic analysis shows that primary prevention remains the most cost-effective approach to address HIV–AIDS:[24] the total cost of meeting Africa's need for condoms has been estimated at $48 million[25] – a far cry from the $10 billion being demanded for treatment.[26] Preventing and treating opportunistic infections are other neglected areas of care that are often cheap and cost-effective.[27] Nevertheless, development agencies, such as UNAIDS, the World Health Organization, the US Agency for International Development and the British Department for International Development, which have traditionally supported prevention programmes, are beginning to respond to pressure.

Despite dramatic epidemic figures, until recently the cultural, political and social stigma of HIV–AIDS led to a muted effort in many poor countries.[28] In part this was due to weak leadership: politicians such as Thabo Mbeki in South Africa, Daniel Arap Moi in Kenya and Robert Mugabe in Zimbabwe neglected practicalities in favour of populist speeches, conspiracy theories or religious fundamentalism. However, those successful HIV–AIDS programmes that do exist have relied on a political context which legitimizes open debate of sensitive issues of sexual behaviour and moral responsibility, distributive justice and access to care, and social capital and community support structures. In general, ethical issues regarding health are weakly conceptualized in developing countries, and there are few opportunities for national debate.[29] The media is not always free from political influence; many people are illiterate and not empowered to participate in national debate. Activist groups or civil society representatives tend to be weaker where governments are less democratic.[30]

This situation compares poorly with that in many rich countries in the 1980s, when AIDS first spread among homosexual and injecting-drug-user groups. Activism by vocal, middle-class American gay communities played a key role in generating research funds and government support for new services as well as in promoting the rights of people with HIV–AIDS.[31] Similarly, open discussion of the benefits of needle exchange programmes garnered political support for these highly controversial interventions all over Europe.[32] In many poor countries, the absence of democratic and participatory debate means that

---

[24] Gilks et al. (1998).
[25] Shelton and Johnston (2001).
[26] Attaran and Sachs (2001).
[27] Abdool Karim et al. (1997) and Bell et al. (1999).
[28] Prual et al. (1991) and Caldwell et al. (1992).
[29] Seidel (1993) and Goldin (1994).
[30] Moore and Putzel (1999).
[31] Epstein (1998).
[32] Stimson (1995).

the elite can use the institutions of power to promote their own access to ARVs instead of innovative public health initiatives.

FROM POLITICAL POSTURING TO PRACTICAL STEPS: AN AGENDA FOR ACTION AND RESEARCH

The politicization of health concerns is not new, but it is extreme. Nevertheless, in the face of practical reality ARVs could, as suggested above, turn out to be a storm in a teacup and drop off the agenda as quickly as they came onto it. Lack of attention to developing countries' political and economic interests risks wasting the enthusiasm generated by media attention. This would be a pity, as the financial and political resources mobilized via this attention could be used to improve access to health care in general, not just to ARVs.

In the places most affected by HIV–AIDS, the storm is just beginning. Doing nothing in response to it is not an option: in most countries, ARVs are already available on the black market for sufferers to purchase as and when they can afford them if they are not able to keep to a regular treatment course. Illegal prescription will cause toxic side effects and the development of viral resistance, but this will be hard to prevent with so few alternatives available to desperate people. However, in the current environment licensed distribution of ARVs will achieve relatively little because health care systems are often too weak to undertake such a complex new treatment programme. Equitable and high-quality provision of ARVs may be feasible one day, but only through long-term political reform of health systems, something government and aid agency staff have been trying to achieve for decades.

In response, some aid agencies have proposed a range of research and pilot initiatives, including developing appropriate ARV regimens for poor countries; evaluating technical and managerial resources required to deliver ARVs (health system capacity and constraints); and assessing the financial costs of expanding ARV programmes to include different population groups through dedicated treatment centres or integrated models of care. However, these responses are highly technical, and underplay crucial problems of poverty, power and equity.

Improving access to ARVs focuses political attention on the parlous state of many countries' health services. Indeed, the argument that lack of decent health services rather than high prices prevents access to drugs has been used disingenuously by the pharmaceutical industry itself. What the pharmaceutical companies are more reluctant to admit is that meaningful reform will require substantial cultural and political change on a foundation of open debate, fair distribution of resources and an environment of hope, not despair. It is up to governments and their donors to support activities specifically designed to foster this fundamental change. These activities might include, for example, delivering ARVs initially to clearly defined, morally uncontentious groups, for prevention of mother-to-child transmission or for victims of rape and needle-stick injuries. Innovative efforts to foster debate on the ethics of access to treatment in societies that do not have a free press, a functional democracy or literate populations will also result in mobilizing wide participation in determining appropriate policy responses. Popular support for action must be mediated by a culturally relevant mixture of elected officials, community representatives and groups of people with HIV–AIDS. Responsibility for these measures should be firmly rooted in the countries most affected by HIV–AIDS and should be locally determined and contextualized.

International actors, meanwhile, should actively involve a wider range of constituencies in international decision-making. Many international fora claim to represent the interests of the poor, but are vulnerable to those of the powerful. For example, with notable exceptions such as Brazil and India, developing-country delegations have been too weak to argue cogently the case for the precedence of public health over intellectual property protection in international trade negotiations. Even in countries such as India, a debate rages over the balance between protecting their nascent pharmaceutical manufacturing industry and promoting public health. The lawyers involved therefore need substantial technical and intellectual capacity, scarce resources in the developing world, to find a politically palatable answer. The United States, by contrast, sent a 400-strong team to the Seattle WTO conference in November 1999 to represent a government heavily funded by the pharmaceutical industry.

Although intergovernmental organizations such as the WTO and the WHO are rarely free from controversy, they are at least predicated on the well-established accountability of sovereign states. In the context of globalization and the rise of private-sector interests, however, these institutions appear antiquated and naïve. For instance, the Gates Foundation is required by US tax laws to spend five per cent of its endowment each year – amounting to some $1 billion – much of which has gone into international health. This figure is similar to the entire budget of the WHO, and the comparison highlights the trend for resources, and with them power, to flow increasingly through non-traditional institutions of unclear legitimacy.[33] Organizations such as the Gates Foundation finance a burgeoning number of public–private partnerships, in which accountability for health impact is even less clear; it may include company shareholders, donor governments or sometimes the partnerships' own executive boards. Beneficiaries are rarely informed of performance, and independent evaluations are the exception rather than the rule.

---

[33] Walt and Buse (2000).

These global institutional trends suggest that rich-country governments concerned with enhancing access to drugs in poor countries need to update and reconsider their policies in a range of areas. It is essential to redress the current balance of influence and power between pharmaceutical companies and poor countries. A further requirement is to act swiftly and coherently on the growing consensus that the current regime of intellectual property protection does not meet the needs of poor countries. Finally, to complement these responses, the fundamental inequities, both global and local, that prevent health systems from providing decent health care need to be recognized and removed.

REFERENCES

Abdool Karim, Q., D. Tarantola, E. As Sy and R. Moodie (1997), 'Government responses to HIV/AIDS in Africa: what have we learnt?' *AIDS*, 11(Suppl. B), S143–9.

Attaran, A. and J. Sachs (2001), 'Defining and refining international donor support for combating the AIDS pandemic', *The Lancet*, 357, 57–61.

Bell, J. C., D. N. Rose and H. S. Sacks (1999), 'Tuberculosis preventive therapy for HIV-infected people in sub-Saharan Africa is cost-effective', *AIDS*, 13 (12), 1549–56.

Boseley, S. (2001), 'At the mercy of the drug giants'. *The Guardian*. London.

Brugha, R. and G. Walt (2001), 'A global health fund: a leap of faith?' *British Medical Journal*, 323, 152–4.

Caldwell, J. C., I. O. Orubuloye and P. Caldwell (1992), 'Underreaction to AIDS in Sub–Saharan Africa', *Social Science and Medicine*, 34, 1169–82.

Consumer Project on Technology (2001), 8–11 April, Høsbjør, Norway, WHO–WTO Secretariat Workshop on Differential Pricing and Financing of Essential Drugs – Participant List, 30 March 2001, *pharm-policy@lists.essential.org: Pharm-policy Digest*, 1 (323), 2001.

Epstein, S. (1998), *Impure Science: AIDS, Activism and the Politics of Knowledge*. London: University of California Press.

Forsythe, S. and C. Gilks (1998), 'Opinion. Policymaking and ARVs: a framework for rational decision making', *Impact on HIV*, 1(1).

Gilks, C., K. Floyd, D. Haran et al. (1998), *Sexual Health and Health Care: Care and Support for People with HIV/AIDS in Resource-poor Settings*. London: Department for International Development, Health and Population Occasional Paper.

Goldin, C. S. (1994), 'Stigmatization and AIDS: critical issues in public health', *Social Science and Medicine*, 39, 1359–66.

International AIDS Vaccine Initiative (2000), *AIDS Vaccines for the World: Preparing Now to Assure Access*. Geneva: IAVI, An IAVI Blueprint.

International HIV–AIDS Alliance (2000), 'Access to treatment', *Allliance News*, 4 (3), 1.

Lurie, P. (1999), *Denying Effective Antiretroviral Drugs to HIV-positive Pregnant Women – The National Government's Flawed Decision*, Public Citizen Health Research Group.

Moore, M. and J. Putzel (1999), *Politics and Poverty: A Background Paper for the World Development Report 2000–01*. Brighton: Institute of Development Studies, University of Sussex.

Organization of African Unity (2001), *Abuja Declaration on HIV–AIDS, Tuberculosis and Other Related Infectious Diseases*. Abuja: African Summit on HIV–AIDS, Tuberculosis and Other Related Infectious Diseases, 24–27 April 2001.

Oxfam (2001a), *Cut the Cost: Patent Injustice: How World Trade Rules Threaten the Health of Poor People*. Oxford: Oxfam.

Oxfam (2001b), *Dare to Lead: Public Health and Company Wealth (Oxfam Briefing Paper on GlaxoSmithKline)*, Oxford: Oxfam.

Oxfam (2001c), *Fatal Side Effects: Medicine Patents Under the Microscope.* Oxford: Oxfam. (See also Chapter 4 in this volume.)

Prual, A., S. Chacko and D. Koch Weser (1991), 'Sexual behaviour, AIDS and poverty in Sub–Saharan Africa' [editorial], *International Journal of STDs and AIDS,* 2, 1–9.

République de Côte d'Ivoire, Ministère de la Santé (2000), Programme National de Lutte contre le SIDA/MST/TUB *HIV/AIDS Drug Access Initiative.* Preliminary report. Geneva: UNAIDS.

Rosenberg, T. (2001), 'Look at Brazil. Patent laws are malleable. Patients are educable. Drug companies are vincible. The world's AIDS crisis is solvable', *New York Times.*

Schieppati, A., G. Remuzzi and G. Silvio (2001), 'Modulating the profit motive to meet needs of the less-developed world', *The Lancet,* 358, 1638–41.

Seidel, G. (1993), 'The competing discourses of HIV–AIDS in sub-Saharan Africa: discourses of rights and empowerment vs. discourses of control and exclusion', *Social Science and Medicine,* 36 (3), 175–94.

Shelton, J. D. and B. Johnston (2001), 'Condom gap in Africa: evidence from donor agencies and key informants', *British Medical Journal,* 323, 139.

Stephens, J. (2000), 'As drug testing spreads, profits and lives hang in balance', *Washington Post,* A01.

Stimson, G. V. (1995), 'AIDS and injecting drug use in the United Kingdom, 1987–1993: the policy response and the prevention of the epidemic', *Social Science and Medicine* 41 (5), 699–716.

Stover, J. and A. Johnston (1999), *The Art of Policy Formulation: Experiences from Africa in Developing National HIV–AIDS Policies.* The Futures Group Occasional Paper. Washington, DC: The Policy Project.

Treatment Access Forum (Various dates), *treatment-access@hivnet.ch.* 2001.

Uganda Ministry of Health (2000), *Uganda Ministry of Health – UNAIDS HIV–AIDS Drug Access Initiative.* Preliminary report. Geneva: UNAIDS

UNAIDS (1997), *Towards the Creation of Strategic Partnerships: Improving Access to Drugs for HIV–AIDS.* Geneva: UNAIDS Report of a consultative meeting.

UNAIDS (1998), *HIV–AIDS Prevention in the Context of New Therapies.* UNAIDS Report of a meeting organized by UNAIDS and the AIDS Research Institute of the University of California at San Francisco. Geneva: UNAIDS.

UNAIDS (2000a), *AIDS Epidemic Update: December 2000.* Geneva: UNAIDS.

UNAIDS (2000b), *Expression of Interest.* Geneva: UNAIDS.

UNAIDS (2000c), Informal Meeting on Open Competition for HIV–AIDS Medicines. Geneva, UNAIDS.

UNAIDS (2000d), *Report of the Meeting on the Evaluation of the UNAIDS HIV Drug Access Initiative.* Geneva: UNAIDS.

UNAIDS (2001), *Fact Sheet: An Overview of the HIV–AIDS Epidemic.* Geneva: UNAIDS.

UNAIDS–UNICEF (2000), *Essential Drugs Used in the Care of People Living with HIV: Sources and Prices.* Geneva: UNAIDS–UNICEF.

VSO (2000), *Drug Deals: Medicines, Development and HIV–AIDS.* London: Voluntary Service Overseas.

Walt, G. and K. Buse (2000), 'Editorial: Partnership and fragmentation in international health: threat or opportunity?', *Tropical Medicine & International Health* 5 (7): 467.

The White House, Office of the Press Secretary (2000), Statement by the President. Washington, DC.

WHO (1998), *WHO Initiative on HIV–AIDS and Sexually Transmitted Infections (HSI): Nine Guidance Modules on Antiretroviral Treatments.* Geneva: WHO.

WHO–UNAIDS (2000), *Key Elements in HIV–AIDS Care and Support.* Draft working document. Geneva: WHO–UNAIDS.

World Trade Organization (1994), Agreement on Trade-Related Aspects of Intellectual Property Rights, Part II: Standards Concerning the Availability, Scope and Use of Intellectual Property Rights. *Article 31: Other Use Without Authorization of the Right Holder.* Geneva: WTO.

13 PROVIDING HEALTH CARE TO HIV PATIENTS IN SOUTHERN AFRICA

Markus Haacker

INTRODUCTION

Southern Africa is the region with the highest rates of HIV infection in the world.[1] The Joint United Nations Programme on HIV–AIDS, UNAIDS, estimates that 11.3 million of a total population of 97 million were HIV-infected in 1999. The adult HIV prevalence rate ranges from about 8 per cent in Tanzania to 36 per cent in Botswana (see Table 13.1).

A comprehensive strategy for coping with the epidemic would be based on improved prevention efforts to reduce the rate of new infections and an expansion of existing health services to provide care to HIV patients. The present study aims not to discuss such a strategy but, more modestly, to evaluate the impact of the HIV–AIDS epidemic on the provision of health services and to highlight some of the obstacles that must be addressed in order to improve the quality of health services in the region.[2]

The first section provides indicators for the quality of health services in the countries covered, such as spending on such services and the availability of health staff and health facilities. The second section analyses the impact of HIV–AIDS on the health sector, addressing the demand on existing health facilities, the toll of HIV–AIDS on health sector personnel, the costs of providing basic health services to HIV patients and the scope for improving access to highly active anti-retroviral therapies (HAARTs). Section three summarizes and concludes.

---

[1] For the purpose of this study, Southern Africa comprises Botswana, Lesotho, Malawi, Mozambique, Namibia, South Africa, Swaziland, Uganda, Tanzania, Zambia and Zimbabwe.
[2] For a broader study of the demographic and economic impact of HIV–AIDS in Southern Africa, see Haacker (2002).

Table 13.1: HIV prevalence in Southern Africa, 1999

Country	Total population ('000)	People living with HIV–AIDS ('000)	Adult HIV prevalence rate (%)	Estimated AIDS deaths
Botswana	1,592	290	35.8	24,000
Lesotho	2,108	240	23.6	16,000
Malawi	10,674	800	16.0	70,000
Mozambique	19,222	1,200	13.2	98,000
Namibia	1,689	160	19.5	18,000
South Africa	39,796	4,200	19.9	250,000
Swaziland	981	130	25.3	7,100
Tanzania	32,799	1,300	8.1	140,000
Uganda	21,209	820	8.3	110,000
Zambia	8,974	870	20.0	99,000
Zimbabwe	11,509	1,500	25.1	160,000
Southern Africa	96,545	11,310	18.0	992,100
Sub-Saharan Africa	596,272	24,500	8.6	2,200,000
Global total (excluding sub-Saharan Africa)	5,362,577	9,800	0.2	600,000

Source: UNAIDS (2000).

THE HEALTH SECTOR IN SOUTHERN AFRICA

The ability of the health sector to cope with the HIV–AIDS epidemic depends on the available resources. Table 13.2 provides several indicators for the quality of health services in Southern Africa. Total per capita health expenditure ranges from $9 (for Malawi) to $203 (for South Africa), corresponding to between 0.2 per cent and 4.1 per cent of the per capita spending for the United States. These differences between countries in spending on health services mainly reflect differences in per capita GDP. As a percentage of GDP, health expenditure ranges from 3.4 per cent (for Swaziland) to 7.5 per cent (for Namibia), which compares with a level of 5.8 per cent for the United Kingdom and 13.7 per cent for the United States.

If the purchasing power of the US dollar differs among countries (owing to lower prices for services and non-traded goods in lower-income countries), health spending in terms of the US dollar is not a good indicator of the quality of services. At purchasing power parity (PPP) exchange rates, total per capita health expenditure ranges from $45 (for Malawi) to $552 (for South Africa),

Table 13.2: Indicators of the quality of health services in Southern Africa

Country	Total per capita health expenditure			Physicians	Nurses	Hospitals	Access to essential drugs
	($, 2000)	(In PPP ($, 2000))	(% GDP, 1997)	(Per 100,000)	(Per 100,000)	(Per '000)	(%)
Botswana	155.0	398.1	4.2	23.8	219.1	1.6	90
Lesotho	21.0	88.8	5.6	5.4	60.1	1.1	80
Malawi	8.9	44.8	5.8	3.0	n.a.	1.3	n.a.
Mozambique	12.7	55.4	5.8	3.0	n.a.	0.9	50
Namibia	113.7	394.1	7.5	29.5	168.0	0.3	80
South Africa	203.0	552.3	7.1	56.3	471.8	0.8*	80
Swaziland	42.6	129.6	3.4	15.1	n.a.	0.7	n.a.
Tanzania	13.0	30.2	4.8	4.1	85.2	0.9	n.a.
Uganda	11.7	56.5	4.1	n.a.	18.7	0.9	70
Zambia	19.8	58.7	5.9	6.9	113.1	n.a.	n.a.
Zimbabwe	33.2	127.0	6.2	13.9	128.7	0.5	70
Memorandum items							
United Kingdom	1,398	1,384	5.8	164.0	497.0	4.2	n.a.
United States	4,956	4,956	13.7	279.0	972.0	3.7	n.a.

* Public hospitals only.
Sources: Cols 1–2 are extrapolations for 2000, using 1997 WHO data on expenditure shares (col. 3) and World Bank estimates of PPP exchange rates. Most of the estimates of health personnel in cols 4–5 refer to 1995 or 1996 (see WHO, 2000). For Malawi and Mozambique, the data on health personnel are from World Bank, *World Development Indicators*, 2001. World Bank (various publications) and the South African Ministry of Health are the sources of data for col. 6. World Bank, *World Development Indicators*, 2001, provides the data for col. 7.

corresponding to between 0.9 and 11.1 per cent of US per capita health expenditure (see Table 13.2).[3]

However, these data on health expenditure are likely to understate the quality of health services compared with industrialized countries, for three reasons: 1) generally, a disproportionate share of health expenditure is accounted for by older people, whereas the age distribution of Southern African countries is tilted towards the young; 2) the numbers may exclude the informal sector,

[3] PPP exchange rates also have the advantage that they respond less to short-term fluctuations of the nominal exchange rate. It is important to bear in mind, however, that PPP exchange rates are estimated on the basis of the prices of a bundle of goods and services that may differ from goods and services relevant for the health sector.

especially traditional healers, who are very important in rural areas; and 3) those who can afford it may seek the most advanced (and costly) services abroad. The national data would not capture these outlays.

An alternative indicator for the quality of health services is the availability of skilled staff. The best-trained health personnel, physicians,[4] are extremely scarce in the poorest countries in the region. For Malawi and Mozambique, the countries with the fewest physicians in the population (about three formally trained physicians per 100,000 people), the availability is only about one per cent of the level for the United States.

In interpreting these numbers, it is important to bear in mind that in the poorer countries, a larger range of health services is provided by staff who are not formally qualified as physicians. As a consequence, the ratio of nurses to doctors in the formal health sector ranges from 10–20:1 in Southern Africa, compared with the ratio of 3–4:1 that is more common in industrialized countries. As the data on health sector personnel are based on formal qualifications and/or employment, they are most likely to exclude the informal sector.

Additionally, Table 13.2 provides data about the number of hospital beds and access to essential medicines. The availability of hospital beds may serve as an additional indicator of the availability of more intensive forms of care (as HIV patients would require in the final stages of the disease). While access to essential drugs in Southern Africa is better than in many other sub-Saharan countries, the data show that significant proportions of the population in the countries covered would not have easy access even to the most basic medications for AIDS-related diseases.[5]

Table 13.3 summarizes available information on the financing of health expenditure in Southern Africa. The share of public vs. private health expenditure differs considerably among countries, with public health expenditure accounting for between 35 per cent and 73 per cent of total health expenditure. Virtually all public health expenditure is financed by taxation; public health insurance does not play a significant role in any of the countries covered. Although some of the countries with high rates of private health expenditure have some form of private health insurance, the share of out-of-pocket health expenditure (as a proportion of total health expenditure) is relatively high in an international context. For six of the 11 economies covered, private health insurance accounts for less than 10 per cent of private health expenditure.

---

[4] Defined as health personnel who have completed a degree of sufficient duration.
[5] Access to essential drugs is defined as the percentage of the population with access within one hour's walk to at least 20 drugs from the WHO's list of essential drugs. The list includes several drugs used to treat opportunistic diseases associated with AIDS.

Table 13.3: The financing of health services in Southern Africa, 1997 (% of GDP)

Country	Total	Public	Private (total)	Private (out-of-pocket)	Private (private insurance and other private)
Botswana	4.2	2.6	1.6	1.5	0.1
Lesotho	5.6	4.1	1.5	1.5	0.0
Malawi	5.8	3.4	2.4	2.1	0.2
Mozambique	5.8	4.1	1.7	1.1	0.5
Namibia	7.5	3.9	3.6	3.6	0.0
South Africa	7.1	3.3	3.8	3.3	0.5
Swaziland	3.4	2.5	0.9	0.9	0.0
Tanzania	4.8	2.9	1.9	1.9	0.0
Uganda	4.1	1.4	2.7	2.0	0.7
Zambia	5.9	2.3	3.6	2.5	1.1
Zimbabwe	6.2	2.7	3.5	2.4	1.1

Source: World Health Organization. The data for Lesotho, Mozambique, South Africa and Zimbabwe are classified as 'complete with high reliability'. For the other countries, the data are classified as 'incomplete with medium to high reliability'. Data may not add up exactly owing to rounding.

THE IMPACT OF HIV–AIDS ON THE HEALTH SECTOR

The HIV–AIDS epidemic has an immediate effect on the health sector: it increases the demand for public and private health services and takes its toll on health sector personnel. This section summarizes the available information on the HIV-related demand for health facilities and personnel, using indicators such as hospital bed occupancy rates or the ratio of trained health personnel to HIV patients. It then provides estimates of the costs of treating HIV patients, based on estimates of the costs and on assumptions about the coverage rates of certain services. As there are some special issues regarding the provision of highly active anti-retroviral therapies, this is discussed in a separate subsection.

The impact on existing health facilities

Very little data are available on the numbers of HIV-positive patients or on actual expenditure for the treatment of HIV–AIDS-related diseases. A statistic that is sometimes reported is hospital bed occupancy rates. A survey of various websites and news agencies suggests that the share of hospital beds occupied by patients with HIV–AIDS-related diseases ranges from 30 to 80 per cent (see Table 13.4). The World Bank estimates that the number of hospital beds needed

Table 13.4: The impact of HIV–AIDS on the health sector

Country	Mortality, all ages, 2000 (%)		Mortality, all ages, 2010 (%)		Hospital beds occupied by HIV patients, various years (%)	AIDS patients per physician
	Total	From AIDS	Total	From AIDS		
Botswana	2.2	1.7	3.6	3.1	60–70	96
Lesotho	1.5	0.6	2.5	1.7	n.a.	228
Malawi	2.2	1.0	2.4	1.4	30–80	250
Mozambique	2.3	0.9	3.0	1.8	30	208
Namibia	1.9	1.2	2.9	2.3	n.a.	41
South Africa	1.5	0.7	3.0	2.3	26–70	17
Swaziland	2.0	1.0	3.2	2.4	50	120
Tanzania	1.3	0.5	1.3	0.7	40–70	97
Uganda	1.8	0.6	1.5	0.6	50	n.a.
Zambia	2.2	1.3	2.1	1.3	60–80	108
Zimbabwe	2.2	1.7	3.2	2.7	50–80	87

Sources: US Bureau of the Census for cols 1–4. The estimates in col. 5 have been obtained from various websites and news agencies. See text for col. 6.

for AIDS patients will exceed the total number of beds now available in Botswana by 2002, in Namibia by 2005 and in Swaziland by 2004.[6] Especially for the worst-hit countries, hospital bed occupancy rates may understate the impact on health facilities, as hospitals may operate above capacity.

As shown in Table 13.2, the availability of physicians and other trained health staff is rather low in some countries of the region. As a consequence, health staff struggle to cope with the very high number of patients with HIV–AIDS-related diseases. If, for example, 10 per cent of those infected were using the services of a physician, then the ratio of HIV-positive patients to physicians would range from 17 (for South Africa) to 250 (for Malawi).[7] These numbers are national averages; the supply of health services tends to be better in the capitals and some larger cities, whereas access even to the most basic services is more limited in rural areas.[8]

As the demand for health services increases, employees in the health sector are also affected by the disease. Assuming that HIV prevalence rates for health-

---

[6] See the relevant World Bank country studies listed in the references section.
[7] The ratio of 10 per cent is used for illustrative purposes.
[8] See, for example, Table 13.2 for access to essential drugs.

sector staff are similar to those of the general population, Haacker (2002) shows that the training of doctors and nurses would have to be expanded by about 25–40 per cent over the 2000–10 period if the countries covered here were just to keep the number of doctors and nurses constant. Increasing workloads and the risk of infection also deter health personnel from working in the areas worst affected by HIV–AIDS, and increase the incentives for emigration, exacerbating the brain drain.

Available demographic projections indicate that the situation in the South African health sector presented in Table 13.4 is likely to deteriorate further. For the year 2000, between 39 and 75 per cent of all deaths in the countries surveyed were AIDS-related, with mortality rates of between 1.3 and 2.3 per cent (for Tanzania and Mozambique, respectively).[9] Following the dramatic increase in HIV prevalence rates in recent years in most of the countries covered here, the numbers of AIDS cases and AIDS deaths is projected to rise further for most countries in the region (see Table 13.4). For South Africa, for example, mortality rates are expected to double between 2000 and 2010 (from 1.5 per cent to 3.0 per cent), reflecting an increase in AIDS-related mortality from 0.7 per cent to 2.3 per cent. Thus, the demand for health facilities and trained health personnel, as well as the losses of trained health staff owing to AIDS, will increase substantially for most of the countries of the region over the coming years.

The costs of prevention of opportunistic diseases and basic treatment

There are two ways of obtaining estimates of and projections for the costs of treating HIV patients: 1) using data on total HIV-related spending for a country and deriving the costs per patient from this; and 2) using case studies to obtain estimates of the costs of treatment per patient and deriving estimates of the total required spending from this. In the literature, the latter approach is referred to as 'scaling up'. As data on aggregate HIV-related spending are not generally available for African countries, most studies follow the scaling-up approach. This approach also has the advantage that the estimates of HIV-related costs are based on common criteria and are comparable among countries. However, the scaling-up method is weak in identifying overhead and fixed costs, such as the share of the costs of administering a hospital that could be attributed to the treatment of HIV patients or the capital costs of building a new hospital to accommodate the rising number of HIV patients. Scaling up requires estimates or targets for the coverage of health services to HIV patients. The coverage of even the most basic health services is limited in several Southern African countries (see Table 13.2), and only a very small proportion of

---

[9] Assuming that those who have died of AIDS would have survived otherwise.

Table 13.5: The cost of treating HIV patients ($)

Treatment	Estimated costs per patient per year	
	Low-income countries	Higher-income countries
Palliative care	25.80	25.80
Prevention of opportunistic infections	36	79
Clinical treatment of opportunistic infections	359	698
HAARTs (drugs only)	1,400	1,400
HAARTs (support)	600	1,000

Source: Bonnel (2001). For palliative care, prevention of opportunistic infections and treatment of opportunistic infections, Table 13.5 reports data from a medium-cost scenario. For highly active anti-retroviral therapy, it reports low-cost estimates. Botswana, Namibia, South Africa and Swaziland are classified as higher-income countries.

HIV patients receives anti-retrovirals. Thus, estimates of the costs of treating HIV patients based on scaling-up are based on a judgment of which rates of coverage are feasible.[10]

A recent study by the World Bank summarizes the available data on the costs of various forms of care for HIV patients, including HAARTs.[11] Its estimates are summarized in Table 13.5.

Table 13.6 uses these estimated costs of treatment per patient to obtain estimates of the impact of HIV–AIDS on the health sector, excluding, for the moment, highly active anti-retroviral therapies. These estimates are based on the assumption that patients would, on average, require health services for the last three years of their lives. For all countries, the estimates are based on the assumptions that the coverage rate for palliative care and prevention of opportunistic diseases is 30 per cent and that the coverage rate for clinical treatment of opportunistic diseases is 20 per cent. As actual coverage rates for the respective countries may differ from those assumed, these estimates should not be interpreted as actual costs. Rather, they provide an indicator of the demand for HIV-related health services that is consistent across countries. (If desired, it can easily be scaled up or down to allow for different coverage rates). Also, the estimates do not include investments in health facilities that may be required to achieve the assumed coverage rates.

---

[10] See Bonnel (2001) for a thorough discussion of this method.
[11] See ibid.

Table 13.6: The impact of HIV–AIDS on HIV-related health services (% of GDP)

Country	Palliative care and prevention of opportunistic infections		Clinical treatment		Total HIV-related health services for assumed rates of coverage		Total expenditure, 1997	Public expenditure, 1997
	2000	2010	2000	2010	2000	2010		
Botswana	0.1	0.1	0.2	0.3	0.3	0.4	4.2	2.6
Lesotho	0.1	0.3	0.5	1.0	0.6	1.3	5.6	4.1
Malawi	0.4	0.5	1.5	2.0	1.9	2.5	5.8	3.4
Mozambique	0.3	0.5	1.1	1.8	1.4	2.3	5.8	4.1
Namibia	0.1	0.1	0.4	0.6	0.5	0.8	7.5	3.9
South Africa	0.0	0.1	0.2	0.3	0.2	0.4	7.1	3.3
Swaziland	0.1	0.2	0.4	0.8	0.5	1.0	3.4	2.5
Tanzania	0.3	0.3	1.1	1.1	1.4	1.4	4.8	2.9
Uganda	0.4	0.3	1.4	1.2	1.8	1.5	4.1	1.4
Zambia	0.2	0.2	0.8	0.9	1.0	1.1	5.9	2.3
Zimbabwe	0.2	0.3	0.8	1.1	0.9	1.3	6.2	2.7

Source: Author's estimates. The estimates are based on coverage rates of 30 per cent for palliative care and prevention of opportunistic diseases and 20 per cent for clinical treatment.

Table 13.6 shows that the required expenditure for palliative care and prevention of opportunistic diseases and for clinical treatment is substantial. Although some regional countries, notably Botswana and South Africa, would be able to, and presumably do, achieve higher coverage rates than the ones assumed here, the demand for HIV-related health services accounts for about one-third of total health expenditure for two of the poorer countries.

However, many of those who need treatment are not able to pay for it, and would have to rely on public health services. Even at the low coverage rates assumed, the costs of treating HIV patients exceed 50 per cent of total public health expenditure for some countries, and exceed total public health expenditure in one case (Uganda). This means that although it would be possible to achieve higher rates of coverage or a higher quality of health service for those who can afford these treatments, access to palliative care, to medication to prevent opportunistic diseases and especially to clinical treatment would be very limited for those who rely on public health services.

The scope for improving access to anti-retroviral therapies

Highly active anti-retroviral therapies are very expensive relative to per capita GDP for the countries of sub-Saharan Africa. Over recent months, a consensus has been reached about improving access to HAARTs in developing countries and providing the required medications at much reduced costs to governments and other agencies working in Southern Africa. Thus, the costs of HAARTs will fall substantially. Some recent studies estimate that if HAARTs were priced at marginal costs for the worst-affected countries it would be possible to provide these treatments for about $1,000 per patient per year, as opposed to costs often exceeding $10,000 in major industrialized countries or about $5,000 in Brazil, a major producer of generic drugs.[12] The estimates below are based on an estimated total cost of $1,100 per patient per year (including the costs of the drugs as well as the required medical support) for the lower-income countries, which is somewhat lower than the World Bank estimates quoted in Table 13.5 and corresponds to the costs suggested by Members of the Faculty of Harvard University.[13] For the higher-income countries, the assumed total cost is $1,500. It is important to remember that these are estimates based on the pricing of HAARTs at marginal cost and that these drugs are not yet available at this cost. Still, a cost of $1,100 per year would exceed per capita GDP for seven of the 11 countries considered here, so that these drugs would not be affordable for a major proportion of the population. Table 13.7 provides estimates of the cost of providing HAARTs, assuming a coverage rate of 10 per cent.[14] Taking into account that the quality of health services in Southern Africa is relatively low, HAARTs are assumed to extend a patient's life by two years on average, and patients are assumed to receive triple therapy for the last four years of their lives. The projections are based on the database of the International Programs Center at the US Bureau of the Census.

At a coverage rate of 10 per cent, the cost of providing triple therapy would initially range from 0.2 per cent of GDP for Botswana and South Africa to 2.4 per cent of GDP for Malawi. By 2010, the cost will rise to between 0.5 per cent of GDP (Botswana, South Africa) to 4.0 per cent of GDP (Malawi), for two reasons. First, as the number of AIDS patients will increase in the near future because of the increase in new infection in recent years, the cost will rise to

---

[12] These figures refer to the total cost of the treatment, not only to the cost of purchasing the drugs. See, for example, Bonnel (2001) or Members of the Faculty of Harvard University (2001).

[13] Members of the Faculty of Harvard University (2001). The classification of lower- and higher-income countries follows Bonnel (2001). See Table 13.5.

[14] For Uganda, Binswanger (2000) reports that about 1,000 patients, that is 0.1 per cent of those living with HIV–AIDS, receive triple therapy with anti-retrovirals. For Malawi, the *Washington Post* (1 November 2000) reports that the number of patients receiving triple therapy in Malawi is about 30, i.e. 0.004 per cent of those living with HIV.

Table 13.7: The cost of highly active anti-retroviral treatments* (% of GDP)

Country	Total HIV-related health services (excluding HAARTs)		Cost of HAARTs		Total HIV-related health services (including HAARTs)		Total expenditure, 1997	Public expenditure, 1997
	2000	2010	2000	2010	2000	2010		
Botswana	0.3	0.4	0.2	0.5	0.5	0.9	4.2	2.6
Lesotho	0.6	1.3	0.7	2.0	1.3	3.2	5.6	4.1
Malawi	1.9	2.5	2.4	4.0	4.3	6.5	5.8	3.4
Mozambique	1.4	2.3	1.7	3.6	3.0	5.9	5.8	4.1
Namibia	0.5	0.8	0.4	0.9	0.9	1.7	7.5	3.9
South Africa	0.2	0.4	0.2	0.5	0.3	0.9	7.1	3.3
Swaziland	0.5	1.0	0.5	1.1	1.0	2.1	3.4	2.5
Tanzania	0.6	0.8	0.7	1.2	1.3	1.9	4.8	2.9
Uganda	0.6	0.6	0.7	0.9	1.3	1.4	4.1	1.4
Zambia	1.0	1.1	1.3	1.7	2.3	2.8	5.9	2.3
Zimbabwe	0.9	1.3	1.1	2.2	2.1	3.5	6.2	2.7

*Assuming a 10 per cent coverage rate.
Source: Author's estimates.

between 0.4 per cent and 5.1 per cent of GDP. Second, the number of those receiving triple therapy will increase as this treatment extends the lives of patients.

Table 13.7 also provides estimates of the total cost of HIV-related services. These numbers are based on the assumption that triple therapy does not change the lifetime cost per patient of other HIV-related costs. Although triple therapy reduces the incidence of other HIV-related illnesses in those receiving it, it also extends their life, so that the net effect on the lifetime cost of treatment is not clear.

The estimated total cost, based on an assumed coverage rate of 10 per cent, shows that owing to substantial reductions in the price of HAARTs, several countries (notably Botswana and South Africa) would be able to provide these medications for a significant proportion of AIDS patients. For example, by 2010, South Africa could achieve a coverage rate for triple therapy of 30 per cent at a cost of 1.4 per cent of GDP. If the costs were $10,000, rather than $1,500, this cost would amount to 10.9 per cent of GDP.

However, for other countries the scope for introducing HAARTs is very limited. Even with the low coverage rates assumed, HIV-related health expenditure would exceed current public health expenditure for several countries. Therefore, it would be difficult to significantly improve access to HAARTs through public health services.[15]

While the scope for providing triple therapy through public health services is very limited, many government employees and people working in the formal sector, whose wages are usually much higher than the average national income, could pay for these drugs at a price of $1,100–1,500. Thus, even if triple therapies will not be available through the public health service, access will increase significantly. Binswanger, for example, reports estimates for Uganda indicating that as the price of anti-retrovirals falls from $10,000 to $600–1,200, the number of patients who can afford these treatments will increase from about 1,000 to 50,000.[16]

One important limitation for improving private access to anti-retrovirals is the lack of a well-developed private insurance sector in most countries. Table 13.3 shows that private insurance accounts for less than one-third of private health expenditure in each of the countries covered here. In particular, policies to expand block insurance of employees through companies, together with a reduction in the price of HAARTs to levels discussed here, could expand the range of patients receiving triple therapy.

SUMMARY AND CONCLUSIONS

The HIV–AIDS epidemic is already a huge burden on the health sector in the countries of Southern Africa. In most of them, more than one-half of all hospital beds are occupied by HIV-positive patients, and the number of AIDS patients per physician exceeds 100. As more people living with HIV are expected to fall ill by 2010, the situation is likely to deteriorate.

The costs of providing health services to HIV patients are substantial. Assuming limited coverage rates of services to HIV patients, the cost of palliative care, prevention of opportunistic infections and clinical treatment (excluding triple therapy) would amount to between 0.3 and 1.8 per cent of GDP in 2000, rising to between 0.4 and 2.5 per cent of GDP in 2010. For some of the poorer countries (Malawi and Mozambique), these costs would amount to about 40 per cent of total health expenditure.

Reducing the prices of highly active anti-retroviral therapies to about $500 per patient per year (and thus the total cost of treatment to $1,100–1,500) would greatly increase the number of those who can afford to pay for them. This applies in particular to government and formal-sector employees, whose wages are much higher than the average national income. Most of private health expenditure is out-of-pocket rather than through private health insurance.

[15] A possible exception is temporary treatments to reduce the rate of mother-to-child transmission.
[16] Binswanger (2000).

Expanding the scope of private health insurance and, where this is not now the case, including triple therapy in the insurance packages would further increase the range of those receiving triple therapy. However, with the possible exception of Botswana and South Africa (and there only to a limited extent), none of the countries in the region will be able to offer general access to highly active anti-retroviral therapies through the public health service.

The quality of health services in the region has already deteriorated significantly. To cope with an increasing number of AIDS patients over the next decade, the affected countries need substantial external assistance in order to build the required health infrastructure and to train the required personnel. Even so, the current cost of providing health services to HIV patients would still account for a very large proportion of total health expenditure for most countries in the region, and attaining just the rates of coverage assumed above would be difficult.

REFERENCES

Ainsworth, Martha and Waranya Teokul (2000), 'Breaking the Silence: Setting Realistic Priorities for AIDS Control in Less-developed Countries', *The Lancet*, 356, pp. 55–60.

Binswanger, Hans P. (2000), 'How to Make Advanced HIV Treatment Affordable for Millions in Poor Countries' (unpublished manuscript) (Washington, DC: World Bank).

Bonnel, René (2001), *Costs of Scaling HIV Program Activities to a National Level in Sub-Saharan Africa: Methods and Estimates* (Washington DC: World Bank).

Forsythe, Stephen (1997), *The Affordability of Anti-retroviral Therapy in Developing Countries: What Policymakers Need to Know*. Family Health International, AIDS Control and Prevention Project.

Haacker, Markus (2002), *The Economic Consequences of HIV–AIDS in Southern Africa*. IMF Working Paper No. 02/38 (Washington, DC: IMF).

Harvard University, Members of the Faculty (2001), Consensus Statement on Anti-retroviral Treatment for AIDS in Poor Countries, Harvard University.

Joint United Nations Programme on HIV–AIDS (UNAIDS) (2000), *Report on the Global HIV–AIDS Epidemic* (Geneva: UNAIDS).

UNAIDS (2000), *AIDS: Palliative Care*. UNAIDS Technical Update (Geneva: UNAIDS).

UNICEF–UNAIDS–WHO–MSF (2001), *Sources and Prices of Selected Drugs and Diagnostics for People Living with HIV–AIDS*.

World Bank (2000), *Botswana – Selected Development Impact of HIV–AIDS* (Washington, DC: World Bank).

World Bank (2001), *Costs of Scaling HIV Program Activities to a National Level in Sub-Saharan Africa: Methods and Estimates* (Washington, DC: World Bank). See Bonnel (2001).

World Bank (2001), *Lesotho – The Development Impact of HIV–AIDS: Selected Issues and Options* (Washington, DC: World Bank).

World Bank (2001), *Namibia – Selected Development Impact of HIV–AIDS* (Washington, DC: World Bank).

World Bank (2001), *Swaziland – Selected Development Impact of HIV–AIDS* (Washington, DC: World Bank).

World Bank (2001), *World Development Indicators* (Washington, DC: World Bank).

World Health Organization (2000), *World Health Report 2000*.

World Health Organization (WHO)–UNAIDS (2000), *Key Elements in HIV–AIDS Care and Support*.

14 SUCCESSFUL PUBLIC–PRIVATE PARTNERSHIPS IN GLOBAL HEALTH: LESSONS FROM THE MECTIZAN DONATION PROGRAM

Jeffrey L. Sturchio and Brenda D. Colatrella

On 21 October 1987, Merck & Co. announced plans to donate MECTIZAN™ (ivermectin),* a new medicine designed to combat onchocerciasis (river blindness), for as long as it might be needed, wherever needed. Merck took this action in collaboration with international experts in parasitology, the World Health Organization (WHO) and other agencies in order to reach those affected by the illness. This unprecedented decision came 12 years after the discovery of ivermectin by Merck scientists and nearly seven years after the first human clinical trials in Dakar, Senegal. Raymond V. Gilmartin, Merck chairman and chief executive officer, has since reaffirmed the company's commitment to donate 'as much MECTIZAN as necessary, for as long as necessary, to treat river blindness and to help bring the disease under control as a public health problem'.[1]

The history of MECTIZAN presents a complex pattern of scientific acumen, perseverance in clinical research, international negotiations, multi-sectoral collaboration and the interaction of health and development. This chapter outlines the history of the MECTIZAN Donation Program, concluding with some observations on lessons learned during its first 15 years and their implications for successful public–private partnerships in global health.[2]

This chapter is based in part on a presentation by Jeffrey L. Sturchio to the Workshop on Differential Pricing and Financing of Essential Drugs, organized jointly by the World Health Organization and the World Trade Organization secretariats, the Norwegian Foreign Ministry and the Global Health Council and held in Høsbjør, Norway on 8–11 April 2001. This presentation may be found on the web at *http://www.wto.org/english/tratop_e/trips_e/hosbjor_presentation_e/21sturchio.e/pdf*. For the final report of the workshop and related documentation, see *http://www.wto.org/english/tratop_e/trips_e/tn_hosbjor_e.htm*.

* Trademark of Merck & Co., Inc., Whitehouse Station, NJ, USA. Merck & Co., Inc., operates in most countries outside the United States as Merck Sharp & Dohme (MSD).

[1] David Lindley, 'Merck's new drug free to WHO for river blindness programme', *Nature*, 329 (29 October 1987), p. 752; John Walsh, 'Merck donates drug for river blindness', *Science*, 238 (30 October 1987), p. 610; Raymond V. Gilmartin's statement of June 1997 is quoted in 'The Story of Mectizan' (1998), accessible on the web at *http://www.merck.com/overview/philanthropy/mectizan/p18.htm*.

[2] The MECTIZAN Donation Program has been widely discussed in the literature on

A DEVASTATING DISEASE

Onchocerciasis is a debilitating, disfiguring and often blinding disease endemic in 35 countries in sub-Saharan Africa, parts of Central and South America and in Yemen in the Middle East. It is a leading cause of blindness in the developing world. The disease is caused by parasitic worms that infiltrate, multiply and spread throughout the human body. The WHO has referred to the disease as 'a scourge of humanity throughout recorded history', with some 120 million people at risk of contracting it, 18 million people infected and an estimated one million people already visually impaired or blinded.[3]

Onchocerciasis is more commonly known as river blindness because the common black fly that transmits the disease to humans breeds in fast-flowing rivers. Black flies pick up the skin-dwelling microfilariae (parasitic worms) by biting infected humans; the disease is then transmitted when the fly bites other human beings and deposits the larvae into them. In some infested areas, people are bitten thousands of times per day. Within infected individuals, these microscopic parasites grow into larger, adult worms that live for approximately 15 years. Continuing the cycle, the adult worms produce and release millions of offspring that swarm throughout the body, causing acute and chronic skin rashes as areas of skin become dry, scaly, and leathery and also skin depigmentation, constant itching and weight loss. In some cases, the itching has been intense enough to drive victims to suicide. The most severe effects of the disease appear when the microfilariae colonize the eyes, creating lesions that can result in sight impairment and eventual blindness. In some villages, more than half of middle-aged and elderly adults were blind. A once common sight was a young boy leading a blind elder by a stick. The blindness associated with the disease also had a dramatic impact in shortening life expectancy: those blinded were reported to have a life expectancy 'one-third that of their sighted peers'.[4]

---

corporate social responsibility, leadership and public–private partnerships in global health. See, for example, Austin and Barrett (2001), Bollier (1997), Bollier, Weiss and Hanson (1991), Dutton and Pratt (1997), Eckholm (1989), Frost, Reich and Fujisaki (2002), Sethi and Steidlmeier (1997), Tavis (1997) and Useem (1998). Sturchio (1992) is based on archival research at Merck.

[3] The quotation comes from remarks by Dr Halfdan Mahler, then Director-General of the World Health Organization, at the press conference in Washington, DC on 21 October 1987 announcing the MECTIZAN donation. For estimates of the number of people at risk from onchocerciasis or already infected or visually impaired, see World Health Organization, 'Onchocerciasis (river blindness)', Fact Sheet No. 95 (February 2000) at http://www.who.int/inf-fs/en/fact095.html and Taylor et al. (1990), p. 116.

[4] Taylor et al. (1990), p. 116. This section draws on the contributions in 'MECTIZAN and Onchocerciasis' (1998) and 'MECTIZAN et Onchocercose' (1998), which provide expert background on the nature of river blindness, the burden of illness in endemic countries, the clinical picture, the social and economic impact of the disease and efforts to control it, as well as perspectives on public–private partnerships in onchocerciasis control.

Adding to the physiological devastation is the socio-economic impact of the disease. Because black flies flourish in areas with swift-flowing water, typically near the most fertile farmland, the risk of disease forces entire communities to abandon fertile plains near rivers and flee to less productive land. Standards of living decline or collapse as members of communities become ill, blind and non-productive, resulting in social disruption and economic deprivation.

In the mid-1970s, aerial sprayings with insecticide in West Africa had reduced but not eradicated black flies in some areas. The only available medicines for the disease, suramin and diethylcarbamazine, could be toxic, producing severe side effects and even visual loss or blindness in some patients. Clearly, additional tools were needed to combat this significant public health problem.

THE DISCOVERY AND DEVELOPMENT OF MECTIZAN

In 1975, scientists at Merck were examining a number of soil samples from the Kitasato Institute in Japan. A sample from a golf course showed properties indicating that it might be effective in fighting parasites in farm animals – eventually leading to the discovery of the highly active chemical family of avermectins. In April 1978, one of these compounds, ivermectin, was tested against gastro-intestinal nematodes in horses, and examination of skin from the treated and untreated horses showed that it was effective against the microfilariae of *Onchocerca cervicalis*. Aware of the relationship between *Onchocerca cervicalis* and *Onchocerca volvulus* (the parasite responsible for human onchocerciasis), Merck scientist Dr William Campbell appreciated the potential significance of this finding for combating human onchocerciasis.[5]

To bring a safe and effective human health product against onchocerciasis into being, Merck Research Laboratories still needed to conduct the exhaustive, meticulous and statistically controlled studies that accompany the progress of any new drug from laboratory to clinic. With support from Dr P. Roy Vagelos, the head of Merck Research Laboratories at that time and later chairman and chief executive officer, Dr Campbell and his colleagues began to investigate the potential of this compound for human use.

Merck's decision in 1980 to begin human trials was as significant as its decision seven years later to donate the drug, if not more so. This decision to pursue the drug's development involved a substantial commitment of resources (time, money and people) that could have been spent pursuing projects with higher profit potential. The problem with ivermectin for onchocerciasis was not that the potential customer base was too small (as with 'orphan drugs') but rather that the potential users were too impoverished to afford the drug at any price.[6]

[5] Sturchio (1992), p. 3. Vagelos (2001) provides a personal perspective on the MECTIZAN story.
[6] Bollier (1997), pp. 281–2.

The process of developing new drug compounds is long, labour-intensive and filled with uncertainty. It is also expensive – particularly in this case owing to the remote locations of people affected by onchocerciasis and the difficulty in reaching appropriate patient populations for clinical testing. Merck had to decide whether to invest in research for a drug that, even if successful, would probably never pay for itself. Further, some worried that if human applications had unanticipated side effects, this could jeopardize sales of the animal product because customers might wonder whether toxic reactions in people would be experienced by animals too.

Although it was recognized early on that the development of a drug for this disease held little promise of a profitable market, it was also recognized that its development could contribute to Merck researchers' basic knowledge and understanding of parasitology. Further, refusal to fund research and testing of a potential new drug discovery could seriously demoralize Merck scientists – among the most essential employees in the company.

The clinical testing and development process was championed by Dr Mohammed Aziz, who, before joining Merck, was a specialist in infectious diseases with the WHO in West Africa. A native of Bangladesh, an expert in tropical medicine and a veteran of WHO public health activities in Sierra Leone, Dr Aziz knew firsthand the suffering that river blindness caused. That awareness and his conviction that ivermectin presented a significant improvement over available therapies motivated his seven-year campaign to amass the necessary clinical evidence to make MECTIZAN available. Had it not been for the drive and commitment of Dr Aziz, joined early on by his colleagues Dr Kenneth R. Brown, Dr Philippe Gaxotte and other dedicated members of the clinical development team, MECTIZAN might have taken much longer to reach those suffering from river blindness.[7]

The first human subjects, in Dakar, received MECTIZAN in February 1981.[8] For larger-scale, Phase II and Phase III trials, Merck recognized it would need to seek outside assistance because infected individuals lived in remote areas of countries where onchocerciasis was endemic, without access to modern medical facilities. In addition, Merck did not have an active commercial business in target countries and thus had minimal knowledge of local health care distribution and delivery systems or contacts with health care authorities in those countries.

---

[7] Sturchio (1992), pp. 4–6. For a profile of Dr Aziz, see Jeffrey L. Sturchio (ed.), *Values & Visions: A Merck Century* (Rahway, New Jersey: Merck & Co., 1991), p. 155.

[8] The results of this first human trial of ivermectin appeared in M. A. Aziz, S. Diallo, I. M. Diop, M. Lariviere and M. Porta, 'Efficacy and tolerance of ivermectin in human onchocerciasis', *The Lancet* (24 July 1982), pp. 171–3 and M. A. Aziz, S. Diallo, M. Lariviere, I. M. Diop, M. Porta, and P. Gaxotte, 'Ivermectin in onchocerciasis', *The Lancet* (25 December 1982), pp. 1456–7.

COLLABORATION WITH THE WORLD HEALTH ORGANIZATION

In 1982, Merck contacted the World Health Organization and requested its assistance in gaining the cooperation of health ministers and practitioners throughout the infected regions so that it could gain knowledge of local health systems, help in identifying relevant patient populations and, eventually, assistance in collecting data on the safety and effectiveness of MECTIZAN in treating human onchocerciasis. The WHO had a long history of involvement and expertise in tropical medicine, and it had local offices throughout the developing world and a close working relationship with ministries of health to develop community health care structures for the distribution of drugs.

Initially, the WHO was sceptical about the idea of a drug that could overcome the side effects induced by similar drugs that required close medical supervision. Its focus was on finding a drug (a macrofilaricide) that could affect or kill the adult worms rather than one (a microfilaricide, such as MECTIZAN) that killed the microfilariae. Furthermore, it had significant investments in its eight-year programme in West Africa, the Onchocerciasis Control Programme (OCP), to control the spread of river blindness by attacking the black fly with aerial spraying of insecticide.

This form of collaboration was uncharted territory for both organizations. Despite differences in organizational cultures and scientific judgment, a working collaboration was forged between the two organizations for conducting clinical trials on ivermectin. For these trials, Merck supplied the drug, managed the regulatory requirements and funded the studies, while the WHO arranged for local medical support and facilities and provided scientists and its political and economic knowledge of the countries.

Phase II trials took place in Senegal, Mali, Ghana and Liberia from 1983 to 1984. The complex tests further confirmed the promise of ivermectin and led to a subsequent set of (Phase III) trials that began in 1985 at the Uniroyal Rubber plantation's medical facility in Liberia.[9]

The results supported Dr Campbell's original findings, confirmed the safety and efficacy of ivermectin for onchocerciasis and established the optimum dosage level. The trials indicated that a single dose taken once a year significantly reduced and effectively eliminated the microfilariae without significant adverse

---

[9] For a thorough review of the results of these trials and others in the clinical development of MECTIZAN, together with ivermectin's safety and effects on transmission of onchocerciasis, see William C. Campbell, 'Ivermectin as an antiparasitic agent for use in humans', *Annual Reviews of Microbiology*, 45 (1991), pp. 445–74. Dr Aziz provides an interim assessment in 'Chemotherapeutic approach to control of onchocerciasis', *Reviews of Infectious Diseases*, 8 (May–June 1986), pp. 500–4. See also K. L. Goa, D. McTavish, and S. P. Clissold, 'Ivermectin: a review of its antifilarial activity, pharmacokinetic properties and clinical efficacy in onchocerciasis', *Drugs*, 42, (4), 1991, pp. 640–58.

reactions. Further, there was minimal need for medical follow-up or monitoring of patients and there were no special handling or storage requirements for the drug. Eliminating the microfilariae significantly reduced the itching and stopped the progression of eye lesions that caused blindness. Unfortunately, restoring the sight of those already blinded by the disease was not possible.

On the basis of these clinical research findings, in 1987 Merck sought and received formal regulatory clearance of the human formulation of ivermectin (now known as MECTIZAN) from the French Directorate of Pharmacy and Drugs.[10]

THE DECISION TO DONATE MECTIZAN

While Merck awaited formal regulatory approval of MECTIZAN for onchocerciasis, its officials began to think about how to get the drug to the millions of people in need of it. Providing it was necessary, but not sufficient. A reliable, effective distribution system that would ensure MECTIZAN reached affected persons in 35 countries in Africa, Latin America and Yemen for more than 15 to 20 years was also needed. The five-year costs for this were expected to be $2 million – and that was just to begin moving the product through the distribution pipeline. The annual cost of distribution was estimated possibly to exceed $20 million before the disease was controlled.[11]

As a private-sector organization, Merck seeks (and the investment community expects) an adequate economic return on its products. But from the start, it realized that the potential commercial market for MECTIZAN was highly uncertain, not only because the victims of onchocerciasis were poor but also because there was no distribution system to reach people in some of the world's poorest and most remote areas. The number of infected people was still an estimate and the extent of the disease outside West Africa was largely unknown. Also unknown was how long it would take to bring the adult worm under control in patients. A commitment to supply MECTIZAN indefinitely could lead to both large and protracted manufacturing and administrative costs. And what potential liability would the corporation face should MECTIZAN cause unexpected adverse reactions?[12]

Simply giving the drug away was not a solution – yet abandoning it was inconceivable. MECTIZAN was the only safe and effective medicine available for onchocerciasis and thus was medically necessary for patients and those at risk. Failure to make MECTIZAN available to those who needed it would have been highly inconsistent with Merck's philosophy and corporate culture.

---

[10] Sturchio (1992), p. 7.
[11] Bollier, Weiss and Hanson (1991), B-4.
[12] Bollier (1997), Tavis (1997) and Sethi and Steidlmeier (1997).

Initially, there was discussion over what price Merck should set for the drug, given that those with the disease and their governments had severely limited resources. Once it realized that those who needed it could not afford it at *any* price, Merck sought a third-party payer. Merck hoped that the WHO, governments of infected areas, donor governments, international health and development agencies or charitable foundations would come forward to purchase MECTIZAN and fund its distribution. This would enable the company to sell the drug at a reduced price and to have it distributed at no cost to the people who needed it but could not afford it. Conversations were held at the highest levels – with the deputy Secretary of State, the White House Chief of Staff, the head of the United States Agency for International Development and other US government policy-makers. But owing to either limited health care budgets or competing health priorities, no one was interested in supporting the drug's purchase or distribution.

There was also debate about donating the drug outright. Merck was financially healthy at the time and could afford to make a significant, long-term commitment. The drug is well suited for mass distribution. As noted above, it requires only one annual dose, it is easy to administer and it could easily be transported and stored in view of its pill formulation and lack of cold-chain requirements. It has a wide margin of safety and requires little in terms of post-treatment monitoring. As a result, treatment is possible in remote places lacking sophisticated medical facilities and having little or no health care infrastructure. However, there was a real concern that a drug donation might create a further disincentive for pharmaceutical companies to conduct research on diseases affecting primarily poor nations – if there was an added expectation that any drugs discovered by such research must be donated to those in need. Another concern was the possible scepticism of recipients about the quality of a free drug.

Giving away the drug, as well as arranging for its distribution, would have been without precedent. But without interested funders, MECTIZAN would remain on the shelf far from victims plagued by skin disease, persistent itching and the fear of blindness. So nearly nine years after the drug's initial discovery, Dr P. Roy Vagelos, by then Merck's CEO, decided that donating it was the right course of action. It would be the most effective way to get MECTIZAN to those who needed it, as quickly as possible. Merck decided not only to donate an unlimited supply of MECTIZAN but also to help create a reliable international network for distributing the drug to those in need.

CHALLENGES AND OBSTACLES

There were significant challenges to providing access to MECTIZAN. Despite its ease of administration (just one annual tablet) and its excellent safety profile, governments were not initially convinced of the feasibility of providing treatment. They lacked the resources needed to distribute the medicine to patients in remote rural areas. Many of the countries hardest hit by onchocerciasis had poorly developed community health infrastructures, which presented numerous distribution and logistical challenges. There were no medical personnel or conventional health systems to facilitate distribution, oversee the drug's administration or monitor adverse reactions. Most of those infected lived in areas accessible only by navigating dirt roads or by walking for days. There were also challenges imposed by the technical issues of drug importation regulations and customs duties. Merck did not have a strong presence in these least developed, endemic countries, or a delivery system in place through which MECTIZAN could be distributed. Establishing a separate delivery system might be viewed by governments as interference, while handing distribution over to an external foundation or health organization might result in unnecessary bureaucracy, competing priorities and greater delays.[13] Further, how would unstable governments and unclear, constantly changing, country-specific customs and documentation requirements impede distribution of the drug?

If MECTIZAN were given out indiscriminately or used improperly, it might cause people to fear it and even to refuse to take it.[14] Adverse reactions had to be identified, medical records had to be kept and distribution programmes had to be logistically feasible. Given the anticipated duration of the drug's use of more than 15 years, a long-term commitment to its distribution was essential.

In addition to the challenges presented by poor health delivery systems, governments had competing health priorities (e.g., malaria, HIV–AIDS), limited local resources and no ready way to determine the value of different initiatives. Finally, political and civil unrest in some countries made arrangements for delivering MECTIZAN to people infected with or at risk of contracting river blindness even more difficult.

CREATION OF THE MERCK MECTIZAN DONATION PROGRAM

Faced with the enormous challenge of distribution, in 1988 Merck established the MECTIZAN Expert Committee (MEC) – a Merck-funded but independent committee of six internationally respected scientists and a chairperson – in order to formulate guidelines and procedures for the responsible distribution of

---

[13] Austin and Barrett (2001).
[14] Bollier, Weiss and Hanson (1991).

MECTIZAN. The goal was to create a dedicated organization external to Merck that would ensure the fledgling donation programme's independence and bring it credibility with potential partners from the outset.[15] The functions of the MEC were to

- develop guidelines, standards and procedures for community-based treatment programmes;
- review applications to implement community-based treatment programmes;
- advise and assist applicants in the implementation of treatment programmes;
- monitor the progress of treatment programmes;
- facilitate the coordination and consolidation of existing programmes and funding initiatives.

In short, the MEC was charged with evaluating requests to use MECTIZAN in community-based treatment programmes and with getting the drug into the hands of those who needed it while ensuring that good medical practices were followed. The latter involved making certain that adverse drug reactions would be identified and reported, that medical records would be kept and that treatment programmes would be reviewed for proper medical and administrative oversight, logistical feasibility and long-term sustainability.

Seeking a pre-eminent leader and visionary in public health, Merck appointed Dr William Foege as the first chairman of the MEC. Dr Foege was the executive director of the Carter Center and a former director of the US Centers for Disease Control. The committee itself included renowned experts in the field of ophthalmology, parasitology, tropical diseases and public health. The MECTIZAN Donation Program (MDP) Secretariat, established at the Task Force for Child Survival and Development in Atlanta, Georgia, was created as the administrative and management arm of the MEC and the MECTIZAN programme.

The requirements for supplying the drug outlined by the MEC included a treatment plan approved by the local ministry of health (MOH); an ability to maintain required medical records and to report any adverse reactions; maintenance of sufficient resources to sustain the treatment programme for a minimum, five-year period; and agreement to integrate the use of MECTIZAN into the existing local health system wherever possible.

For its part, Merck made a commitment to provide the drug free of charge for as long as needed; to pay for all costs associated with shipping, customs and clearance to the consignee (although in-country distribution costs are borne by

[15] On the early operation of the MEC, see H. Bruce Dull, 'MECTIZAN donation and the MECTIZAN Expert Committee', *Acta Leidensia*, 59 (1 and 2), 1990, pp. 399–403; Dull and S. E. O. Meredith, 'The MECTIZAN Donation Programme – a 10-year report', *Annals of Tropical Medicine & Parasitology*, 92, Supplement 1 (1998), pp. S69–71; and W. H. Foege, '10 years of MECTIZAN', *Annals of Tropical Medicine & Parasitology*, 92, Supplement 1 (1998), pp. S7–10.

numerous partners, including non-governmental development organizations (NGDOs) and government health ministries); and to fund the MEC and the MDP Secretariat. In the early years of the programme, the company played a major role in informing governments of the drug's availability and use by assigning a full-time medical director to liaise with African countries. Today, Merck remains involved in programme management: it ensures that the donation process and procedures adhere to corporate policies; reports programme data, including quantities of tablets shipped; funds and assists in the creation of educational materials; builds and maintains the important relationships involved in this public–private partnership; and communicates internally and externally about the programme's progress. Merck also continues to meet the important public health responsibility associated with drug safety, monitoring and reporting. Merck scientists and clinicians have remained involved in the programme since its inception.[16]

With approval from the MECTIZAN Expert Committee, the first MECTIZAN tablets were shipped and the first patients treated in autumn 1988. The delivery of MECTIZAN was greatly facilitated by the Onchocerciasis Control Programme, which made an immediate launch of ivermectin treatment programmes possible within OCP countries in West Africa by providing national governments and NGDOs with technical and logistical support. Building on the achievements of the OCP and this collaborative partnership, a new regional programme for Africa, the African Programme for Onchocerciasis Control (APOC), was launched in 1995 by the World Bank with the purpose of treating onchocerciasis in the 17 affected countries outside West Africa. By raising approximately $130 million over 12 years to fund efforts to create sustainable, community-directed MECTIZAN treatment programmes, APOC aims to eliminate onchocerciasis as a public health problem and socio-economic constraint in the non-OCP countries in Africa. In the six countries of Latin America where the disease is endemic, the Onchocerciasis Elimination Programme of the Americas (OEPA), a multi-country, multi-agency, multi-donor effort, has been established in order to coordinate MECTIZAN distribution and to help eliminate the disease as a public health problem by 2007. MECTIZAN is now delivered through programmes such as the OCP, APOC and OEPA, as well as treatment programmes outside these larger, organized initiatives.[17]

[16] Coyne and Berk (2001).
[17] For a useful analysis of the interrelation of these various programmes, see D. E. Etya'alé, 'MECTIZAN as a stimulus for development of novel partnerships: the international organization's perspective', *Annals of Tropical Medicine & Parasitology*, 92, Supplement No. 1 (1998), pp. S73–77. See also Benton (2001), available at *http://www.worldbank.org/afr/findings/english/find174.htm*; the relevant essays in 'MECTIZAN and Onchocerciasis' (1998) and 'MECTIZAN et Onchocercose' (1998); and the Onchocerciasis Control Programme and African Programme for Onchocerciasis Control web sites at *http://www.who.int/ocp/apoc/index.htm* and *http://www.worldbank.org/gper/apocadmin.htm*.

THE EVOLUTION OF A UNIQUE PUBLIC-PRIVATE PARTNERSHIP

Today the Merck MECTIZAN Donation Program is a unique multi-sectoral coalition involving Merck, the MECTIZAN Expert Committee, the World Health Organization, the World Bank, UNICEF, the Carter Center, dozens of national ministries of health, representatives of the international donor community, more than 30 non-governmental development organizations and many local community health workers. The WHO continues to play a leading technical role in onchocerciasis control while the World Bank plays the leading financial role.[18]

The active participation of non-governmental development organizations has been particularly important to the continuing success of the MDP. In the early years of the programme, NGDOs working in the area of blindness prevention throughout Africa served as a catalyst for the delivery of MECTIZAN. They continue to play a critical role, particularly in countries where local health services lack appropriate and necessary resources. NGDOs

- collaborate with MOHs to ensure that all affected communities are treated;
- mobilize funds for the programme;
- assist the MOH in preparing national plans and project proposals;
- provide technical expertise to the treatment programmes;
- engage in community mobilization and operational research;
- monitor, evaluate and report on programmes;
- develop communication tools and distribute educational materials about the drug and the treatment;
- train community distributors and supervise community-directed treatment.

In addition to the international partnership, there are also local partnerships that help to sustain the MECTIZAN Donation Program. In many African countries, a National Onchocerciasis Task Force (NOTF) – a partnership among the MOH, local and international NGDOs involved in onchocerciasis control efforts and the WHO – has been established to facilitate treatment programmes. The NOTFs help to strengthen the country's epidemiological surveillance capability and to facilitate via their own staff the local delivery and distribution of MECTIZAN at various levels, including individual communities.

Close collaboration among these diverse organizations – the private sector, multilateral agencies, ministries of health, local and international NGDOs, financial donors and affected communities – has been the hallmark of the MDP. The success of this partnership lies in the ability of diverse organizations to set aside their own agendas and biases, to accept one another's structural and philosophical differences and to work towards the common goal – the distribution of

---

[18] Coyne and Berk (2001).

MECTIZAN to the affected populations until onchocerciasis is eliminated as a public health problem and socio-economic constraint.

THE IMPACT OF THE PARTNERSHIP

The Merck MECTIZAN Donation Program is now the largest ongoing donation programme of its kind. There are active treatment programmes in 33 of the 35 countries in sub-Saharan Africa, Latin America and Yemen where onchocerciasis is endemic. Some 700 million MECTIZAN tablets have been donated and shipped since the inception of the programme, and the two hundred millionth treatment took place in 2001.

Over 25 million individuals who would otherwise lack access to appropriate and needed pharmaceuticals are treated annually.[19] Those with serious infections are spared a life of darkness, while those with dermatological manifestations of the disease are provided relief from the chronic discomfort of itching. The transmission of the disease has been reduced and many premature deaths have been prevented. Since the inception of the MDP, some 16 million children have been spared the risk of infection in 11 countries in West Africa alone, owing to a spraying programme combined with MECTIZAN treatment. More than 600,000 cases of blindness will have been prevented by 2002.[20] In some countries, infection rates have dropped dramatically, from over 50 per cent to near zero.

The achievements of the programme extend beyond its immediate health benefits to socio-economic improvement, capacity-building and sustainability and to strengthened health systems in infected countries. Communities also benefit from the increased productivity of their members. It has been estimated that investments in programmes aimed at controlling onchocerciasis have yielded economic returns of nearly 20 per cent, primarily from increased agricultural output.[21] Economic gains result too from the resettlement of land freed from disease: the World Bank reports that 25 million hectares of arable land have been recovered – enough to feed 17 million people.[22]

LESSONS LEARNT

What lessons have we learnt from the MECTIZAN experience? What has it taught us about how to mobilize resources in public–private partnerships to address significant health problems – and to do so in a way that significantly reduces the disease burden over the long term?

[19] Ibid.
[20] Benton (2001).
[21] Hopkins and Richards (1997).
[22] Benton (2001).

In one sense, of course, MECTIZAN is unique, in that effective treatment requires only one annual dose, easily administered and with no major side effects. But it nonetheless provides an instructive case study in the interrelations of scientific and clinical research, corporate social responsibility and the challenges of providing access to health care and development. Some of the critical factors for success include:

- the need to focus scientific and clinical research resources on feasible targets; for clearly important health priorities;
- the importance of partnerships between public-sector and private-sector organizations (including non-governmental development organizations) to control a disease) and for those partnerships to be informed by the needs of the people whose lives are directly affected;
- the essential role of distribution mechanisms and health care infrastructure in ensuring that medicines such as MECTIZAN reach those who need them.

Partnerships

The case of MECTIZAN clearly demonstrates the power and possibilities of strong, transparent and creative public–private partnerships in helping to address the enormous public health challenges facing developing countries today. The value of partnerships in advancing the cause of global health cannot be overstated. The complexity of the issues we face, the entrenched nature of the diseases we fight and the fragility of the health care infrastructures we seek to build and/or strengthen are all beyond the ability of one organization or country to address alone.

Partnerships work best when based on clear objectives, trust, complementary expertise and mutual benefits. Individual organizations must be willing and able to set aside their own agendas in favour of shared commitments and responsibilities that are implemented with transparency and accountability. Organizational differences should be embraced rather than feared or ignored. Individual expertise needs to be identified and applied to well-defined goals. Sustainable resources should also be identified, and there is a need for mechanisms to evaluate the impact, both health and economic, of partnership initiatives.

The continuing need for coordination, communication and commitment from all stakeholders in the process is also crucial to success. Furthermore, it is critical that the public and private sectors work together in a way that enables the people who are most directly affected to determine their own needs and priorities. Partners should respect the culture of the environments in which programmes operate. And finally, the important relationships upon which partnerships are based must be nurtured continually in order to keep the partnership strong and successful.

The Merck MECTIZAN Donation Program is an example of an effectively functioning global partnership based on cooperation among diverse organizations and governments, the provision of necessary resources, long-term commitment and a comprehensive, sustainable approach to a complex, multi-country problem.

Infrastructure

Merck's responsibility in meeting global health needs goes beyond discovering and developing a medicine like ivermectin, and beyond merely making charitable contributions. In over a decade of experience, we have learned that simply removing cost as a barrier (by providing medicine free of charge) is not enough in itself to ensure that the medicine gets to the people who need it most. There must be a secure, efficient and effective distribution system through which drugs can flow and an affirmed, reliable agreement on the part of recipient governments that allows for the unobstructed entry of medicines. MECTIZAN has taught us that even the simplest pharmaceutical intervention faces tremendous challenges in delivery.

Sustainability

The MECTIZAN programme also shows that for a donation project to succeed, a commitment to ensure sustainability is as critical as the promise to supply a product. The MDP example is one instance of how drug donation programmes can be sustainable. A key success factor was Merck's unconditional guarantee of the necessary quantities of MECTIZAN for as long as necessary. Doing well is a precondition to doing good: an enabling policy environment (including, for instance, adequate TRIPS-compliant intellectual property protection standards) is a prerequisite for a company to have the wherewithal to mount a major philanthropic programme such as the MECTIZAN Donation Program and to make an open-ended commitment of supplies. This commitment provided needed assurance to NGDOs and MOHs that a long-term investment in addressing onchocerciasis was feasible. It made it more worthwhile to invest substantially in creating a distribution system and solid systems for training and supervising all personnel, particularly the thousands of community health workers.

The MDP case also suggests that donation programmes should, where possible, be integrated into a country's health care system. At the start of MECTIZAN distribution, most treatment programmes depended on mobile teams visiting communities, doing a diagnosis and then organizing mass treatment as required. But as these mobile teams were not sustainable over the 15 to 25 years required for treatment, a better approach had to be developed. Experience showed that communities, once fully informed, were capable of organizing their own treatment. In fact, communities can not only organize but also direct and manage their treatment in what is called community-directed treatment – in this case community-directed treatment with ivermectin (CDTI).

CDTI, a process built on the experience of the members of the community, enhances its decision-making and problem-solving capacity. The community exercises authority over decisions. The community is informed about the detailed tasks of distribution, but it decides who should distribute and whether or not such persons are strictly volunteers or should receive some compensation. The community plans the distribution of the drug, deciding on acceptable methods of distribution (e.g. central place, house-to-house) and timing. This approach ensures sensitivity to community decision-making structures and social customs and allows for innovation as needed. The community is the lead stakeholder in the provision of services, which creates a sense of ownership and thus increases the likelihood that these activities will be integrated into the community's health agenda. While start-up fieldwork may increase the immediate workload of the community distributor, an empowered community takes more responsibility for programme implementation, thus reducing the health workers' workload over the longer term. The goal is that after five years, communities will be ready to continue treatment alone with minimal help and supervision.

The strategy of CDTI has been employed to ensure sustainability by having MECTIZAN delivered to patients by village health workers as part of regular health care delivery. In fact, a remarkable 61,930 communities in affected regions are now planning and managing MECTIZAN distribution. This local ownership has increased local commitment to the programme.[23]

Capacity-building

The cooperative nature of the Merck MECTIZAN Donation Program has also helped to strengthen the primary health care system in many countries where MECTIZAN is delivered: indeed, the delivery infrastructure and treatment strategies have resulted in the delivery of other health services.

---

[23] On CDTI, see Hopkins (2001); William R. Brieger (ed.), *Implementation and Sustainability of Community-Directed Treatment of Onchocerciasis with Ivermectin: A Multicountry Study*, Final Report to the UNDP–World Bank–WHO Special Programme for Research and Training in Tropical Diseases, TDR/IDE/RP/CDTI/00.1 (Geneva: WHO–TDR, 2000); and Brieger et al. (2002). For the number of communities involved in CDTI (until the end of August 2001), see African Programme for Onchocerciasis Control, Joint Action Forum, *Year 2001 Progress Report*, JAF 7.4 (October 2001), p. 6.

Many in the international public health community have expressed concern about the vertical nature of increasing numbers of disease-specific donation programmes and the undue burden they may place on already overwhelmed local governments. However, in the case of MECTIZAN, the training of local (country and community-level) health care workers in census-taking and in the distribution, administration and monitoring of MECTIZAN treatment has supported onchocerciasis control efforts in countries where the disease is endemic. Subsequently, these enhanced skills have enabled health care personnel to apply their knowledge to other initiatives that support a country's health objectives, resulting in grassroots, community-based health systems available to address other diseases. The CDTI approach serves as an 'entry point' at which additional health interventions might be introduced. The community-based distributors, equipped with important new skills and their census data, serve as the foundation upon which a functioning, enhanced health care system can develop.[24]

The approach implemented in Africa to address another tropical disease, lymphatic filariasis, provides an example. In October 1998, following regulatory approval by the French Regulatory Agency for the use of MECTIZAN in lymphatic filariasis, Merck announced the expansion of the MECTIZAN Donation Program to this disease in African countries where onchocerciasis and lymphatic filariasis coexist. To accomplish this, albendazole (GlaxoSmithKline) was added to the MECTIZAN distribution system already established for onchocerciasis control in Africa. The donation of MECTIZAN for lymphatic filariasis was launched in 2000 in Ghana, Nigeria, Togo and Tanzania; the programme was extended to four additional countries in 2001 – Burkina Faso, Uganda, Côte d'Ivoire and Benin. The treatment of lymphatic filariasis is benefiting from the existing delivery structure for onchocerciasis.[25]

An expressed goal of participating NGDOs is to explore opportunities for other health and development activities using the MECTIZAN distribution system as an entry point. Several NGDOs involved in MECTIZAN distribution

---

[24] Hopkins (2001) and Coyne and Berk (2001).
[25] See World Health Organization, 'Major private sector partner, Merck, welcomed to lymphatic filariasis control effort', Press Release WHO/76, 23 October 1998, available at http://www.who.int/inf-pr-1998/en/pr98-76.html; World Health Organization, *Building Partnerships for Lymphatic Filariasis: Strategic Plan*, WHO/FIL/99.198 (Geneva, Switzerland: WHO, September 1999), available at http://www.who.int/ctd/filariasis/docs/Strategi.pdf; World Health Organization, *Eliminate Filariasis: Attack Poverty*, Proceedings of the First Meeting of the Global Alliance to Eliminate Lymphatic Filariasis, Santiago de Compostela, Spain, 4–5 May 2000, WHO/CDS/CPE/CEE/2000.5 (Geneva: WHO, 2000), available at http://www.who.int/ctd/filariasis/docs/main_english.pdf; *Community-Directed Treatment for Lymphatic Filariasis in Africa: Report of a Multi-Centre Study in Ghana and Kenya*, UNDP–World Bank–WHO Special Programme for Research and Training in Tropical Diseases, TDR/IDE/RP/CDTI/00.2 (Geneva: WHO/TDR, 2000); and Ottesen (2000).

(Christoffel-blindenmission, Helen Keller Worldwide, Organisation pour la Prévention de la Cecité and Sight Savers International) have successfully added Vitamin A to the MECTIZAN delivery system in many African countries, including Cameroon, the Central African Republic, Mali and Nigeria. Moreover, the interaction with patients during MECTIZAN delivery and distribution has afforded health care workers the opportunity to diagnose other conditions, including cataracts.

The MECTIZAN Donation Program has also contributed to the enhancement of local health systems through the development of a cadre of international scientific experts and resources, on-the-job training in field activities for over 1,000 professionals, the empowerment of communities through CDTI and the training of at least 30,000 community distribution workers. They, as suggested, may now offer the potential for other public health interventions at a community level.[26] Finally, community-directed treatment with ivermectin requires the annual collection of census data. With the help of the rural health dispensary personnel, community distributors record data such as size of population, age, gender, pregnancy etc. These data offer additional information relevant for potential health interventions.

One might plausibly argue that the MDP is not simply a drug donation programme but rather a public health initiative carried out by a multi-sectoral public–private partnership. The initial decision to donate MECTIZAN served as a catalyst for much broader, and effective, health interventions, as well as a learning tool for those involved in onchocerciasis control.

Implications for future access programmes

Donation programmes have never been promoted as the solution to the global access crisis, nor should they be. But they do offer one mechanism for providing access to care and treatment for those in need, and they should be evaluated on a case-by-case basis (depending on the disease, the medication, the available infrastructure and other relevant criteria). Although donation programmes may not be perfect, they should be encouraged where appropriate.

To a certain extent, Merck's MECTIZAN Donation Program has encouraged other pharmaceuticals companies to pursue research and new collaborative efforts in an effort to address the needs of poor countries. It has served as a model for new donation programmes such as the International Trachoma Initiative (undertaken by Pfizer in collaboration with the Edna McConnell Clark Foundation and the WHO) and GlaxoSmithKline's partnership with the WHO, Merck and other partners to eliminate lymphatic filariasis. The MECTIZAN

---

[26] Coyne and Berk (2001).

Donation Program is widely considered to be a highly successful example of public–private partnership in international health and a paradigm for the pharmaceuticals industry's donation programmes.[27]

CONCLUSIONS

Through the continuing collaboration of the international, multi-sectoral health coalition for treating those afflicted with onchocerciasis or at risk of contracting the disease, there is hope that within the next decade it can be eliminated as a major public health problem and socio-economic development constraint.

The Merck MECTIZAN Donation Program, which has helped millions of people in the developing world, is an instructive case, reminding us that even when medicines are free, questions of infrastructure, transparency, distribution, logistics, partnership and sustainability shape the prospects for long-term health benefits. The history of the decision to donate MECTIZAN to those in need illustrates the complexity and drama of the discovery and development of modern drugs. The decision involved the interdisciplinary collaboration of Merck's basic and clinical research groups and the creative approach of Merck management and its many partners in solving the complex problems associated with onchocerciasis and distributing a new medicine in some of the poorest regions of the world. Their solution – the creation of a unique and multifaceted partnership – demonstrates that important public health outcomes are possible when public- and private-sector organizations work together to apply their complementary resources and expertise to achieve a common goal.

These lessons are instructive in considering approaches to other medical conditions and other programmes of care and treatment in the developing world. Although simple solutions remain elusive, the MECTIZAN case, by demonstrating what can be accomplished in the face of numerous complexities and challenges, is a cause for optimism.

---

[27] See, for example, Wehrwein (1999); McNamara (2001); and the studies cited in note 2 above. On the broader issues of public–private partnerships in global health, see Buse and Walt (2000a, 2000b), Buse and Waxman (2001), Reich (2000), Reich (2002), Widdus (2000), Walt and Buse (2001), and other essays in the August 2001 issue of the *Bulletin of the World Health Organization* (vol. 79, no. 8).

REFERENCES

Austin, James E. and Diana Barrett (2001), 'Merck Global Health Initiatives (A)', Harvard Business School Case 301-088 (26 January).
Benton, Bruce (2001), 'The Onchocerciasis (River Blindness) Programmes: Visionary Partnerships', World Bank Africa Region, Findings No. 174 (January). Available at http://www.worldbank.org/afr/findings/english/find174.htm.
Bollier, David (1997), 'Merck & Company: Quandaries in Developing a Wonder Drug for the Third World', in *Aiming Higher: 25 Stories of How Companies Prosper by Combining Sound Management and Social Vision*. New York: American Management Association, 280–93.
Bollier, David, Stephanie Weiss and Kirk O. Hanson (1991), 'Merck & Co., Inc.: Addressing Third-World Needs'. Cases (A), (B), (C) & (D). Stanford, California: Business Enterprise Trust. Available from http://www.hbsp.harvard.edu as Cases 9-991-021, 9-991-022, 9-991-023, and 9-991-024.
Brieger, William R., Sakiru A. Otusanya, Ganiyu A. Oke, Frederick O. Oshiname and Joshua D. Adeniyi (2002), 'Factors Associated with Coverage in Community-Directed Treatment with Ivermectin for Onchocerciasis Control in Oyo State, Nigeria', *Tropical Medicine and International Health*, 7 (January), 11–18.
Buse, Kent and Gill Walt (2000a), 'Global Public-Private Partnerships: Part I – A New Development in Health?', *Bulletin of the World Health Organization*, 78 (April), 549-61.
Buse, Kent and Gill Walt (2000b), 'Global Public-Private Partnerships: Part II – What Are the Health Issues for Global Governance?', *Bulletin of the World Health Organization*, 78 (May), 699-709.
Buse, Kent and Amalia Waxman (2001), 'Public–Private Health Partnerships: A Strategy for WHO', *Bulletin of the World Health Organization*, 79 (August), 748–54.
Coyne, Philip E. and David W. Berk (2001), 'The Mectizan (Ivermectin) Donation Program for River Blindness as a Paradigm for Pharmaceutical Industry Donation Programs', World Bank Working Paper (December).
Dutton, Jane E. and Michael G. Pratt (1997), 'Merck & Company: From Core Competence to Global Community Involvement', in Noel M. Tichy, Andrew R. McGill and Lynda St Clair (eds), *Corporate Global Citizenship: Doing Business in the Public Eye*. San Francisco: New Lexington Press, 150–67.
Eckholm, Erik (1989), 'River Blindness: Conquering an Ancient Scourge', *New York Times Magazine* (January 8).
Frost, Laura, Michael R. Reich and Tomoko Fujisaki (2002), 'A Partnership for Ivermectin: Social Worlds and Boundary Objects', in Reich (ed.), *Public–Private Partnerships for Public Health*, Harvard Series on Population and International Health. Cambridge, Massachusetts: Harvard Center for Population and Development Studies, 87–113.
Hopkins, Adrian D. (2001), 'Onchocerciasis (River Blindness)', Presentation to the NGDO Coordination Group for Onchocerciasis Control Meeting, September.
Hopkins, Donald R. and Frank Richards, Jr (1997), 'Visionary Campaign: Eliminating River Blindness', in *1997 Medical and Health Annual*. Chicago, Illinois: Encyclopedia Britannica.
McNamara, Robert S. (2001), 'Look How Successful an Aid Partnership Can Be', *International Herald Tribune* (20 December).
'MECTIZAN and Onchocerciasis: A Decade of Accomplishment and Prospects for the Future: The Evolution of a Drug into a Development Concept', Special issue of *Annals of Tropical Medicine & Parasitology*, 92, supplement 1 (April 1998), S5–179.
'MECTIZAN et Onchocercose – dix années de MECTIZAN en Afrique: des partenariats pour un succès prolongé'. Special issue of *Cahiers d'etudes et de recherches francophones/Santé*, 8 (1) (January–February 1998), 3–90.
Ottesen, Eric A. (2000), 'The Global Programme to Eliminate Lymphatic Filariasis', *Tropical Medicine and International Health*, 5 (September), 591–4.
Reich, Michael R. (2000), 'Public-Private Partnerships for Public Health', *Nature Medicine*, 6 (June), 617–20.

Reich, Michael R. (ed.) (2002), *Public–Private Partnerships for Public Health*, Harvard Series on Population and International Health. Cambridge, Massachusetts: Harvard Center for Population and Development Studies.

Sethi, S. Prakash and Paul Steidlmeier (1997), 'The Benevolent Corporation? Merck and Co., Inc. Gives Away the Cure for River Blindness', in *Up Against the Corporate Wall: Cases in Business and Society*, sixth edition. Upper Saddle River, New Jersey: Prentice Hall, 422–35.

'The Story of MECTIZAN'. Whitehouse Station, New Jersey: Merck & Co., 1998. Available at *http://www.merck.com/overview/philanthropy/mectizan/home.html*.

Sturchio, Jeffrey L. (1992), *The Decision to Donate MECTIZAN: Historical Background*. Rahway, New Jersey: Merck & Co.

Tavis, Lee A. (1997), 'River Blindness: The Merck Decision to Develop and Donate MECTIZAN', in *Power and Responsibility: Multinational Managers and Developing Country Concerns*. Notre Dame, Indiana: University of Notre Dame Press, 244–75.

Taylor, Hugh, Michel Pacqué, Beatriz Muñoz and Bruce M. Greene (1990), 'Impact of mass treatment of onchocerciasis with ivermectin on the transmission of infection', *Science*, 250 (5 October), 116–18.

Useem, Michael (1998), 'Roy Vagelos Attacks River Blindness: "The Drug Was Needed Only by People Who Couldn't Afford It"', in *The Leadership Moment: Nine True Stories of Triumph and Disaster and Their Lessons for Us All*. New York: Times Business, 10–42.

Vagelos, P. Roy (2001), 'Social Benefits of a Successful Biomedical Research Company: Merck', *Proceedings of the American Philosophical Society*, 145 (December), 575–78.

Walt, Gill and Kent Buse (2000), 'Partnership and Fragmentation in International Health: Threat or Opportunity', *Tropical Medicine and International Health*, 5 (July), 467–71.

Wehrwein, Peter (1999), 'Pharmacophilanthropy', *Harvard Public Health Review* (Summer), 32–9.

Widdus, Roy (2001), 'Public–Private Partnerships for Health: Their Main Targets, Their Diversity, and Their Future Directions', *Bulletin of the World Health Organization*, 79 (August), 713–20.

15 STREET PRICE: A GLOBAL APPROACH TO DRUG PRICING FOR DEVELOPING COUNTRIES

Anna Thomas

INTRODUCTION

Mr Phiri has been ill for a long time – he is HIV-positive. Not having any drugs is the biggest problem. The home-based care team help – they give him and his family counselling, make him comfortable and help clean the house. But they can't do anything for his symptoms. The family know that there are drugs to help him, but they can't afford to buy them from the private hospital and the public hospital doesn't have the drugs. Mr Phiri was the breadwinner, and now that he's sick the family don't have enough money to buy food. They can't grow enough in the garden because they're too busy looking after him. Sometimes the family are so desperate to make Mr Phiri feel better that they find a few kwacha and buy any cheap medicines from the grocery store.

Elke Bedehasing, VSO Nurse Tutor, St Luke's Hospital, Malawi

The high prices of drugs impact enormously on the well-being of communities throughout the developing world and on the daily work of VSO doctors, nurses and pharmacists who live there. The development disaster that is HIV–AIDS

VSO is an international development agency that works through volunteers. The article on which this chapter is based was edited by Ken Bluestone, Silke Bernau and Rachel Bishop. Additional research was carried out by Lucy Tweedie and Miranda Lewis. The author also thanks Philippa Saunders (Essential Drugs Project), Eva Ombaka (Ecumenical Pharmaceutical Network), Fritha Melville, Sarah Kyobe, Patrick Wajero, Matthew Bell and Mark Goldring for their invaluable comments.

We are very grateful to the VSO volunteers in India, Uganda, Kenya and Malawi and to the many other people in those countries who contributed their time and expertise to the research for this article. Special thanks to Sam Malamba (UNAIDS, Uganda), Chris Ouma (ActionAid Kenya), and Anand Grover (Lawyers' Collective, India) and to the VSO programme staff for their help. The views in this chapter are those of the VSO alone and are not necessarily shared by everyone who took part in the research. Any errors are the sole responsibility of VSO.

In this chapter, equity-pricing signifies a means to ensure systematically that developing-country purchasers with similar levels of financial resources have equal access to the lowest possible drug prices. Differential pricing refers to any situation where different prices are charged for different markets. North is used to mean developed countries and South to mean developing countries.

has turned the spotlight on drug prices, and a window of opportunity for action has opened. This opportunity has recently been strengthened and defined by extensive public debate on the issue. The British government continues to be active in this debate,[1] most recently by convening the high-level Working Group on Differential Pricing to investigate solutions. Drug prices are also a priority matter at the EU level,[2] and a meeting of stakeholders including industry, governments, international organizations and NGOs, convened by the World Health Organization (WHO) and the World Trade Organization (WTO) in April 2001 in Høsbjør, Norway discussed the issues in detail.[3]

This chapter adds to the debate by setting out the essential criteria that any solution to the problem of high drug prices for developing countries must meet, from the perspective of VSO partners and stakeholders in several developing countries. The current policy approaches cannot fulfil these criteria. VSO proposes that the international community should set up a new global equity-pricing framework, based on the needs of developing countries, which includes a price database and a forum for global price negotiations. This framework would benefit all stakeholders, in North and South.

This proposal should be considered alongside issues under discussion concerning the Agreement on Trade-Related Aspects of Intellectual Property Rights (TRIPS). Although TRIPS is not the focus of this article, VSO strongly supports the full use of TRIPS safeguards, giving developing countries the maximum number of options to produce or purchase low-cost drugs. The Declaration on TRIPS and Public Health agreed at Doha in November 2001 confirmed countries' right to use these safeguards. VSO also supports examining potential improvements to the terms of TRIPS for developing countries. Indeed, the two discussions are not mutually exclusive, as competition is an inevitable part of any adequate approach to systematic equity-pricing.

THE CONTEXT: HIGH PRICES

Why is price important?

In developing countries, the prices of many drugs that could save lives and reduce suffering are too high for either individuals or governments to afford. In the context of HIV–AIDS, this can mean that young adults, the backbone of society, are needlessly sick. The high price of medicines not only limits access to vital treatment but also reduces the efficacy of health systems as a whole. It is VSO's experience that people do not use health services unless they believe

---

[1] UK Cabinet Office (2001).
[2] Commission of the European Communities (2001).
[3] WHO–WTO (2001).

effective drugs will be available and affordable. 'We can't afford the bus fare, only to get to the health centre and find there aren't any drugs,' said a patient of one VSO partner in Malawi. In the context of HIV–AIDS, commentators argue similarly that if affordable drugs are available, people are far more likely to volunteer for HIV testing, as they know they have something to gain. Care and prevention are inextricably linked.[4]

As well as being a humanitarian crisis, the HIV–AIDS epidemic is an economic and development disaster, which is seriously jeopardizing the attainment of international development targets in some parts of the world.[5] Given the extreme financial pressures facing developing countries' health systems, high medicine prices are clearly an important factor that must be addressed.

Over the past year, however, some parties have argued that high prices should not be a focus of debate and that the development of health systems and the financing of drug purchases should be focused on instead. The WHO argues that all these issues, together with rational drug selection and use, are crucial pieces of the 'access jigsaw'.[6] This article focuses on price while recognizing that it is not the only issue.

The special nature of drugs

Drugs are unique commodities. They are essential goods, but their production requires substantial technological input and therefore a fairly high level of industrialization. The development of new drugs requires an even higher order of technological sophistication. Few, if any, other products both are essential and require high technological input. Thus, the pharmaceutical industry has a unique social responsibility. Solving the problem of high drug prices demands creative thinking. The essential nature of drugs makes a solution imperative, but the cost of a high knowledge input to their conception and production must be covered.

Newer drugs, higher prices

Most of the more expensive drugs have been developed (or applied to their current uses) relatively recently. Although older drugs provide optimum treatments for many conditions and health problems, newer drugs are the only option or have significant advantages in other cases. The HIV–AIDS epidemic has drawn attention to the high prices of newer drugs because the anti-retrovirals (ARVs), which slow down the HIV virus, have no older substitute. 'The price issue in general has become clear and loud because of anti-retrovirals,' according to

---
[4] UNAIDS (2000).
[5] International Development Committee (2001).
[6] See Chapter 11 (WHO–WTO) in this volume.

Martin Oteba of the Ugandan Ministry of Health. Similarly, some newer drugs for HIV–AIDS-related opportunistic diseases are the best or only treatment option. Examples include fluconazole, which is used for a type of AIDS-related meningitis and for debilitating oral thrush, and ciprofloxacin, an antibiotic that can be used to treat many opportunistic infections, including resistant tuberculosis (TB). Moreover, drugs in development will continue to supersede current ones.

It has been argued that the absence of some newer high-priced drugs from the WHO Essential Drugs List demonstrates that they are unimportant for developing countries' public health. This argument is incorrect. Cost is a criterion for inclusion on the Essential Drugs List, meaning that an expensive drug is less likely than a cheaper one to be included on the list. Thus, the exclusion of a drug does not tell the whole story of its potential for public health benefit. In any case, the WHO has now committed to a new process of selection based on evidence rather than expert consensus.

Why are prices high?

High prices are set partly to cover investment in the research and development (R&D) of new products. Lack of transparency makes detailed discussion of these costs impossible, and there is considerable evidence that the issue is often overstated.[7] Nevertheless, R&D costs clearly need to be allowed for in calculating prices.

To facilitate return on innovation, new drugs are patented, preventing market competition for a set time. To a large extent, this releases companies from competitive downward price pressures for this period. Patents apply throughout the developed world and in many parts of the developing world, and as TRIPS is fully implemented, all members of the WTO will be bound by 20-year patents on products and processes.

The R&D of most truly innovative drugs takes place in the developed world. Even in India, for example, which has a highly developed pharmaceutical industry, basic research into new molecules accounted for only a fraction of the research that even the biggest companies carried out until 2000.[8] In the developed world, prices are set at levels that recoup R&D investment and make comfortable profits. In the developing world, the target market for new drugs is generally the affluent middle class. Indeed, expensive drugs are usually available in private hospitals

---

[7] A recent report argues that the cited cost of $500 million per drug is an exaggeration, that much R&D is publicly funded, that fewer than a quarter of 'new' drugs marketed are truly innovative and that spending on marketing is higher than that on R&D. See *Treatment R&D Myths – The Case Against the Drug Industry's R&D Score Card*, Public Citizen, 2001.
[8] VSO interview with Mr D. G. Shah, Indian Pharmaceutical Alliance, 6 March 2001. For more details, see Chapter 7 by Granville and Leonard in this volume.

and retail pharmacies but are often completely unavailable in the public sector of developing countries. As one African R&D industry representative said, 'Our products are expensive, because we go to the places where we know people can afford them. We don't lie, but we do persuade doctors to prescribe them ... for example [a particular antibiotic] is still under patent here, so we can charge whatever we like for it.' This commercial strategy applies to the sale of many products in the developing world. It is a rational strategy from a commercial perspective – it allows similar principles of pricing and marketing to be followed on a global basis. But this approach ignores the fact that the millions of people who need these drugs, and their governments, simply cannot afford them.

Looking for a different approach

Other approaches to pricing could increase access to drugs without damaging commercial interests, and different approaches are required within industry and government respectively. Confident policies are needed that will enable new drugs that enhance public health to be widely available to developing countries at prices far below the highest international prices.

For this to happen, the pharmaceutical industry and Northern policy-makers need to accept that the vast majority (if not all) of the R&D costs for HIV–AIDS-related medicines whose patents are owned in the North must be covered in the North. This would enable the selling of higher volumes at lower prices in the South. It would also mean that companies could take a more relaxed approach to intellectual property protection in the South. This, however, is not a new proposal. For example, the International AIDS Vaccine Initiative proposes that 'the poorest countries pay only the marginal costs of producing vaccines while richer countries and populations bear the full costs of research and development'.[9]

Two specific changes are needed to make this approach feasible. First, much tighter provisions are needed to ensure that cheaper drugs do not flow from the South back to the North, to maintain financial returns in the North. Second, the R&D-based companies need to change their attitude to sales in developing countries; they must aim to sell a high volume of drugs at a small return per unit.

This approach is possible. R&D is currently funded almost entirely from sales in the North. For example, only 10 per cent of GlaxoSmithKline's sales of

---

[9] Submission on behalf of the National AIDS Trust Vaccines Programme to the International Development Committee inquiry into HIV–AIDS and Social and Economic Development (2000). Ensuring current R&D is paid for in the North would not solve the problem of providing incentives for R&D for 'neglected diseases' that occur only in poor countries. Such R&D is happening only in a small minority of cases at the moment. However, this is a major issue in itself, demanding a separate set of policy solutions. It is beyond the scope of the current chapter.

anti-HIV drugs are outside the United States and Europe. Moreover, some of this 10 per cent is from other Northern markets.[10] Further, the entire African pharmaceuticals market constitutes only about 1.5 per cent of the global total.[11] It is encouraging that one major R&D company, GlaxoSmithKline, has publicly stated: 'We have accepted that we will recover our [R&D] costs in developed-country markets.'[12] Indeed, it was pointed out in the WHO–WTO conference in Høsbjør that a high-volume, low-priced approach would be economically feasible and would be in the interests of consumers in the South and manufacturers while not adversely affecting Northern consumers.[13]

Within this context, the rest of this chapter is based on three assumptions:

- Developing countries should be able to gain access to key drugs for HIV–AIDS at dramatically lower prices than developed countries.
- R&D-based companies are willing to reassess current pricing strategies and to sell at dramatically lower prices in the South as long as they are able to maintain current Northern price levels through adequate market segmentation.
- R&D for new drugs that is carried out for Northern pharmaceutical companies should be paid for in the North.

ESSENTIAL CRITERIA FOR EQUITY-PRICING

Clearly, new policy approaches are necessary, and VSO believes they should be based on the needs of developing countries. Through interviews with VSO partners and other stakeholders in Uganda, Kenya and India, VSO has established a set of 10 criteria, to be used as a guideline for policy-makers working on solutions for equity-pricing (see below).

The interviewees included volunteers and their employers, other NGOs, government representatives, UN organizations and industry (mainly the local pharmaceutical industry). They represent viewpoints on the key issues frequently emphasized by the stakeholders. And even though there was not a consensus of everyone interviewed, their viewpoints were interesting because their emphases differ significantly from those in many Northern discussions of pricing issues.

Ugandan, Kenyan and Indian perspectives differed on certain aspects of these issues, for example, because of those countries' different pharmaceuticals production capacity. Uganda has little domestic pharmaceuticals production, while Kenya produces one-third of medicines purchased by its public sector. Ideas about how equity-pricing works are well developed in these countries.

[10] *GlaxoSmithKline Annual Report* (2000).
[11] *SCRIP Yearbook 2000* (2000).
[12] Viehbacker (2001).
[13] WHO–WTO (2001).

In contrast, India produces three-quarters of its medicines domestically, with much price competition and as yet no product patents. Differential pricing by Northern companies is much less relevant for many stakeholders in India. They feel the debate should focus on how India can continue to meet its own need for pharmaceuticals at a low price in the context of TRIPS, although they are aware of the changes that the agreement may create. 'After 2005 we're not going to be able to manufacture a lot of stuff here,' said an Indian activist. There is much concern about the impact of TRIPS in all three countries, and much conviction that it will increase prices. Some Indian policy-analysts are extremely sceptical about differential pricing: they do not believe prices will be set as low as those reached by Indian companies and they believe it may undermine India's own production of medicines.

However, despite the differences in the three countries' pharmaceutical production capacity, stakeholders in all three believe that competition (whether from domestically produced drugs or imports) is a key element of fair drug pricing. In Kenya in 2001, a strong NGO campaign resulted in the successful writing of TRIPS safeguards into law.

The 10 criteria

Minimum level Prices should tend towards a minimum level for poor countries. This is likely to mean prices close to or at the marginal cost of production. Also, where generic versions are available, it means that a price significantly higher than other prices for similar products on the world market would be unacceptable. It does not, however, mean that prices should tend towards zero.

Equity Countries at a similar low level of development should have access to drugs at the same low prices – there needs to be a level playing field. Poor sections of the population of middle-income countries with high levels of inequality should also have access to low-priced drugs. This implies criteria for eligibility based on development indicators and disease levels and a transparently negotiated process for agreeing what these indicators should be.

Sustainability Price reductions should be long-term and predictable, and the mechanism by which they are achieved should be credible to all. Many developing-country stakeholders believe that price competition through the manufacture of generic drugs is essential to sustainability, as it is the only feasible mechanism for ensuring that low prices are reached and maintained. 'Prices won't go up again, because things are going in the direction of generics,' says Dorothy Ochola, formerly of the Ugandan UNAIDS Drug Access Initiative.[14]

[14] See her Chapter 10 in this volume.

The understanding of sustainability implicit here differs from the definition of the R&D-based industry, for which sustainability means that low prices should be set at a level with enough margin so that it is confident of being able to maintain them comfortably. This could conflict with the minimum price criterion.

Range Price reductions should not be limited to anti-retrovirals, which have been the main focus for prices so far. Medicines for HIV-related opportunistic diseases and for palliative care should be included too. This chapter focuses on drugs for HIV–AIDS and opportunistic diseases, but similar principles should also be applied to other key drugs for diseases endemic in developing countries.

Quality A global pricing framework should ensure that only manufacturers who comply with acceptable quality standards are included.

Unconditionality Price reductions should not be contingent on conditions that may damage other aspects of developing countries' ability to gain access to drugs (or on conditions that could harm any other aspect of their development). Examples of these conditions would be an agreement to buy only from a particular company for a fixed time or an agreement not to make full use of the right to implement and use TRIPS safeguards.

Self-reliance Mechanisms for price reduction should strengthen the self-reliance of developing countries in two areas. First, their ability to operate as equal partners should tend to increase. This is particularly relevant to price negotiation. Second, mechanisms should support the expansion of developing countries' production of pharmaceuticals (where possible and relevant) in order to create a degree of independence of supply and for economic and employment reasons.[15]

Accountability Governance of equity-pricing should be run by a public body, at the international level, with the involvement of stakeholders from both developing and developed countries.

Transparency To ensure accountability and equity, the prices being offered would need to be published and to be well publicized. Details of the process for reaching low prices should be transparent, as should the process of reaching the criteria for eligibility.

Market segmentation Prices in developed countries must be maintained, which means that low-priced drugs must be prevented from flowing back to developed

---

[15] See Chapters 7 and 8, by Granville and Leonard and by Reekie, in this volume.

countries and that political pressures to reduce developed-country prices to developing-country levels must be resisted.

Additional issues

Three major issues emerged from interviews with developing-country stakeholders that also need to be addressed by national and/or international actors. These issues, however, are not included in the 10 central criteria because they may not be dealt with most effectively through policies focusing on drug *pricing*.

Integration Systems to deliver reduced-price drugs should be integrated, as far and as soon as possible, into existing health care systems and strategies rather than be organized as parallel vertical systems – extra systems set up specifically to deal with one particular problem. This is a core principle, necessary to maximize efficiency and minimize distortion of budget allocation. According to a recent report on the demise of Africa's health systems,

> vertical programmes have increasingly been perceived to have hindered the development of effective health systems; they often duplicated existing activities; they distracted health personnel who had to focus on the immediate outcomes of individual projects rather than long-term development of systems; and they were only sustainable as long as donor priorities stayed the same and funds continued to flow. They have led to fragmentation of health systems.[16]

Rational use It is imperative that all medicines, especially ARVs, are taken correctly. This reduces the risks of unsafe drug use and the emergence of resistant pathogens, thus maintaining the effectiveness of the drugs.

Further debate and consultation is needed about drugs with a risk of resistance. It is needed, for example, about whether national governments should make a particular level of commitment to developing rational-use systems (to ensure that the most appropriate drugs are used) before they are offered equity prices. Resistance is a serious consideration but, on the other hand, there is a danger of 'creeping conditionality'. Developing countries may argue that if drugs are widely and cheaply available through legal channels in all sectors, there is less chance of a black market developing that would be even less controlled and more prone to engendering resistance. There is also a strong belief that although resistance is important, it should not be an excuse to withhold drugs. According to a long-time international health worker, 'There was the same discussion ... that vaccines were not safe to introduce in developing countries. We're seeing it all again.' However, many developing-country stakeholders are extremely concerned about the impact of poorly controlled cheap drugs.

[16] MEDACT–Save the Children (2001).

Currently, the situation in many cases is that the pharmaceutical industry is deciding how conditions relating to rational use should be set. Whether this is the most appropriate mechanism for such a sensitive area is a matter for careful consideration.

Internal equity   It is widely recognized that all drugs will not be available or affordable to everyone in the short term and that this should not be used as a reason to stall progress. 'Dollar-a-day medicines give hope, even though not everyone can afford them, and for HIV–AIDS, hope is a big medicine,' says Sophia Mukasa Monico of the Ugandan AIDS Support Organization. However, national and international actors need to consider how limited distribution can be arranged in the fairest way.

EXISTING METHODS OF ACQUIRING LOWER-PRICE DRUGS FOR DEVELOPING COUNTRIES

Many mechanisms already exist that help developing countries to acquire drugs at prices lower than those in the North. They divide into two categories: situational factors, which are part of the existing commercial environment, and intentional initiatives, which are deliberate initiatives aimed at reducing prices for Southern countries.

Situational factors

Commercial strategy   Manufacturers already set drug prices at differing levels for different developing (and developed) countries. This is because prices are set according to specific conditions in targeted markets. These different levels arise from commercial strategy – they are not intended to be a way of increasing access for the poor, and they may result in high prices as well as low ones in developing countries. But the phenomenon does give developing countries an opportunity to engage in parallel trade, thereby reducing prices.

Generic competition   Competition may occur if the drug is off-patent globally or it may occur in countries where product patents are not applicable, for example India. Where there is adequate competition, and an adequate market, price reductions can be dramatic. Prices become lower in the private sector, and public purchasers have the opportunity to achieve low prices through competitive tender. This mechanism for drug price reduction may be greatly reduced with the full implementation of the TRIPS Agreement if countries are not able to use TRIPS safeguards.

> **Box 15.1: Price comparisons between Kenya and India**
>
> | Drug | Price (£) in Kenya | Price (£) in India |
> |---|---|---|
> | Fluconazole (200 mg) | 9.70 (brand) | 0.50 (generic) |
> | Ciprofloxacin (500 mg) | 2.57 (brand) | 0.10 (generic) |
> | Acyclovir (200 mg) | 2.00 (brand) | 0.10 (brand) |
> | Acyclovir | 0.56 (generic) | 0.10 (generic) |
>
> This box is based on a VSO straw poll of prices available in several retail pharmacies in India in February 2001 and in Kenya in May 2001. In Kenya, fluconazole is patented and ciprofloxacin is presumed to be patented (there was no generic version available). Both these patents are nearing the end of their term. Acyclovir recently came off patent. In India several generic companies have manufactured each drug for several years.
>
> In each country, some portions of the prices are not set by the manufacturer. In Kenya the wholesaler's mark-up can be up to 25 per cent and the retailer's mark-up can be as much as 33 per cent. In India there were, at the time of research, national and local taxes on drugs of about 40 per cent of the manufacturer's price, as well as wholesaler and retailer mark-ups (which are regulated). The Indian government has now cut taxes on some drugs for HIV–AIDS. These factors, although important, do not explain the overall price differences observed, which are an order of magnitude higher.
>
> *Source:* All information in this box is derived from VSO research and interviews, February–May 2001.

Intentional initiatives

(a) Voluntary industry initiatives

(i) 'Negotiated price offers' The differential pricing of drugs by R&D companies occurs sporadically on a voluntary company-by-company, country-by-country and drug-by-drug negotiated basis. The most prominent of these price offers has been for ARVs, under the UNAIDS Accelerating Access programme. The terms for each country are reached by individual negotiation.

(ii) Differential pricing strategies Some companies have developed their price offers and published the conditions under which they commit differential pricing to take place. This may involve publishing the price being offered for particular drugs and/or publishing the criteria by which certain countries are eligible for low prices. GlaxoSmithKline is one such company.

(iii) Donations Some companies have donated drugs instead of offering price reductions for HIV–AIDS. Examples in the HIV–AIDS field are Pfizer's donation of fluconazole and Boehringer Ingelheim's donation of nevirapine.

> **Box 15.2: Lower-cost anti-retrovirals in Uganda: combining negotiation and competition**
>
> Since 1997, Uganda has been one of four countries involved in a partnership between UNAIDS and the R&D-based pharmaceutical industry that is looking at ways to deliver HIV–AIDS care, including ARVs, in developing countries. A pilot project has demonstrated the feasibility of this delivery of ARVs, although on a small scale – about 3,000 Ugandans now have access to them,[a] but 800,000 Ugandans are HIV-positive.[b]
>
> Price reductions for this project have been achieved by a combination of negotiation and competition. Uganda obtains reduced-price drugs through a negotiated Accelerating Access agreement. These price reductions are variable in extent – by April 2001, six drugs were available at less than 50 per cent of the previous price, but the price of six others had fallen by less than 5 per cent.[c]
>
> Dr Peter Mugyenyi of the Joint Clinical Research Centre (JCRC), one of the Kampala hospitals involved in the pilot project, believed he could obtain lower prices, and started purchasing generics. This led to a price cascade. 'We started buying generics last year. Then the R&D companies came and said they would match the price. Generics then cut their prices further, so the brand names cut theirs again. Now that's what I call negotiation,' he said. Since February 2001 these prices have fallen further.
>
> | Year | Cost ($)* per month of triple cocktail** at the JCRC |
> | --- | --- |
> | 1996 | 942 |
> | 1998 | 800 |
> | 1999 | 550 |
> | 2000 | 400 |
> | 2001 | 100 (generic) (170 (through Medical Access)) |
>
> * Exchange rate as of February 2001.
> ** Zidovudine, lamivudine and nevirapine.
>
> A UNAIDS report on the pilot projects states: 'In the field of price reductions of drugs, the Initiative has been a continued learning experience. This has finally led to a mixed model of price reduction mechanism combining negotiations and competition ... the Drug Access Initiative clearly shows that open competition including generics is an element of price reductions'.[d]
>
> [a] Mugyenyi (2001).
> [b] UNAIDS (2000).
> [c] Ochola (2001).
> [d] UNAIDS (2001).

(b) Negotiation and purchase by international organizations

International organizations purchase some drugs and vaccines directly from the pharmaceutical companies. Examples include the United Nations Children's Fund programme for vaccines, the United Nations Fund for Population Activities

> **Box 15.3: Vertical programme to reduce TB drug prices**
>
> In 2001, the WHO started to use a competitive bidding mechanism in buying off-patent drugs in bulk for distribution to qualified developing countries. A six-month course of TB drugs, which had cost it $15–20, now cost $10.[a]
>
> Meanwhile, the WHO is also dealing with multi-drug-resistant TB. Some key drugs for this condition are patented. All the necessary drugs were identified as being produced only by the patent-holder, as having a single, although unpatented, producer or as having multiple suppliers. Where drugs were under a monopoly, a single negotiator (Médecins Sans Frontières) represented all potential markets, to increase negotiating power: 'Where numerous negotiating bodies compete for the same products, prices are often higher because multiple sources of demand compete for a limited supply.' The size of the markets (both guaranteed and potential) were estimated, and negotiations were conducted on this estimate. Drugs were supplied only to TB treatment projects judged to be technically sound.
>
> To encourage the development of competition, a 'tiered-tender' system was used. This means that where there is competition, the lowest-price bidder gets the highest percentage of the contract (e.g. 50 per cent), but other manufacturers also get a portion (e.g. 20–30 per cent). This approach 'does not result in the immediate lowest price but should yield lower prices in the long term'. Also, the drugs were submitted for inclusion on the WHO's Essential Drugs List. Inclusion on the list is said to facilitate in-country drugs registration and also to increase generic manufacturers' confidence in the potential global market.
>
> Price reductions for drugs that were under monopoly production at the beginning of the programme were as much as 95–97 per cent of prices in the developed countries.
>
> *Source:* R. Gupta et al., 'Responding to Market Failures in Tuberculosis Control – Supplementary Material', *Science Magazine*, 293 (5532), 10 August 2001, p. 1049.
> [a] *New York Times* News Service, 22 June 2001.

(UNFPA)'s programme for contraceptives and the WHO's TB programme. Where competition is present, these organizations may invite suppliers to tender. Where there is no competition, they have sometimes negotiated dramatic price reductions with single-source suppliers.

(c) Facilitated tender

International organizations may facilitate tenders from developing countries by publishing indicative information on the range of drug prices. A group of international organizations is currently undertaking this for HIV–AIDS drugs.

WILL THE CURRENT INITIATIVES FULFIL THE 10 CRITERIA?

The criteria for equity-pricing are clear and comprehensive, and there are many initiatives already addressing the pricing issue. Can stakeholders expect the criteria to be met reliably and consistently by the current initiatives, and perhaps extensions of them, in the near future? This section examines to what extent current pricing initiatives meet or fall short of the essential criteria.

'Price offers' by companies

Equity is not addressed by ad hoc price cuts. Clearly low prices are available only where they are offered. Motives for this have been assumed. To one contact in Kenya, it appears that 'the industry doesn't want to discuss prices with a region as a bloc. I think they want to go country by country because we are economically weak and therefore weak in our ability to negotiate individually. With their economic power, the research companies could buy the whole country if they wanted to.' Where companies publish prices and criteria for eligibility, equity is improved, but the fact that the companies rather than a democratically sanctioned public body decide eligibility presents a difficulty.

Minimum price is a difficult issue to discuss, as the marginal costs of production are not available. However, it is clear that some of the price reductions for ARVs are not approaching the prices offered by generic companies, which are the best indicator we have of marginal cost (see Table 15.1). It is also widely assumed in discussion among experts from international organizations that further price reductions are feasible, with $150 to $200 per year for a triple cocktail treatment[17] frequently mentioned. According to Dr Palitha Abeykoon of the WHO in India, a reduction to the $150 per year level for anti-retrovirals would make an enormous difference to levels of access in India.

There are major concerns in developing countries about the *sustainability* of price offers: 'If someone gives you an offer today, he can withdraw it tomorrow,' said Samuel Ochieng of the Consumer Information Network of Kenya. The pharmaceutical companies state that they are committed to maintaining their differential price offers, but there is no legal or market mechanism to reinforce this commitment.

The *range* of drugs for which differential prices have been offered is poor. So far, the focus has been on ARVs. There have been no offers of low prices for fluconazole or for ciprofloxacin (apart from in the WHO's TB programme), for example.

Developing-country governments emphasized in their June 2001 paper to the WTO Special Session on TRIPS and Access that patent-related conditions must not be connected with equity-pricing. Despite assurances to the contrary,

---

[17] See Box 15.2 above.

Table 15.1: Comparison between prices of drugs from various manufacturers

Drug	Daily dose	Manufacturer	Discount price/day ($)
Lamivudine	2x150mg	GlaxoSmithKline	0.63
		Hetero	0.27
		Cipla (non-profits)	0.30
		Aurobindo	0.25
Zidovudine	2x250mg	GlaxoSmithKline	1.49
	2x200mg	Hetero	0.53
	2x300mg	Cipla	0.84
	6x100mg	Aurobindo	0.50
Nevirapine	2x200mg	Boehringer Ingelheim	1.22 (adult), free for MTCT*
		Hetero	0.55
		Cipla (non-profits)	0.54

* Mother-to-child transmission.
Source: *Sources and Prices for Selected Drugs and Diagnostics for People Living with HIV–AIDS* (UNICEF, UNAIDS, WHO, MSF, May 2001).

there is still a concern about *conditionality* among those on whom the conditions would be imposed. This concern also emerged from stakeholder interviews. Related to this is a fear of legal retaliation if countries do use TRIPS safeguards: 'We should be allowed to use alternative sources if they are cheaper – but legal threats will deter us,' said Martin Oteba of the Ugandan Ministry of Health.

Price *transparency*, where it exists, is generally unsystematic. Thus it is not as useful as it could be as a generator of equity and unconditionality.

The current initiatives do ensure physical *market segmentation*, but they do this by placing restrictions on purchase and delivery systems, which may reduce the number benefiting from the drugs. Improved legal mechanisms for segmentation could replace the need for these restrictions. There is no political agreement to prevent developed countries using prices in developing countries as benchmarks.

Donations

The issues concerning donations are similar to those concerning price offers, which means that they fall short in many of the same criteria, in particular *equity* and *range*. As with price offers, there are also problems about possible *conditionality*.

Donations clearly do meet the *minimum price* criterion. But issues of *sustainability* are compounded in the case of donations: 'My big worry is the sustainability of the free drugs coming in – HIV is here for a long time,' said Sophia Mukasa Monico of the Ugandan AIDS Support Organization. There is no guarantee for developing countries that they will be maintained. Moreover, donated drugs have to be paid for by the donor, while drugs priced around marginal cost are revenue-neutral for the donor. Thus donations are not sustainable for companies on a large scale where several products are involved. This also affects developing countries' *self-reliance*. One Ugandan government official said, 'We don't want more charity – the companies must realize that they can sell more to us.' This does not mean that drug donations are never useful. They do not, however, provide a sustainable systematic approach to providing treatment for HIV–AIDS.

Negotiation and purchase by international organizations

Large international purchasing programmes probably come closer to the *minimum price* criterion for single-source drugs than the other initiatives mentioned in this chapter. This is because they are likely to represent a large guaranteed market, which gives them price-negotiating power much greater that of individual developing countries – one of the major advantages of this type of programme. If they are publicly run, they are also more likely than privately run initiatives to meet the *transparency* and *accountability* criteria.

There are problems relating to other criteria, however. One problem concerns *range*. Most existing large purchasing programmes deal with a relatively limited number of products. The HIV–AIDS epidemic may be simply too large and complex for a single large purchaser to meet the need for drugs: it involves too many different drugs for too many countries.

The biggest problem with this type of programme as a global solution is the transfer of power from the recipient countries to the purchaser, which reduces *self-reliance* by a significant amount. Sometimes the distribution of the drugs is also vertical rather than integrated, which risks distorting national priorities.[18] Nonetheless, large purchasing programmes are likely to remain a useful part of the palette of solutions.

Generic competition

Many developing-country stakeholders believe that competition is the only mechanism needed to bring drug prices down. The competition mechanism, where it works well, does indeed meet many of the important criteria: the *minimum price* is approached, low prices are *sustained* through competition, countries have an *equal* opportunity to purchase on the global market, developing countries are *self-reliant* in their choices of drug purchase and, because they are not beholden to anyone, there can be no *conditionality*.

---

[18] MEDACT–Save the Children (2001).

The competition mechanism should be a principal part of a systematic approach to drug pricing. On its own, however, it does not ensure *range* – some drugs, even when they are off-patent, are made by only a few generic manufacturers. For example, the drug amphotericin is important for the early treatment of AIDS-related meningitis. According to the WHO, 'its manufacture is difficult and there is little generic competition'.[19]

In addition, developing countries sometimes appear to need better information in order to find the cheapest sources of high-quality generics. This applies whether drugs are patented or not. According to Sam Malamba, a Ugandan working on drugs access, 'Often people are not aware of the lowest prices they could obtain. Information-sharing is really important.' For example, the Ugandan government's listed price for a 200-mg fluconazole tablet is £1.29 – considerably higher than the Indian pharmacy (not government) price of about £0.50. There are many possible reasons for this, but one is that information on the cheapest sources is not available. Currently, the *transparency* criterion is not being met.

Most importantly, to rely on generic competition alone, in the context of the TRIPS Agreement deadlines, may be insufficient for some countries.

At least in the short term, differential pricing mechanisms and better information systems are needed so as to complement price reductions achieved through competition. This section clearly demonstrates that current and fragmentary initiatives, in particular individual price offers and donations, meet the criteria poorly. A new approach to policy is needed.

A FRAMEWORK FOR GLOBAL PRICING THAT FITS THE CRITERIA

The international community needs to develop a systematic, global approach to equity-pricing. This would ensure the highest possible degree of equity, increase the range of low-priced drugs, reduce the risk of conditionality and improve the assurance of market segmentation. A systematic approach would remove some of the problems inherent in the current piecemeal initiatives. As one government official states, 'We need a system. Uganda can't negotiate with a wide enough range of companies; they all want preferential treatment.'

VSO suggests a framework for global equity-pricing that would meet the criteria. The framework is very simple. It combines and develops several elements that already exist rather than proposing 'global regulation'. It should work in conjunction with other approaches to increasing medicine access, but it is not designed to address all aspects of the issue. Competition is crucial to the efficient working of this framework. The framework could operate within the current TRIPS Agreement, provided the purchase of generic medicines under compul-

[19] UNICEF, UNAIDS, WHO, MSF (2001).

sory licence is a realistic option. It would work better under a revised intellectual property system that increases developing countries' options to use generic medicines.

The equity-pricing framework

The equity framework has five elements: strengthened market segmentation, a drugs source and price database, scaled-up negotiation, flexible price caps and national and regional tenders. Within this framework, each pharmaceutical company (R&D and generic) should offer a price at or approaching the marginal cost for each of its HIV–AIDS drugs, including those for palliative care and opportunistic diseases, to eligible developing-country purchasers. (The eligibility of drug, country and purchaser should be negotiated by the international community.) These prices should be published on a constantly updated database, which would create competitive downward pressure on prices and give purchasers a simple, transparent mechanism for finding and purchasing best-value medicines of acceptable quality. A global forum of developing-country purchasers should negotiate further price reductions with the pharmaceutical companies, particularly for drugs for which competition is lacking. Once negotiated, these reduced prices would constitute a price cap for a company and be published on the database. Purchasers could buy at database prices or they could use confidential tender procedures to fulfil their specific contract needs or to gain further price reductions (see Figure 15.1).

Strengthened market segmentation

There is consensus among most stakeholders that market segmentation is necessary and desirable, and achievable. One example is the malaria drug marketed under two different trade names: Riamet and Coartem. In India, GlaxoSmithKline uses packaging for anti-retrovirals written entirely in Hindi script. To ensure the commercial viability of equity-pricing, products in lower-price markets must be kept separate from those in the higher-price markets. This should be done in three ways:

- Companies should use physical means, such as making tablets in different colours or using different packaging, to differentiate drugs intended for low- and high-price markets. This is already being done successfully.[20]
- The large pharmaceutical markets, i.e. North America, western Europe, Japan and Australasia, should enact legal measures to prevent the backflow of

[20] WHO (2001).

Figure 15. 1: The equity-pricing framework

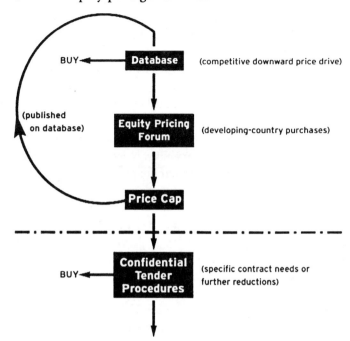

medicines sold at equity prices from low-priced countries. Experience with existing programmes and legal instruments suggests this could be achieved.[21]
- The governments of countries with large pharmaceutical markets should sign a public agreement that their prices will not be benchmarked against the low prices in developing countries.

Although effective separation between the markets of developed and developing countries is crucial, it is important that parallel trade among developing countries, as another mechanism for ensuring minimum prices,[22] is still permitted.

Within developing countries, companies currently concentrate on the affluent middle class. It is probably not possible to maintain a price differential within countries through legal mechanisms, because its enforcement would be extremely difficult. However, it may be possible to maintain some degree of internal market segmentation by physical means (for example, different colours or brand names) and by differential marketing – this would be an extension of current practice. Although watertight internal segmentation cannot be guaranteed, this difficulty should not stop the implementation of equity-pricing or limit eligibility for this pricing only to, for example, least developed countries.

---

[21] WHO–WTO (2001).
[22] On parallel trade, see Chapter 3 by Maskus and Ganslandt in this volume.

A source and price database

Companies, both R&D and generic, should offer eligible purchasers a price per unit for each of their products. There may be a single low price, which appears to be the most workable option,[23] or more than one price for different categories of purchaser. Several companies, for example GlaxoSmithKline, Merck and Cipla, have unilaterally offered single low prices for ARVs to particular purchasers. These prices would then need to be published on a database that identifies companies, individual products and their prices. (Different companies producing similar products would of course set their prices independently.) Price publication conduces to equity, and accountability. It encourages open competition, which is the best way to achieve the minimum price and which is also the only way to ensure price sustainability.

The database should include off-patent drugs, patented drugs and generic versions of patented drugs, which may not be patented in all countries or may be purchased under compulsory licence. It should be updated continuously with price changes, which would be expected owing to competitive downward pressures. The database should also be a source of information on available drug prices, helping countries to find potential suppliers. The database should be maintained by a UN organization. A pre-qualification process should exclude companies that have failed to meet acceptable quality standards. The opportunity to qualify for inclusion in the database should be widely advertised to companies, on an international basis. A group of international organizations (WHO, UNICEF, UNAIDS and MSF) already run a database, with pre-qualification, showing the range of HIV–AIDS drug prices.

Scaled-up negotiation

Where there is an adequate number of manufacturers of a product, competition alone may achieve minimum prices. However, where there is only a single manufacturer (for example, of a new drug) or where patent laws do not allow competition, negotiation is required. This may also apply if there are only a few manufacturers and competition is not optimum.

Prices should be negotiated between the pharmaceutical companies and an Equity Pricing Forum. The forum should be a price-negotiating body, not a purchasing body – purchasing should still be done by countries or regions. The forum should represent all countries eligible for equity prices and should consist of representatives from each developing region who have authority over drug purchasing, together with international organizations. Its membership should rotate. It should not have representation from the pharmaceutical industry, either

---

[23] WHO (2001).

generic or research-based. It should operate as part of an existing international organization. There has been discussion about the Global Health Fund acting as a global price negotiator. The process for assembling the forum, and its rules of operation, should be published.

The forum may be the most difficult part of the framework, but negotiation of prices by international bodies increases developing countries' negotiating power, and has been effective in delivering low prices. It is the best option for bringing about minimum prices where there is inadequate competition, and for doing so in a way that fits the 10 criteria.

Flexible price caps

The Equity Pricing Forum should negotiate voluntary price caps for the eligible drugs and purchasers. Price capping is the most sustainable way of bringing about the lowest prices for developing countries if generic competition cannot do so. (Many countries, including Britain, use some form of price capping system in their domestic drug-pricing arrangements.) The price caps should be published on the database. Where competitors exist, they would be expected to undercut the price caps. The price cap should not be lower than the marginal cost of production. It could be increased by renegotiation with the forum. As with all prices on the database, there would be either a single price for eligible countries or more than one for different categories of purchaser, depending on which system of eligibility is chosen.

The price cap should follow four guidelines:

- Where generic versions of a drug exist, their prices should be used as an indication of marginal cost.
- To provide an estimate of market size, forum members should come to negotiations with an approximate idea of the budget for the drug under negotiation that is available over a set time for the purchaser from their region or organization.
- The basis for negotiation should be the principle of payment according to ability to pay.
- A guideline price formula may be used.

Tendering

The drugs should be available to purchasers without further negotiation at the prices on the database. Drugs are frequently purchased by tender, and regional tenders are increasingly discussed (although not feasible in all regions). Eligible purchasers, whether national or regional, should have the option to ask companies to tender for their particular requirements, with the published prices as guidelines, if that tendering would serve to reduce prices still further. The database, and its pre-qualification, would give purchasing countries better information on which to base their decisions about tenders.

Which drugs, countries and purchasers would be eligible for equity prices?

The question of which drugs, countries and purchasers would be eligible for equity prices needs to be negotiated by the international community. All drugs useful for people with HIV–AIDS, including drugs for opportunistic diseases, drugs for palliative care and anti-retrovirals, should be eligible. This is likely to include some drugs omitted from the current Essential Drugs List – one of the criteria for inclusion on the list is price, which excludes some important drugs that are currently too expensive. Many drugs for HIV–AIDS-related disease, such as antibiotics, are also used for HIV-negative people. These should be available at equity prices for other indications.

All least developed countries, and any developing countries that have a high prevalence of HIV–AIDS, measured either in absolute numerical terms or as more than a certain percentage of the population, should be eligible for low-priced drugs. Drugs at the prices on the database should be available to governments, NGOs, international organizations and private-sector employers for use only in the eligible countries. Where there is no major risk of resistance developing to a drug or in countries with an adequate prescribing system for the control of access, the drug should be available also to private-sector wholesalers and retailers. The public sector, however, should take priority.

RECOMMENDATIONS

> The UK Government needs to share some of the outrage reasonable people everywhere feel about a world whose wealth is so obscenely distributed.
>
> Polly Toynbee, *The Guardian*, 31 August 2001

Medicines, taken for granted by people in the North, are too expensive for the world's poor, many of whom are also in the grip of an unprecedented HIV–AIDS epidemic. As awareness has grown, the fundamental injustice of this situation has angered the media and the public in developed countries, in a way that few specific issues affecting faraway developing countries ever do. Solutions with genuine substance rather than short-term spin need to be implemented urgently.

VSO believes that a systematic global framework for achieving equity drug pricing is necessary, and feasible. This must be developed in parallel with discussions about how to ensure competition in medicine pricing through the use of TRIPS safeguards and the potential reform of TRIPS. To achieve a systematic framework, governments of developed and developing countries, international organizations and R&D-based and generic pharmaceutical companies should make a commitment to the following 10 principles, as outlined above:

1. Prices must tend towards the minimum possible level for poor countries.
2. All countries at a similar level of development or disease burden must have access to medicines at the same low prices.
3. Pricing must be long-term and predictable.
4. All medicines for HIV-related opportunistic diseases, palliative care and treatment of the HIV virus must be eligible for equity-pricing.
5. Equity-priced drugs must comply with acceptable quality standards.
6. Equity-pricing must not entail conditions damaging to other aspects of access to drugs or to other aspects of development.
7. Equity-pricing policies must strengthen developing countries' self-reliance.
8. Any pricing framework must be accountable and publicly governed.
9. The prices being offered must be transparent.
10. The Northern and Southern markets must be separated effectively.

In addition, VSO recommends the following to specific stakeholders.

The British government should

- Ensure that its Working Group on Differential Pricing develops concrete proposals to take forward a Global Equity Pricing Framework that creates equity of price access among countries and affords sustainability through the use of generic competition as an intrinsic part of the framework.
- Make a commitment to ensuring market segmentation between the United Kingdom and developing countries.
- Promote a global approach to equity-pricing at the next World Health Assembly and gain political commitment from developed countries to refrain from benchmarking their drugs prices against equity-priced drugs.

The EU should

- Develop concrete proposals to take forward a Global Equity Pricing Framework.
- Develop union-wide legislation to ensure market segmentation between the EU and developing countries.
- Encourage member states to pledge not to benchmark their drug prices against equity-priced drugs.

The international community should

- Establish an Equity Pricing Forum, in consultation with WHO member states.
- Strengthen existing initiatives, to allow for the development of a published source and price database.

Developing country governments should

- Prioritize HIV–AIDS in national health planning.
- Actively seek out all opportunities for reducing HIV–AIDS treatment costs.
- Continue to develop systems to ensure the rational use of drugs, particularly anti-retrovirals, as part of an integrated approach to health system development.
- Develop mechanisms for global and regional negotiations on the price of drugs with other stakeholders.

The R&D-based pharmaceuticals industry should

- Agree in principle that R&D should be paid for in the North.
- Agree in principle to a systematic approach to global equity-pricing, to using a price database and to global price negotiations.
- Physically separate the market, by formulating and packaging drugs differently for developing countries.
- Publish the low prices available to developing countries on existing and future databases.

The generic pharmaceutical industry (in all countries) should

- Proactively consider ways of increasing the production of essential drugs for developing-country markets.
- Agree in principle to a systematic approach to global equity-pricing, to using a price database and to global price negotiations.

CONCLUSION AND SUMMARY

In developing countries, the price of many drugs that could save lives and reduce suffering are too high for either individuals or governments to afford. This situation is encountered daily by VSO doctors, nurses and pharmacists throughout the developing world, and has a massive impact on the communities where they work. In the context of HIV–AIDS it can mean that young adults, the backbone of society, are needlessly sick. As well as being a humanitarian crisis, this is an economic and development disaster.

From extensive interviews with VSO volunteers and partners, government representatives, pharmaceuticals companies, UN organizations and NGOs in several developing countries, VSO has derived a set of criteria (listed in the Recommendations section above) that must be met if any solution to the problem of high drug prices for developing countries is to be found.

Current piecemeal approaches to drug pricing cannot fulfil these criteria. VSO believes that a systematic, global approach to pricing would ensure the highest possible degree of equity, increase the range of low-priced drugs for developing countries, reduce the risk of conditionality and improve assurance of market segmentation. To ensure the sustainability of low prices, price competition involving the availability of generic drugs must be an intrinsic part of a global pricing approach.

VSO proposes that the international community should set up a new global equity-pricing framework, based on the needs of developing countries. VSO proposes a simple framework, which does not involve 'global regulation'. It expands and systematizes elements of initiatives that already exist. The framework should operate as part of the responsibilities of an existing UN organization.

Within the framework, each pharmaceutical company (R&D and generic) should offer a price at or approaching marginal cost for each of its HIV–AIDS drugs – including those for palliative care and opportunistic diseases – to eligible developing-country purchasers. The eligibility of drugs, countries and purchasers should be negotiated by the international community. The prices of drugs should be published on a constantly updated database, which would create competitive downward price pressures and give purchasers a simple, transparent mechanism with which to find and purchase best-value medicines of acceptable quality. A global forum of developing-country purchasers should negotiate further price reductions with the pharmaceutical companies, particularly for drugs for which there is no competition. Once negotiated, this reduced price would constitute a price cap for that company and be published on the database. Purchasers could buy at database prices or they could use confidential tender procedures to fulfil their specific contract needs or to gain further price reductions.

This proposal is intended to operate alongside current discussions of the TRIPS Agreement. Although TRIPS is not the focus of this article, VSO strongly supports full use of TRIPS safeguards, because they give developing countries the maximum number of options for producing or purchasing low-cost drugs. VSO also supports an examination of potential improvements to the terms of TRIPS for developing countries. Indeed, the two discussions are not mutually exclusive, as competition is an inevitable part of any adequate approach to systematic equity-pricing.

Growing awareness in the era of HIV–AIDS of the fundamental injustice of high drug prices in developing countries has angered the media and the public in developed countries in a way that few issues affecting developing countries ever do. Solutions with genuine substance rather than short-term spin need to be implemented urgently. The British pharmaceutical industry now has an important opportunity to make a substantial difference to poor people's access to drugs through the measures proposed above for ensuring sustainable global price reductions. There is also a critical opportunity for the British government to provide dynamic moral and political leadership to the international community and secure an effective response to this humanitarian crisis and development disaster.

REFERENCES

Commission of the European Communities (2001), Programme for Action: Accelerated Action on HIV–AIDS, malaria and tuberculosis in the context of poverty reduction. COM (2001) 96 Final.

GlaxoSmithKline Annual Report, 2000.

International Development Committee (2001), *HIV–AIDS: The Impact on Social and Economic Development.* The Stationery Office.

MEDACT–Save the Children (2001), *The Bitterest Pill of All – the Collapse of Africa's Health Systems.*

Mugyenyi, P. (2001), 'The Urgent Need for HIV Treatment in Africa', presentation at International HIV–AIDS Conference. Kampala, April.

Ochola, D. (2001), 'Current Experience with Differential Pricing of HIV–AIDS-related Drugs in Uganda', presentation at workshop on Differential Pricing and Financing of Essential Drugs, Høsbjør, Norway, 8–11 April 2001.

SCRIP Yearbook 2000, PJB Publications Ltd, 2000.

Submission on behalf of the National AIDS Trust Vaccines Programme to the International Development Committee inquiry into HIV–AIDS and Social and Economic Development, 2000.

Treatment R&D Myths – The Case Against the Drug Industry's R&D Score Card, Public Citizen, 2001.

UK Cabinet Office (2001), *Tackling the Diseases of Poverty,* Performance and Innovation Unit.

UNAIDS (2000), Report on the Global AIDS Epidemic.

UNAIDS (2001), 'UNAIDS HIV Drug Access Initiative: Pilot Phase', *UNAIDS Best Practice Digest,* 2000. *New York Times* News Service, 22 June.

UNICEF, UNAIDS, WHO, MSF (2001), *Sources and Prices of Selected Drugs and Diagnostics for People Living with HIV–AIDS.*

Viehbacker, C. (GlaxoSmithKline) (2001), 'Pharmaceuticals and Intellectual Property – Overcoming the Impasse', Foreign Policy Centre Global Health Lecture No. 4, 24 May.

WHO (2001), 'More Equitable Pricing for Essential Drugs: What Do We Mean and What Are the Issues?', background paper for the WHO–WTO workshop on Differential Pricing and Financing of Essential Drugs, Høsbjør, Norway, 8–11 April 2001.

WHO–WTO (2001), Report on the Workshop on Differential Pricing and Financing of Essential Drugs, Høsbjør, Norway, 8–11 April 2001.